THE RUSSIA SANCTIONS

In *The Russia Sanctions*, Christine Abely examines the international trade measures and sanctions deployed against Russia in response to its 2022 invasion of Ukraine. Abely situates contemporary sanctions within their larger historical and economic backgrounds and provides a uniquely accessible analysis of the historic export controls and import restrictions enacted since 2022. She argues that these sanctions have affected, and will continue to affect, global trading patterns, financial integration, and foreign policy in novel ways. In particular, she examines the effects of sanctions on energy, food, fertilizer, the financial system, and the global use of the US dollar, including trends of de-dollarization. Coverage includes sanctions against oligarchs, the freezing and seizure of assets, and steps taken to make sanctions more effective by promoting financial transparency worldwide.

Christine Abely is an assistant professor at New England Law | Boston. She previously practiced international trade and sanctions law and is a licensed customs broker. Her work has appeared in *The Hill, Just Security*, and numerous academic journals.

The Russia Sanctions

THE ECONOMIC RESPONSE TO RUSSIA'S INVASION OF UKRAINE

CHRISTINE ABELY

New England Law | Boston

Shaftesbury Road, Cambridge CB2 8EA, United Kingdom

One Liberty Plaza, 20th Floor, New York, NY 10006, USA

477 Williamstown Road, Port Melbourne, VIC 3207, Australia

314–321, 3rd Floor, Plot 3, Splendor Forum, Jasola District Centre, New Delhi – 110025, India

103 Penang Road, #05-06/07, Visioncrest Commercial, Singapore 238467

Cambridge University Press is part of Cambridge University Press & Assessment, a department of the University of Cambridge.

We share the University's mission to contribute to society through the pursuit of education, learning and research at the highest international levels of excellence.

www.cambridge.org
Information on this title: www.cambridge.org/9781009361187

DOI: 10.1017/9781009361224

First published 2024

A catalogue record for this publication is available from the British Library

A Cataloging-in-Publication data record for this book is available from the Library of Congress

ISBN 978-1-009-36118-7 Hardback
ISBN 978-1-009-36119-4 Paperback

Contents

Contents

Acknowledgments

I owe a debt of gratitude to the exemplary reporting worldwide on the Russian invasion of Ukraine, its global economic effects, and the sanctions and trade measures imposed in response. The timeline compiled by Chad Bown at the Peterson Institute for International Economics was particularly helpful in drafting the chapter about the first week of the invasion.

Thank you to Matt Gallaway, Jadyn Fauconier-Herry, and Laura Blake at Cambridge University Press, as well as Marijasintha Jacob Srinivasan. Thank you to Victoria George for her work creating the index of this book.

I would like to thank the organizers and participants of conferences at which I received invaluable comments and feedback, including the Junior International Law Scholars Summer Workshop, the Junior International Law Scholars 2023 Conference, the conference of the American Society of International Law International Economic Law Interest Group, the AALS Financial Regulation Section Conference, the Sydney Centre for International Law Works-in-Progress Conference, the New England Law | Boston Junior Faculty Colloquium, and the Money as a Democratic Medium Conference. Thank you to Stacie Strong, Perry Mehrling, Erin Fitzgerald, Aliza Bloom, Ellen Farwell, Eliot Tracz, Bhamati Viswanathan, Lynn Muster, Jason Giannetti, Ben Heath, Stratos Pahis, David Zaring, Paolo Saguato, Jeffery Zhang, Nizan Packin, Matt Bruckner, Nathan Arriba-Sellier, Heidi Schooner, Charlotte Ku, Steven Koh, Guillermo Garcia Sanchez, Daimeon Shanks, Haley Anderson, Stephen Cody, Rachel Ngo Ntomp, and all others who provided helpful comments on this manuscript. I truly appreciate your time and assistance. Thank you to Lawrence Friedman and Rachel Wechsler for their assistance during the proposal stage of the project. Thank you to Christos Nikolos for research assistance on the issue of the withdrawal of private companies from doing business in Russia.

Thank you to my family: my parents, Bob and Sue Mandell; my husband, Jim; and my two daughters, Keira and Grace.

Introduction

This is the account of an extraordinary year of sanctions and international trade measures imposed against Russia after its invasion of Ukraine in 2022. That year saw the use of economic warfare on a global scale. The coordination of national action was a remarkable feature of the 2022 sanctions, demonstrating the commitment of a large portion of the international community to the principle of territorial integrity.

The 2022 sanctions were directed against specific parties and sectors and thus considered to be targeted in nature. More broad-based comprehensive sanctions had been deployed in other areas of the world with staggering effect and increasing frequency in recent years. So too had targeted sanctions been increasingly implemented in a variety of geographic areas and for a plethora of reasons. What was unique about 2022, however, was the extent to which the sanctions against Russia were coordinated among so many nations. Coordination of legal provisions between countries was not always so uniform with respect to other sanctions programs, especially those imposed by the United States. For example, sanctions on Cuba were US-imposed and broadly criticized internationally, while sanctions placed on Iran by the United States differed in significant ways from those imposed by other authorities. Also unusual was the fact that the 2022 sanctions were placed on so many targeted individuals and entities in Russia, a power more important to the world trading and financial system than other sanctioned nations like North Korea. Though they would technically be considered as targeted measures, the 2022 sanctions were enacted on such a scale as to bear similarities to the comprehensive sanctions regimes directed at other jurisdictions.

But the imposition of sanctions against Russia in 2022 was by no means universal. Large portions of the world refrained from taking part in the economic response against Russia, or even from condemning the Russian invasion of Ukraine. The 2022 Russian invasion began to divide the world into those nations who economically divorced themselves from Russia in response, and those who did not.

Of course, a portion of the sanctioning nations' response to Russia consisted in providing direct military assistance to Ukraine. Those countries also provided humanitarian aid around the world to Ukrainians displaced by the invasion, as well as to the inhabitants of other nations affected by the rise in food and energy prices that year. These issues of humanitarian and military aid are largely outside the scope of this book and are not described in detail herein. But they were as central to the response against Russia as were the economic sanctions and international trade restrictions that are the focus of this book.

This book attempts to relate the economic and legal history of a short time period characterized by a remarkable number of newly enacted sanctions. Not all of the sanctions provisions enacted by every sanctioning jurisdiction are described within this book. This volume instead tries to convey the content and scope of the most significant and most commonly imposed measures. It likewise attempts to give some sense of the breadth of the restrictions and the sheer number of nations that became part of the sanctioning effort. Some of the complexities of the sanctions measures and of other areas of international law have likewise been simplified or omitted.

The year 2022 brought the Russian invasion of Ukraine, an extraordinary challenge to the international community and the rule of law. This is the story of how the sanctioning nations responded to that challenge with economic sanctions, export controls, and import restrictions. It is also, quite possibly, the story of how that year would begin to change the global commercial landscape forever.

1

Before the Invasion

OFAC . . . administers and enforces economic and trade sanctions . . . against targeted foreign countries and regimes, terrorists, international narcotics traffickers, those engaged in activities related to the proliferation of weapons of mass destruction, and other threats to the national security, foreign policy or economy of the United States.

—US Office of Foreign Assets Control, Department of the Treasury

The sanctions imposed against Russia beginning in late winter 2022 were sweeping, historic, and rolled out with stunning rapidity. Their effects would soon ripple across the world in ways both big and small. American consumers saw gas prices at the pump climb above $4 or even $5 per gallon.[1] Moscow commuters crowded behind subway turnstiles, searching for coins when their Apple and Google Pay access was cut off.[2] Some ships shifted their routes; others stopped loading and unloading in Russia entirely.[3] Monuments in Europe dimmed their lights to conserve energy as consumers worried about energy prices and the coming winter.[4] Meanwhile, Russian troops fought on, shelling Mariupol into near-entire destruction and committing atrocities in Bucha and elsewhere.[5]

The 2022 sanctions were notable for their extraordinarily coordinated nature and the extent to which they targeted Russia, a country deeply intertwined with the global economy.[6] Nations, though, have long used sanctions as economic tools to attempt to achieve foreign policy goals and other ends. The sanctions against Russia were largely enabled by existing legal frameworks that had earlier been developed and expanded, especially during the last century and even more markedly during the past few decades. In particular, the United States, the European Union, and other jurisdictions had already turned to sanctions before 2022 to respond to Russia's invasion and annexation of Crimea, its cyberattacks and human rights violations, and other harmful acts against other nations and its own citizens. While the 2022 sanctions against Russia were historic in the breadth of their restrictions against a major world economy, they built upon a long history of sanctions use and a recent ratcheting up of sanctions against Russia itself.

Economic sanctions and international trade measures have long been used by the United States and other countries to target hostile foreign governments and individuals, and for other purposes such as advancing foreign policy interests. Sanctions restrict the ability of regulated parties, including both entities and individuals, to carry out transactions with sanctioned parties, countries, or regions. They most often govern the actions of persons with the nationality of, or located within, the enacting jurisdiction, but may also in certain instances require conformity in other areas and by additional persons; in these cases, sanctions are applied extraterritorially. The severity of sanctions ranges widely. Sanctions may, for instance, involve a total asset freeze; they might restrict a certain sector of the economy; or they might place restrictions on select financial activities such as dealing in debt.[7] These are only a few examples of the myriad ways in which sanctions may be crafted to reach their attempted ends.

Originally developed and deployed during times of war, the use of sanctions expanded greatly during the latter half of the twentieth century, especially as used by the United States and increasingly by the European Union.[8] Sanctioning entities are often termed "senders." Nations against whom sanctions are imposed are "targets."[9] Sanctions may be imposed multilaterally (by way of the United Nations, for example) or by individual jurisdictions.[10] Unilateral sanctions are often termed "restrictive measures," particularly within the European Union, because of the concept that the legal term "sanctions" necessarily refers to sanctions imposed multilaterally.[11] Unilateral sanctions are also variously termed "autonomous sanctions," or "non-UN" sanctions.[12] This book uses the general term "sanctions" to refer to both unilateral economic sanctions as well as multilateral ones.

Trade restrictions are often used alongside sanctions to achieve similar foreign policy ends. These may appear in the form of restrictions on either exports or imports. Export controls limit not only the shipment of physical items to certain destinations, but also affect the transfer of software and intangible controlled information, often even after it has left the jurisdiction imposing the relevant export controls.[13] A physical item exported from the United States to another country generally remains subject to US export controls even upon subsequent re-export to a third country.[14] Often used to control how high-tech items travel around the world, export controls may also be used to deny a party the ability to obtain US-origin items.[15] Bans on certain imported products, too, may be used in response to hostile nations, as can raising tariffs (taxes on imported items) short of an outright ban, subject to the rules of the World Trade Organization (WTO) pertaining to WTO Members.[16]

In the United States, sanctions are administered by the Office of Foreign Assets Control (OFAC) in the US Department of the Treasury.[17] Export controls for the most common types of items are administered by the Bureau of Industry and Security (BIS) within the US Department of Commerce.[18] The US Department of State controls strictly military items, while certain other agencies, such as the Department of Energy, have jurisdiction over some other types of exports, such as nuclear technology.[19] Legislative authorities for sanctions in the United States include various laws such as the International Emergency Economic Powers Act (IEEPA) and the Trading with the Enemy Act (TWEA).[20] Export control authority in the United States is currently provided by the Export Control Reform Act of 2018, among other authorities.[21]

The Office of Foreign Assets Control has existed since 1950, as the successor to the Office of Foreign Funds Control established in 1940.[22] Economic sanctions were used early on in American history. The Treasury Department imposed and administered sanctions during the War of 1812 and the Civil War.[23] The Allied powers, which would come to include the United States, carried out a blockade of Germany during World War I. Used during the interwar period[24] and expanded during World War II, economic sanctions were also deployed with increasing frequency during the latter half of the twentieth century and into the present day, particularly by the United States.[25] Likewise, the United States instituted export controls during World War I, which took on broader scope during World War II and the Cold War years.[26]

Other nations and jurisdictions administer their own sanctions and export controls, including the European Union, the United Kingdom, Canada, Japan, Australia, and others. The United Kingdom's Office of Financial Sanctions Implementation (OFSI) is currently the parallel entity to the United States' OFAC. It was established within HM Treasury in 2016.[27] In 2017, OFSI was granted the ability to assess monetary penalties for violations of financial sanctions.[28] Sanctions in the UK are issued under the authority of the Sanctions and Anti-Money Laundering Act of 2018, which was established in preparation for Brexit, the exit of the United Kingdom from the European Union.[29] Canada imposes its sanctions under the United Nations Act, the Special Economic Measures Act, and the Justice for Victims of Corrupt Foreign Officials Act.[30] Australia imposes both UN sanctions as well as its own autonomous sanctions, the latter under the Autonomous Sanctions Act 2011 and Autonomous Sanctions Regulations 2011.[31] Other nations impose sanctions under similar legislative authorities.

The European Union has imposed restrictive measures since 1994, after the Maastricht Treaty establishing the European Union came into effect in November 1993.[32] The Council of the European Union is responsible for making decisions as to the imposition of sanctions upon the basis of recommendations made by the High Representative of the Union for Foreign Affairs and Security Policy, to promote the objectives of the EU Common Foreign and Security Policy (CFSP). Arms embargoes and travel bans require only a Council Decision to bind Member States. Restrictive measures that are economic in nature require implementation by way of Council Regulations made by the European Commission along with the High Representative.[33] Some Member States of the European Union, such as the Netherlands, do not impose their own sanctions beyond those mandated by the European Union and the United Nations.[34] Others, such as France, impose their own autonomous sanctions at the national level as well.[35] France, for instance, administers certain anti-terrorism sanctions domestically.[36]

The UN Security Council passes binding resolutions regarding sanctions, which must then be implemented by UN Member States at the national level.[37] The UN Security Council consists of five permanent members (China, France, Russia, the United Kingdom, and the United States), as well as ten nonpermanent members serving for two-year terms.[38] Since 1966, the United Nations has imposed sanctions for a variety of reasons, such as apartheid in South Africa, the white supremacist government in Southern Rhodesia, and the testing of nuclear weapons by North Korea.[39]

Export controls, like sanctions, may also be imposed unilaterally or by way of multilateral agreement. The Wassenaar Arrangement is one such multilateral regime. It coordinates a large number of export controls relevant to many "dual-use" items.[40] These are items that can be used for both military and civilian use.[41] In practice, dual-use items include many common products, such as consumer laptops or commercial GPS units.[42] Other multilateral export control arrangements include the Australia Group (for chemical and biological weapons), and the Missile Technology Control Regime, among others.[43] These multilateral agreements are then put into effect through domestic legislation in their member countries.[44]

The United States implements economic sanctions, including unilateral measures, particularly frequently.[45] It maintains a variety of sanctions programs designed to address a broad range of threats around the world, from transnational criminal organizations to the rough diamond trade.[46] However, neither the pre-2022 sanctions against Russia nor many of its other programs are as all-encompassing as its comprehensive sanctions in place against Syria, Iran, Cuba, and North Korea, with the exception of the comprehensive sanctions put in place after Russia's invasion of Crimea.[47] In some of these cases, the US sanctions are paralleled by the sanctions measures of other jurisdictions; but in others, the US sanctions are more far-reaching and aggressive than those imposed against the same target by other jurisdictions.

COMPREHENSIVE SANCTIONS

The United States, along with other jurisdictions in certain instances, administers several sanctions programs that are sweeping in the scope of their restrictions. These sanctions programs are often among the most controversial sanctions measures implemented by the United States, due to both the breadth of their restrictions and the extent to which US law often operates extraterritorially to penalize conduct by non-US actors outside the United States. These programs are termed "comprehensive" sanctions, as distinguished from the "targeted" or "smart" sanctions aimed at specific individuals, entities, or sectors rather than entire countries or regions.[48]

Iran has been subject to a variety of US sanctions measures since 1979, when American diplomats were taken hostage in Tehran.[49] The current US sanctions broadly prohibit financial transactions by US persons or from the United States with Iran. The Iran and Libya Sanctions Act of 1996 introduced secondary sanctions, which were designed to retaliate against Iran's nuclear program by punishing non-US parties who engaged in prohibited transactions with Iran.[50] As described further within Chapter 4 on extraterritoriality, these secondary sanctions have been a particular point of tension between the United States and the Member States of the European Union, which historically has not implemented sanctions secondarily.[51]

The European Union implemented its own broad restrictive measures against Iran only later, after the existence of Iran's nuclear program became known early in the new century.[52] The European Union, along with the United States, subsequently enacted a series of nuclear-related sanctions and restrictive measures. These included prohibitions on the import of certain types of energy supplies including crude oil and natural gas, along with an asset freeze on the Central Bank of Iran and myriad other provisions.[53] The UN Security Council also passed its own sanctions again Iran, having passed three rounds of resolutions in 2006, 2007, and 2008 to implement sanctions.[54]

The Joint Comprehensive Plan of Action (JCPOA) was agreed in 2013 and finalized in 2015 between Iran and the five permanent members of the UN Security Council (the United States, China, France, Russia, and the United Kingdom), as well as Germany (the P5 + 1).[55] On Implementation Day of the JCPOA (January 16, 2016), the International Atomic Energy Agency verified that Iran had met its obligations as of that time, and the European Union, United States, and the United Nations lifted many of their nuclear-related sanctions against Iran. In practice, this meant that most of the prohibitions imposed by the European Union and the United Nations were lifted.[56] But the United States maintained a host of sanctions against Iran for a variety of nuclear- and nonnuclear-related reasons, and so implementation of the JCPOA meant that, of the US sanctions against Iran, for the most part only the secondary sanctions that often forced non-US parties into a choice of doing business with either the United States or with Iran were lifted.[57] The sweeping primary sanctions against Iran relevant to parties subject to US sanctions jurisdiction remained largely intact.[58]

The United States withdrew from the JCPOA in 2018, during the administration of President Trump.[59] Iran adhered to the terms of the deal for over a year afterward.[60] Thereafter, in 2020, the United Kingdom, France, and Germany issued a statement voicing their concerns about Iran's reduced compliance with the full terms of the agreement, including with respect to enrichment of uranium.[61] As of April 2023, the Biden administration has not caused the United States to rejoin the JCPOA.[62]

The sanctions maintained against Cuba by the United States are also extensive. These sanctions, however, are US-imposed and do not have the same international support as do certain other sanctions programs.[63] They originated when President Kennedy declared an embargo in February 1962, less than a year after the failed Bay of Pigs invasion.[64] The United States also froze Cuban assets in the United States. Travel restrictions were subsequently imposed after the Cuban Missile Crisis. The sanctions imposed against Cuba do contain certain exceptions, as for humanitarian activities. Travel restrictions were loosened during the Obama administration, allowing for twelve categories of exceptions, including educational activities; athletic competitions; activities by private foundations, or educational or research institutes; and others.[65] Even so, most types of financial transactions by US persons with or in Cuba remained barred, and the Trump administration reimposed some sanctions on Cuba by redesignating the country as a state sponsor of terrorism.[66] This move barred some types of previously permitted travel to Cuba as well as remittances from the United States; some of these Trump-era restrictions were unwound during the Biden administration.[67] Internationally, the sanctions imposed by the United States against Cuba have been highly controversial.[68] In 2021, the UN General Assembly voted for the twenty-ninth straight year to condemn the US embargo of Cuba, with only the United States and Israel voting against the resolution, three other countries abstaining from the vote, and 184 voting in favor of the condemnation.[69]

Syria has become subject to comprehensive sanctions more recently. When the Syrian civil war erupted in 2011, the Assad Regime used chemical weapons against the Syrian people and murdered civilians.[70] The US sanctions authorities responded first by sanctioning certain Syrian officials, and eventually sanctioning the Government of Syria itself and prohibiting the provision of services to Syria or investments in that country.[71] The European Union, Canada, Australia, the Arab League, and others also imposed unilateral sanctions against Syria.[72] Multilateral sanctions, however, were not imposed by the United Nations against Syria, as Russia and China exercised their veto in the UN Security Council against such measures.[73]

The sanctions in place with respect to North Korea are extremely restrictive, having been imposed by many nations in response to the regime's nuclear and missile testing. Nine rounds of UN sanctions against North Korea have been imposed since 2006, due to the country's nuclear test that year.[74] The UN sanctions were supplemented by a variety of additional unilateral measures from countries including the United States, Japan, and South Korea.[75] China, however, continues to maintain economic relations with North Korea.[76] In 2022, China and Russia vetoed additional UN sanctions against North Korea, despite their nine prior decisions since 2006 not to exercise that power.[77]

In each of the comprehensive sanctions programs, exceptions from the broad sanctions restrictions do exist as part of the legal framework. Generally, humanitarian activities, and certain transactions in support of that work, can be carried out in each of these locations.[78] For instance, US law permits the export of agricultural commodities, food, medicine, and medical devices to Iran.[79] As described within this book, however, regulated parties tend to overcomply with sanctions and so legal exemptions may be less effective than their language might suggest.

EFFECTS OF SANCTIONS

When sanctions are deployed with full force, the effects can be staggering. During the effective period of secondary sanctions, Iranian crude oil exports plunged over 50 percent.[80] The impacts are even more severe when sanctions are widely coordinated across nations, as the example of North Korea demonstrated. Yet these economic weapons bring a human cost. Despite the exceptions for the provision of humanitarian services and the supply of food and medicine, sanctions and export controls have often prevented countries from obtaining essential resources for their populations. As a group of nonprofits stated in an open letter to President Biden, sanctions slowed access in Iran to supplies to fight COVID-19.[81] In Yemen, sanctions triggered "a years-long famine and the largest cholera outbreak anywhere in history."[82] The Syrian economy suffered greatly from sanctions, including through a collapse of its currency, hyperinflation, and food shortages.[83] UN sanctions were criticized as worsening standards of living and contributing to humanitarian crises in Haiti, Iraq, and Afghanistan.[84] As described further in Chapter 7, economic sanctions and trade restrictions can create or exacerbate humanitarian crises by directly restricting the import of certain goods, such as medical equipment, into a country. Despite the presence of exemptions for many types of humanitarian activities and imports, sanctions can cause regulated parties to reduce risk by over-complying with sanctions. Sanctions can also interfere with the regular economic and trade functions of a particular area, and worsening economic conditions can foster human suffering.

And despite the economic fallout sanctions can wreak, they have not always been fully effective in accomplishing their goals, especially where sanctions have large-scale objectives such as regime change. The Communist Party has ruled Cuba throughout decades of sanctions.[85] Sanctions did not effect a change in regime after the 1979 Iranian Revolution.[86] It was Operation Desert Storm, and not the sanctions that preceded it, that forced Saddam Hussein to withdraw Iraqi forces from Kuwait.[87] And as events would prove, the sanctions enacted in response to Russia's 2014 annexation of Crimea ultimately failed to prevent further Russian aggression.

But a goal of sanctions, generally, is to provide some deterrent[88] or punitive effect short of military action or physical war.[89] With a limited range of nonmilitary responses available, an imperfect economic weapon may be preferable to military escalation. While sanctions themselves can be an inadequate tool for regime change, they can nevertheless be used to promote certain worthwhile goals, such as human rights protection. Indeed, apartheid in South Africa ended after the coordinated imposition of economic sanctions, along with a broader commercial boycott.[90] Yet evidence suggests that the imposition of economic sanctions can worsen human rights abuses, despite the good intentions with which they were enacted.[91] Sanctions are therefore a controversial tool whose odds of success, at the time of their imposition, are often uncertain.

THE RECENT PRE-INVASION SANCTIONS AGAINST RUSSIA

The United States, the European Union, and other powers repeatedly ratcheted up incremental sanctions against Russia in the years immediately preceding 2022. As described in further detail in the next section of this chapter, Russia, under the leadership of President Vladimir Putin, invaded and annexed the Crimean Peninsula of Ukraine in February and March of 2014.[92] The United States responded by enacting sanctions specifically targeting economic activity in that region, restricting the flow of exports of goods, services, and technology to Crimea and prohibiting new investment there by US persons as well.[93] Imports of goods, services, and technology from Crimea into the United States were also prohibited. The Office of Foreign Assets Control also introduced sanctions targeted at certain sectors of the Russian economy, including oil and gas exploration in deepwater Russian locations or offshore in the Arctic.[94] Other nations and jurisdictions imposed similar, coordinated measures in response to the Russian invasion of Crimea, including the European Union, the United Kingdom, and Canada.[95]

The impetus for sanctions grew when in July 2014, Russian-backed separatists in Ukraine shot down Malaysian Airlines Flight 17, killing 283 passengers and 15 crew members.[96] The event led to calls for increased sanctions against Russia to respond to its support of the separatist groups that threatened Ukraine's territorial sovereignty.[97] That same month, the European Union announced sanctions against Russian individuals and entities linked to the Russian government.[98]

Other sanctions measures addressed different bad acts by Russian actors and the Russian state. For example, the death of Sergei Magnitsky in Russian custody led to a wave of human rights–related sanctions against Russia. Magnitsky was a Russian lawyer who uncovered tax fraud and corruption linked to the Kremlin.[99] He was arrested in late 2008 by the Russian Ministry of the Interior. While in custody, he was refused treatment for pancreatitis.[100] A Russian human rights council concluded that on the night of his death in November 2009, Magnitsky was beaten by eight guards with rubber batons. An ambulance crew called to help him was left waiting for over an hour.[101] He died shortly thereafter. He was thirty-seven years old. "He died from heart failure," said Putin.[102]

As detailed in the investor Bill Browder's two books on the topic, Browder and others lobbied governments worldwide to respond to Magnitsky's death by enacting sanctions on Russian human rights violators.[103] Magnitsky bills passed around the world, starting with the United States' Magnitsky Act in 2012.[104] Similar laws were then passed in Canada, the United Kingdom, the European Union, Australia, and other nations. Russia responded to the US legislation within two weeks of its passage, banning Americans from adopting Russian children.[105]

The 2017 Countering America's Adversaries through Sanctions Act (CAATSA) also imposed sanctions on Russia, along with sanctions on Iran and North Korea. These sanctions against Russia were designed to respond to interference in the 2016 US presidential election, along with Russian activities connected with the invasion of Crimea and the ongoing civil war in Syria. Leading up to the 2016 election, Russian hackers had stolen voter information, emailed election administrators, and even accessed Hillary Clinton's emails.[106] Special Counsel Robert S. Mueller III, indicting Russians for these actions, in particular noted the role of the Russian Internet Research Agency. This "troll farm" had created thousands of fake social media accounts posing as Americans to sow disinformation about the upcoming election.[107]

Among other provisions, CAATSA mandated sanctions of various types pertaining to Russia based on issues of cyber security, corruption, sanctions evasion, human rights abuses, certain types of crude oil projects, export pipelines, arms transfers to Syria, privatization of state-owned assets, and others.[108] It also introduced prohibitions concerning certain types of new debt and equity related to sanctioned Russian energy companies and financial institutions.[109] As these last provisions were restrictions directed at particular sectors of the Russian economy, they were called "sectoral" sanctions.[110]

The US Treasury in 2018 made subject to full blocking sanctions (the nature of which are described in further detail in this chapter) entities and individuals involved with election interference, including the Internet Research Agency and those who had funded or assisted it.[111]

Businesses in the United States and abroad had also faced disruptive cyberattacks from Russia. Among these was the NotPetya attack, which caused globally $10 billion in damage, spreading out from Ukraine to Europe, the United States, Australia, and others. It hit entities like the pharmaceutical company Merck, shipper A.P. Moller-Maersk, and even Russian state oil company Rosneft as the cyber virus advanced, unchecked, back into Russia.[112] Ransomware – software freezing access to systems or data until the victim made a payment – from Russian sources had already targeted US infrastructure and critical operations, such as hospitals. Sanctions were announced in 2021 against Russia in part due to the hacking activities of the Russian Intelligence Services, including the Federal Security Service and the Main Intelligence Directorate.[113]

The United States and the European Union implemented sanctions in response to Russia's use of chemical weapons to poison Sergei Skripal and opposition leader Alexei Navalny.[114] Skripal was an alleged Russian double agent who was passing intelligence to British authorities. In March 2018, he and his adult daughter Yulia were found unconscious on a bench in Salisbury in the UK, the result of exposure to the nerve agent Novichok.[115] Navalny, too, had been poisoned with Novichok. He became extremely sick on a flight within Russia in August 2020 and was evacuated to Germany. Hospitalized and diagnosed there, he was imprisoned on his return to Russia.[116] The US Secretary of State made a determination that Russia's use of Novichok against Navalny triggered actions under the Chemical and Biological Weapons Control and Warfare Elimination Act of 1991.[117] This triggered measures from the United States in 2021, including further export restrictions on items controlled for export for reasons of national security, as well as US opposition should Russia seek loans from international financial institutions, and a prohibition on US banks providing loans or credit to the Government of Russia except for food and agricultural commodities and products.[118]

When the US Department of the Treasury fully blocks persons and entities, as for example it did under the Magnitsky Sanctions or the cyber-related sanctions, it does so by naming individuals and entities to OFAC's Specially Designated Nationals and Blocked Persons (SDN) List.[119] Naming a party to the SDN List results in that party being subject to full blocking sanctions.[120] When that occurs, no US party, or party within the United States, may engage in a financial transaction with the SDN.[121] Nor can the US party facilitate, approve, finance, or guarantee a transaction by a foreign person that would be prohibited if the US person had engaged in that transaction directly themselves.[122] Blocking generally involves freezing assets, rather than seizing them (absent any link to criminal activity or other indication that the funds have been obtained improperly). Ownership of such assets remains the property of their blocked owners, but access to them is denied by way of the blocking.[123] Likewise, the United Kingdom implements targeted asset freezes, applicable to parties named on OFSI's Consolidated List.[124] The European Union maintains a consolidated list of persons, groups, and entities subject to EU financial sanctions, including blocking sanctions.

In November 2020, Russia responded to the sanctions enacted against it by banning the import of agricultural products from the United States, the European Union, Canada, Australia, and other jurisdictions that had enacted economic sanctions against Russia.[125] Food and agriculture exports from Lithuania, Latvia, and Estonia to Russia were negatively impacted by these actions in particular.[126]

The Russian sanctions in place before February 2022 were much more restricted in scope than are the sanctions in place against comprehensively sanctioned countries (excepting those applicable to the Crimea region, which are comprehensive in nature). While a variety of sanctions measures blocked or limited certain transactions with Russia, overall the pre-2022 sanctions did not touch the bulk of Russian economic activity. The US sanctions against Russia during that time (excepting the Crimea sanctions) lacked the comprehensive nature of certain other US sanctions programs. While Crimea was a comprehensively sanctioned region, financial transactions with parties elsewhere in Russia could be carried out so long as they did not involve a party on the SDN List, or involve a more limited restriction such as a sectoral sanction or a CAATSA restriction. The pre-2022 sanctions against Russia were on the whole limited in nature, and were designed to respond in proportion to the harmful Russian activities that had occurred over the past decade.[127]

THE COMING SIGNS OF INVASION

Russia's aggressive intentions with respect to Ukraine became increasingly clear in recent years. Since 2014 in particular, when Russia invaded and annexed Ukraine's Crimean peninsula, it seemed a distinct possibility that Putin might in the near future launch an attempted takeover of additional Ukrainian regions or perhaps even the entire country.

Part of the Soviet Union, Ukraine became an independent nation in August 1991 upon declaration of the Ukrainian parliament. This occurred after the fall of the Berlin Wall the previous year, and shortly before the formal dissolution of the Soviet Union in December 1991.[128] The country voted to become independent from the USSR in December 1991. A turnout of 84 percent of eligible voters cast over 90 percent of votes for independence.[129]

The historic state of Rus', Christianized in 988 and captured by the Mongols in 1240, was centered on the present Ukrainian capital of Kyiv.[130] Moscow emerged as a major city only later. Putin often cited the state of Rus' as the justification for escalating Russian incursions into Ukrainian territory, ignoring both the centuries of subsequent history in the territory that would become Ukraine and the fact that power in Rus' had been centered on Kyiv, rather than Moscow.[131] He authored an article in July 2021 emphasizing what he characterized as a common history between Russia and Ukraine.[132] The piece echoed many of the same themes he earlier used to justify the takeover of Crimea. Ukraine was a modern creation, Putin said, but he claimed that truly it was part of "historical Russia." "One fact is crystal clear," he argued. When the Ukrainian state was created, "Russia was robbed, indeed." Yet Putin's claims were clearly contrary to the thirty years' history of Ukraine as a sovereign nation.[133]

The new century saw both pro-democratic popular movements in Ukraine and a growing Russian determination to exert control over the country. The Ukrainian election of 2004 pitted Russian-backed Viktor Yanukovych against Viktor Yushchenko, a former prime minister who had attempted energy sector reforms.[134] The Orange Revolution resulted when Yanukovych was declared the winner of a fraudulently run election. Protestors gathered in Kyiv's Maidan Nezalezhnosti (Independence Square) to support Yushchenko.[135] The movement foiled

Yanukovych's attempt to claim the presidency and allowed Yushchenko to take office.[136] During the campaign, Yushchenko was poisoned with dioxin, an herbicide also used in Agent Orange.[137] The circumstances of his poisoning remained mysterious and Russia denied any involvement, but Yushchenko himself believed that Russia was responsible.[138]

Yanukovych returned to power in 2010, when he was elected president.[139] In 2013, he suspended talks toward an association agreement with the European Union in favor of moving toward joining a Russian-led customs union.[140] In response, protests broke out in Ukraine at the end of 2013 and violence peaked in February and March of 2014. "Ukraine is Europe," protestors in Maidan chanted.[141] The conflict was variously referred to as the Maidan Revolution and the Revolution of Dignity.[142] Yanukovych fled on February 21, 2014, eventually ending up in Russia.[143] On February 22, the Ukrainian parliament voted to dismiss him from the presidency.[144]

Crimea was soon the site of protests, both pro-Russian and pro-Ukrainian.[145] At the end of February, unidentified pro-Russian gunmen took control of the Crimean parliament building,[146] and subsequently two airports.[147] Armed troops took control of the peninsula in what soon became apparent was a Russian state-organized incursion.[148] Though Putin originally denied Russian involvement, he would later admit the presence of Russian forces in Crimea.[149]

In what was largely characterized as a sham referendum, Crimea voted on March 16 to break from Ukraine and unify with Russia.[150] The vote returned 97 percent in favor of joining Russia, with 83 percent turnout, and with voting occurring under armed security and without international observers.[151] (A later report briefly posted by Putin's Council on Civil Society and Human Rights suggested that the turnout had actually been much lower.) Voters chose between either unification with Russia or greater autonomy within Ukraine, without a choice to maintain the current status of Crimea within Ukraine.[152] On March 18, Putin delivered an address, claiming Crimea for Russia. This was perhaps done either as part of a planned broader scheme of territorial expansion into Ukraine, or as a plan concocted to respond to the pro-democratic nature of the Maidan Revolution.[153] The peninsula was an "integral part" of Russia, Putin claimed.[154]

The annexation of Crimea was internationally condemned as illegal. The other nations within the informal Group of Eight forum (G8) (Canada, France, Germany, Italy, Japan, the United Kingdom, and the United States) indefinitely suspended Russia from the group, becoming the G7.[155] The Parliamentary Assembly of the Council of Europe adopted a resolution stating that the "illegal annexation" had "no legal effect" and the Council would therefore not recognize it.[156] The US White House issued a statement: "No decisions should be made about the future of Ukraine without the Ukrainian government. ... Russia's actions are dangerous and destabilizing."[157]

But even at that time, it was apparent that Russian ambitions for Ukraine's territory were not yet satisfied, as evidenced by Russia's support of separatists in the

Donetsk and Luhansk oblasts. These provinces were part of the Donbas region of Ukraine. After Stalin's forced agricultural collectivization had killed millions of Ukrainians by famine in the 1930s, the Soviet Union sent Russians en masse to the region to live.[158] In April 2014, pro-Russian protestors stormed government buildings in Donetsk and Luhansk; the area experienced fighting between Russian-backed rebels and Ukrainian state forces since that time.[159] Also in 2014, the Ukrainian parliament granted the areas temporary self-rule.[160] Over 14,000 people had died in the Donbas region in the ensuing years, and over a million more had fled to Russia.

A particular point of Russian contention was Ukraine's public desire to join the North Atlantic Treaty Organization (NATO). Ukraine had adopted legislation in 2017 stating its commitment to attain NATO membership.[161] The Ukrainian parliament had also voted in 2019 in favor of a constitutional amendment stating the goal of NATO and EU membership, which the Ukrainian president Petro Poroshenko then signed into effect.[162] Later, Putin would use Ukraine's NATO ambitions as a justification for the 2022 invasion; some argued that this was a mere pretext rather than a genuine trigger.[163]

Volodymyr Zelensky, a former actor, was elected President of Ukraine in 2019.[164] He would soon have to face the existential threat of Russia to Ukraine, as it was becoming clear that Russia was soon to take drastic offensive action. The immediate warning signs developed in spring 2021, when the Russian military appeared near the Ukrainian border, and stayed after military exercises ended.[165] The military presence swelled again in November. Videos on social media showed tanks and missiles being moved in the south and west of Russia.[166] In December 2021, headlines grew increasingly urgent: "Russia planning massive military offensive against Ukraine involving 175,000 troops, US intelligence warns." Satellite images from space revealed Russian military activities in Russia and Belarus, close to Ukraine: a new field hospital, a pontoon bridge, antitank attack helicopters.[167] Ukraine and the world waited uneasily as this intelligence pointed toward what Russia was planning.

As 2022 began, world leaders sought to prevent a Russian invasion. It was later reported that in January, the Director of the US Central Intelligence Agency made a secret trip to Kyiv to warn Zelensky of the Russian plan to invade through Belarus and to capture the airport in Hostomel, Ukraine, as part of the attack.[168] Publicly, the United States warned repeatedly of "sanctions with massive consequences" were Russia to move further into Ukraine.[169] In mid-February, German Chancellor Olaf Scholz met with Zelensky in Kyiv and then with Putin in Moscow to pledge German financial support to Ukraine and to try to dissuade Russia from further violation of Ukrainian territorial sovereignty.[170]

In the coming weeks and months, Russia would shred its tenuous peace with Ukraine, and in turn, its own ties with the world economic system.

2

Invasion

The First Week

MONDAY, FEBRUARY 21

If Ukraine was to join NATO it would serve as a direct threat to the security of Russia.
— President Vladimir Putin[1]

The first steps of the 2022 Russian campaign against Ukraine came the day after the Beijing Olympics' closing ceremony. Putin signed a decree recognizing two portions of the Donbas region of Ukraine as independent – the so-called Donetsk People's Republic (DNR) and the Luhansk People's Republic (LNR).[2] He ordered troops into the two regions; for "peacekeeping," Putin claimed.[3] Later intelligence reports would reveal that the timing was not accidental. Chinese officials had in fact asked Russia to delay the invasion until after the close of the games.[4]

Putin broadcast a message over Russian state television, to the Russian people, to "compatriots" in Ukraine, and to the world.[5] He spoke for an hour, attempting to justify the military action. He claimed that Ukraine was an "integral part" of Russian "history, culture, spiritual space."[6] Per Putin, Ukraine was beset by "the rise of far-right nationalism," by "Russophobia," and by "Neo-Nazism." His particular concern was the Ukrainian desire to join NATO. Putin saw this possibility as a threat to the security of Russia itself. But the invasion fit with Putin's long-standing obsession of reclaiming the former power of the Soviet Union and his vision of an expansionist, imperialist Russia.

In his speech, Putin acknowledged that the Russian offensive would likely provoke a response: "[T]hey are threatening us with sanctions. But I think they will impose those sanctions." In his view, however, those sanctions were inevitable, regardless of what Russia did: "They will always find an excuse to introduce more sanctions regardless of the situation in Ukraine."

Putin was correct about one thing: Sanctions would be forthcoming, even if the initial response of the United States, the European Union, and other pro-Ukrainian jurisdictions were "cautious."[7] Later that same day, President Biden announced Executive Order 14,065, which introduced sanctions prohibiting a US person or company from making any new investment in either of the so-called republics.[8] No goods, services, or technology could be imported from the United States after having passed through those regions. Nor could goods, services, or technology be sent to those regions by a US person, or from the United States. These prohibitions resembled the US sanctions that had earlier been issued with respect to Crimea, which placed broad restrictions on transactions and exports in the sanctioned region itself, but which were geographically limited to the Crimea and Donbas regions.[9] The White House stressed that these sanctions were "distinct from the severe and swift economic measures" that the United States and its allies would issue were Russia to launch a broader invasion of Ukraine.[10]

Likewise, the European Union announced limited sanctions, blocking the assets of five individuals and implementing travel bans against them. The individuals sanctioned were members of the Russian State Duma who had been elected to represent Crimea and its city of Sevastopol after its illegal annexation, as well as leaders of the Sevastopol electoral commission.[11] They were so sanctioned for undermining Ukrainian sovereignty. The United Kingdom stated that it planned to announce its own measures the next day.[12]

The United Nations Security Council held an emergency session late that evening at Ukraine's request. Rosemary DiCarlo, the United Nations Under-Secretary-General for Political and Peacebuilding Affairs, commented: "The risk of major conflict is real and needs to be prevented at all costs."[13] The group would meet again two days later.

TUESDAY, FEBRUARY 22

Who in the Lord's name does Putin think gives him the right to declare new so-called countries on territory that belonged to his neighbors?
—President Joseph Biden[14]

On Tuesday, the Russians remained in Ukraine, and the world remained on edge. Although Russian troops were still only in the Donbas region, it was apparent that Russia would not halt its advance there. "The invasion of Ukraine has effectively already begun," said Scott Morrison, the Prime Minister of Australia. "Russia is at peak readiness to now complete a full-scale invasion of Ukraine, and that is likely to occur within the next 24 hours."[15] Boris Johnson, Prime Minister of the United Kingdom, agreed: "Putin is establishing the pretext for a full-scale offensive."[16]

The economic response to the Russian aggression continued, including a particularly high-profile measure taken with respect to the controversial Nord Stream 2 pipeline. The pipeline had been built to transport natural gas from Russia to northern Germany.[17] Although the €10 billion project (paid for in part by Russian state-owned Gazprom, as well as by Western gas companies) was physically complete, it required Germany's certification to begin operations.[18] As a condition to certification, the German Economic Ministry had issued an opinion in October 2021 that the pipeline was not a security threat to Germany.[19] Olaf Scholz, the German chancellor, now stated that the certification process would be halted by the withdrawal of that opinion, and that the German Economic Ministry would "make sure that this pipeline cannot be certified at this point in time."[20] In reply, Dmitry Medvedev, former President of Russia and current deputy chairman of the Russian Security Council, tweeted: "Welcome to the brave new world where Europeans are very soon going to pay €2.000 for 1.000 cubic meters of natural gas!"[21]

Consistent with their actions the day before, the United States and the United Kingdom announced new financial sanctions in response to Russia's recognition of the so-called DNR and LNR regions as "independent."[22] Significantly, the United States blocked VEB and PSB, two Russian state-owned banks, placing them on the SDN List. VEB was a major source of funds for economic development projects within Russia.[23] PSB had ties to the Russian Ministry of Defense and the country's defense sector.[24] The United Kingdom sanctioned five other banks, including one with close ties to the Kremlin and another institution linked to the Russian defense industry.[25] Several individuals, including oligarchs (described in Chapter 8) were personally sanctioned by the United Kingdom as well. The United States also issued Directive 1A under Executive Order 14,024, which extended existing Russian sovereign debt prohibitions to cover participation in the secondary bond market for bonds issued after March 1, 2022.[26] (Participation by US parties in the primary market for such bonds had already been prohibited by Directive 1 under Executive Order 14,024, issued in April 2021.)

Similar to the messaging the day before, the United Kingdom noted that these were only the "initial" round of sanctions against Russia.[27] The United States agreed. "[I]f Russia goes further with this invasion, we stand prepared to go further," declared President Biden.[28] It was clear, as Russia prepared for a broader invasion, that economic sanctions would be drastically expanded when that moment came.

WEDNESDAY, FEBRUARY 23

We want to determine our own course and build our own history: peacefully, calmly, and honestly.

—President Volodymyr Zelensky[29]

By Wednesday, Russia's intentions of a general invasion were becoming increasingly clear. The Ukrainian parliament declared a state of emergency.[30] US wheat prices rose to a 10-year high.[31] Malware was reported to be targeting organizations in Ukraine, and the websites of Ukraine's parliament and foreign ministry went down amid a distributed denial-of-service attack.[32]

Again on Wednesday, more coordinated sanctions and trade restrictions were issued to address the developing Russian threat. With Germany having halted certification of the Nord Stream 2 pipeline the day before, the United States imposed sanctions on the company that owned and had planned to operate it, as well as on the entity's corporate officers.[33] Nord Stream 2 AG and those individual officers would now appear on OFAC's SDN List, and their assets were fully blocked.

The European Union issued its first sanctions package of 2022 against Russia.[34] These measures included sanctions on all 351 members of the Russian State Duma, since they had voted to support Putin's decision to recognize the Donetsk and Luhansk oblasts as independent republics. The European Union sanctioned individuals including Russian government officials, oligarchs, senior military officers, and those responsible for spreading disinformation against Ukraine. The package contained an import ban on goods from the non-Ukrainian-governed portions of the Donetsk and Luhansk regions. The European Union also introduced financial sector sanctions to prohibit financing of the Russian government and central bank.[35]

Australia also imposed sanctions, imposing travel bans and financial sanctions on eight members of Russia's Security Council and imposing sanctions specific to certain sectors of the Donetsk and Luhansk regions.[36] It also imposed sanctions on certain Russian financial institutions similar to those announced by the United States and the United Kingdom the day before. Japan, too, announced similar measures; it would ban exports from and imports to the Donetsk and Luhansk regions, and also prohibit Russian sovereign bond issuance and trading in Japan.[37] Iceland's prime minister confirmed that the country would be joining with the EU sanctions.[38]

UK Prime Minister Boris Johnson was criticized for not having yet imposed more stringent sanctions against Russia.[39] UK Foreign Secretary Liz Truss wrote in *The Times* that additional measures would be imposed "[s]hould Russia refuse to pull back its troops": "Nothing is off the table in our response to Putin's aggression."[40]

Late that evening, Ukrainian President Volodymyr Zelensky spoke to the Russian people directly in his native Russian via the messaging service Telegram: "You know our character, you know our people, and you know our principles. You know what we value. So stop and listen to yourselves, to the voice of reason, to the voice of common sense."[41] His words would go unheeded.

THURSDAY, FEBRUARY 24

Today I initiated a phone call with the president of the Russian Federation. The result was silence.

—President Volodymyr Zelensky[42]

Russian troops in Belarus crossed the Ukrainian border in the early morning hours on Thursday. Air raid sirens sounded as shelling began. Zelensky announced martial law[43] and said sabotage groups had entered Kyiv.[44] Putin televised his message: "I decided to conduct a special military operation," he said, allegedly to protect the Donbas region.[45]

One after another, world leaders condemned the invasion. Finnish President Sauli Niinstö commented: "Russia has massively expanded hostilities in Ukraine and now the mask has come off. Only the cold face of war is visible."[46] The European Council held a special meeting and issued conclusions "on Russia's unprovoked and unjustified military aggression against Ukraine."[47] Among its declarations, it stated: "[t]he European Council deplores the tragic loss of life and human suffering caused by the Russian aggression."

Sanctions followed swiftly, with major packages announced by the United States and the United Kingdom on the 24th, and the European Union's second sanctions package to be issued on the 25th. These sanctions were different from those of the immediately preceding days. The new measures were designed to begin undermining the core of the Russian economy itself, not merely those banks linked to the defense sector or a few powerful oligarchs. These sanctions were still not so wide-reaching as those in place against Iran, North Korea, or the other comprehensively sanctioned areas. But though technically targeted in nature, they barely resembled other targeted sanctions regimes, which were far more selective.

Two things in particular were noteworthy about the sanctions announced this day. First was the systemic importance of the sanctioned entities to the Russian economy and financial system. The second was the extraordinarily coordinated and rapid nature of the sanctions response by a large number of nations, undertaken through multilateral cooperation but not through the United Nations.[48] While sanctions had certainly often been imposed outside of the UN framework in the past, fully autonomous EU sanctions separate from any existing UN program had previously largely been more targeted or thematic in nature.[49] The US announcement of sanctions issued on February 24 highlighted the extent of coordination:

> Putin's threatening actions and now his unprovoked aggression toward Ukraine are being met with an unprecedented level of multilateral cooperation. The United States welcomes the commitments by Australia, Canada, the European Union, Japan, and the United Kingdom that they will also take similarly forceful actions to hold Russia accountable – demonstrating the strength of our partnerships and deepening the impact on Russia more than any action we could have taken alone.[50]

One category of sanctions was those targeting significant Russian financial institutions. Several key banks were subject to full US blocking sanctions and asset freezes by the United Kingdom. OFAC, for instance, placed on the SDN List VTB, Russia's state-owned and second-largest bank. It held almost 20 percent of Russian banking assets.[51] It was "one of the largest financial institutions the [United States] Treasury" had ever blocked, a move intended to send an "unmistakable signal" that Russian aggression would be met with economic retaliation.[52] So too did the United

Kingdom announce an asset freeze on VTB.[53] Other banks fully blocked by the United States included state-owned Otkritie (Russia's seventh-largest financial institution, and a systemically important credit institution); Sovcombank (Russia's ninth-largest bank overall and the third-largest private financial institution in Russia by amount of assets); and Novikombank (another Russian state-owned bank).[54]

The United States also announced the imposition of correspondent banking and payable-through account sanctions separate from full blocking sanctions. Correspondent banking constitutes the network of inter-bank relationships, often across national borders.[55] Correspondent banks hold accounts for other banks, to be used for various purposes including foreign exchange services, international wire transfers, and check clearing.[56] Payable-through accounts allow customers of foreign banks access to check clearing services and the US financial system.[57] (Correspondent and payable-through account sanctions are described in greater detail in Chapter 3)

The correspondent and payable-through account sanctions did not fully block the property of a sanctioned bank in the same way that being named to the SDN List and thereby incurring full blocking sanctions did.[58] However, they did have a significant impact on the banks on which they were placed. They limited the ability of those banks to open accounts or maintain accounts at other banks abroad and thereby easily transact certain types of business for its customers. The correspondent banking sanctions also severely restricted sanctioned banks' access to US dollars through the channels of global banking networks.[59]

OFAC imposed correspondent banking sanctions on Sberbank, the largest financial institution in Russia. It held about a third of the country's assets, and was majority-owned by the Russian government.[60] Similarly, the United Kingdom placed sanctions on Sberbank on March 1 to prohibit its correspondent banking and sterling clearing activities.[61]

OFAC made thirteen Russian entities subject to debt and equity restrictions, which prohibited the issuance of debt of more than fourteen days' maturity and new equity for their benefit.[62] These entities included Gazprombank, which was Russia's third-largest financial institution, along with Sberbank, Russian Agricultural Bank (Russia's fifth-largest financial institution), Gazprom (the world's largest natural gas company), Rostelecom (Russia's largest telecommunications company), Alrosa (the world's largest diamond mining company), Sovcomflot (Russia's largest maritime and freight shipping company), and others, including transportation- and energy-related entities.

Another element of the economic response consisted of extensive export controls. High-tech items of US origin or exported from the United States used by the defense, aerospace, and maritime sectors, including "semiconductors, computers, telecommunications, information security equipment, lasers, and sensors," would by default now be denied for export to Russia.[63] Military end-users in Russia were also newly restricted from receiving any exports of US-origin items or items from the

United States. Similar measures were coordinated with and forthcoming from the European Union, Japan, Australia, the United Kingdom, Canada, and New Zealand.

OFAC also sanctioned Belarusian individuals and entities associated with the defense and financial sectors for supporting and facilitating the Russian invasion.[64] These included Belinvestbank and Bank Dabrabyt, Belarus's fourth- and eleventh-largest banks, respectively, based on their connections with the Government of Belarus. As OFAC referenced in its press release announcing these sanctions, Belarusian President Alexander Lukashenko had been fraudulently elected to a sixth term in 2020 and had become increasingly dependent on Russia to maintain power.[65] The country had earlier been made subject to sanctions by various jurisdictions including the United Kingdom, the European Union, and the United States for repression of peaceful protests following the invasion.[66] Belarus was now supporting Russia in its invasion of Ukraine, allowing Russia to launch its attack toward Kyiv through a convenient route in Belarusian territory.[67] On March 1, the United Kingdom announced its first package of sanctions against Belarusian actors for their support of the Russian invasion, including four senior defense officials and two state military enterprises (an aircraft repair plant and a semiconductor manufacturer).[68] The US export controls announced against Russia on February 24 would, on March 2, be implemented against Belarus as well.[69]

All of these measures, however, left one sector largely untouched: energy. Within the US regulatory framework, general licenses provided carve-outs from sanctions restrictions.[70] As part of Thursday's measures, General License 8 allowed the banks newly penalized by full blocking and correspondent account sanctions to continue to carry out energy-related transactions.[71] "Related to energy" was broadly defined to include a variety of sources like oil, natural gas, petroleum, coal, wood, biofuels, and others. The exemption extended to activities like extraction, production, transport, and transmission, along with many more. Thus, these sanctions created a regulatory exemption for transactions related to the flow of energy from Russia to proceed unimpeded. While the energy sector was exempt from the sanctions restrictions, it was still subject to export controls and sectoral sanctions that limited new investment and financing.

Meanwhile, Russia's offensive continued. Hanna Maliar, Ukraine's deputy defense minister, posted on Facebook calling for Ukrainians to resist the Russian invasion. Google searches for how to make a Molotov cocktail spiked. Ukrainian TV stations broadcast instructions on how to make the weapons.[72]

As the CIA had warned Zelensky, Russian helicopters attacked Antonov Airport in Hostomel. They destroyed the massive Antonov An-225 Mryia aircraft, which had been used on medical supply trips during the COVID-19 pandemic.[73] Zelensky ordered a general mobilization to defend Ukraine, under which men between the ages of 18 and 60 were no longer permitted to leave the country.[74]

FRIDAY, FEBRUARY 25

We are facing a full-fledged invasion of a country by another one. It is not a special forces operation, like Russia intends us to believe. It is a fully fledged invasion with bombing, killing of civilians, with confrontations between two armies. This is the worst thing that has happened in Europe ... since the end of the Cold War. And nobody knows what is happening afterwards. Nobody knows which are the real intentions of Putin.

—Josep Borrell, High Representative of the European Union for Foreign Affairs and Security Policy[75]

By Friday, the battle for Kyiv had begun.[76] Missile strikes came in the early morning hours. Air defense downed a Russian aircraft, which hit an apartment building on its way down.[77] Long lines of cars formed as Ukrainians fled into Poland and Romania.[78] Ukrainian lawmaker Kira Rudik posted a photo of herself on Twitter holding a gun: "I learn to use #Kalashnikov and prepare to bear arms. It sounds surreal as just a few days ago it would never come to my mind."[79]

Friday brought the second major round of sanctions from the European Union, following their conclusions and public announcement the day before that action would be taken in coordination with the United Kingdom, the United States, and the other sanctioning powers.[80] As with the sanctions of other jurisdictions the day before, financial sanctions were greatly expanded from the initial measures taken earlier in the week. Russian state-owned entities could no longer be traded on EU exchanges. Export controls were tightened, including those on semiconductors. EU parties could no longer sell aircraft or parts to Russian airlines.[81] The EU sanctioned Putin personally, as well as Sergey Lavrov, the Russian minister of foreign affairs. The United States did likewise, also sanctioning two members of Russia's Security Council directly responsible for the invasion of Ukraine in addition to members of the council already sanctioned.[82] Australia, too, would soon sanction Putin and all members of the Russian Security Council not already subject to its sanctions.[83]

Taiwan announced its intent to join with the democratic sanctioning parties. The Taiwanese vice-president Lai Ching-te commented: "The principle of self-determination cannot be erased by brute force."[84] China refused to condemn the Russian invasion.[85]

In the evening came word from President Zelensky, who filmed a video from Kyiv. He confirmed that he remained in Ukraine and in Kyiv. "We are all here. Our troops are here. Civil society is here. And we are here. We are defending the independence of our country. We will continue to do so."[86]

The UN Security Council voted on a draft resolution condemning Russia's actions. The resolution failed. Russia, a permanent member of the Security Council, exercised its veto, precluding passage of the resolution.[87] Fifty countries issued a joint statement in response: "Russia has abused its power today to veto our strong resolution. But Russia cannot veto our voices. Russia cannot veto the

Ukrainian people. Russia cannot veto their own people protesting this war in the streets. Russia cannot veto the UN Charter. Russia cannot, and will not, veto accountability."[88]

SATURDAY, FEBRUARY 26

The United Nations was born out of war to end war. Today, that objective was not achieved. But we must never give up. We must give peace another chance.
— UN Secretary-General António Guterres[89]

The Russian invasion continued to meet with fierce opposition in Ukraine.[90] "Russian forces are not making the progress they had planned," reported the UK Ministry of Defense.[91] Gunfire in Kyiv killed a six-year-old and injured several others. Russian artillery heavily damaged an apartment building in Kharkiv, killing one person. The mayor of Vasylkiv, Natalia Balasynonvich, reported fighting in the town and over 200 Ukrainians wounded.[92]

The imposition of new sanctions measures continued. The United States, the European Union, France, Germany, Italy, the United Kingdom, and Canada issued a joint statement "commit[ting] to ensuring that selected Russian banks [would be] removed from the SWIFT messaging system."[93] As further discussed within Chapter 3, disconnecting those banks from the messaging system that facilitated the settlement and clearing of cross-border transactions would isolate Russia from key portions of the global financial system. These countries also agreed to create a task force to enforce the new sanctions.

Private entities responded to the invasion as well. Google, YouTube, and Facebook cut off Russian state-owned media company RT from monetizing its videos on their platforms. [94] Within days, TikTok and Facebook would block RT in the European Union entirely, and in March YouTube would block Russian state-owned media channels around the world. [95] Individual states within the United States also took actions variously significant and symbolic. New Hampshire enacted a ban on the sale of Russian alcoholic beverages, such as vodka, at state liquor outlets.[96] A number of other states had or would take similar actions, like Utah, Virginia, Pennsylvania, Oregon, North Carolina, and West Virginia.[97]

At the United Nations, the Security Council sought to take action notwithstanding Russia's veto of the resolution the day before to demand Russia's immediate cessation of the invasion and withdrawal.[98] The Security Council called an emergency session of the UN General Assembly on February 27,[99] which opened on February 28.[100] On March 2, the General Assembly adopted a resolution condemning the Russian invasion, and "[r]eaffirming its commitment to the sovereignty, independence, unity and territorial integrity of Ukraine within its internationally recognized borders."[101] The resolution stated: "The military operations of the Russian Federation inside the sovereign territory of Ukraine are on a scale that the international community has not seen in Europe in decades. .... [U]rgent action is needed to save this generation from the scourge of war." 141 UN Member States voted for the resolution; five against it; and thirty-five abstained.[102]

SUNDAY, FEBRUARY 27

Sanctions are most effective if many countries introduce the same restrictions. We are therefore in close contact with the EU and our neighbouring countries, and preparations for implementing the wide-ranging package of sanctions are in full swing.
            –Prime Minister of Norway Jonas Gahr Støre.[103]

The UN Office of the High Commissioner for Human Rights reported that by 5:00 PM the day before, there had been at least 240 civilian casualties in Ukraine, with at least 64 dead.[104] It also reported that more than 160,000 people had already been internally displaced, and over 116,000 had fled Ukraine for other nations. Missiles hit oil and gas facilities in Kharkiv and in Vasylkiv, near Kyiv, causing fires and explosions so large that officials in Kharkiv notified residents that the explosion had not in fact been caused by a nuclear bomb.[105]

The sanctioning powers continued to express their support for Ukraine. EU President Ursula von der Leyen issued a statement: "For the first time ever, the European Union will finance the purchase and delivery of weapons and other equipment to a country that is under attack. This is a watershed moment."[106] In a televised interview the same day, she spoke of Ukraine's future in the European Union: "[O]ver time, they belong to us. They are one of us and we want them in."[107]

Those jurisdictions that had already announced sanctions continued to expand their response to Russia, as well as devote attention to the initial enforcement of the new measures. The European Union and Canada announced the closure of their airspace to all Russian airplanes, as Germany had done the day before.[108] Canada announced later on Sunday that it would investigate a flight operated by Russian airline Aeroflot, traveling from Florida to Moscow, that had entered Canadian airspace in violation of the new ban.[109] German airline Lufthansa had announced that it would itself avoid Russian airspace and halt service to destinations in Russia.[110]

Additional countries continued to join the sanctions response and support Ukraine in other ways. Japan announced that it would join in the SWIFT disconnections announced the day before.[111] Norway announced that it would align with the EU sanctions. Its sovereign wealth fund would divest from Russia.[112] In addition, it would be providing humanitarian aid and military equipment to Ukraine. As the Prime Minister of Norway Jonas Gahr Støre pointed out, "Norway has strict policies regarding exports of military equipment, but Ukraine now faces extraordinary circumstances."[113] German Chancellor Scholz announced that Germany would send 1,000 antitank weapons and 500 Stinger surface-to-air missiles to Ukraine; it had until that point as a matter of policy refused to send lethal weapons to Ukraine as a conflict area.[114]

Private entities from the sanctioning nations continued to support the economic response. Google Maps suspended its live traffic mode in Ukraine as refugees continued to stream toward the Polish border and for the safety of Ukrainians still in the country.[115] UK energy company BP announced that it would sell its 19.75 percent share in Rosneft, the Russian energy company.[116] BP had taken a stake in Rosneft in 2013, when Rosneft bought BP's interest in TNK-BP, a Russian oil company that was created as a partnership between BP and a group of several Russian billionaires.[117]

But support for the sanctions was not universal worldwide. Brazilian President Jair Bolsonaro stated that his country would not take part in the sanctions against Russia and raised the possibility that the sanctions might negatively affect Brazilian agriculture.[118] His skepticism over sanctions would be echoed by many other countries as well.

AFTER

These sanctions of the first week were just the beginning of the economic response to Russia's invasion of Ukraine. In 2022, Kyiv did not fall; nor did Ukraine surrender to Russia. The sanctioning powers sought to continue and increase their support for Ukraine through the use of economic sanctions and other measures as Russia continued to wage war. Yet the sanctions did not cause Russia to stop its invasion, either immediately or at any point throughout 2022.

Significant sanctions continued to be announced in the next month and throughout 2022, most notably with respect to energy and access to the global financial system. For example, on February 28, the United States announced a freeze on the assets of the Russian central bank.[119] Significantly, the European Union banned imports of oil and natural gas from Russia. Many of the correspondent-account sanctions originally imposed were converted to full blocking sanctions as the conflict continued.

Additional countries joined in the response, like Albania,[120] Monaco, Liechtenstein, South Korea, Singapore, and even the famously neutral Switzerland.[121] New Zealand passed sanctions measures mirroring those of the coalition states, even though it did not have its own autonomous sanctions regime. Previously, the country had generally enacted sanctions only in conformity with UN Security Council requirements.[122] Other countries would decline to join with the sanctions, including South Africa,[123] Brazil,[124] Indonesia, India, Israel,[125] Mexico,[126] Serbia,[127] Venezuela,[128] and perhaps with greatest effect, China. Many countries in South America, Africa, and Asia declined to join in the sanctions response.[129] Those countries that sanctioned Russia contained about 36 percent of the world's population,[130] though they did constitute a major share of world GDP.[131] A more detailed list of countries joining in the economic response against Russia is detailed within an appendix of this book. The following chapters explore in depth the various types of measures making up the economic response to Russia, as well as their effects, which were felt around the world.

3

The Financial Sanctions and Impact on the Global Financial System

We are going to strike the Russian banks. We want to isolate Russia financially. We want to cut off all the links between Russia and the global financial system.

—French Finance Minister Bruno Le Maire[1]

Financial sanctions were key to the overall economic strategy against Russia. In turn, these measures, along with the other types of sanctions enacted, greatly affected the world financial system. In addition to blocking the property of particular individuals and entities, the sanctions sought to undermine Russian power by denying Russia access to the world financial system. They did so by disconnecting major Russian financial institutions from the messaging capabilities that normally allowed those banks to effectively carry out cross-border transactions by easily exchanging financial information with banks located outside of Russia. In addition, the sanctions directly targeted the ability of many significant Russian financial institutions to conduct key cross-border financial functions, like dollar clearing and settlement. They also blocked property held by Russian banks abroad and prevented access to large portions of Russia's foreign exchange reserves.

These sanctions against the Russian financial sector would be perhaps the most important of the sanctions measures announced throughout 2022. Russia was integrated deeply enough within the world financial system such that measures to isolate the country from it caused significant hardship. Russia, however, was not so systemically important to the world financial system that the financial sanctions would cause undue harm to the sanctioning powers. The financial sanctions were therefore fundamentally different from the energy sanctions, for example. Russia had comparatively much greater power in the world energy system and thus could lead in developing alternative systems for energy distribution that excluded the sanctioning powers. It could create no convincingly viable alternative financial network.

Henry Farrell and Abraham Newman's conception of weaponized interdependence articulates the idea that some states have the ability "to leverage interdependent relations to coerce others."[2] In Daniel Drezner's words, weaponized interdependence is "a condition under which an actor can exploit its position in an embedded network to gain a bargaining advantage over others in a contained system."[3] This power may be exerted by way of the panopticon effect, whereby "advantaged states use their network positions to extract informational advantages vis-à-vis adversaries," and by the choke-point effect, whereby such states "can cut adversaries off from network flows."[4]

The nations sanctioning Russia could utilize chokepoint effects with respect to the global financial system due to the dominance of both the SWIFT messaging system and the dollar (and to a lesser extent, the euro). Farrell and Newman have identified global finance as an area in which "market actors created institutions and technologies to overcome the transaction costs associated with decentralized markets and, in doing so, generated potential sites of control."[5] As Farrell and Newman have pointed out, disconnecting banks from the SWIFT network is a potent tool that can create severe effects due to the centralized nature of the platform. So too are the US dollar and the euro centrally important to the global financial economy.[6] Sanctions restricting their use with Russian parties would have significant and immediate effect.

The financial and other sanctions placed on Russia in 2022 were targeted, or smart, sanctions. Less broadly designed than comprehensive sanctions, they were intended to exert maximum effect with minimum collateral effects.[7] But the 2022 sanctions on Russian parties were placed on so many systemically significant entities, including financial institutions, and had such profound implications for dollar- and euro-denominated trade, that these targeted sanctions were much broader than many other instances of targeted sanctions. Although these were targeted sanctions, they appeared nearly comprehensive in effect.

In turn the financial sanctions, along with the other economic restrictions placed on Russia, had a profound effect on the global financial system. From newly volatile currencies to attempted de-dollarization, the sanctions created significant new challenges and incentives to change. Their impact will not be fully understood for years to come.

SWIFT

As described in Chapter 2, removal of certain Russian banks from the SWIFT network was one of the most notable components of the economic response against Russia. The inter-bank messaging system, designed to facilitate financial transactions, links entities in over 200 countries.[8] At the time of the invasion, over 300 Russian financial institutions were connected to SWIFT.[9] As an entity organized under Belgian law, SWIFT is required to follow the laws of Belgium and the European Union.[10] (EU sanctions regulations were directly applicable within Member States, including Belgium.)[11] SWIFT is subject to oversight by the G-10 central banks.[12]

SWIFT disconnection has been used as a foreign policy tool in the past. Certain Iranian banks were cut off from SWIFT access first in 2012 and then again in 2018/2019.[13] These measures were achieved by way of an EU Council Regulation, which then required action from SWIFT as an entity subject to that provision.[14] This followed pressure from the US in 2012 on the European Union to disconnect those banks, including by way of consideration of legislation in the US Congress concerning the potential of sanctions on providers of financial messaging systems that also provided messaging services to the Central Bank of Iran and other sanctioned financial institutions in Iran.[15]

Russia's annexation of Crimea in 2014 triggered speculation that Russian financial institutions might be removed from the SWIFT platform. SWIFT issued a statement that it would not itself remove Russian financial institutions from the platform. It would, however, abide by any European-imposed sanctions ordering it to do so, as the network was required to by law.[16] To address the potential future removal of its banks from SWIFT, Russia began to develop its own financial messaging system, the System for Transfer of Financial Messages (SPFS).[17] At the time of the invasion in 2022, the SPFS connected about 400 financial institutions within Russia and about fifty other entities outside of the country.[18]

SWIFT disconnection could trigger deeply disruptive effects because of the network's unique position in enabling financial transactions around the world through the exchange of financial information. Farrell and Newman have identified SWIFT as an example of a central hub in a global network of financial messaging. In the example of the removal of Iranian banks from SWIFT, a chokepoint effect was created that left Iranian banks without financial messaging alternatives because of the structure of the network around that central hub.[19] To this point, Farrell and Newman quoted Joanna Caytas, who noted the outsized impact that SWIFT disconnection could cause "due to the vital importance of the embargoed services and near-complete lack of alternatives with comparable efficiency."[20]

Almost immediately after the 2022 Russian invasion of Ukraine there were widespread calls for SWIFT access to be cut off for at least some Russian banks. While removing certain Russian banks from SWIFT would not itself prohibit cross-border transactions involving those entities, as a practical matter such transactions would become much more difficult should the removals occur.[21] No financial messaging network existed that connected as many financial entities globally as did SWIFT.

The sanctioning powers did not immediately issue a decision to remove any Russian banks from SWIFT. As President Biden noted, some European allies were opposed to punitive measures involving SWIFT. German officials called for a "targeted and functional limitation of SWIFT," and sought ways to limit the "collateral damage of a decoupling from SWIFT."[22]

As discussed in Chapter 2, however, the European Union agreed to enact SWIFT sanctions, and the platform removed seven Russian banks as required by law. These were VTB, VEB, Bank Rossiya, Bank Otkritie, Novikombank, Promsvyazbank, and

Sovcombank. As described in the next section, all of these banks had previously been made subject to another type of financial sanctions.[23] Sberbank, Russia's largest bank, was not included in this March round of SWIFT removals, nor was Gazprombank, the country's third-largest bank. (Some nations had urged that at least some Russian banks remain connected to SWIFT to allow for energy purchases from Russia.)[24] Sberbank was eventually removed from SWIFT in June.[25] More banks were removed in June: the Credit Bank of Moscow, the Russian Agricultural Bank, and the Belarusian Bank for Development and Reconstruction.[26] Three Belarusian financial institutions were also removed from SWIFT shortly after the March removals.

These financial institutions, once disconnected from SWIFT, sought alternative methods to communicate financial information. Use of Russia's own SPFS system expanded to 50 new entities to a total of 440 in September, with 100 users non-resident in Russia.[27] Early in 2023, Iran reported that it had connected its own financial messaging service, SEPAM, to SPFS.[28]

SANCTIONS ON RUSSIAN BANKS

But the core of the financial sanctions against Russia was not the SWIFT removals, but rather the direct sanctioning of Russian banks. These sanctions took the form of correspondent and payable-through account restrictions, as well as full blocking sanctions.

As previously described, correspondent and payable-through account sanctions affected the ability of targeted banks to process transactions denominated in currencies of the sanctioning powers on behalf of their customers. Clearing and settlement describe the process by which financial institutions handle payments, often involving converting funds from one currency into another, and by which obligations between financial institutions are satisfied, either in real time or on a deferred basis.[29] Correspondent and payable-through account sanctions had earlier been used in other contexts as well, perhaps most notably with respect to Iran. With respect to Russia, Directive 2 pursuant to US Executive Order 14,024 was issued on February 24, shortly after the invasion. It listed those Russian banks for whom US institutions could no longer open or maintain correspondent or payable-through accounts, or process transactions involving those entities.[30] OFAC's CAPTA List contained foreign financial institutions subject to correspondent account or payable-through account sanctions.[31]

In addition to the use of correspondent accounts, US dollar-denominated transactions are often cleared through payment systems that involve the use of parties located in the United States, such as the Clearing House Interbank Payments System (CHIPS).[32] In 2022, CHIPS was "the largest private sector USD clearing system in the world."[33] Its public-sector counterpart is Fedwire, a real-time gross settlement system owned by the US federal reserve banks.[34] While CHIPS processes both domestic and cross-border payments, "approximately 95% of CHIPS payments [have] a cross-border leg."[35] Correspondent and payable-through account sanctions affected the ability of parties so sanctioned to access such payment systems.[36]

Full blocking sanctions, as contrasted with correspondent banking sanctions, impeded not only the currency-processing relationships between the sanctioned banks and financial institutions in the sanctioning nations. They also essentially cut off the possibility for all dealings in property, broadly defined, between sanctioned parties and parties subject to the laws of the sanctioning states. Fully blocked entities were also subject to an asset freeze of their property held in sanctioning nations. The use of the US dollar itself with fully blocked parties could also provide the nexus for US sanctions enforcement jurisdiction.[37]

Part of the early response to the Russian invasion of Ukraine included US prohibitions against any US person engaging in transactions involving the Central Bank of Russia, the Russian National Wealth Fund, or the Russian Ministry of Finance.[38] This had the effect of freezing the assets of those entities held within the US or by US persons.[39] At the same time, the United Kingdom also prohibited UK persons from entering into financial transactions with these entities, having the same effect.[40] So too did the European Union announce a ban on transactions with the Russian Central Bank at the same time.[41]

Other nations and jurisdictions, including The Bahamas,[42] Singapore,[43] Japan,[44] and South Korea,[45] also sanctioned entities in the Russian financial sector. The US and Canada also enacted sanctions against the Russian Direct Investment Fund (RDIF), a Russian sovereign wealth fund whose valuation was estimated at just under $175 billion at the beginning of February 2022. The RDIF had been created in 2011 by order of the Russian government to incentivize direct investment in Russia (but was considered by the US government to be a means for enriching Putin).[46]

Some financial institutions that were initially targeted by only the lesser correspondent or payable-through account sanctions were later made subject to full blocking sanctions as the Russian military continued to wage war in Ukraine. Such was the case with Sberbank, which was originally targeted only by correspondent and payable-through account sanctions but in April was made subject to the more stringent US and UK full blocking sanctions.[47] Likewise, in the European Union, Sberbank was initially made subject only to the SWIFT sanctions as well as to sanctions limiting access to EU capital markets.[48] In July, however, the European Union also fully blocked Sberbank. Similarly, Alfa Bank, Russia's largest private bank and the country's fourth-largest bank overall, was initially targeted by the United States with debt and equity restrictions only. It was likewise made subject to full blocking sanctions by the United States at the same time in April as was Sberbank.[49]

The coalition states continued to make additional Russian banks subject to full blocking sanctions throughout 2022 as the conflict continued and as targeted financial institutions took actions to evade the sanctions. For example, in April

OFAC designated Transkapitalbank as an SDN. The private commercial bank had "suggested options to evade international sanctions" to financial institutions in Asia and the Middle East, including by offering to process dollar-denominated payments through its own alternative to SWIFT.[50]

The blocking sanctions against these Russian banks, including the Russian central bank, effected a freeze on Russia's foreign reserves held in the sanctioning nations. By April, the United States had blocked over 60 percent of Russia's banking assets, while the European Union had blocked 26 percent.[51] Russia stated publicly that the joint sanctions against its central bank had frozen about $300 billion of the institution's assets, nearly half of its foreign currency reserves.[52] In May, the European Union reported that it had frozen about $24.5 billion of the central bank's assets; about $100 billion had been frozen by the United States.[53]

Russia had to some extent been aware of the possibility that its US dollar foreign reserves might be frozen should extensive sanctions be triggered. Russia had been increasing foreign currency reserves since its financial crisis in 1998, with an uptick in the accumulation of gold reserves in particular around the time of and subsequent to its invasion of Crimea.[54] In the year prior to January 2022, the Russian central bank increased its renminbi holdings from 13 percent to 17 percent of its total currency reserves.[55] The Russian National Wealth Fund, a sovereign wealth fund created in 2008, in mid-2021 announced its intentions to convert its US dollar holdings into other currencies, including euros, yuan, and gold.[56]

Russia, however, either could not or did not fully prepare for the sort of sanctions that were enacted in 2022, where it lost access to reserves in numerous currencies and states within a short period of time. Limiting Russia's access to much of its foreign exchange reserves had the purpose of "limit[ing] Russia's ability to finance the war against Ukraine," as those reserves "(in the absence of sanctions) could be used to acquire goods and services from abroad."[57]

Other financial sanctions accompanied the major provisions of the 2022 sanctions already described. EU measures, among other restrictions, prohibited deposits over a certain value from Russian nationals or residents and the sale of euro-denominated securities to Russians.[58] In October, the United Kingdom announced that it would suspend for sanctioned entities the ordinary process used to manage the orderly failure of Russian banks; pursuant to that regular process, Russian actions were recognized under UK law.[59]

Remittances abroad in numerous locations were affected by the sanctions and also by world events. US sanctions of March 11 prohibited the exportation of US dollars in cash to Russia. A general license issued at the same time, however, provided an exception for noncommercial, personal remittances from the United States or by a US person to persons located in the Russian Federation, or to US persons located in the Russian Federation.[60] In September, the European Union issued a statement affirming the importance of financial remittances from Ukrainians in the European Union to Ukraine, announcing commitments to making these remittances affordable, transparent, and accessible.[61] Worldwide, remittances to Ukraine were expected to rise over 20 percent in 2022.[62]

Remittances from Central Asia to Russia, though not directly affected by the sanctions or actions taken by Russia in response, were indirectly affected by way of a recession in Russia and an initial post-invasion drop in the value of the ruble.[63] By mid-year, Kyrgyzstan forecast a 20 percent decline in remittances from Russia in 2022 compared with the prior year.[64] In contrast, remittances from Russia to Georgia and Armenia rose sharply in 2022 as Russians sent money to other countrymen now in those nations who had fled conscription.[65]

PAYMENT ALTERNATIVES AND DE-DOLLARIZATION

Much of the power of the financial sanctions came from the dominance of the US dollar and euro in world trade. Using the dollar in transactions with sanctioned parties, for instance, could incur liability for the transacting party, even if that transacting party was not located in a sanctioning state. (This mechanism is described further in Chapter 4.) Before the invasion, approximately 40 percent of global trade in goods was denominated in US dollars.[66] Russia denominated about half of its exports in dollars; this was a significant decline from 2013, when 80 percent of its exports were dollar-denominated.[67] Consistent with attempts by Russia to de-dollarize trade in light of the growing likelihood of additional future US sanctions, Russia and China announced a bilateral currency swap deal in 2014, which was extended in 2017.[68]

The global use of the US dollar and the euro created the same sort of chokepoint effects when correspondent or full blocking sanctions were introduced as Farrell and Newman described in the context of SWIFT, lending disproportionate effect to sanctions affecting the use of these currencies. To comply with 2022's expansive new sanctions, parties around the globe began to de-dollarize trade with Russia. Russia, in turn, increasingly sought to rely on non-sanctioning states to facilitate trade and financial transactions, most notably China. Transactions between the two countries directly could be carried out in yuan through China's own payment system, the Cross-Border Interbank Payment System (CIPS), which settled and cleared renminbi-denominated transactions.[69] CIPS allowed direct participants (mostly foreign affiliates of Chinese financial institutions) to communicate necessary information about these transactions through either the CIPS system or SWIFT, while indirect participants (about 60 percent of which were located outside of China as of 2022) were able to use the CIPS clearing and settlement capabilities in conjunction with SWIFT messaging only.[70] VTB and Alfa Bank, both sanctioned, introduced money transfers from Russia to China in yuan without using SWIFT.[71] The central bank of India created a settlement system for rupee-denominated transactions.[72] Sberbank allowed its clients to open correspondent accounts at its branches in India to more easily carry out transactions in rupees.[73]

Many private entities, however, terminated their payment services in Russia, either to comply with newly enacted sanctions or because of popular sentiment, or some combination of both. Visa, Mastercard, and American Express all suspended doing business in Russia at the beginning of March. This meant that Russian-issued cards would still work within the country, but such cards would no longer work outside of Russia. In turn, cards issued outside of Russia would not work inside Russia.[74] Japanese credit card company JCB took similar measures.[75] Discover Card halted its prior plans to establish a branch office in Russia.[76] Some Russians were nevertheless able to obtain Visa cards by traveling to Uzbekistan to get them; indeed, a Russian tour operator even offered a special package trip.[77] Apple Pay ceased supporting payments using Russian Mastercard and Visa cards almost immediately after the invasion. (According to Russian bank Sberbank, however, Apple neglected to remove the payment capability with the Russian Mir platform until the end of March.)[78] It was anticipated that China's UnionPay might increase card services in Russia, but in April it ultimately decided against doing so for fear of sanctions implications.[79]

Payment systems that still continued to function in Russia had to take care to comply with sanctions. In September, OFAC issued sanctions compliance guidance for instant payment systems. These platforms allowed for near-instantaneous transfer of funds between users.[80] They functioned similarly to PayPal and Venmo (though the guidance did not implicate the activities of these particular parties, since Venmo was only available to US residents and PayPal had suspended services in Russia in early March following the invasion).[81] The guidance provided compliance advice for such systems subject to US sanctions, including recommendations to "incorporate sanctions compliance during the design and development process" to include sanctions compliance controls. OFAC also encouraged the development of systems using "sanctions compliance features, tools, and contractual clauses," and noted the importance of "enabling communication among participating financial institutions" to better handle potential sanctions issues. The use of instant payment systems had raised sanctions compliance issues in the past. For example, PayPal had settled an enforcement action in 2015 with OFAC for $7.7 million. OFAC had alleged that the company failed to screen transactions involving Iran, Cuba, and Sudan, and parties sanctioned by the Weapons of Mass Destruction Proliferators and Global Terrorism Sanctions Regulations.[82]

Russia sought alternative payment options. The Central Bank of Russia planned to implement a digital ruble, with banks to be connected to the platform in 2024. Russian's own Mir payment system, which issued cards domestically in Russia beginning in December 2015,[83] allowed Russians to make payments in countries including Armenia, Belarus, Kazakhstan, Kyrgyzstan, Tajikistan, Turkey, Uzbekistan, and Vietnam. Venezuela also connected to the system. The issuance of certain new cards, however, was stymied by a chip shortage. Russia sought microchips from China to manufacture new Mir bank cards.[84] Sberbank began to reuse chips from unactivated bank cards.[85]

The Mir system was also impeded by further sanctions measures. OFAC published guidance in mid-September noting that although Mir and its operator, the National Payment Card System Joint Stock Company (NSPK), were not themselves sanctioned entities, the payment system might be used in connection with financial transactions with sanctioned parties. Foreign financial institutions that "entered into new or expanded agreements with NSPK [would] risk supporting Russia's efforts to evade US sanctions" by expanding the use of Mir, and would themselves risk being blocked by US sanctions.[86] These were an example of secondary sanctions – namely, instances where parties not originally subject to US sanctions jurisdictions would be made the target of sanctions for dealing in certain ways with US-sanctioned persons or entities.[87] Around this time, the United States sanctioned personally a number of executives and officials associated with the Mir payment system, including Vladimir Komlev, the Chairman and CEO of NSPK,[88] and Olga Skorobogatova, First Deputy Governor of the Central Bank of Russia, who was responsible for overseeing the Mir payment system.[89]

In response to this potential for triggering US sanctions, several Turkish banks ceased using the Mir system.[90] Certain banks in Kazakhstan, Turkey, and Vietnam did the same.[91] A major Tajikistani bank and an Uzbekistani payment processing center also suspended use of Mir cards, citing technical issues.[92]

INVESTMENT

Some of the sanctions imposed against Russia came in the form of prohibitions against the making of new investments in Russia. The United States, for example, announced a ban on new investments by US persons in the Russian energy sector.[93] An executive order followed on March 11 that would allow for the imposition of bans against new investments by US persons in further Russian economic sectors that might be determined in the future.[94] Bans on new investment into Russia entirely were announced on April 6 by the United States[95] and the United Kingdom,[96] and on April 8 by Japan.[97] The EU in mid-April announced a ban on new investments in the Russian energy sector,[98] followed in December by a ban on new investments in the mining sector.[99]

The term "new investments" was defined by US regulations to include both a contribution of funds or other assets, as well as loans or other specified extensions of credit[100] including overdrafts, currency swaps, purchases of debt securities, purchases of loans, the issuance of standby letters of credit, drawdowns on existing letters of credit, and more.[101] "New investments" included, for example, the purchase of commercial real estate in Russia; the entry into an agreement in Russia that would provide royalties or ongoing profits; the purchase of equity in a company located in Russia;[102] and the purchase of natural resource rights in Russia. Generally, the ban on new investments did not include maintaining a previously established investment, winding down already-established investments, or entering, performing, or financing an ordinary commercial sales contract (assuming that all other applicable sanctions provisions were appropriately complied with).[103]

These investment bans, along with private actions voluntarily taken to stop doing business in Russia, caused a significant decline in the total foreign direct investment (FDI) inflows into Russia. Incoming FDI into Russia had been profoundly affected by COVID-19. Russia's incoming FDI fell 70 percent in 2020, due to the pandemic and low world market prices for Russia's natural resource exports.[104] While FDI into Russia increased in 2021, the 2022 invasion led to a steep drop in inbound FDI.[105]

SOVEREIGN DEBT

The financial sanctions also had effects on sovereign debt, as payments on such debt were impeded by the newly imposed sanctions. It seemed that Russia had anticipated the issue of payment difficulty for sovereign debt should sanctions be enacted en masse. For example, researchers noted that after the imposition of sanctions related to Russia's invasion of Crimea, the Russian government started to include an Alternate Payments Clause in its dollar-denominated bonds that allowed for payment in alternative currencies, and in some cases the ruble, if for reasons beyond its control it could not make payments in the currency specified by the bond terms.[106]

But not all bonds contained such a provision, and the sanctions impeded bond payments where the relevant terms specified that payment be made in a particular currency, such as euros or US dollars, that now involved sanctions restrictions. In June, Russia defaulted on its foreign currency debt for the first time since Lenin had caused a default in 1918. (A default on ruble-denominated debt had occurred in 1998.)[107] Payments required in dollars and euros could not be made, because Russia sent payment to clearinghouse Euroclear but the sanctions prevented the forwarding of payments to the holders of the debt. Russia denied that the event could be characterized as a default, blaming the sanctions for creating artificial barriers to payment. "A foreign-currency payment was made back in May, and the fact that funds were not transmitted to recipients is not our problem," said Russian government spokesman Dmitry Peskov.[108] Russia announced a new procedure under which it would consider Russia's obligations to make payments on Eurobonds to be completed. This would occur when payments were deposited in an account at the Russian National Settlement Depository.[109]

OTHER CURRENCY EFFECTS

The sanctions, along with the invasion itself and other world events, helped spur currency volatility both immediately after the invasion and throughout 2022. During

March 2022, the first sets of sanctions "triggered runs on Russian banks, capital flight, and a 60 percent depreciation of the ruble in less than two weeks."[110] In response, Russia raised interest rates to 20 percent and implemented capital controls.[111] Namely, Russians could not withdraw more than $10,000 in foreign currency or take more than $10,000 in cash out of the country. Nor were they permitted to transfer funds to their own foreign bank accounts. Exporters were required "to convert 80 percent of their foreign-currency revenues into [rubles]."[112]

The ruble soon rebounded. Russian capital controls and other restrictions were eased in May, with the exporter conversion requirement lowered to 50 percent. By June, the ruble had risen to its highest value against the dollar since 2015, for an increase of 45 percent against the dollar since January 2022.[113] The high prices for gas and oil in the world energy market helped maintain the strength of the ruble.[114]

Other currencies were also affected by the events of 2022. By August, the euro fell to its lowest rate against the dollar since 2002, the last time the euro had traded at par with the dollar.[115] The slide in the euro relative to the dollar was due to both the strength of the dollar and fears of a European energy crisis, as well as to lower interest rate hikes from the European Central Bank than from the US Federal Reserve.[116]

Japan in particular faced challenges in maintaining the strength of its currency. "We are deeply concerned about the rapidly increasing volatility in the foreign exchange market," stated Shunichi Suzuki, Governor of the International Monetary Fund for Japan. He elaborated that "speculative activities" were triggering "unprecedentedly sharp and one-sided movements" in the level of the yen.[117] The currency had declined relative to the US dollar as Japan maintained low interest rates while other jurisdictions such as the United States raised them.[118] Japan purchased yen on the foreign exchange market twice in October to strengthen the yen.

Inflation hit globally as nations faced rising costs of food and energy. Though sanctions were often not the sole cause of inflation, the increased prices they fostered contributed to the issue, as discussed further in Chapters 5 and 7. A number of African central banks raised interest rates in order to address inflation. Between December 2021 and September 2022, for example, Nigeria raised its interest rates 14 points (+2 percent); Ghana raised its rates 22 points (+7.5 percent).[119] Russia itself reported an annual inflation rate of 11.9 percent in 2022.[120]

In October, the G7 Finance Ministers and Central Governors issued a statement pledging that they would "continue to closely monitor global markets … and welcome the monitoring and analysis of the Financial Stability Board."[121] They also "reaffirm[ed] [their] exchange rate commitments as elaborated in May 2017" in light of the volatility of currencies during 2022. The Financial Stability Board is an international body whose mission was to promote global financial stability through assessment of vulnerabilities, policy development, and monitoring.[122] The May 2017 commitments referenced are the FX Global Code, which set forth "global principles of good practice in the foreign exchange market."[123] These included commitments for clear and accurate information sharing; robust risk management and compliance; and efficient and transparent confirmation and settlement of transactions in the wholesale foreign exchange market.[124] As acknowledged by the G7 statement, these commitments faced challenges in the volatile currency markets of 2022.

Cryptocurrency prices were also affected by the invasion, with prices falling in the immediate economic aftermath and crashing further by May.[125] At the time the first sanctions were enacted in February, it was feared that bad actors would flock to cryptocurrency in order to evade sanctions regulations.[126] Widespread sanctions evasion by use of cryptocurrency, however, was not observed. This was potentially due to several causes, including that Russia lacked a large-scale cryptocurrency infrastructure, and that everyday items could not be purchased with cryptocurrency.[127] The illiquidity of the crypto markets also contributed to its unexpected unpopularity as a tool for sanctions evasion.[128]

The sanctioning states engaged in the imposition of sanctions and in enforcement in order to address the sanctions evasion activities that did occur by way of cryptocurrencies. The European Union placed a ban on the provision of crypto asset services to Russia, initially in April only for wallets over €10,000 but then extended in October to cover all services no matter the wallet size.[129] OFAC in April added Bitriver and ten of its Russian-based subsidiaries to the SDN List for carrying out virtual currency mining in Russia.[130] In September, OFAC issued sanctions compliance guidance for the virtual currency industry.[131]

ANTI-MONEY LAUNDERING

Russia's invasion of Ukraine also affected its standing within the Financial Action Task Force (the FATF). The FATF is an international body that was founded in 1989 "to prevent the utilization of the banking system and financial institutions for the purpose of money laundering."[132] Since its formation, it has developed standards on combating money laundering and worked to coordinate their implementation among over 200 jurisdictions.[133] Russia had been a member of the FATF since 2003.[134] Russia faced significant money laundering issues (further described in this book within Chapters 8 and 10), which a 2019 FATF Mutual Evaluation characterized as "a widespread and persistent trend of non-compliance with preventive AML/CFT [anti-money laundering/combating the financing of terrorism] obligations particularly in the financial sector."[135] The country, however, was not considered by the FATF to be a high-risk jurisdiction (on the FATF blacklist), nor was it one subject to increased monitoring (on the FATF grey list).

The Russian invasion of Ukraine led the organization to "express[] its grave concern about the invasion's impact on the money laundering, terrorist financing and proliferation financing risk environment as well as the integrity of the financial system, the broader economy and safety and security."[136] The organization also commented that the invasion was in opposition to "the FATF core principles," and "represent[ed] a gross violation of the commitment" made by FATF members.[137] One group of commentators argued that the FATF should add Russia to its blacklist.[138] In June, the organization "severely limit[ed]" Russia's involvement in the body by prohibiting the country's taking on "any leadership or advisory roles" or participating "in decision-making on standard-setting, FATF peer review processes, governance and membership matters." Nor could the country provide "assessors, reviewers, or other experts for FATF peer-review processes."[139] In September, Russia was "sidelined" within the organization, and was suspended in February 2023.[140]

CONCLUSION

The financial sanctions were among the most potent of the economic weapons deployed against Russia. The dominance of the dollar and euro worldwide ensured that the financial sanctions would have far-reaching effects. While Russia sought to develop its own financial infrastructure and to work with China to develop alternative payment systems, those networks could not be developed quickly enough or deployed widely enough to significantly blunt the impact of the sanctions in the short term. Yet in the long term, it seemed that sanctions might hasten Russia's move away from the dollar and the euro, and provide the impetus for long-lasting financial ties with China.

4

Extraterritoriality

The United States is determined to sanction people and companies, no matter where they are located, that support Russia's unjustified invasion of Ukraine.

—US Treasury Secretary Janet Yellen[1]

The sanctions came from a host of nations and jurisdictions: the United States, the United Kingdom, the European Union, Japan, and many others. But the enactment of sanctions against Russia was by no means universal among nations. Large portions of the world abstained from imposing economic penalties in response to the invasion. Such countries included China, India, and numerous states in Africa, South America, and the Middle East.[2] Yet parties in even those states that had not announced sanctions against Russia could also in many instances be subject to the extraterritorial application of sanctions provisions.

This was because of extraterritoriality: the application of sanctions to reach conduct beyond the borders and to nonnationals of the jurisdiction that had enacted the particular legal restriction. Sanctions may be imposed extraterritorially through applying primary sanctions – the sanctions prohibiting transactions by parties regulated by the sender state with a sanctioned party – to activities occurring outside of the sender state or to activities of parties who might not be nationals of the sender states, so long as there is some sufficient nexus to the sender state.[3] Sanctions can also be imposed extraterritorially through the use of secondary sanctions, which are sanctions imposed for dealing with primarily sanctioned parties.[4]

The extraterritorial application of the primary sanctions against Russia by the sanctioning jurisdictions certainly increased their reach dramatically, affecting conduct and parties that would not otherwise have been made subject to sanctions restrictions. The possibility of being made subject to secondary sanctions also provided a strong incentive for otherwise nonregulated parties to observe sanctions restrictions even beyond their strict legal obligations. The extraterritorial application of sanctions multiplied their effects – in ways both intended and deleterious to global welfare.

EXTRATERRITORIAL APPLICATION OF SANCTIONS AND INTERNATIONAL LAW ISSUES

The extraterritorial application of sanctions has been variously defined as lacking a territorial connection between the sanctioned conduct and the jurisdiction issuing the sanctions; lacking such a substantial territorial connection; or nonexclusive coexisting multiple jurisdictional authority over the same conduct.[5] While the sanctions imposed by the United States have been applied extraterritorially to perhaps the greatest extent, both historically and with respect to the 2022 sanctions against Russia, the sanctions of other nations also often extend beyond their borders.

The extraterritorial application of sanctions has long been the subject of debate, both as a matter of policy and of legality. Some scholars have argued that the extraterritorial application of unilateral sanctions can in certain instances violate customary international law.[6] (Customary international law consists of those customs, created independently of treaty obligations, which are considered to be binding or which serve as evidence of binding principles upon states.[7]) Customary international law allows for prescriptive jurisdiction ("a [s]tate's authority to lay down legal norms"[8]) in the presence of "a genuine connection between the subject of the jurisdiction and the state seeking to regulate."[9] A state can exercise prescriptive jurisdiction on territorial grounds, namely over "persons, property, and conduct within its territory."[10] It may also exercise prescriptive jurisdiction under the effects doctrine, namely, "with respect to conduct that has a substantial effect within its territory."[11] Those effects also have to be direct. The nationality principle allows for state exercise of prescriptive jurisdiction over "the conduct, interests, status, and relations of its nationals outside its territory."[12] Passive personality allows the state to "prescribe law with respect to certain conduct outside its territory that harms its nationals."[13] Finally, the protective principle allows for prescriptive jurisdiction extraterritorially over nonnationals with respect to conduct "directed against the security of the state."[14] The protective principle may be used for certain other limited purposes, including to address "espionage, certain acts of terrorism, murder of government officials," "conspiracy to violate immigration or customs laws" and others. All states are also permitted to exercise prescriptive jurisdiction over "certain offenses of universal concern," including "genocide, crimes against humanity, war crimes," and others.[15]

While these doctrines provide justification for the extraterritorial application of sanctions in theory, they do not always fully justify the actual use of sanctions as applied extraterritoriality in practice. For example, the territorial principle provides what some scholars considered a rather tenuous justification for the application of

US sanctions based solely on the use of the US dollar.[16] While dollar clearing activities technically involve conduct occurring in the United States, which may be used as the grounds for asserting US jurisdiction, a financial transaction may otherwise occur entirely outside of the United States.[17]

The use of US sanctions to reach foreign subsidiaries of domestic companies in certain instances is an expansive use of the nationality principle.[18] This control theory has been rejected elsewhere as an appropriate ground for use of the nationality principle.[19] Indeed, the European Union and Canada both have rejected the application of primary sanctions to foreign subsidiaries of their own domestic companies.[20] The International Court of Justice commented on the nationality principle in the *Barcelona Traction* case, in which it found that the nationality of a company for the purposes of investor protection was to be determined based on the state of incorporation of the entity, not of the nationality of its controlling shareholders.[21] This conclusion is at odds with the expansive construction of the nationality provision envisioned by the common extraterritorial application of US sanctions.[22]

The argument against the use of the nationality principle to impose extraterritorial sanctions is particularly compelling where secondary sanctions, for instance, are applied in the form of penalties rather than in the form of access restrictions; access restrictions are not subject to the same sort of concerns about overreach of US law.[23] Access restrictions by way of sanctions include limiting the ability of non-US parties to access the US financial system or markets, for example, whereas secondary sanctions as penalties can result in civil or criminal fines.[24]

Likewise, the other principles are sometimes questioned as justifications for the most expansive application of sanctions extraterritorially. The effects doctrine can lack clarity over what a direct or substantial effect would constitute.[25] The protective principle may justify the extraterritorial use of sanctions, but only where there is evidence of some threat to which the sanctions are responding.[26] States are prohibited from imposing their own national sanctions measures if those measures violate an international treaty obligation to which they were bound.[27]

Each of these principles provide a justification for the extraterritorial application of law. Of course, sanctions often have extraterritorial effects as well. Debates over the extraterritoriality of sanctions have generally focused on justifications for their extraterritorial application, which is also the focus of this particular chapter. Extraterritorial effects of the 2022 sanctions against Russia are discussed at length in each chapter of this book.

MECHANISMS OF EXTRATERRITORIAL APPLICATION OF SANCTIONS LAWS

The US sanctions regulations are structured in several ways to allow for their extraterritorial application. The most notable forms of extraterritorial sanctions include primary sanctions applied extraterritorially, along with secondary sanctions that are applied to non-US parties outside of the United States. Primary sanctions are applied to penalize conduct including that occurring outside of the United States and engaged in by non-US parties. Secondary sanctions are sanctions which are imposed against non-US parties based on their support of sanctioned parties, even where such conduct is legal under the terms of primary sanctions.[28]

US sanctions often prohibit transactions with sanctioned parties undertaken within the United States *or* by US parties. The disjunctive "or" is key. Foreigners can be penalized if they were within the United States when they entered into prohibited transactions. US corporations (and in certain instances, their foreign subsidiaries abroad when owned or controlled by those US entities) can be penalized even when the relevant conduct occurred overseas.[29]

The type of conduct prohibited by the US sanctions is extremely broad, which carries even greater prohibitive effect when applied to non-US parties or to conduct occurring outside of the United States. The Ukraine/Russia-related sanctions regulations of the US, which mirror language found in many other US sanctions programs, state that "[a]ll property and interests in property" with a US jurisdictional nexus and belonging to designated parties "are blocked and may not be transferred, paid, exported, withdrawn or otherwise dealt in."[30] A comprehensive prohibition exists with respect to the Crimea region of Ukraine, and prohibits "the exportation, reexportation, sale, or supply, directly or indirectly, from the United States, or by a United States person, wherever located, of any goods, services, or technology to the Crimea region of Ukraine."[31] As earlier described, similar comprehensive restrictions were enacted with respect to the so-called DNR and LNR regions of Ukraine. The US sanctions regulations also contain prohibitions against US persons, wherever located, from "approv[ing], financ[ing], facilitat[ing], or guarantee[ing]" a transaction by a non-US party that would be unlawful if the US person carried it out directly themselves.[32]

OFAC sanctions also apply extraterritorially to prohibit parties, US or otherwise, from causing a violation of the sanctions regulations.[33] This provision was added to IEEPA within the IEEPA Enhancement Act of 2007. The causation provision was little-used as an enforcement tool by OFAC at first. Most US sanctions enforcement cases that might have relied on the causation provision instead applied a theory of indirect supply of services, which achieved the same effects as the use of the causation provision. In recent years, however, OFAC has increasingly deployed the causation tool as an independent ground for liability based on conduct that had occurred outside of the United States, against both financial institutions and other entities.

The extraterritorial application of sanctions provisions has generally been viewed favorably by US courts to the extent it has been addressed. For example, the court in the *Zarrab* criminal case commented that sanctions issued pursuant to the authority of IEEPA and the US Iranian Transactions and Sanctions Regulations (ITSR) would likely be able to overcome the presumption against extraterritoriality should that issue be considered by a court.[34] (The court in the *Zarrab* case did not in fact rest its decision on that basis, since a domestic nexus existed in the form of the exportation of services from the United States.[35]) The presumption against extraterritoriality is applied by US federal courts to many US statutes.[36] But as the *Zarrab* decision pointed out, the IEEPA and ITSR providing the basis for criminal charges in that case "reflect the United States' interest" with respect to foreign policy toward Iran. As such, IEEPA, the statutory authority underlying many of the US sanctions programs, provides a relatively strong case for the extraterritorial application of US law notwithstanding the presumption against extraterritoriality applied by US courts.[37]

The United States is the most prominent proponent of the use of extraterritorial sanctions. The primary sanctions measures of other nations, however, have often applied extraterritorially to some extent as well, perhaps most commonly to regulate the activities of nationals of a sanctioning nation when those individuals are located abroad. In 2018, the United Kingdom enacted the Sanctions and Anti-Money Laundering Act (SAMLA), which reaches activities occurring either in the United Kingdom or by a UK person anywhere in the world. The United Kingdom's OFSI has stated that a violation of the UK sanctions requires some sort of UK nexus, but that the activity does not have to occur within UK borders; such a nexus might be satisfied by, for example, "transactions using clearing services in the United Kingdom."[38] Australia's sanctions can apply to the activities of Australian citizens and Australian-registered business entities located overseas.[39]

US export controls are also applied in an extraterritorial manner.[40] The trade measures imposed against Russia are described further in Chapter 6. The export controls promulgated by the United States apply to activities outside of US territory in several ways. US jurisdiction attaches to US-made items wherever located. In addition, the export controls limit not only initial exports of US-made items from the United States, but also reexports, which occur when US-made items travel from one foreign country to another. In-country transfers, whereby US-made items are transferred from one end-user in a particular foreign country to another end-user in that same country, are also subject to the US export control regulations. Even non-US made items with a certain percentage of US content, or made using US technology, can be subject to US export controls by way of the Foreign Direct Product Rule. Indeed, as further described in Chapter 6, changes to the FDP Rule were certainly a notable part of the 2022 economic response to Russia's invasion of Ukraine.

HISTORICAL USE OF EXTRATERRITORIAL SANCTIONS

The increasing extraterritorial application of US sanctions, often resulting in higher penalties for non-US parties than for US-based entities,[41] has been the source of contention between the United States and many other nations in recent years. The extraterritorial application of US sanctions has long been controversial. In particular, Member States of the European Union have often opposed the extraterritorial application of US sanctions, characterizing such use as a violation of national sovereignty. In 2021, HR/VP Josep Borrell commented:

> [T]he [European Union] has always been firm and vocal in condemning any extraterritorial application of sanctions. We are also opposed to the growing use of secondary sanctions, as well as the use of sanctions as a trade and economic tool. For the [European Union], sanctions are exclusively a foreign policy tool. And in any event, they must respect international law... We must not counter extra-territoriality with extra-territoriality.[42]

In one early dispute over extraterritoriality between the United States and certain European countries, the extraterritorial reach of US export controls in connection with the Euro-Siberian gas pipeline was challenged. The United States opposed the pipeline project on the grounds that it would foster excessive European dependence on gas from the USSR, as well as provide aid to the USSR and allow the USSR access to American technology.[43] In 1982, the United States amended its export regulations to extend jurisdiction to US-owned subsidiaries and to items already having legally left the United States, to the objections of European parties and states.[44] Agreement was reached between the United States and European nations several months later to remove the export controls.[45]

Perhaps most notably, the extraterritorial application of the Iranian sanctions imposed by the United States faced opposition from around the world. In addition to the extraterritorial application of primary sanctions, the US sanctions regime against Iran also implemented secondary sanctions that reached to penalize conduct of non-US actors outside of the United States. The potential for US secondary sanctions imposed on non-US nationals for activities concerning Iran was dramatic-ally enhanced through the Iran Sanctions Act of 1996,[46] the 2010 Comprehensive Iran Sanctions Accountability and Divestment Act (CISADA),[47] the 2012 Iran Threat Reduction and Syria Human Rights Act (TRA) and the 2013 Iran Freedom and Counter-Proliferation Act (IFCA).[48] The JCPOA was signed in 2015, resulting in the lifting of US secondary sanctions measures in 2016, but these secondary sanctions were later reimposed when the United States withdrew from the JCPOA during the Trump administration.[49]

The US sanctions against Cuba have also been applied extraterritorially. In 2019, Title III of the Helms-Burton Act (also known as the Cuban Liberty and Democratic Solidary [LIBERTAD] Act) was reactivated, allowing for potential action under Title IV. The provision allowed for a private right of action in the US federal courts against third parties, based on allegations of knowingly and intentionally trafficking in the confiscated property of US nationals.[50] The Helms-Burton Act was enacted in 1996, but Title III was suspended by presidential statutory authority until during the

Trump administration.[51] After the statute's 1996 enactment, the European Union brought action against the United States in the WTO[52] and retaliatory legislation was passed by Canada, Mexico, and the European Union, in the case of Mexico and the European Union to block recognition of the Helms-Burton Act.[53] The Council of the European Union issued a statement in response after the reactivation in 2019, stating that the European Union "deeply regret[ted] the full activation," and that the decision to do so was "a breach of the commitments undertaken in the EU-US agreements of 1997 and 1998" which would "cause unnecessary friction and undermine[] trust and predictability in the transatlantic partnership."[54]

The European Union implemented a blocking statute to address the extraterritorial aspects of the US sanctions against Iran and Cuba, which were viewed as an inappropriate incursion into national and EU sovereignty. Council Regulation (EC) No. 2271/96 was enacted in 1996 and "nullif[ied] the effect in the EU of any foreign court ruling based on" specified foreign laws, and "allow[ed] EU operators to recover in court damages" resulting from the extraterritorial application of those specified laws.[55] In December 2021, the European Union's Court of Justice (CJEU) issued its first judgment clarifying the nature of the regulation.[56] It found that an EU entity could breach the blocking statute by complying with the specified extraterritorial aspects of the listed sanctions laws, even in the absence of a US order requiring its compliance.[57] It also found that the statute applied in civil disputes.

Similar legislation has been enacted elsewhere to counteract the extraterritorial aspects of various sanctions measures, usually those that had been imposed by the United States. Other blocking statues include, for example, that of Canada, which prohibits extraterritorial compliance with the US sanctions against Cuba.[58] China's blocking statute, the Anti-Foreign Sanctions Law enacted in 2021, creates a reporting requirement for Chinese companies when foreign sanctions law prohibits them from economic activities with sanctioned parties.[59]

Another measure taken by some EU Member States to combat the extraterritorial application of US sanctions was the establishment of the Instrument in Support of Trade Exchanges (INSTEX). It was founded under French law in 2019 and owned by the nations of France, Germany, the United Kingdom, Belgium, Denmark, the Netherlands, Norway, Finland, Spain, and Sweden.[60] It was created to facilitate trade between Iran and the European Union in light of the United States' withdrawal from the JCPOA.[61] It was set up as a payment clearinghouse that netted European payments against other European payments, and Iranian payments against other Iranian payments.[62] It focused on facilitating humanitarian trade between the EU and Iran but was dissolved in 2023 after Iran had agreed to only a single transaction.

The use of sanctions on an extraterritorial basis mirrors the increasing extraterritorial application of other statutes. For example, China in 2020 enacted the Hong Kong National Security Law. Under its Article 38, jurisdiction extends extraterritorially to reach nonnationals of China or Hong Kong, even outside China, based on listed offenses.[63] The EU General Data Protection Regulation (GDPR)'s Article 3 extends the scope of the GDPR to the processing of personal data of EU nationals to locations outside of the EU where processing relates to offering them goods and services or monitoring their behavior occurring inside the European Union. Likewise, EU antitrust law applies extraterritorially, for example, by satisfying a qualified effects test.[64] More informally, China deployed economic pressure against Lithuania for allowing Taiwan to open an office in that country, as well as against Slovenia for attempting to deepen its relationship with Taiwan.[65] These measures mirror the formal use of secondary sanctions elsewhere.[66] While the extraterritorial application of sanctions laws has long been controversial, the use of other statutes on an extraterritorial basis suggests the potential for an increasing global deployment of such extended jurisdictional application.

ISSUES CREATED BY EXTRATERRITORIAL APPLICATION OF SANCTIONS

Beyond the debate over the legality of applying sanctions extraterritorially, sanctions that apply outside of an enacting jurisdiction are also controversial because of the negative consequences in which a broad application of sanctions may result. A major issue associated with the use of sanctions, and multiplied by the use of sanctions extraterritorially, is that of overcompliance. Overcompliance in the private sector occurs when "companies take more extensive actions than strictly necessary," and where they "effectively limit their economic activities beyond what is strictly necessary under an extraterritorial sanction."[67]

Overcompliance has historically been an issue with respect to the application of primary sanctions within a jurisdiction. This is especially true when those sanctions have been applied comprehensively to a region or jurisdiction. The effects of overcompliance grow in magnitude when primary sanctions are applied extraterritorially or secondary sanctions are enacted. Secondary sanctions, for example, create incentives to overcomply with sanctions. Counterparties are discouraged from doing any business with sanctioned parties due to the risk that they might also become sanctioned in turn.[68] The extraterritorial application of primary sanctions also propagates problems of overcompliance globally. Banks can be force multipliers of trends in overcompliance, as they may compel their customers to abide by their own interpretations of sanctions obligations. In a financial system in which the US dollar is the leading medium of exchange, the use of the US dollar as a jurisdictional hook to apply financial sanctions extraterritorially has great practical effect. As discussed in Chapter 3, the reliance of the world on the US dollar and on the euro multiplies the effects of sanctions, weaponizing the interdependence of the world financial system. Where sanctions laws have greater geographic reach, the possibility of overcompliance with those regulations similarly grows. So too do secondary sanctions trigger overcompliance. The threat that engaging in nominally legal commerce can lead to becoming a sanctioned party oneself is a strong disincentive to engaging in transactions with sanctioned parties.

Overcompliance entails the risk of serious negative consequences. Broad sanctions helped trigger a humanitarian crisis in Iraq. More recently, the sanctions against Iran caused drastic increases in the cost of basic goods. They impeded Iranians' access to medical supplies and treatments, and reduced living standards in a myriad of other ways.[69] The COVID-19 pandemic was particularly deadly in Iran, and seemingly made worse at least in part by overcompliance with existing sanctions. This resulted despite the humanitarian exemptions that were intended to alleviate such suffering.[70] The extraterritorial application of primary sanctions and the threat of secondary sanctions to parties outside of an enacting jurisdiction, while making any particular set of sanctions more effective in theory, exacerbate the problem of overcompliance as counterparties seek to avoid the potential legal implications of sanctions.[71]

EXTRATERRITORIALITY OF SANCTIONS AGAINST RUSSIA

Like many other US sanctions programs, sanctions imposed by the United States against Russia before 2022 allowed for secondary sanctions to be imposed against non-US parties engaged in certain activities with sanctioned Russian parties. CAATSA contained provisions mandating the implementation of secondary sanctions in certain instances, such as where non-US persons knowingly carried out significant transactions with the Russian defense sector. For example, the United States implemented sanctions on Turkish entity SSB in 2020, after SSB procured a surface-to-air missile system from Rosoboronexport, which the US Department of State characterized as "Russia's main arms export entity."[72] The term "significant transactions" as used in CAATSA has been controversial, given that the term is not defined within the statute or by the agency.[73]

Executive Order 14,024, issued April 15, 2021, allowed persons and entities to be sanctioned if they were determined by the US Secretary of the Treasury, in consultation with the Secretary of State, "to have materially assisted, sponsored, or provided financial, material, or technological support for, or goods or services to or in support of" persons blocked pursuant to the order, or activities including malicious cyber-enabled activities, interference in US elections, transnational corruption, or assassination of a US person or national of a US ally or partner, among others. The order also provided for the possibility of sanctions against citizens or nationals of Russia if they provided such support for a sanctioned government. This last provision created the potential for secondary sanctions against Russian nationals and citizens for supporting the government of Syria, for example.

The United States had also passed legislation allowing for the imposition of secondary sanctions in connection with the construction of the Nord Stream 2 pipeline.[74] Namely, the law allowed for the imposition of sanctions against vessels engaged in pipe-laying at 100 feet or more below sea level in connection with the project. Secondary sanctions could also be imposed against foreign persons who sold, leased, or provided vessels for construction, or facilitated those activities; facilitated deceptive or structured transactions to provide vessels for construction; provided necessary underwriting services or insurance or reinsurance for those vessels; provided necessary services or facilities for technology upgrades, retrofitted, installed welding equipment for, or tethered those vessels; or provided necessary testing, inspection, or certification necessary for the project. Earlier legislation allowed for sanctions to be placed on parties who invested at least $1 million (or $5 million over 12 months) in Russian energy export pipelines or the equivalent value in goods, services, or support.[75]

So too were secondary sanctions used by the United States to respond to Russia's 2022 invasion. They were not immediately implemented against parties providing support to Russia, but their possible use was highlighted as the conflict continued, especially after Putin's illegal annexation of four Ukrainian territories. The economic response against Russia was a coordinated effort among numerous nations, a number of which had previously stated their opposition to secondary sanctions. The coordinated nature of the response may explain the initial lack of secondary sanctions used in the economic response to Russia.

But later in 2022, secondary sanctions were increasingly raised as a possible tool to respond to Russia as the conflict continued and the coalition of sanctioning nations sought additional economic tools. In September, OFAC issued an FAQ and response raising the possibility of secondary sanctions in connection with one designated party. NSPK, the operator of the Mir payment system, was not itself designated as a sanctioned entity. Nevertheless, OFAC stated that non-US financial institutions "that enter[ed] into new or expanded agreements with NSPK risk[ed] supporting Russia's efforts to evade US sanctions" and could themselves be blocked by way of secondary sanctions for providing material support to activities carried out in order to evade the US sanctions or to aid blocked persons.[76] Allowing for secondary sanctions in connection with the Mir payment system served to address a key mechanism by which Russian parties were trying to avoid existing sanctions relating to payments.[77] Earlier in the year, while not explicitly threatening secondary sanctions, a US representative had signaled to India the importance of not attempting to aid Russia in avoiding sanctions on the US dollar: "There are consequences to countries that actively attempt to circumvent or backfill the sanctions. . . . We are very keen for all countries, especially our allies and partners, not to create mechanisms that prop up the rouble, and those that attempt to undermine the dollar based financial system."[78]

In October, the United States signaled its intent to "more aggressively" deploy secondary sanctions against parties providing material support to Russia's military-industrial base.[79] It did so, for example, in November, when it sanctioned two UAE-based transportation firms and an Iranian unmanned aerial vehicle (UAV) manufacturer, as well as two Iranian individuals, for providing UAVs to Russia. Russia then used these drones to attack civilian infrastructure in Ukraine.[80] Likewise, the United States had in September named as SDNs Chinese Sinno Electronics and Armenian Taco LLC for their relationship with Radioavtomatika, a Russian defense procurement company that had itself been earlier sanctioned by the United States.[81]

Not all US measures imposed in the later part of the year featured secondary sanctions, however. The US Treasury clarified that the G7 price cap on oil would not implicate secondary sanctions for non-US parties who did not use the services of the sanctioning or G7 powers.[82] Several US legislators put forward their own proposal for a price cap that would provide for the imposition of secondary sanctions.[83] The version eventually adopted by OFAC, however, did not contain a mechanism for secondary sanctions to designate non-US parties dealing in oil over the price cap.

Primary sanctions and trade restrictions were also enforced on an extraterritorial basis. In June, the United States added five Chinese companies to the Entity List (parties on which were prohibited from receiving exports without a license, with a presumption of license denial).[84] These additions were made because they were alleged to have directly violated US export controls by "continu[ing] to contract to supply Russian entity listed and sanctioned parties after Russia's further invasion of Ukraine," contrary to US export controls.[85]

The sanctions of other nations also had extraterritorial aspects during the 2022 economic response. New Zealand's Russia Sanctions Act 2022 provided for extraterritorial jurisdiction for offenses occurring wholly outside of New Zealand, so long as the defendant was a New Zealand citizen or an entity incorporated under New Zealand law, among other possible jurisdictional hooks.[86] Notably, the EU's eighth sanctions package included a measure to allow the listing of persons who facilitated the circumvention of already-imposed sanctions,[87] a provision akin to the sort of secondary sanctions long imposed by the United States.[88] Both EU and non-EU nationals could be listed for having facilitated sanctions evasion. This change in the EU position on sanctions that could be applied extraterritorially could likely be attributed to the unique nature of the Russian threat. So too had the view of extraterritoriality under EU law perhaps shifted in recent years, as laws in other areas like privacy (most notably in the case of the GDPR) and antitrust had been applied outside of the EU with increasing frequency and effect.[89]

The coordinated nature of the 2022 response to Russia in many nations deemphasized the conflicts that could be created by applying sanctions extraterritorially, most notably in the case of US sanctions applied to EU parties. Because the scope of many of the sanctions measures was consistent across the jurisdictions enacting sanctions, and because many jurisdictions participated in the economic response, primary sanctions applied in similar ways across much of the world. Only where sanctions conflicted in some meaningful way, and where an actor could engage in a given activity under national law but for the presence of some foreign prohibition, would extraterritoriality raise issues that were of practical significance. Thus in the case of the Russia sanctions, the European Union and the United States faced fewer conflicts between the extraterritorial application of US sanctions and the provisions of national and EU law than in the cases of the US sanctions against Iran or Cuba.

Large portions of the world, however, were not part of the sanctioning coalition. Non-sanctioning nations were often subject to and affected by the extraterritorial application of the sanctions. Many African nations, for example, were not participants in the 2022 sanctions, but were nevertheless affected by the extraterritorial application and effects of the sanctions. These were often caused by the prohibitions against providing services to or dealing in the property of major Russian financial institutions. The effect of such measures was to restrict the use of the currencies of sanctioning nations with parties designated as targets, even in transactions with parties from non-sanctioning nations.

Thus, the extraterritorial application of sanctions created effects that were felt around the world, even in jurisdictions and by nationals of countries that had not themselves joined in the economic response to Russia. While the debate around the extraterritorial application of sanctions had long centered on EU–US relations, the coordination between those two jurisdictions now meant that the debate over extraterritoriality shifted to other global focal points.

The extraterritoriality of sanctions against Russia created many of the same issues that extraterritorial sanctions had created in the context of comprehensively sanctioned regimes. The use of targeted sanctions applied against Russia and globally was intended to lessen the humanitarian impacts that earlier, more comprehensive sanctions regimes had triggered. But the sanctions against Russia, while technically targeted in nature, were used against so many targets as to approach somewhat of a comprehensive sanctions regime in reality. The use of extraterritorial and secondary sanctions against Russia thus raised many of the same types of issues as would the use of such sanctions in connection with a comprehensively sanctioned regime.[90] As described further in Chapter 7, 2022 also brought efforts from the United Nations and unilaterally sanctioning powers to reduce barriers to humanitarian assistance to sanctioned areas. While the extraterritorial application of sanctions would continue to pose issues in other spheres, the humanitarian sanctions exceptions were an attempt to deal with the most severe of the unintended consequences of sanctions.

CONCLUSION

The 2022 Russia sanctions represented somewhat of a departure from the usual practice of applying sanctions extraterritorially in practice. The United States, perhaps recognizing its European allies' historical aversion to extraterritorial sanctions, tempered its initial sanctions response to focus more on primary sanctions and only later in the year increased the use of secondary sanctions. The European Union, on the other hand, in its eighth sanctions package announced new criteria for listing non-EU parties that closely mirrored the secondary sanctions long used by the United States, representing a departure from its usual practice of limiting itself to primary sanctions only. While the European Union and the United States had long been at odds regarding the extraterritorial use of sanctions, perhaps the Russia crisis – along with other recent developments in European law, like the expansive use of antitrust and privacy authority – would signal a new move toward something like consensus in this area.

5

The Energy Problem

Russia is blackmailing us. Russia is using energy as a weapon.

—Ursula von der Leyen, European Commission President[1]

You have this new revisionism suggesting that we have to be pumping oil like crazy and we have to be moving into long-term infrastructure building, which would be absolutely disastrous.

—John Kerry, US Special Presidential Envoy for Climate[2]

Sanctions on energy were key to the broader sanctions strategy against Russia. But the economic fallout from such restrictions would not be borne by Russia alone. Because of the importance of Russian oil and other forms of energy to the global energy market and to Europe in particular, attempting to cut off the Russian energy supply to large portions of the world was extremely difficult. The move necessarily inflicted harm on those nations imposing and enforcing sanctions.

Nor did the economic harm from the energy sanctions fall evenly upon each of the sanctioning powers. The domestic politics of imposing energy sanctions were very different for those countries that relied heavily on Russia to meet their energy needs than they were for countries with ample natural energy resources of their own. For that reason, the fluid multilateral cooperation that largely characterized the sanctions effort was more difficult for energy-related sanctions than for those imposed against other sectors. And because of the worldwide need for Russian energy supplies, the energy sanctions in many instances were more limited and contained more exceptions than did other legal prohibitions against Russia.

The economic effects of the energy sanctions were also more complicated and caused more harm to the sanctioning nations than did those in other areas. As energy prices rose, Russia reaped financial gains and the energy-importing sanctioning powers suffered. The energy sanctions were extensive enough to cause harm to the sanctioning nations reliant on Russian energy, but not universally imposed by nations such that Russian revenue from oil sales were immediately seriously diminished. And while the rise in energy prices might have been an impetus to move to clean energy over time, the immediate need for energy and metals drove sanctioning powers to prioritize current requirements and postpone measures to attain climate goals.

BACKGROUND

Oil sanctions and trade restrictions had been imposed in a variety of contexts in the past.[3] The United States placed export controls on oil shipments to Japan even before the United States entered World War II.[4] In 1979, the United Nations imposed an oil embargo against South Africa.[5] Likewise, the United States' Comprehensive Anti-Apartheid Act of 1986 contained a prohibition against exporting crude oil or refined petroleum to South Africa.[6] In the 1980s, the United States barred the import of oil from Libya, along with the sale of US-origin oil drilling and refining equipment.[7] This was eventually followed by UN sanctions on Libya including, among other measures, a prohibition on the export of oil- and gas-related equipment to Libya. OPEC also employed trade restrictions on oil when it launched and maintained an embargo against the United States from 1973 to 1974.[8] In turn, to help ensure US supply, US crude oil could not legally be exported from 1975 to 2015.[9] The Consolidated Appropriations Act, in 2016, removed that restriction.[10]

More recently, the United Nations had imposed an embargo against Iraq, including with respect to sales of oil. In 1996, the United Nations established the Oil-for-Food Program. It allowed Iraq to sell oil to pay for humanitarian necessities; the program, however, was plagued by corruption.[11]

A prominent recent example of sanctions on energy supplies was those sanctions placed on the Venezuelan state-owned company PdVSA. In 2019, the company was designated by OFAC as an SDN, pursuant to certain general licenses that allowed certain activities with respect to the entity.[12] The move prevented PdVSA from exporting oil to the United States, and also prohibited US companies from providing light crude to PdVSA needed to dilute its heavy oil to allow it to flow through pipelines.[13]

So too had energy sanctions been used against Russia itself. The United States had earlier imposed sanctions on certain sectors of the Russian economy, including oil and gas exploration in Russian deepwater, Arctic offshore locations, and shale formations in Russia and Belarus.[14] This caused the US company ExxonMobil to leave a previously planned partnership to develop resources in the Kara Sea in the Arctic with Russian state-owned oil company Rosneft, a project later resumed by Rosneft alone.[15]

The energy crisis of 2022, characterized by high prices and limited supplies, had preinvasion roots. Oil producers in recent years had become wary of making significant new investments to expand capacity; prices in recent years had been too low to justify these capital expenditures.[16] Oil prices crashed in 2014–16, partly due to increased US shale oil production.[17] The COVID-19 pandemic triggered another drastic downturn in oil prices as worldwide oil demand fell nearly 30 percent in April 2020 from the prior year.[18] While the price of oil by January 2022 had recovered from its pandemic lows, world events were about to drive it to the other extreme.[19]

THE ENERGY SANCTIONS AND TRADE RESTRICTIONS AGAINST RUSSIA

Russia is a major energy supplier to the world and derives much of its income from energy sales. In 2020, Russia exported a total of $74.4 billion in crude petroleum,[20] including to China ($23.8 billion), the Netherlands ($9.26 billion), Germany ($6.38 billion), South Korea ($5.03 billion), and Poland ($4.22 billion).[21] As of 2021, it was the world's second-largest natural gas producer, and the largest natural gas exporter.[22] Given the importance of energy exports to the Russian economy, at the outset of the invasion it appeared that energy sanctions on Russia had the potential to cut export revenue dramatically, and deal a powerful blow to Russia's ability to wage a sustained conflict.

The sanctioning powers, however, were differently situated with respect to their reliance on Russian energy. The United States, in contrast to Germany and its billions of dollars of crude petroleum imported from Russia in 2020, imported only a net of $979 million in crude petroleum from Russia that same year. Other sanctioning nations, like Canada and Australia, were likewise less reliant on Russian energy. As such, coordinating energy sanctions on Russia across multiple jurisdictions would prove more challenging than for other sectors.

Canada acted quickly to enact an embargo on Russian crude oil imports, as Prime Minister Trudeau announced the measure on February 28.[23] The ban was "largely symbolic," since Canada was itself a major energy producer and had last imported Russian oil in 2019.[24] Its own imports in recent years had come largely from the United States, with additional supplies from Saudi Arabia, Iraq, and others.[25]

As described earlier, the first set of US sanctions enacted against certain Russian financial institutions contained general licenses carving out energy-related transactions. Even though there was no immediate ban on Russian energy imports into the United States, it seemed that one might be forthcoming, given the popular will to act against Russia and given the large volume of revenues Russia derived from energy supply sales. On March 3, the bipartisan Ban Russian Energy Imports Act was introduced in the US Congress. Though ultimately never enacted, the draft legislation declared that Russa's invasion of Ukraine was a national emergency that represented "an unusual and extraordinary threat to the national security, foreign policy, and economy" of the United States. The legislation would have directed President Biden to prohibit imports of crude oil, petroleum, petroleum products, liquefied natural gas (LNG), and coal "in which the Russian Federation or a national of the Russian Federation has any interest."[26] When asked that same day about a possible ban on Russian energy supplies, White House Press Secretary Jen Psaki defended the existing sanctions carve-out: "[W]e do not have a strategic interest in reducing the global supply of energy. And that would raise prices at the gas pump for the American people, around the world, because it would reduce the supply available. . . . [I]t also has the potential to pad the pockets of President Putin, which is exactly what we are not trying to do."[27]

Oil companies, anticipating import bans of Russian oil by additional nations, announced various actions winding down or ceasing certain business activities in Russia. Within days of the beginning of the invasion (and after having been summoned by the UK business secretary to a meeting to explain its ties to Russia),[28] BP announced its intent to give up its 20 percent ownership interest in Rosneft, the Russian energy company historically owned and controlled by the Russian state.[29] Shell terminated joint ventures with Gazprom, the Russian state-owned energy company. Shell soon after faced public criticism when it bought Russian crude oil at a discounted price, after other industry actors had begun to reduce dealings in Russia.[30]

A US ban on Russian energy imports was soon forthcoming. On March 8, President Biden signed an Executive Order banning the import into the United States of Russian oil, liquefied natural gas, and coal.[31] The United Kingdom also announced that day that it would cease importing Russian oil by the end of 2022.[32] As the UK government noted, 8 percent of its oil demand was supplied by Russia, but the United Kingdom itself was also an oil producer.[33] Australia also announced a similar ban, to go into effect on April 25.[34] (Only 1.2 percent of its oil imports in 2021 came from Russia.)[35]

A decision to ban Russian energy supplies from entering the European Union was not forthcoming as quickly. Many Member States within the union were heavily dependent on Russian energy imports. Europe imported much of its energy needs; in 2020, the European Union imported 58 percent of the gross energy supplies it consumed.[36] Of its total energy needs, the European Union imported 83 percent of its natural gas in 2021, along with 91.67 percent of its crude oil and petroleum products consumed.[37]

Nearly a third of EU households used natural gas; about 40 percent of the European Union's gas consumption went to household use.[38] Pre-pandemic, almost half of oil and petroleum used in the European Union went to road transportation, including cars; 19 percent went to industrial uses.[39] The pandemic had curtailed travel of EU citizens and reduced overall demand for oil and petroleum by 10 percent.[40]

Much of the European Union's energy needs were met by Russia. Over 24 percent of the total gross energy consumed in the European Union was imported from Russia, the single largest outside source of EU natural gas, oil, and coal supplies.[41]

Forty-three percent of the EU's imported natural gas came from Russia, as did 29 percent of its imported crude oil.[42] Over half of the European Union's imported coal was supplied by Russia. Other major energy suppliers to the European Union included Algeria and Qatar for natural gas; Saudi Arabia, the United Kingdom, Kazakhstan, and Nigeria for crude oil; and Norway for both. The United States and Australia also supplied the European Union with coal.

At the end of May, EU Member States agreed on a ban on the import of Russian crude oil transported by sea, which constituted 90 percent of the oil imported from Russia.[43] The ban would go into effect December 5, 2022.[44] In effect, the measure exempted Hungary, because it received its oil through land by pipeline.[45] Bulgaria was granted a temporary exception through 2024; Croatia was also given a more limited exception for a shorter period of time.[46] Petroleum products would also be banned from import into the European Union, effective February 5, 2023.[47] Coal from Russia was banned from import into the European Union beginning in August 2022.

IMMEDIATE IMPACTS

The invasion and sanctions resulted in both immediate and longer-term consequences, affecting both prices and trading patterns of energy throughout the world.

The sanctions caused dramatic increases in energy prices. West Texas Intermediate (WTI) crude futures spiked almost immediately after the invasion, reaching a high at the beginning of March. Prices then dropped off but continued to see-saw upwards, reaching another near-high at the beginning of June. The average price of gas in the United States reached $5 per gallon in June, for the first time ever (in nominal dollars, unadjusted for inflation).[48] WTI crude futures then trended lower throughout the rest of June, July, and August; US average gas prices followed suit, falling below $4 per gallon by the end of August.

Gas prices were a highly visible component of emerging inflation in the United States, which reached 9.1 percent in June and 8.5 percent in July for the preceding twelve-month period.[49] Motor fuel, consisting mostly of gasoline, made up nearly 4 percent of the Consumer Price Index (CPI) used by the US Bureau of Labor Statistics to measure inflation.[50] The CPI also reflected the rising costs of Russian energy by way of the fuels and utilities index (4.6 percent of the CPI), which consisted in large part of household energy.[51] But while energy was a significant component of inflation, it was certainly not the only one. The US fiscal and monetary stimulus intended to offset a pandemic-era economic downturn contributed to inflation as well.[52] Thus, the US inflation rate remained relatively high even as gas prices fell throughout the summer.[53] So too in the European Union did rising energy prices contribute to inflation, where the annual inflation rate in the European Union reached 9.8 percent in July.[54]

The soaring gasoline prices were popularly blamed on corporate greed. In August, UN Secretary-General António Guterres commented: "[T]his grotesque greed is punishing the poorest and most vulnerable people."[55] President Biden also viewed gasoline companies as a significant cause of America's gas woes. In a letter to BP, Chevron, Exxon Mobil, Marathon Petroleum, Phillips 66, Shell and Valero, President Biden accused them of profiteering from the energy crisis and unfairly limiting refining capacity.[56] Exxon Mobil responded, arguing that it had kept investing in refining capacity during the pandemic, "when we lost more than $20 billion and had to borrow more than $30 billion to maintain investment to increase capacity to be ready for post-pandemic demand."[57] The company suggested ways for the federal government to respond to the crisis, including waiving provisions of the Jones Act and some fuel specifications, "promot[ing] investment through clear and consistent policy that supports US resource development," and "streamlined regulatory approval and support for infrastructure such as pipelines."[58]

Others also called for a repeal of some Jones Act restrictions. The Jones Act was a 1920 US statute "requir[ing] that vessels transporting cargo from one US point to another US point be US-built, and owned and crewed by US citizens."[59] Critics of the law argued that it increased costs of shipping Texas and Alaskan oil to the Northeast and the West Coast and thus provided an advantage to imported oil in those markets.[60] The governors of the New England states wrote to the US Secretary of Energy in July, requesting a possible suspension of the Jones Act along with other measures, like the development of a modernized strategic energy reserve and immediate coordination between the states and federal government to prepare for the coming winter.[61]

In addition to drastic changes in the price of energy, the sanctions also affected trading patterns and the volume of energy flows. China stepped up its purchases of Russian oil, importing 55 percent more in May 2022 than it had a year earlier.[62] India also increased its oil purchases from Russia.[63] Russian oil also continued to flow to Turkey.[64] Faced with the new competitor of Russia, Iran cut prices of its oil that it sold to China.[65] In July, the National Iranian Oil Company and Gazprom signed a memorandum of understanding to develop oil and gas fields in Iran, construct pipelines for the export of oil from Iran, and work on LNG projects.[66]

The sanctioning powers also sought new energy trading partners and increased their purchases from existing suppliers. Norway became the largest supplier of natural gas to the European Union, providing about one-third of the natural gas used there.[67] Norway also increased its sales of oil to the European Union. The United States increased its oil purchasing from Mexico and Latin America.[68] Germany agreed to a fifteen-year deal, beginning in 2026, with Qatar to supply Germany with two million tons of LNG each year.[69] The gas would be delivered to a new LNG terminal in Brunsbüttel, Germany that was projected to be operational by that time. This facility was planned prior to the Russian invasion of

Ukraine.[70] In November, Germany completed the construction of its first floating LNG terminal.[71]

The Organization of Petroleum Exporting Countries (OPEC) consisted of thirteen member countries, most located in the Middle East and Africa.[72] OPEC+ consisted of ten additional states, including Russia. The OPEC+ group met every month to determine oil output, pursuant to the Declaration of Cooperation agreed to in 2016.[73] In June, OPEC+ announced that it would increase production in July and August 2022. This relatively modest increase was not expected to significantly alleviate high consumer gasoline prices in the United States.[74] In October, when oil prices had declined to about $85 per barrel, the group considered a large reduction in oil production in an apparent attempt to raise oil prices above $90 per barrel once again.[75]

China and Russia envisioned a deeper energy relationship in the long term. In early February, before the invasion, the countries had agreed to a thirty-year Russian commitment to supply natural gas to China.[76] As of the summer of 2022, construction on a new Power of Siberia 2 pipeline linking the two countries through Mongolia was anticipated to begin in 2024.[77]

Longer-term supply shifts were also possible with respect to Africa. Algeria was not at first able to increase petroleum exports immediately after the Russian invasion of Ukraine. This was due to a prior lack of foreign investment, which had shortchanged production capacity.[78] In July, however, Italy and Algeria agreed to increase natural gas sales from Algeria to Italy.[79] Energy companies including Eni (Italy), Occidental (United States), and Total (France) would also invest in the development of Algerian oil production.

PREPARING FOR WINTER

It soon became clear that significant energy shortages could result throughout Europe in the coming winter. For example, the International Monetary Fund forecast by mid-year that Hungary, Slovakia, and the Czech Republic could suffer a shortage of up to 40 percent of normal gas consumption levels.[80] To help address the potential crisis, the European Union adopted a regulation to fortify gas storage reserves before winter. It required Member States to fill their underground gas storage to at least 80 percent before the coming winter.[81] The European Commission introduced a voluntary plan for rationing natural gas by cutting consumption by 15 percent, in order to conserve supplies ahead of winter.[82] In Germany, Berlin stopped lighting many tourist attractions. Hanover introduced an energy savings plan that would, among other measures, turn off public fountains and shut off hot water in municipal buildings.[83] The German government in August introduced its own energy plan that would reduce the temperature in public buildings and planned to give priority on the railroads to oil and coal over passenger transport.[84]

The falling gas prices towards the end of the summer did not alleviate concerns about possible price spikes in the coming winter, especially given the EU ban on imported Russian oil that would go into effect in December. The G7 countries agreed to a price cap, both to try to ensure the continued flow of energy at or below a set price, as well as to limit Russian profit from sales of energy supplies at high prices.[85] The price cap was structured by each sanctioning power as a ban on its citizens or those within its territory from dealing in services related to the maritime transportation of oil from Russia, including services related to insurance and shipping.[86] An exception to the ban existed if parties could prove that the Russian oil was purchased at or below the value of the price cap. OFAC confirmed that the US price cap framework did not include secondary sanctions; the restrictions would apply only to parties subject to US sanctions regulations and would not involve the designation of other parties for otherwise non-prohibited dealings in oil over the price set by the cap.[87] Legislators in the United States, however, worked on developing legislation to create the potential for such secondary sanctions to be imposed on non-US parties, even outside of the United States, for dealings in oil sold over the maximum price.[88]

A cap to limit the price of natural gas in the European Union was agreed to in December 2022. The cap would go into effect if gas prices reached €180 per megawatt hour for three days.[89]

As it turned out, the winter of 2022–23 did not result in the extreme energy crisis that many had feared. Warm temperatures in the fall and early winter meant that gas remained stored at fairly high levels within the European Union.[90] The alternative sources of energy procured by EU Member States leading up to winter were helpful in alleviating pressure on energy prices.[91]

ENFORCING THE ENERGY SANCTIONS

The energy shortages of 2022 spurred increasing covert shipments of fuel. Despite the imposition of sanctions, some oil of at least partly Russian origin flowed clandestinely to the United States and the European Union. Some came via refineries in India; some was handed off by ship in the Mediterranean Sea and then directed to China, India, and Europe.[92] Both before and after sanctions were imposed, some tankers carrying Russian oil turned off tracking capabilities, whether to avoid public scrutiny or perhaps to facilitate illicit oil dealing in violation of the sanctions against Russia once those sanctions came into effect.[93] In April 2022, Russia shipped over 11.1 million barrels in tankers without a known destination, a new trend arising post-invasion.[94] Governments began scrutinizing energy shipments more closely. For example, US Customs and Border Protection halted an oil tanker from unloading in Louisiana for four days in order to verify its cargo; the oil on board was determined to come from Kazakhstan, not Russia, and unloading was allowed to proceed.[95]

The EU price cap framework included a provision for monitoring by the European Commission of possible evasion through activities like re-flagging of ships to states outside of the European Union.[96] These measures were designed to address the concerns of nations such as Greece, Malta, and Cyprus whose ships were heavily involved in transporting Russian oil and would suffer from this type of re-flagging.[97]

THE ECONOMIC EFFECT ON RUSSIA AND RUSSIA'S ECONOMIC RESPONSE

The energy sanctions differed somewhat from many other sanctions and trade restrictions placed on other Russian goods and services because of the fundamental nature of oil as an easily-traded, relatively fungible commodity.[98] The impact of the sanctions could therefore be blunted by the redirection of non-sanctioned oil to other destinations, as Russian oil helped to fulfill the demand of buyers not legally required to observe the mandates of the sanctions.[99] Notwithstanding this potential offset, a significant gap soon opened up between the price of Russian oil and the Urals oil benchmark, as fewer buyers were able to purchase Russian oil in compliance with sanctions, or willing to take on the compliance risk. Russian oil sellers also faced increased costs for shipping oil to Asia rather than to Europe.[100]

Even though the overall volume of Russian oil and gas exports fell, Russian revenues from those exports rose sharply, because of the higher prices for oil worldwide.[101] Gas and oil sanctions were a double-edged weapon for the European Union and other sanctioning powers. While the major sanctioning powers sought to limit Russia's financial resources through restricting its oil and gas sales, they were themselves subject to the economic fallout such a decision necessarily triggered. These sanctions were also an extremely imprecise instrument, since the short-term demand for oil and natural gas was relatively price inelastic. Russian oil and gas revenues rose even while the volume of sales dropped. Indeed, as the sanctions drove the price of oil upwards, paradoxically those sanctions provided a new means of financial support for Russia to wage war in Ukraine.[102] Oleg Ustenko, chief economic advisor to the president of Ukraine, blasted the piecemeal nature of the sanctions regime. "The failure to impose a genuine embargo on Russian oil and gas is turbocharging Putin's revenues and financing war crimes in Ukraine."[103] In the longer term, however, the Russian oil industry depended on key exports from other nations that were now restricted, like drilling equipment and software.[104]

The energy sanctions were soon met by measures imposed by Russia. In July, Gazprom provided force majeure notice to some of its European buyers of gas, stating that it would not provide contractually agreed-upon shipments of natural gas and that the provision also applied retroactively with respect to contractual shortfalls in supply.[105] The force majeure clauses in its contracts allowed Gazprom to be relieved of its obligations to supply gas in the case of extraordinary events. The

German energy company Uniper, that country's largest importer of Russian gas, formally rejected Gazprom's notice.[106]

Among the most concerning of Russia's retaliatory measures was the uncertainty around whether natural gas would continue to flow from Russia to Germany through the Nord Stream 1 pipeline, which had opened in 2011.[107] The pipeline was owned by an entity whose major shareholder was Gazprom. The Nord Stream 2 pipeline, as previously mentioned, had been sanctioned in February before it could become operational. Natural gas stopped flowing through the Nord Stream 1 pipeline on July 11, when the pipeline was shut down for ten scheduled days of annual maintenance.[108] It was feared that Russia would keep the pipeline nonoperational for longer in retaliation for the sanctions measures that had been imposed upon it.

To speed the resumption of energy flows through Nord Stream 1, Germany sought the return of a repaired turbine from Canada despite the presence of Canadian sanctions, and urged an exception so that the lack of a part would not serve as a real or pretextual reason for the pipeline halting operations. [109] Canada agreed to make an exception to the existing sanctions measures to return the repaired turbine. Ukraine objected to the exception being granted. "[T]he latest Canadian-German agreement . . . is the adjustment of the sanctions regime to the whims of Russia," declared Ukraine's Ministries of Foreign Affairs and Energy in a statement, arguing that the decisions "violat[ed] international solidarity," and went "against the principle of the rule of law."[110] Canada would later revoke that exception in December.[111]

Russia resumed natural gas flows through Nord Stream 1, at the same 40 percent capacity that had been present immediately prior to the shutdown.[112] Shortly thereafter, however, Russia reduced the capacity to 20 percent, citing the need for repairs.[113] Energy flows through the pipeline were finally halted indefinitely at the beginning of September.

In late September, both the Nord Stream 1 and Nord Stream 2 pipelines began to leak natural gas. While they were nonoperational at the time, they were filled with natural gas.[114] This resulted in a large discharge of the greenhouse gas methane.[115] Seismic data revealed the cause of the leaks to be undersea explosions. By the end of 2022, it was not yet known who had sabotaged the pipelines.[116]

Russia countered the energy sanctions in other ways as well. At the end of June 2022, Putin declared the nationalization of Sakhalin-2, an oil and gas field that supplied approximately 4 percent of the world's LNG; foreign investors could request to retain their shares within one month.[117] JERA, the largest power generation company in Japan, signed a deal in August to continue to buy LNG from Sakhalin-2.[118] In April 2023, a Russian paper reported that Putin had approved compensation of over $1.2 billion to Shell, a stakeholder in the project prior to nationalization.[119] It was not the first time Sakhalin-2 had been the subject of alleged nationalization. In 2006, the majority Russian government-owned Gazprom bought

50 percent plus one share of the equity in the project, following purported pressure by the Russian government to do so.[120]

In October, Putin nationalized the Sakhalin-1 pipeline and terminated Exxon Mobil's ownership interest, leading Exxon Mobil to exit Russia entirely.[121] The company had owned a 30 percent stake in the project. No compensation from the Russian government to Exxon was immediately reported, and Exxon termed the action an expropriation.[122] The Japanese government and a consortium of investors retained their ownership in Sakhalin-1, as they had done with respect to Sakhalin-2.[123]

DEVELOPING ALTERNATIVE ENERGY SOURCES

In the energy market upheaval of 2022, the sanctioning powers and others sought energy supplies from alternative sources. This included both identifying other suppliers of fossil fuels and expediting the development and deployment of clean energy alternatives.

The sanctioning powers turned to other energy suppliers to replace some of the newly created energy shortfall. In July 2022, the European Union strengthened ties with Azerbaijan to further develop a non-Russian source of natural gas.[124] Human Rights Watch and other groups criticized the agreement, arguing that Azeri opposition members had been or remained wrongfully imprisoned and that the European Union's agreement failed to negotiate meaningful political change within Azerbaijan.[125] Germany turned to developing access to chilled LNG by building floating terminals to receive shipments by sea. Germany had historically favored oil and gas transported by pipeline.[126] The Biden administration's offshore drilling plan limited drilling in certain areas but left open the possibility for new drilling leases in the Gulf of Mexico and offshore Alaska.[127]

Before the Russian invasion, nations had increasingly realized that addressing climate goals was of pressing importance. The burning of fossil fuels, including oil, natural gas, and coal, was currently the primary driver of climate change.[128] Global warming was projected to raise the average temperature of the Earth by likely at least 2.7 degrees Fahrenheit by 2100 without "aggressive mitigation of greenhouse gas emissions."[129] The UN Secretary-General called the 2021 Report of the Intergovernmental Panel on Climate Change "a code red for humanity."[130] Recent rates of sea level rise were "unprecedented over the past 2,500-plus years."[131] Sea levels were projected to rise by 2100 anywhere to between one and over six feet.[132] Climate change also exacerbated the problem of fuel shortages, as temperatures reached new heights in the summer of 2022 and energy was needed to power cooling systems.[133]

The EU Green Deal, approved in 2020, was Europe's plan to address climate change by cutting emissions at least 55 percent by 2030 and making the European

Union climate neutral (meaning, net-zero emissions) by 2050.[134] The European Union had earlier enacted Regulation 2017/1938, which attempted to prevent gas supply disruptions.[135] It provided the framework for a "solidarity mechanism" that would be triggered should "an extreme gas crisis" occur.[136] The prior November, the United Nations had held its 26th Conference of the Parties (COP26), related to the Paris Agreement and climate change, in Glasgow.[137] Twenty countries, including the United States and Canada, reached a deal at the meeting to end international public financing for fossil fuels, but no similar agreement was made regarding domestic subsidies.[138]

The climate crisis had made the need clear to develop alternative energy sources, which was only heightened as the Russian sanctions drove energy prices higher and restricted supplies.[139] Indeed, the high prices and extremely volatile nature of energy post-invasion lowered relative price barriers to the development of clean energy.

But developing alternative energy sources would be difficult in the short term. The United States lacked both the clean energy infrastructure and the structural incentives that might allow clean energy to fill the gap left by the sudden absence of Russian oil.[140] The sharp increase in gas prices created a strong incentive to increase oil and gas production domestically. In Europe, coal consumption actually increased in 2022, even though imports of Russian coal into the union were banned beginning in August.

Increasing consumption of non-Russian fossil fuels would not help ease the climate crisis. The US Special Presidential Envoy for Climate, John Kerry, urged the world not to lose its focus on climate: "But what we cannot allow to happen, is what is beginning to happen, which is a false narrative being created by those very people who never wanted to deal with the climate crisis anyway."[141] In September, China's climate envoy warned the European Union not to move backward on its climate commitments.[142]

Russia was a major supplier of metals like nickel, palladium, lithium, and others that were necessary for electric car batteries, solar panels, wind turbines, and other clean energy infrastructure components.[143] Metals from Russia not otherwise banned (like silver, gold, iron, and steel were) faced a 35 percent import tax into the United Kingdom. Worldwide, metal prices, especially nickel, rose sharply after the invasion.[144] Developing alternative energy sources faced other trade challenges in the United States as well. Solar panels imported from China were held up overseas as the US Department of Commerce investigated trade violations regarding forced labor on solar panels from China.[145]

Alternative energy sources could also be controversial. In Europe, the energy shortage caused an increased demand for wood pellets. These were produced by logging, often in old-growth forests in Central Europe.[146] In 2018, scientists had urged the EU Parliament to change the directive "that would let countries, power plants and factories claim credit toward renewable energy targets for deliberately cutting down trees to burn them for energy."[147] Germany's economics ministry announced that the life of two nuclear power plants would be extended through April 2023 instead of being shut down at the end of 2022.[148]

The rising price of energy brought increased attention toward promoting clean energy. In June, President Biden authorized use of the Defense Production Act to speed US production of solar panel parts and improve US solar manufacturing capabilities.[149] The Inflation Reduction Act was signed into law in the United States in August. It contained key provisions related to clean energy, including consumer tax credits for electric and fuel cell vehicles and energy-efficient home updates, and reducing greenhouse gas emissions by a billion metric tons by 2030.[150]

THE ENERGY FUTURE

On the whole, the energy sanctions were a rare example of the 2022 sanctions where the sanctioning alliance achieved few visible results in the short term, and perhaps threatened the popular will to impose future sanctions. The factors that had achieved so much more in other sectors, like banking – rapid coordination, comprehensive restrictions, and more robust enforcement – were missing here. And perhaps the sanctions could trigger a more rapid move to clean energy – but so too could they stagnate progress toward that goal. The world continued to face a broader energy crisis than the one precipitated by the Russian invasion of Ukraine, and the way forward – either with respect to strengthening the energy sanctions or to solving the climate crisis – remained unclear.

6

Trade as a Weapon

The impact of our export controls will only continue to bite harder the longer Russia sustains its aggression.

—Alan Estevez, US Under Secretary of Commerce for Industry and Security[1]

Sanctions were not the only tool deployed against Russia by the coalition of nations responding to its invasion of Ukraine. As referenced in earlier chapters, import restrictions (limiting and placing restrictions on goods from Russia entering into other countries) and export controls (restricting goods that could be shipped to Russia and to certain Russian end-users) were used as well. Limiting dual-use exports to Russia had at least two purposes: to prevent the Russian military from obtaining supplies it needed to wage war, and to sap resources from Russian industry to weaken the nation's economic standing as a whole. Measures restricting imports from Russia were enacted both to reduce revenue accruing to Russia, as well as for symbolic reasons. While sanctions had some of the most immediately noticeable effects, export controls had the long-term potential to slow the growth of the Russian economy as high-tech items from the sanctioning nations gradually became unavailable in Russia.[2]

IMPORTS FROM RUSSIA

IMPORT BANS ON PRODUCTS FROM RUSSIA

Russia's most valuable exports to the rest of the world, both pre- and post-invasion, were energy-related. Russia exported $484 billion worth of goods in 2021, around 37 percent of which was crude petroleum, refined petroleum, petroleum gas, and coal briquettes.[3] Food and fertilizer were another high-value source of Russian exports abroad. Notably, Russia exported a large quantity of wheat and nitrogen-based fertilizers; wheat comprised about 1.8 percent of the value of Russia's exports in 2021. Russia also exported other grains and agricultural products. Russian metal exports were also significant, including semi-finished iron, nickel (used in the production of stainless steel and car batteries), cobalt (used for rechargeable batteries), vanadium (used in energy storage and steel production), gold (3.9 percent of Russia's exports by value in 2021), lead, platinum, tungsten, manganese, zinc, and copper.[4] Russia also exported wood and wood products.

Part of the initial economic response to the invasion was the ban of certain imports from Russia, principally with respect to natural gas and petroleum. Import bans on numerous products also followed in subsequent rounds of sanctions. For example, US Executive Order 14,068, issued on March 11, prohibited the importation into the United States of Russian-origin fish, seafood, alcoholic beverages, and nonindustrial diamonds. This import ban affected $1 billion in Russian export revenue.[5] The European Union prohibited imports from Russia of iron, steel, wood, cement, seafood, and liquor. The United Kingdom imposed an import ban on Russian-origin silver, wood products, and luxury goods.[6]

Another notable import restriction included the ban on importing gold from Russia, adopted in June by the United States, the United Kingdom, the European Union, Australia, Japan, and Canada. After crude petroleum, refined petroleum, and petroleum gas, gold was Russia's next most valuable export, totaling $19.1 billion in 2021.[7] Some viewed the June ban as primarily symbolic in nature. By that time, the combination of private entities' voluntary cessation of business in Russia and with Russian entities, along with the effects of the sanctions, had already greatly reduced imports of Russian gold into the sanctioning nations.[8]

Not all imports from Russia into the United States or other sanctioning nations were prohibited. Indeed, the Associated Press found in August that more than 3,600 shipments from Russia had arrived in the United States since the Russian invasion, including those of wood, metals, and rubber.[9] While this number represented a sharp decline from the 6,000 shipments that had arrived during the same time in 2021, it demonstrated that the import restrictions were by no means comprehensive.[10]

Aluminum, in particular, remained free from a ban on imports into the United States or the European Union in the initial stages of the sanctions response.[11] In 2018, the United States had designated as an SDN United Company RUSAL, owned by Oleg Deripaska, whom the United States also sanctioned at the same time.[12] At that point, RUSAL produced 7 percent of the world's aluminum supply. During that same time period, the US aluminum supply became affected by the Trump-era Section 232 tariffs, which imposed a 10 percent tariff on aluminum imports into the United States not from Canada or Mexico. The Section 232 sanctions, along with the restrictions on RUSAL, sent the price of aluminum soaring. OFAC lifted sanctions on RUSAL in early 2019 after an agreement was reached to lessen Deripaska's control over RUSAL and to reduce his ownership of the company below

50 percent.[13] Now in 2022, the earlier sanctions-induced volatility in the price of aluminum, along with worldwide shortages of the metal, was a compelling force against the immediate imposition of an aluminum import ban. Industry groups in October urged European authorities against such a ban, arguing that it would hurt European companies.[14] And indeed, aluminum was not among the Russian-origin metals banned from import into the sanctioning coalition of nations. Not until 2023 would the United States announce a 200 percent tariff on the import of aluminum articles of Russian origin, and even then the measure was not an outright ban.[15] Canada would eventually ban imports of aluminum and steel from Russia in March 2023.[16]

Similarly, titanium was not made subject to an import ban because of its strategic importance to the sender states. Titanium, used in the manufacture of airplanes, was a key export from Russia to the United States and other sanctioning powers. Mid-year, the European Union blocked a proposal for sanctions on VSMPO-Avisma PJSC, a Russian metals company. Doing so avoided a potential retaliatory export ban by Russia of titanium to the European Union.[17] Private entities, though, took actions to limit their sourcing of titanium from Russia, notwithstanding the lack of any legal restriction which would require them to do so. Boeing, for example, stopped purchasing titanium from Russia soon after the invasion, suspending its long-term contracts with suppliers there.[18] Airbus continued its titanium purchases from Russia throughout most of 2022, but late in the year announced that it would extricate itself from Russian supply relationships within months.[19]

The legal prohibitions against Russian imports generally did not extend to imports of finished products from other countries where raw materials had originally been sourced from Russia. Specifically, US import restrictions did not apply to Russian-origin materials that were substantially transformed in another country or otherwise met legal requirements such that they were no longer considered to be Russian-origin products under US law.[20] For example, fish caught in Russia were not subject to the import ban on Russian seafood when they were processed in China. This had significant effect; almost a third of wild-caught fish imported from China in 2019 were estimated to have been caught in Russia.[21] Sally Yozell, Director of the Environmental Security program at the Stimson Center, testified that this shortcoming in country of origin labeling and traceability resulted in this "significant loophole."[22]

In response to the import bans on many of its products, Russia announced its own import restrictions. Namely, it banned the export of over 200 products such as timber, vehicles, and medical, agricultural and telecommunications equipment. The ban extended to exports to about forty-eight countries.[23]

MFN TREATMENT AND THE LEGAL FRAMEWORK OF THE WTO

The trade measures taken by the sanctioning nations and Russia were subject to an international framework of rules, certain legal provisions of which would be at issue with respect to the economic response to Russia. The World Trade Organization (WTO) had existed since 1995 to help facilitate the reduction in barriers to trade between Members and to resolve trade-related disputes between them. It had evolved from the General Agreement on Tariffs and Trade (GATT), which was signed in 1947 and came into effect in 1948.[24] The GATT was designed to lower tariffs and other barriers to trade following the World War II, in part to move away from the global protectionism of the 1930s and its associated economic harms and geopolitical tensions.[25]

WTO Members extended certain trade benefits to all other Members. Generally, each WTO Member was required to extend to all other Members most favored nation (MFN) status.[26] The MFN principle required WTO Members to extend the same trade benefits equally to, and not discriminate among, all Members with MFN status.[27] A cornerstone of the global trading system, the MFN principle appeared in the first article of the GATT.[28] National treatment required imported and domestic goods to be treated equally once imported goods entered the domestic market.[29] Trade disputes between WTO Members were to be resolved through the WTO dispute settlement system, involving consultations between the disputant governments, adjudication by panels appointed by the Dispute Settlement Body, and the possibility of appeal to the Appellate Body (though in 2022 the Appellate Body was nonfunctional due to vacancies on the Appellate Body for which appointments were blocked by the United States).[30] Russia had been a Member since 2012[31] and the sanctioning nations were also WTO Members. Ukraine, too, had been a Member of the WTO since 2008.[32] Belarus was not a WTO Member at the time of the Russian invasion of Ukraine. It had been negotiating WTO accession since 1993, but work on its accession had been halted after the widely condemned election of Lukashenko in 2020.[33]

The trade-related measures against Russia included the import bans described above, as well as actions to remove the benefit of MFN treatment from Russian-origin goods imported into the sanctioning nations. In April, both houses of the US Congress voted to remove Russia's most favored nation trade status by revoking its permanent normal trade relations status,[34] legislation subsequently signed by President Biden into law.[35] The other G7 nations (Canada, France, Germany, Italy, Japan, and the United Kingdom) also agreed to take action to revoke Russia's most favored nation status, as did Albania, Australia, Iceland, Moldova, Montenegro, New Zealand, North Macedonia, and South Korea.[36] So too was Belarus widely stripped of its MFN status for its support of the Russian invasion.[37]

Following those actions, the Russian parliament drafted legislation to withdraw Russia from the WTO (along with the World Health Organization).[38] By June, however, Russian media sources claimed that Russia would not in fact withdraw from the WTO or other organizations including the WHO, or a number of other international organizations. Belarus was penalized for its support of Russia's invasion by being deemed "unfit" for WTO membership by a group of jurisdictions including the United States and the European Union. As grounds, the group cited Belarus's "complicity in Russia's aggression, which [was] incompatible with the values and principles of the WTO and of a just rules-based order."[39]

Revoking Russia's MFN status raised the tariffs on many of the goods imported from Russia into the United States. Tariffs are taxes levied on imported goods, usually calculated as a percentage of those goods' value.[40] National tariff schedules, largely harmonized at the international level, set forth applicable tariff rates based on classifications of types of goods. The Harmonized Tariff Schedule of the United States sets forth duty rates in a Column 1 and Column 2. Column 1 details the rate applicable to most favored nations (further divided into countries in free trade agreements with the United States and those not). Column 2 contains the duty rate for countries that do not have most favored nation status. (Column 2, generally, contains the tariff rates originally set forth by the 1930 Smoot-Hawley Tariff Act.)[41] Despite the exclusivity that the term "most favored nation" might imply, immediately before the Russian invasion of Ukraine, Cuba and North Korea were the only countries in the world whom the US made subject to the duty rates of Column 2.[42]

MFN treatment does not always confer a significant reduction in a tariff rate under US law. Sometimes the duty rates in Column 1 and Column 2 are identical; a loss of most favored nation status does not affect the import tariffs for such goods. For example, a major portion of the exports from Russia to the United States were often natural resources that did not have a significant or even any difference in the tariff rates set forth in Column 1 and Column 2.[43] But often the rates set forth in Column 2 were significantly higher. In such cases, imports from a nation that lacked most favored nation status would be subject to much higher duty rates upon import into the United States than imports of the same type of product from a nation with most favored nation status. For example, tariff rates on titanium products, many of which the United States imported from Russia, rose significantly when Russia lost MFN status.[44] The cost of higher tariffs was paid by importers in the United States, to be borne by those US importers or passed on to consumers. Regardless of whether the importer or the consumer ultimately paid the higher tariff, a US importer had a clear incentive to source goods of the same type from a nation with MFN status either in order to minimize its own costs or to make the price of its product more competitive.

Like the United States, other jurisdictions also maintain different tariff schedules for countries receiving MFN and non-MFN treatment, often resulting in an increase in tariffs on Russian-origin goods when MFN status was removed. Canada is one such country. Prior to the Russian invasion of Ukraine, it subjected only North Korea to non-MFN rates, since it did not participate in the US-imposed measures against Cuba.[45] The European Union and New Zealand, however, did not have a separate tariff schedule for non-MFN countries, and so the removal of MFN status from Russia did not immediately result in Russian-origin products being made more expensive to import.[46]

One other tariff-related change made with respect to Russian-origin imports occurred in November, when the US Department of Commerce re-classified Russia from a market to a nonmarket economy. Russia thereby joined a list of eleven other countries so classified, including China, Belarus, Vietnam, Armenia, Azerbaijan, Georgia, Kyrgyzstan, Moldova, Tajikistan, Turkmenistan, and Uzbekistan.[47] The nonmarket designation affected the application of the US antidumping and countervailing duty laws. Essentially, the move allowed data used in the calculation of such duties about Russian companies' actual costs and prices to be substituted for data based on a similar country with market-based costs and prices.[48] Antidumping duties are imposed on imported goods to offset the difference between the market value of the good in the exporting country and the price of the good being sold ("dumped") at a lower price in the importing country.[49] Countervailing duties are intended to offset government subsidies associated with the production of the relevant imported goods.[50] Ultimately, the effect of this move was somewhat limited by the drop in the level of imports into the United States from Russia during 2022.[51]

The trade restrictions – meaning the import bans and loss of MFN treatment – imposed by the sanctioning nations and Ukraine against Russia were all potentially subject to WTO provisions regarding the scope of permissible trade barriers. The existing WTO rules against the unilateral creation of trade restrictions, however, are subject to certain defenses, including that of measures necessary for reasons of national security. Specifically, the national security defense contained in Article XXI states, among other provisions, that "nothing in" the GATT "shall be construed ... (b) to prevent any contracting party from taking any action which it considers necessary for the protection of its essential security interests ... (iii) taken in time of war or other emergency in international relations." The use of the national security defense does not require any preclearance by or notification to other WTO Members.[52]

Shortly after Russia commenced its invasion, Ukraine notified the WTO General Council that it was exercising its national security rights under Article XXI of the GATT 1994, Article XIV bis of the GATS, and Article 73 of the TRIPS Agreement. Specifically, it "decided to impose a complete economic embargo and no longer apply the WTO agreements in its relations" with Russia.[53]

The national security defense has been invoked on several occasions by various states, as it was in 1982 when the European Economic Community, Canada, and Australia suspended imports from Argentina in light of the Falklands conflict.[54] Argentina opposed this invocation and sought an interpretation of Article XXI. The Contracting Parties to the GATT subsequently adopted in November 1982 a Decision Concerning Article XXI of the General Agreement setting procedural guidelines relating to measures taken under Article XXI.[55] The Ministerial Declaration of November 29, 1982, at Paragraph 7(iii), stated that "the contracting parties undertake, individually and jointly, ... to abstain from taking restrictive trade measures, for reasons of a non-economic character, not consistent with the General Agreement."

The national security defense was also at issue in 2016, after Ukraine initiated a WTO complaint against Russia challenging transportation restrictions in the region.[56] In response, Russia invoked the national security defense in Article XXI (b)(iii). The WTO panel adjudicating the dispute concluded that Russia had indeed met the requirements for invoking XXI(b)(iii). While the panel found that use of the national security exception was within the purview of the state, there were some limited grounds on which the WTO panel could review that use. Specifically, the panel noted that "it is for a Member itself to decide on the 'necessity' of its actions for the protection of its essential security interests."[57] Nevertheless, a WTO panel could review "(i) whether there was any evidence to suggest that the Member's designation of its essential security interests was not made in good faith, and (ii) whether the challenged measures were 'not implausible' as measures to protect those essential security interests." This decision and the deference granted to a nation to determine measures necessary to protect its own essential security interests suggested that a WTO panel would be likely to uphold the Ukrainian economic embargo against Russia should Russia initiate a WTO complaint based on Ukraine's invocation of Article XXI.[58] (The United States had taken the position in another case that the national security defense was entirely nonjusticiable.[59] In any case, the clear national security concerns relevant to the Russian invasion of Ukraine seemed to indicate that this was a situation in which the WTO would accept the use of the national security defense to impose trade barriers against Russia.)

Russia, however, questioned the legality of the import restrictions levied against it by the sanctioning nations, issuing a statement circulated to WTO Members at its request. The Russian statement argued that the import bans and "implementation of import tariffs above MFN rates," along with the export controls imposed by those same sanctioning jurisdictions were "clearly inconsistent" with provisions of GATT and GATS (the General Agreement on Trade in Services, a WTO treaty which became effective in 1995).[60] Russia argued that the actions of the sanctioning nations were overly politicizing the WTO, and that isolating Russia within the organization "would lead to paralysis of the basic functions of the WTO, namely providing a forum for trade negotiations and administering trade agreements."[61] It also argued that the import restrictions against it were hurting the world economy, by creating inflationary effects and "jeopardizing the global food security."

Despite Russia's protests, the imposition of import restrictions against Russian-origin goods displayed no fundamental weaknesses of the global trading system. Instead, 2022 illustrated the value of the national security exception in allowing modifications to the global trading regime during times of emergency such as the Russian invasion. Certainly, the WTO faced other challenges, such as reactivating the Appellate Body or delineating the boundaries of the national security exception in cases like the US-China trade dispute initiated during the Trump administration.

But the WTO continued to serve as a framework to preserve global economic order in the rest of the world, despite Russia's aggressive military action.

EXPORT CONTROLS

The trade-related response to Russia included not only restrictions against Russian-origin imports, but also new controls on what items could be sent to Russia, especially to Russian military end-users. Export controls had the potential to cause some of the most potent long-term effects to Russia by limiting the country's access to products created using sophisticated levels of technology.

Export controls are coordinated multilaterally through a variety of organizations, including the Wassenaar Arrangement for the control of dual-use goods. (These are products that have both a military and nonmilitary purpose, broadly construed.) Formed in 1996, the group agrees upon export controls for such goods that are then implemented by way of domestic legislation by member countries.[62] An earlier export control organization was the Coordinating Committee for Multilateral Export Controls (COCOM), which was active from 1949 to 1994. The purpose of COCOM was to control exports of certain items to the Soviet Union, China, and communist nations of Eastern Europe.[63]

The Wassenaar Arrangement is more expansive and includes many more nations than did COCOM. COCOM member countries were limited to Belgium, Canada, Denmark, France, West Germany, Greece, Italy, Japan, Luxembourg, the Netherlands, Norway, Portugal, Turkey, the United Kingdom, and the United States, and later Spain and Australia. The organization initially controlled items in a manner "disproportionately driven by American interests," given the position of the United States immediately after World War II.[64] The Wassenaar Arrangement, in contrast, had forty-two participating states at the time of Russia's invasion of Ukraine. Notable additions to the Wassenaar Arrangement besides the initial COCOM group included India, Russia, South Africa, Turkey, and a number of other European nations, including Ukraine. As of 2022, Taiwan was not a member country of the Wassenaar Arrangement, but upon the Russian invasion of Ukraine in February 2022 stated that it was following the Wassenaar Arrangement framework with respect to export controls upon Russia.[65]

Russia's participation in the Wassenaar Arrangement posed new difficulties in the wake of the invasion, creating an impediment to the consensus necessary to update the list of dual-use goods that would be subject to export controls.[66] Unilateral export controls, and export controls that were coordinated multilaterally outside of the Wassenaar Arrangement or other groups that included Russia, therefore would take on increasing importance in 2022 and perhaps beyond.

Other multilateral export control groups of which Russia was a member in 2022 included the Missile Technology Control Regime (MTCR). Russia was the chair of the organization for twelve months from October 2021 to October 2022;

Switzerland then took over the chair position.[67] Russia was not a member of the Australia Group, a multilateral group that coordinated the control of materials and technology that could lead to the proliferation of chemical and biological weapons, but maintained its own unilateral export controls on some such controlled items.[68]

Whether coordinated multilaterally or imposed unilaterally, export controls are usually broad in nature and cover many different types of physical items and intangible information. Dual-use export controls, for example, extend to certain physical items; equipment; software; and "technology," which in the United States is defined as "information necessary for the development, production, use, operation, installation, maintenance, repair, overhaul, or refurbishing of an item."[69] The Wassenaar Arrangement maintains a lengthy list of dual-use items that are subject to controls. The United States implements these controls but also supplements them with its own unilaterally imposed export controls, all detailed on the Commerce Control List (CCL) or designated within a catch-all category, EAR99. Dual-use items are controlled for a variety of different reasons, such as national security, nuclear nonproliferation, antiterrorism, and others. An item may require a license from the US government before export depending on the particular reason(s) for control and the country for which the item is destined; those licenses may be granted in some instances but might be denied in others, and might be subject to a presumption of denial depending on the particular circumstances. Other export control restrictions may also apply depending on the particular end-user for whom the export is destined.

As many types of items and information are controlled, so too are many activities subject to export controls. US jurisdiction, for example, attaches to US-origin items' export (shipment from the United States to a foreign country), reexport (shipment from one foreign country to another), and in-country transfer (conveyance of an item within one foreign country to a different end-user in that same foreign country), among other activities. US export controls apply not only to US-origin items, but also to items that have previously been present in the United States. Foreign-made commodities can be subject to US export controls if those items incorporate a certain amount of US-origin content. In certain instances, even the shipment of foreign-made products can be controlled by US law if those products were produced directly with the use of US technology or software. This last provision is known as the US Foreign Direct Product (FDP) Rule.[70] When applied, it extends US export control jurisdiction over items that would not otherwise be subject to US export controls, including any requirement of an export license or other export prohibitions.

The FDP Rule was triggered most notably in recent years with respect to Huawei, the Chinese smartphone maker. Huawei, the second-largest smartphone manufacturer in the world, was added to BIS's Entity List in 2019 for alleged violations of IEEPA, connections with the Chinese government, and concerns about Chinese government surveillance.[71] The effect of that action was to limit Huawei's access to

US-made products. BIS took further action against Huawei in 2020, by triggering the FDP Rule. This brought within US export jurisdiction foreign-made items that were the direct product of certain types of information or equipment that were themselves subject to US export controls. The move was intended to limit Huawei's access to semiconductors.

The FDP Rule was modified on February 24, in the immediate response to the Russian invasion. The new measure created two provisions to restrict the export of foreign products destined for Russia or Belarus. First, the Russia/Belarus FDP rule applied to items produced outside of the United States that were either "the direct product of US-origin software or technology subject to the EAR [Export Administration Regulations]," or "produced by certain plaints or major components thereof which [were] themselves the direct product of certain US-origin software or technology subject to the EAR."[72] The rule applied when such an item was destined for Russia or Belarus, or would "be incorporated into or used in the production or development of any part, component, or equipment produced in or destined to Russia and Belarus." Exceptions existed for EAR99-designated items, which as BIS pointed out "includes many consumer items used by the Russian and Belarusian people." This rule had the effect of restricting many US-origin and foreign-made direct product higher-tech items that were specifically listed on the CCL, while still allowing the export of consumer goods to ordinary Russian consumers.[73]

BIS also created a second, more stringent FDP Rule specific to items destined for Russian or Belarusian military end-users (the Russia/Belarus MEU FDP Rule). Unlike the Russia/Belarus FDP rule for nonmilitary end-users, the Russia/Belarus MEU FDP rule applied to items both listed on the CCL and also designated as EAR99. The Russia/Belarus MEU FDP Rule therefore restricted US-origin and foreign-made direct products where the Russian or Belarusian end-user was a military one, even with respect to relatively innocuous items. Both rules expanded the scope of US export controls to apply to foreign direct product items, including those produced in non-sanctioning states, to which US export controls would not normally apply.

Later export controls restricted items associated with quantum computing from export to Russia and Belarus. Quantum computing has applications to cybersecurity and intelligence, including cryptography.[74] Russia had announced advances in its quantum computing capabilities in the year before the invasion, as well as in 2022.[75] Export controls sought to slow the development of Russian quantum computing capabilities in light of its military aggression in Ukraine.

Further export controls were also enacted during 2022 to limit arms shipments that could be delivered to the private military company the Wagner Group.[76] The organization was a group of mercenaries that had reportedly committed war crimes and had been present in Ukraine since the Russian invasion of Crimea.[77] It was closely tied to the Russian state.[78] The entity was found to have received shipments of rockets and missiles from North Korea since November 2022.[79] The Wagner

Group had already been sanctioned by the United States since 2017 and was also sanctioned by multiple other jurisdictions. It had also been on the Entity List since 2017. In December 2022, its Entity List designation was modified to designate it as a Russian or Belarusian end-user. This implicated the military end-user restrictions applicable to Russia/Belarus, instead of subjecting the Wagner Group to merely the nonmilitary Russia/Belarus end-user category it had been previously subject to. This further limited the Wagner Group's ability to obtain items produced outside of the United States that were subject to the Foreign Direct Product rule, such as, for instance, EAR99 items restricted for Russian military end-users but not nonmilitary ones.[80]

Beyond the export controls on higher-tech items, or on those items destined for military end-users, numerous jurisdictions also banned the export of luxury goods to Russia, including the United States, Canada, the European Union, the United Kingdom, and Japan.[81] The US measure affected exports of less than $550 million each year.[82] Japan's ban included cars worth over 6 million yen (over $48,000 at the time), among many other items.[83] This move was intended to penalize the oligarchs by restricting their access to luxury goods, and also served as a symbolic condemnation of Russia's invasion.[84]

The export controls and other sanctions soon affected Russia's ability to obtain products and components in a variety of settings. US Secretary of Commerce Gina Raimondo reported that Russia was repairing tanks with semiconductors from dishwashers and refrigerators.[85] Airlines, too, suffered from a lack of imported parts.[86] Even where items could be legally imported into Russia, their supply was often interrupted, whether because of the sanctions related to transport and insurance or because companies had stopped doing business in Russia broadly. For instance, the flow of medical devices from the European Union and the United States into Russia was largely interrupted at the start of the conflict, returning to half of its earlier level in April, for those reasons.[87]

But the export controls by no means comprehensively blocked Russian access to the items controlled. Transshipments of restricted products occurred through third countries, attempting to evade enforcement. Products that had been shipped to Russia before the invasion still remained in-country and in reality could be reused, even if their in-country transfer was technically prohibited after the post-invasion imposition of export controls. BIS was particularly concerned about certain types of products being diverted to Russia and Belarus that could be useful to the Russian military. These included antennas, cameras, GPS systems, Inertial Measurement Units (IMUs), integrated circuits, marine thrusters, sonar systems, spectrophotometers, vacuum pumps, wafer (semiconductor) fabrication equipment and substrates, and others.[88]

To combat product shortages, Russia also allowed imports to be made without the permission of trademark holders. Normally, a trademark owner could prevent the import of goods into Russia that had been lawfully purchased in a third country (parallel imports).[89] Protection against parallel imports can be economically helpful for an intellectual property rights owner because parallel import protection allows it to better maintain price differentials and maintain efficient distribution systems.[90] In May, Russia published a list (later updated) of trademark holders and products to whom such intellectual property protection no longer applied, such as Apple watches, Sony Playstations, and later Lego and BMW.[91] Such newly authorized parallel imports allowed certain products to continue to reach Russia even though their producers had already announced they would stop doing business with Russia, since they no longer had control over the products once they were sold in the third country.[92] This allowed the Russian public to continue to purchase these goods.[93] In June, the Russian parliament formally legalized parallel imports. Russia also undermined intellectual property protection when it issued Decree No. 299 on March 6, which provided that zero compensation would be available to intellectual property rights holders if they committed unfriendly actions against Russian entities or persons.[94]

As with other aspects of the economic response, third-party nations often stepped in to fill the demand no longer filled by sanctioning states. As described in other chapters of this book, the sanctions and export controls were followed by significant changes in trading patterns, notably with respect to energy supplies, food, and fertilizer. Trade data showed that throughout 2022, China was supplying Russia with a variety of dual-use goods. The data indicated a significant increase in the shipment of computer chips and chip components.[95] Chinese semiconductors, however, were often defective or lacked the quality of the now-restricted chips from the sanctioning nations.[96] Indeed, the US government noted in a summary of the sanctions' effects that the percentage of defective microchips from China had risen drastically after the imposition of sanctions, up to 40 percent a year after the invasion.[97] In addition, certain nations stepped in to provide arms to Russia throughout 2022.

Iran, in particular, was suspected to be providing arms to Russia during this time.[98] The European Union, the United Kingdom, and the United States argued that Iran supplied drones to Russia that were used in attacks on Ukraine.[99] All three sanctioned Iranian individuals and/or Russian military personnel for their role in those transactions.[100] Iranian pilots trained on Russia Sukhoi Su-35 fighter jets in the spring of 2022, raising the possibility that Russia would sell those planes to Iran in the future.[101] North Korea, too, was allegedly supplying Russia with artillery shells and rockets.[102]

Conclusion

The export and import restrictions imposed against Russia had several goals: to limit revenue to Russia; to hinder Russia's ability to wage war; and ultimately, to hasten the withdrawal of the Russian military from Ukraine. Export controls did impact

Russian industry. As with sanctions, however, evasion was a factor undercutting their potency. Enforcing the export controls would remain a continuing goal for the sanctioning nations as 2022 drew to a close.

The year's trade restrictions illustrated how Russia was becoming more and more isolated within the global economic institutions, like the Wassenaar Arrangement and the WTO, in which it was a member. The WTO, with its national security defense that seemed well-suited to allowing the enactment of trade restrictions in situations such as this, seemed likely to survive any tension caused by the imposition of import measures against Russia. Its own challenges, such as reviving its nonfunctional Appellate Body, would come from other sources, a full discussion of which is beyond the scope of this book. The Wassenaar Arrangement, however, which required unanimity to create controls on new items, was now hampered by Russia's place in the international body. It would remain to be seen whether the arrangement would be supplanted in the future by a new sort of multilateral export coordination in which Russia would not have a place to exert such power.

7

Food Insecurity

The world faces acute food and nutrition challenges. Conflict, climate change and the lasting impact of COVID-19 are having devastating effects on local and global food systems and the people who rely on them. Russia's unprovoked aggression against Ukraine has significantly worsened these challenges and vulnerabilities.

—EU High Representative Josep Borell, US Secretary of State Antony Blinken, and
UK Foreign Secretary James Cleverly[1]

What we are seeing are direct targets on Ukraine's means of agricultural productivity, in all aspects – from fields where we see Russia having planted landmines, to dairy sheds, where they are attacking sheds and killing cattle, to silos where grain is stored, to railroads, where grains are transported from farms to markets, all aspects. There's nothing that's been left untouched by this war.

—Caitlin Walsh, Center for International and Strategic Studies[2]

The year 2022 saw widespread disruptions in the supply of food and fertilizer around the world. Ensuring the food supply became a key priority, both for Ukraine and for countries around the world.

The war itself was a direct cause of food supply disruption. Ukraine's exports of grain to the world were disrupted due to damage to Ukrainian wheat fields and a Russian blockade of Ukrainian ports, among other factors.[3] These impediments added to wider food supply and supply chain issues that had arisen during the COVID-19 pandemic.

Whether the sanctions themselves caused food supply disruptions was a matter of intense debate.[4] The sanctions broadly exempted food supplies from direct prohibitions.[5] They did, however, affect food and fertilizer supply indirectly, by way of overcompliance and disruptions in world trade patterns.[6] The relative importance of these indirect effects were greatly exaggerated by Russian disinformation campaigns, which sought to characterize the food crisis in the developing world as having been precipitated by the sanctioning powers, while omitting the impact that direct military action had played in causing food shortages. The sanctioning powers responded by highlighting the lack of direct sanctions on food and fertilizer, and by noting that it was Russia's own aggression that had provoked their economic response.[7]

Recognizing the presence of the growing food crisis, the sanctioning powers took steps to try to minimize the impact of the sanctions on the continued transport of food and fertilizer globally. Yet despite these legal exemptions, the world faced challenges in its efforts to ensure the free trade of food globally, both between sender and target nations as well as to third-party nations.

SANCTIONS AND FOOD SECURITY

Issues of sanctions and food security have long been intertwined, and evidence suggests that sanctions often have had a role in contributing to or triggering food shortages. Though sanctions programs regularly contain exceptions for humanitarian activities and shipments, the presence of these legal carve-outs are sometimes not enough to avoid catastrophic civilian consequences. Iraq faced a humanitarian crisis after the imposition of comprehensive sanctions in 1990, including the death of numerous children.[8]

Sanctions can also affect the availability of food to much of a targeted nation's population. The imposition of sanctions and trade restrictions can often spark inflation as imported products become scarce and domestic products in turn become subject to greater demand, leaving consumers in the targeted nations with greatly reduced purchasing power.[9] Iranians experienced 45 percent inflation in 2021 following the 2018 re-imposition of secondary sanctions by the United States.[10] They reported cutting back food purchases, including staples, and research showed that it became harder to obtain the foods for a healthy diet.[11]

In some cases, it can be difficult to ascertain to what extent particular food crises were caused by sanctions, the acts of the regimes that sanctions targeted, or some combination of both. The humanitarian crisis in Afghanistan was one such instance in which harm to civilians was inflicted both by the government and the economic effect of sanctions. By 2022, Afghanistan, subject to a central bank asset freeze and under the rule of the Taliban, was suffering from widespread hunger.[12] Child malnutrition rose sharply between 2020 and 2022, amid newly imposed sanctions and a withdrawal of international aid after the Taliban takeover of the country.[13] Human Rights Watch reported that over 90 percent of Afghans faced some form of food insecurity, and that the banking system was failing on a basic level to function amid sanctions.[14] Women and girls suffered economically from the Afghan government's restrictions on their ability to work and travel freely.[15] Human Rights Watch called for efforts by the United States and the United Nations to provide exemptions from sanctions to allow the Central Bank of Afghanistan to connect to the global banking system, or in the alternative to develop mechanisms and review policy to better enable transactions in support of humanitarian activities.[16] It also urged the Taliban to stop violating human rights in the country, especially against women and girls.[17]

So too did Syrians face economic crisis both by way of sanctions and the government those sanctions targeted. The Syrian civil war started in 2011, during which the government of Bashar al-Assad used chemical weapons and laid siege to cities, starving their inhabitants.[18] By 2021, over 12 million Syrians were food insecure, over half the population.[19] North Korea faced a massive famine in the 1990s, while it was under sanctions imposed by the United States but before nuclear-related sanctions were imposed in the early 2000s by the UN Security Council, the European Union, the United States, and others.[20] The 1990s famine was the result of flooding and the deeply repressive North Korean government.[21] The economic sanctions contributed to the further breakdown in the functioning of the North Korea economy, along with the actions of the North Korean dictatorship and its increased isolation since the COVID-19 pandemic.[22] Research demonstrated that the presence of the nuclear-related comprehensive sanctions rendered the provision of humanitarian aid more burdensome. This was due to reasons including the work necessitated for aid providers to understand their compliance obligations, as well as the restricted availability of banking services since financial institutions generally have a low appetite for sanctions-related risk.[23]

It is evident that some relationship exists between the imposition of sanctions and resulting humanitarian effects, especially when economic sanctions are deployed in a more comprehensive manner, are paired with trade restrictions,[24] or are broadly applied extraterritorially.[25] Overcompliance and de-risking amplify the effects of sanctions on a sanctioned populace. Overcompliance refers to the trend whereby regulated parties take actions broader than those strictly required to comply with the terms of sanctions, thus widening the scope of sanctions' effects. This often has humanitarian impacts on medicine and food, even where such items are not technically subject to sanctions restrictions.[26] Alena Douhan, UN Special Rapporteur on unilateral coercive measures, explained in a Guidance Note how overcompliance by the financial sector can cause deleterious effects:

> Documented cases show that over-compliance with sanctions prevents, delays or makes more costly the purchase and shipment to sanctioned countries of goods, including humanitarian goods and services such as essential food, medicine, medical equipment and spare parts for such equipment, even when the need is urgent and if of life-saving nature. Such practices also prevent international organizations and humanitarian NGOs from transferring funds to pay their employees in sanctioned countries, and block people in these countries from accessing their property, meeting their financial obligations, exercising business activities and handling normal day-to-day interactions, including ordering goods, transferring money for or getting money from their families, making simple payments for

ordinary needs and purposes, booking flights and hotels, and participating in international cooperation including in the spheres of art, science, sport, culture and many others. They also impede their access to justice, including in national and international court and investment tribunals, to respond to accusations and defend themselves, thus denying such fundamental rights as the presumption of innocence, due process, the right to defence and to a fair hearing and trial.[27]

Thus, even where sanctions or trade restrictions provide an exemption for humanitarian activities or importation of goods, the mere presence of sanctions can pose certain difficulties to the provision of those activities or items.[28] Namely, the realities of overcompliance and de-risking, especially in the banking, insurance, and transportation sectors, can have a chilling effect that in practice prevents humanitarian activities from actually occurring.[29]

Research also indicates that sanctions often fail to work against dictatorships and other non-democracies.[30] Indeed, economic sanctions can even be followed by a target government escalating its human rights violations,[31] a decline in political rights,[32] or reduced civil liberties in the target nation.[33] Sanctions can spur domestic dissent and in turn more severe government crackdowns; so too can sanctions foster greater corruption as those sanctions diminish a government's fiscal resources.[34]

EFFECTS OF THE 2022 SANCTIONS

As commentators noted, the rising food prices of 2022 did not originate solely with Russia's invasion of Ukraine or with the ensuing sanctions. The pandemic had negatively impacted supply chains and raised food prices in the process.[35] To contain an outbreak of African swine fever, China in 2019 had slaughtered many of its pigs, which along with losses due to the disease triggered a rise in meat prices.[36] The invasion, however, drastically exacerbated the problem, due to the disruption of Ukrainian agricultural exports.

Conflict between Russia and Ukraine raised the possibility that a significant portion of the world's wheat supply might be affected. Russia was the world's largest wheat exporter, with 17 percent of world exports in 2021; Ukraine was the world's fifth, with 10 percent.[37] Together their wheat constituted about 13 percent of the world wheat supply (since some other nations produced their own wheat but did not export a large proportion of it).[38] Other major wheat producers included China and India, though most of those nations' supplies went to domestic consumption instead of export.[39] Other major exporters of wheat included Canada, the United States, and France.[40] Since wheat and other agricultural staple prices are relatively inelastic, disruptions to the world wheat supply had dramatic market effects.[41] This resulted in the greatest negative impact where food prices constituted a relatively high percentage of per capita income.[42]

The Russian invasion of Ukraine disrupted Ukraine's supply of wheat to the rest of the world in several ways. Russian ships blockaded Ukrainian ports in the Black Sea, preventing wheat exports.[43] The invasion and bombardment caused physical damage to grain storage facilities; satellite images analyzed by the Ukraine Conflict Observatory revealed that by September, around one in six such facilities had been damaged, destroyed, or were at that point controlled by Russia.[44] Russian bombardments set Ukrainian wheat fields alight.[45] Russia was accused of deliberately burning them, as well as intentionally targeting grain storage facilities.[46] By December, Ukraine's grain exports for that particular season were down over 29 percent from the same point in the prior year.[47]

Initially, it was feared that the invasion would disrupt Russian grain production as well.[48] In March, Russia suspended exports of grains including wheat, meslin, rye, barley, and corn to other nations in the Eurasian Economic Union, which included Armenia, Belarus, Kazakhstan, and Kyrgyzstan, in order to ensure sufficient domestic supply.[49] Kazakhstan, in turn, imposed limitations on its own wheat exports in mid-April.[50] Egypt banned exports of wheat, flour, and pasta from April until September. Kosovo and Serbia also banned wheat exports. India banned the export of wheat beginning in May.[51] The food export restrictions announced by various nations were permitted by way of certain WTO rules, which allowed for temporary restrictions on the export of food so long as countries complied with conditions including "tak[ing] into account the impact on importing countries' food security," "notify[ing] the WTO as soon as possible, and as far in advance as possible," and "be[ing] prepared to discuss the restriction with importing countries and to supply them with detailed information when asked for it."[52] The WTO Director-General Ngozi Okonjo-Iweala addressed the organization's ministerial meeting in June by urging nations to limit food export restrictions and prohibitions.[53] At that time, at least thirty nations had imposed food export controls.[54] The Food and Agriculture Organization, the IMF, the World Bank, the World Food Programme, and the WTO issued a joint statement urging solutions to the looming food crisis including facilitating food trade by releasing stores of grains and fertilizers, and "[r]emoving export restrictions and adopting inspections and licensing processes that are more flexible." To achieve this, they highlighted the importance of achieving transparency through better monitoring and through notifications to the WTO.[55]

The actual disruption to Russian wheat production turned out to be much more limited than that which occurred in Ukraine. Indeed, it was a productive year for Russian wheat. As it became clear that Russia would not suffer grain shortages, Russia's ban was lifted in early April, sooner than planned.[56] The Russian Union of Grain Exporters announced that it expected total 2022 exports from July to December to have increased 10 percent from the 2021 figure.[57]

In the immediate days after the launch of the invasion, however, the limited impact of the war on the 2022 Russian harvest was not yet known. The world feared that both Ukraine and Russian grain exports would be reduced drastically as a result. The invasion thus caused a near-immediate effect on the price of food supplies globally. The Food Price Index of the UN Food and Agriculture Organization

(FAO) ended 2022 up 14.3 percent from its level in 2021, which was itself 28 percent higher from 2020 due to the pandemic.[58] It reached its 2022 high in March, generally declining throughout the rest of 2022. Wheat prices were particularly affected.

Developing nations faced particular stresses as a result of the increased prices, as nations such as Turkey, Vietnam, and Indonesia were major importers of grain from Russia.[59] As mentioned, households in developing nations also spent a larger proportion of their income on food and were particularly susceptible to increases in food prices.[60] Oxfam reported that bread prices in Yemen rose 35 percent during the week of the Ukrainian invasion; per Oxfam, Yemen imported 42 percent of its grain from Ukraine.[61] A particularly severe situation existed in Lebanon, where food prices quadrupled by October 2022 since the prior year. This was attributable to Lebanon's reliance on food supplies from Russia and Ukraine; the country's financial crisis since 2019; and an explosion in 2020 that had destroyed privately held grain supplies and limited storage capacity.[62] North Korea seemed to be facing a food crisis and high corn and rice prices by late 2022 and early 2023, after floods in 2022.[63]

The problematic food situation was further exacerbated by the fact that Russia's usual exports of fertilizer had been interrupted by the effects of sanctions, particularly those restricting shipping.[64] Ship operators had announced that they would no longer service Russian ports. In 2021, Russia was the world's largest exporter of nitrogen fertilizer and the second-largest of potassic and third-largest of phosphorous fertilizers; Belarus was also a significant exporter of fertilizer.[65] A number of developing countries, in particular, relied on Russia to source "at least a fifth of their [fertilizer] imports."[66] Andrey Melnichenko, a Russian billionaire who was the founder of the fertilizer producer EuroChem, lobbied authorities in South Africa, arguing publicly that sanctions affected the flow of food and fertilizer to Africa.[67]

As the price of wheat rose, alternative foods were increasingly relied upon. In Togo, a bread made with corn flour instead of wheat flour became popular.[68] Bakers in the Ivory Coast began to make bread by substituting cassava flour for some of the wheat flour.[69] In 2021, the UN General Assembly at the proposal of India had named 2023 as the International Year of the Millets, which took on renewed importance after the 2022 Russian invasion of Ukraine.[70] The 2022 disruption in the wheat supply caused by the invasion highlighted the importance of this wheat alternative in developing food supply resiliency. But the centrality of wheat to the diet of people worldwide meant that disruptions in its supply could not be easily or immediately remedied.

In July, Ukraine and Russia reached an agreement to release 22 million tons of Ukrainian grain from behind a Russian naval blockade.[71] This was the Black Sea Grain Initiative, which was monitored through a Joint Coordination Centre consisting of representatives of Ukraine, Russia, Turkey, and the United Nations.[72] The announcement of the deal helped spur an immediate reduction in wheat prices.[73] Russia suspended its participation in the agreement on October 29, but soon thereafter resumed it, on November 2.[74] The agreement was renewed in November for an additional three months.[75]

Trade patterns in grains shifted in notable ways. China announced in late February that it would lift all previous restrictions on imports of Russian wheat into China (a move agreed upon with Russia in early February, before the invasion). Russian wheat imports had previously been limited due to concerns over agricultural disease.[76] A price differential opened between Russian wheat and wheat from other nations not as affected by the sweeping sanctions, making Russian wheat more attractive to parties in nations not in the sanctioning coalition. Egypt, for example, imported 24 percent more wheat from Russia in March 2022 than in March 2021.[77] The Taliban and Russia in September agreed to a deal for the supply of wheat from Russia, along with oil and gas.[78]

UNDERSTANDING THE RELATIONSHIP BETWEEN SANCTIONS AND FOOD SECURITY, AND ADJUSTING SANCTIONS TO PROMOTE FOOD TRADE

What ultimately was responsible for the rising food prices of 2022 was subject to intense debate. Putin, of course, argued that the crisis was not the fault of the Russian invasion of Ukraine but that of the retaliatory sanctions.[79] Russian propagandists spread a variety of false theories online, blaming food shortages on environmentalists, "globalists" (used as shorthand for Jewish people), and hoarding by other nations.[80] China and the United States sparred over the cause of the food crisis. USAID Administrator Samantha Power said that China was hoarding food and fertilizer amid the crisis.[81] Zhao Lijian, Chinese Foreign Ministry Spokesperson, argued that the United States had itself contributed to the food crisis by way of the sanctions.[82]

The sanctioning powers sought to dispel this narrative that the sanctions were responsible for growing food insecurity. The US Department of State noted the Russian disinformation campaign that blamed food shortages on sanctions and was targeting the Middle East and Africa, "amplified by Kremlin-controlled state outlets such as RT Arabic, RT en Francais," and Chinese state-controlled media.[83] The United States declared: "Food insecurity has risen because of Putin's war of choice."

In June, the Council of the European Union issued conclusions stating that "[t]here are no sanctions on Russian exports of food to global markets," and speaking out against "Russian information manipulation and interference which falsely blames sanctions for the deteriorating global food security situation."[84] It also highlighted recent EU contributions to combat the food crisis, including to the Southern Neighborhood, the Sahel and Lake Chad regions, and the Horn of Africa.[85] The Council proposed a four-strand approach that would address food insecurity over both the short and the long term by providing emergency relief, transforming the food system, facilitating trade of Ukrainian agricultural exports and global food and fertilizer trade, and further engaging in multilateral action.

Likewise, OFAC in July issued a fact sheet on food security, highlighting that it had not sanctioned the sale or transport of fertilizer, agricultural equipment, or medicine into Russia, and also that it had issued a general license to authorize certain transactions related to agricultural commodities (including fertilizer) and equipment.[86] It also noted the support of the United States for the United Nations' efforts "to bring both Ukrainian and Russian grain to world markets and to reduce the impact of Russia's unprovoked war on Ukraine on global food supplies and prices."[87] And though fish and seafood from Russia could no longer be legally imported into the United States, those restrictions did not affect the supply of Russian fish and seafood elsewhere.

Both the United Nations and individual countries took action to help promote trade in fuel and fertilizer, as well as to ensure the continued provision of humanitarian aid in regions where sanctions applied. In November, a joint statement was released by representatives of the European Union, the United States, and the United Kingdom, acknowledging the food crisis and providing details of new measures that would address the situation (quoted at the beginning of this chapter).[88] Changes to the sanctions laws to ameliorate difficulties exacerbated by sanctions included the issuance of EU guidance. Likewise, US General License 6B authorized all transactions prohibited by the Russian Harmful Foreign Sanctions Regulations that related to activities including the production, manufacturing, sale, or transport of agricultural commodities and agricultural equipment. "Agricultural commodities" was defined to encompass food for humans or animals, as well as fertilizers and seeds.[89] Similarly, the United Kingdom issued a General License that exempted acts that would otherwise violate sanctions related to agricultural commodities, including food, fertilizer, and seeds.[90]

But the sanctions, though their terms did not themselves prohibit trade in food and fertilizer, were nevertheless not without effect on the flow of food supplies around the world. As earlier described, parties from sanctioning nations were wary of doing business with Russia even where sanctions provisions allowed them to do so. This trend of overcompliance chilled even the legal trade with Russia in wheat and the provision of related services like transportation.[91] For example, although sanctions themselves did not prohibit trade in Russian fertilizers, Russian fertilizers became stuck in European ports due to difficulties posed by sanctions with respect to payments and transit issues when fertilizer shipments were made that had some relation to sanctioned individuals.[92]

To address such problems, the European Union's ninth sanctions package in December contained a derogation proposed by nations including France, Germany, the Netherlands, Belgium, Spain, and Portugal, but initially opposed by Poland and Lithuania.[93] The provision allowed for national governments to unfreeze the funds of certain individuals who had had significant roles in the fertilizer trade before the sanctions were imposed, if those actions were reported to the European Commission.[94]

CONCLUSION

Though just one cause of food insecurity around the world, the 2022 Russian invasion of Ukraine demonstrated the need for greater food security worldwide. This fact had recently been highlighted during the COVID-19 pandemic. So too was food security an increasingly pressing issue as the effects of climate change mounted.[95] Narrowly tailoring sanctions to minimize their impacts on the global food supply, and tackling challenges raised by overcompliance, would be one piece required to solve the food insecurity puzzle in the years ahead.

8

The Oligarchs, and Others

The blood of the Ukrainian people is on their hands. They should hang their heads in shame.
— Liz Truss, British Foreign Secretary[1]

THE INDIVIDUALS SANCTIONED

Sanctions against wealthy Russian oligarchs were a high-profile element of the economic response to Russia's invasion of Ukraine. Individuals had long been sanctioned personally by the US and other governments. These included human rights abusers,[2] arms dealers,[3] terrorists, and drug traffickers. And, as in the case of the most recent sanctions against Russia, they included wealthy individuals who had allegedly siphoned their wealth from the Russian state and used those funds to further support the regime that had enriched them.[4] Government officials, too, were made personally subject to sanctions, especially those who were connected with the Russian defense industry, benefited from the Russian takeover of Crimea, or otherwise undermined the integrity of the Ukrainian state.

The sanctions enacted in 2022 against Putin himself were unusual. The US did not often sanction heads of state personally. OFAC commented that "President Putin joins a very small group that includes despots such as Kim Jong Un, Alyaksandr [Lukashenko], and Bashar al-Assad."[5] Lukashenko, the president of Belarus, had been personally sanctioned by the United States in 2021, a year after taking office based upon a fraudulent election.[6] Syria's Bashar al-Assad had been sanctioned by the US since 2011.[7] North Korea's Kim Jong Un became subject to US sanctions in 2016, after a 2014 UN Commission of Inquiry report linked Kim to human rights abuses.[8] Muammar al-Qaddafi, the leader of Libya, had been subject to sanctions imposed by the UN Security Council.[9]

Sanctions on Russian oligarchs had been a distinct possibility since the enactment of the Countering America's Adversaries through Sanctions Act (CAATSA) in 2017.

In 2018, the US Department of the Treasury issued a report identifying the most significant Russian oligarchs, determined by their closeness to the Russian government and their net worth, as required by CAATSA Section 241.[10] The CAATSA report did not itself make the listed oligarchs subject to any sanctions, but the reporting requirement was seen as a possible precursor to sanctions on those identified.[11] The report was to include an assessment of the likely effects of making Russian oligarchs subject to secondary sanctions. It was submitted to five Congressional committees as required by the statute.

In 2022, the enactment of sanctions against the oligarchs brought with it high-publicity enforcement. The yachts, in particular, were some of the most visible symbols of wealth seized when the oligarchs began to be personally sanctioned.[12] The US Department of Justice launched its Task Force KleptoCapture in March 2022, an interagency task force set up to investigate and enforce violations of the sanctions.[13] Less than a month later, it had its first success with its seizure of *Tango*, a $90 million, 255-foot-long superyacht owned by Viktor Vekselberg. He had been sanctioned by the United States and was under investigation for tax fraud, money laundering, and other crimes.[14] There were other such yachts seized from oligarchs, some even bigger and even more expensive than the *Tango*.[15]

The Russian oligarchs held assets around the world.[16] Roman Abramovich was owner of the United Kingdom's Chelsea Football Club before the league disqualified him, ordering him to sell the team. He was worth around $8.3 billion, having grown rich from his close ties with Putin. Once known as a "stealth oligarch,"[17] he made friends in Hollywood and on Wall Street, threw parties on St. Barts with the likes of Prince and Paul McCartney, and collected property in London, Tel Aviv, New York, Aspen, and elsewhere.[18] Sanctioned by the European Union and the United Kingdom, he was spared from similar US measures after Zelensky urged Biden to hold off so that Abramovich could assist in peace talks with Russia.[19] He did go to those peace talks – and was seemingly poisoned there, suffering "peeling skin" and "piercing pain in the eyes."[20]

Some who had profited from ill-gotten Russian wealth were less well-known. Twenty-six-year-old Polina Kovaleva lived in London and was an active Instagram user. She was also the stepdaughter of Sergey Lavrov, Russian Minister of Foreign Affairs.[21] Maria Pevchikh, Head of Investigations at the Anti-Corruption Foundation, detailed on Twitter how at twenty-one, Kovaleva had paid cash for a £4.4 million Kensington apartment. The United Kingdom responded to Pevchikh's tweets, sanctioning Kovaleva personally.[22]

Alina Kabaeva, Putin's purported girlfriend, was initially not made subject to sanctions by either the European Union or the United States.[23] She was a former rhythmic gymnast and Olympian, and also a former legislator in the lower house of the Russian Federal Assembly. It was rumored that Putin had become involved with her before his 2014 divorce, and that she had allegedly had three of his children. Billionaires, Russian officials, and Putin's two daughters could be sanctioned. US sanctions officials, however, initially determined that Alina Kabaeva should not.[24] She was eventually sanctioned by the European Union in June[25] and by the United States in August.[26]

The 2022 provisions placed sanctions on many more Russian oligarchs than had been subject to such measures in the past. Even so, some argued that they still did not reach enough powerful people in Russia. Alexei Navalny was a prominent Russian opposition leader imprisoned in early 2021 after what was widely regarded abroad as a sham trial.[27] From prison in 2022, he called for heavier punitive measures on the oligarchs. He pointed to the fact that Abramovich had not yet been sanctioned by the United States, and he commented that the sanctions on only forty-six of Russia's 200 richest people (per Forbes) did not "sound very much like an all-out war on Putin's oligarchs" to him.[28]

Indeed, not all wealthy Russian elites were initially made subject to sanctions. In late March, Bloomberg found that out of Russia's twenty wealthiest individuals, the United States had sanctioned only four; the European Union, nine; and the United Kingdom, ten.[29] Many of the initially unsanctioned were later targeted, like Leonid Mikhelson, Russia's second-wealthiest person (sanctioned in April); Vagit Alekperov (a co-founder and CEO of Lukoil who resigned his position after being made individually subject to UK sanctions in April); Vyacheslav Kantor (major shareholder of fertilizer group Acron and sanctioned by the United Kingdom in April); Alexander Abramov (sanctioned by Australia in April and the United Kingdom in November[30]); and Andrey Guryev (owner of the second-largest estate in London, after only Buckingham Palace, and sanctioned by the United States in August[31]). Among those who largely avoided sanctions from the allies of Ukraine: Vladimir Lisin (sanctioned by Australia but not the European Union or the United States[32]); Dmitry Rybolovlev; and Leonid Fedun. (Ukraine itself sanctioned individuals as well, including Lisin, Rybolovlev, and Fedun.)

In 2018, the United States had sanctioned Oleg Deripaska, a former business partner of Abramovich, and the founder of RUSAL, one of the world's largest aluminum producers. Deripaska was also sanctioned by the United Kingdom following the 2022 invasion of Ukraine. In September 2022, the United States indicted Deripaska and several of his associates for conspiring to evade the sanctions against him.[33] Sanctions on RUSAL had caused significant increases in the price of aluminum before they were lifted in a deal struck that reduced Deripaska's control over the company.[34] While the United States in 2022 initially hesitated to impose individual sanctions on other entities and oligarchs connected with commodities, in December it sanctioned Vladimir Potanin, who was the CEO and largest shareholder of Norilsk Nickel – a major supplier of palladium and to a lesser extent nickel.[35] Potanin had already been sanctioned by the United Kingdom and Canada.[36]

The sanctions against individuals also extended to Russian propagandists. In March, the United Kingdom announced sanctions on Sergey Brilev, a Russian

TV anchor, and state media organizations including TV-Novosti, owner of RT, and Rossiya Segodnya, owner of Sputnik. Both Sputnik and RT were news networks either owned or controlled by the Russian state. Other sanctions included executives and directors associated with Sputnik, RT, and Gazprom-Media.[37] Likewise, the European Union's ninth sanctions package targeted notable propagandists for the Russian government.[38]

In addition to asset freezes and prohibitions, the actions taken against individuals included travel restrictions. The EU and UK sanctions against the oligarchs, for example, included travel bans. Ordinary Russians, however, were still permitted to travel to the sanctioning jurisdictions. The European Union suspended the EU–Russia visa facilitation agreement that had been adopted in 2007, and simplified the process for obtaining short-term visas.[39] The sanctioning powers stopped short, however, of imposing a comprehensive ban on Russian travel, despite Zelensky's urging that such a prohibition be implemented.[40]

Sanctions also affected the ability of wealthy Russians to obtain residency or citizenship in other countries. The signs of the coming invasion led the United Kingdom in mid-February to suspend its Tier 1 investor visa program. The provision had permitted UK residency for those investing £2 million in the United Kingdom, along with their families.[41] Investors could then apply for permanent residency after five years (three years for investments of £5 million or more and two years for investments of £10 million or more). The Financial Action Task Force (FATF) initiated a project to investigate the use of citizenship by investment.[42] Israel, a non-sanctioning nation, formed a committee concerning the sanctions, including the issue of how to prevent Russian oligarchs with Israeli citizenship from evading sanctions.[43] A number of Russian billionaires held dual citizenship, including Mikhail Prokhorov, who obtained Israeli citizenship in April 2022 through the Law of Return.[44]

ASSET SEIZURE

In the US, the authority to seize (instead of simply to freeze) assets of the Russian oligarchs comes not from US sanctions regulations themselves, but from other legal provisions allowing for forfeiture of assets linked to illegal activities. Forfeiture through the use of the US legal system can be effected either by way of civil or criminal forfeiture actions. Criminal forfeiture actions are filed against parties convicted of crimes in the United States. Civil forfeiture suits are filed by the United States against property itself that has some link to criminal activity.[45] But barring some link to criminal activities, assets in the United States that were frozen pursuant to sanctions could not be seized, whether to be used for the rebuilding of Ukraine or for any other purpose. While the oligarchs could not access their funds after the imposition of full blocking sanctions against them, their funds had not been confiscated by the United States.

In April, the US House of Representatives passed the Asset Seizure for Ukraine Reconstruction Act, which stated that it was "the sense of Congress" that "[t]he President should take all constitutional steps to seize and confiscate assets under the jurisdiction of the United States of foreign persons whose wealth is derived ... through corruption linked to or political support for the regime of Russian President Vladimir Putin" and whom had been sanctioned. That would allow seized assets to be sold off to generate funds to be directed to Ukraine.[46] The legislation also directed the establishment of an interagency working group to "determine the constitutional mechanisms" under which such asset seizure could be achieved. The American Civil Liberties Union had argued against the passage of the bill in an earlier form, on the ground that it would not afford the notice required by the Due Process Clause of the Fifth Amendment of the US Constitution.[47] The bill was therefore amended to the non-binding form[48] that passed the House.

US President Biden announced a plan that would add a new crime of possessing "proceeds directly obtained from corrupt dealing with the Russian government," create a new administrative process for the forfeiture of property seized from sanctioned individuals, and update the Racketeer Influenced and Corrupt Organizations (RICO) Act to include sanctions evasion within the definition of racketeering activity.[49] (A further discussion follows in Chapter 10 regarding the lack of seizure authority where no criminal nexus was present, such as with respect to Russian central bank assets.) In September, the REPO Task Force (discussed in Chapter 10) was convened by US officials to "accelerate oligarch asset forfeiture efforts" in coordination with the EU and G7 countries.[50] Discussed at that meeting were legislative efforts that would expedite asset seizures and strengthen their enforceability in US courts. These legislative proposals, and others, are further discussed in Chapter 10.

ENFORCEMENT

Even without expanded enforcement authorities, sender nations were able to seek asset forfeiture where some link to criminality could in fact be demonstrated. One civil forfeiture action was filed in US federal court in November, when prosecutors sought to seize more than $5 million owned by Konstantin Malofeyev.[51] He was a major financer of separatists in Crimea and had been designated as an SDN in 2014.[52] The 2022 forfeiture action was based on allegations of conspiracy to violate US sanctions and violations of US sanctions. Specifically, Malofeyev had hired an American citizen to work for him in operating television stations, and he had also conspired to transfer a $10 million investment in violation of the full blocking sanctions against him.[53] In early 2023, he was ordered to forfeit those funds after he failed to contest the forfeiture action.[54]

The oligarchs and other sanctioned individuals often sought to circumvent the interdictions that had been placed on them. Heightened enforcement was necessary to detect and crack down on sanctions evaders. At the time the first of the sanctions were enacted, the US Financial Crimes Enforcement Network (FinCEN) issued an alert detailing red flags that could signal that oligarchs were attempting to launder funds and evade sanctions.[55] These included warnings specific to real estate; artwork; and "other high-value assets, such as luxury yachts and vehicles." One oligarch, Suleiman Kerimov, had his $325 million superyacht sailed to Fiji from Mexico to avoid American sanctions. The plan failed. Fijian authorities detained it there anyway as American officials sought its return.[56] (In November, the United States sanctioned Kerimov's family members and asset manager Alexander-Walter Studhalter, a Swiss national who was alleged to have aided Kerimov in evading US sanctions.)[57]

Numerous enforcement actions sought to penalize those individuals engaging in sanctions evasion and to deter others from similar conduct. In September, Deripaska was indicted by the US based on allegations of sanctions evasion following his 2018 designation by OFAC as an SDN.[58] He was alleged to have used the US financial system with respect to certain luxury properties, receiving hundreds of thousands of dollars, using others to obtain US goods and technology, and having his associates assist his girlfriend in giving birth in the United States.

Canada in December announced that it was seizing the assets of an entity owned by Roman Abramovich and seeking their forfeiture.[59] Abramovich had been designated as an individual sanctioned by Canada's Special Economic Measures (Russia) Regulations (SOR/2014-58). This was the first time Canada had sought to use those regulations to effect such a seizure and forfeiture, after the legislature had enacted the relevant provisions earlier in 2022 by way of C-19, the budget implementation act.[60] The amendments allowed for the forfeiture and seizure of property under either the Special Economic Measures Act or the Justice for Victims of Corrupt Foreign Officials Act (Sergei Magnitsky Law). The amendments also provided information-gathering and sharing powers between parties within the Canadian government and law enforcement to effect such seizures.[61]

FINANCIAL TRANSPARENCY

A major impediment to the enforcement of sanctions against the oligarchs was that their financial holdings were often hidden.[62] Shell companies, for example, helped enable oligarchs to evade sanctions where the beneficial ownership information of those entities was not readily available. The global financial system lacked key safeguards to ensure the financial transparency that would allow for the efficient enforcement of sanctions.

Putin, himself subject to sanctions, almost certainly had access to a vast hidden fortune. Publicly, Putin's net worth was unclear.[63] Bill Browder, in 2017 testimony before the Senate Judiciary Committee, estimated that Putin owned assets worth $200 billion. [64] The Panama Papers, published beginning in 2016, had disclosed how funds from Russia had moved via Bank Rossiya, Swiss intermediaries, and Mossack Fonseca (the Panamanian law firm from which the papers were leaked), to the Russian Commercial Bank of Cyprus (a subsidiary of VTB at the time) and offshore to a firm in the British Virgin Islands, and eventually to close associates of Putin.[65] These included Putin's best friend, Sergei Roldugin, a cellist.[66] It was assumed that at least some of the money that went to Putin's close associates benefited the Russian president himself, even though it was not held in his own name.

In recent years, information had been revealed demonstrating the need for greater financial transparency to allow for the effective taxation of hidden funds and to prevent parties from stashing criminally linked or otherwise ill-gotten gains. The problem was especially flagrant with respect to large quantities of Russian assets held abroad. The Pandora Papers, published beginning in late 2021, had shed light on the magnitude of the oligarchs' asset concealment around the world.[67] These papers consisted of nearly 12 million documents collected by the International Consortium of Investigative Journalists (ICIJ).[68] They had revealed previously secret information about a huge number of financial holdings and transactions, including those of wealthy Russians, that showed how wealth was hidden in offshore jurisdictions, often for tax evasion or other corrupt purposes.[69] Likewise, an investigation by the BBC and Finance Uncovered detailed the use of English Limited Partnerships to launder funds, including from Russian sources, after the passage of anti-money laundering provisions in 2016 and 2017 governing other types of UK business entities.[70]

The ability of wealthy Russians to launder their assets posed a challenge to the efficacy of sanctions. Indeed, significant sums of money had flowed out of Russia and been hidden abroad in the years leading up to the invasion. In 2017, researchers estimated that Russians might own similar amounts of financial wealth in-country and abroad.[71] About $1 trillion of Russian wealth was estimated to be "dark money" held offshore, about one-quarter of which was tied to Putin or his contacts.[72] Where money could not be easily traced back to the sanctioned oligarchs, it became much more difficult to enforce the sanctions imposed against them.[73]

Numerous jurisdictions recognized the need for greater financial transparency, both preinvasion as a result of the revelations made by the various ICIJ papers, and in 2022 as money laundering grew in importance as a sanctions evasion tool. In January 2021, the United States had enacted the Corporate Transparency Act. By the time of the Russian invasion of Ukraine, however, the US Treasury Department had not yet implemented the Act's provisions. In May 2022, Senators Elizabeth Warren (D-MA), Sheldon Whitehouse (D-RI), Marco Rubio (R-FL), and Ron Wyden (D-OR) sent a joint letter to Secretary of the Treasury Janet Yellen and Acting Director of FinCEN Himamauli Das, urging FinCEN to "immediately accelerate" its finalization of the Act.[74] The letter was later joined by other legislators, including Chuck Grassley (R-IA), Bob Menendez (D-NJ) and Bill Cassidy (R-LA).[75]

In September, FinCEN announced a final rule to create a reporting requirement to mandate the disclosure of the beneficial ownership of organizations "created in or registered to do business" in the United States, to go into effect in 2024.[76] In 2022, the United Kingdom enacted the Economic Crime (Transparency and Enforcement) Act. This law increased transparency by requiring certain foreign entities with real estate holdings to disclose their ownership.[77] The Swiss Federal Council in October instructed the Federal Department of Finance to draft a bill to address financial transparency and beneficial ownership disclosures.[78] Germany's Sanctions Enforcement Act II of 2022 mandated the addition of land register data to its already-existing transparency register.[79]

The European Union's 5th AML (Anti-Money Laundering) Directive, which went into effect in 2020, had granted public access to company beneficial ownership registers maintained by EU Member States.[80] In November 2022, however, the Court of Justice of the European Union (CJEU) issued a ruling stating that public access to entity beneficial ownership information had to be balanced against the fundamental rights of the parties subject to and affected by the disclosure regime, notably with respect to their privacy rights.[81] Soon after the decision was issued, the national registers of Luxembourg and the Netherlands were no longer publicly available.[82]

There were also calls for greater cross-border financial transparency. The objectives here included goals such as fostering easier enforcement of existing sanctions regimes, deterring and penalizing tax avoidance, and detecting other criminal activities. Some parties, like the Financial Transparency Coalition, the Independent Commission for the Reform of International Corporate Taxation, and economists Thomas Piketty and Gabriel Zucman, called for the establishment of a global asset registry. This would provide information about beneficial ownership to the public across jurisdictional boundaries.[83] Its proponents argued that the register would ameliorate wealth inequality by creating a new tool to combat tax avoidance and evasion.[84] Another proposal, by sociologist Brooke Harrington, called for the imposition of sanctions on key well-connected wealth managers who hid much of the oligarchs' wealth offshore.[85]

PROCEDURAL BARRIERS

The EU sanctions against individuals were time-limited pursuant to an urgent designation procedure and had to be renewed periodically. An individual could be designated for fifty-six days on an urgent basis if they had already been sanctioned by another jurisdiction; the fifty-six-day period could then be renewed one additional time. (After the expiration of the second fifty-six days, the individual could remain subject to sanctions on an extended basis if certain findings had been made.) The UK sanctions contained similar provisions allowing for an urgent designation but limiting the urgent designation and its renewal to the same timelines. The UK powers for the urgent designation were introduced after the invasion, in order to allow for the sanctioning of individuals with the same speed as with which the United States and the European Union were making designations at that time.[86]

Ahead of a meeting of the Council of the European Union in September, Hungary requested that individual sanctions against three Russian oligarchs be lifted.[87] It backed off its demand shortly thereafter, but the matter illustrated the tensions between Hungary and the other Member States of the European Union with respect to sanctions.[88]

EFFECTS OF THE SANCTIONS ON INDIVIDUALS

For those oligarchs who were made subject to sanctions, the economic consequences could be significant. Travel bans excluded them from many nations they had previously frequented. Russian oligarchs lost an estimated $95 billion in 2022.[89] Abramovich alone lost access to over $10 billion in 2022, over half of his net worth.[90] Evidence indicated that sanctions on individual oligarchs had observable negative effects on the stock prices of companies on whose boards sanctioned oligarchs served as directors.[91]

Beyond just the economic effects, the sanctions on individuals carried social stigma.[92] Some of the oligarchs used social media to oppose the Russian invasion, like Oleg Tinkov through Instagram (calling Ukrainian deaths "unthinkable and unacceptable"), perhaps hoping either to avoid sanctions or protest the imposition of already-imposed measures.[93]

Some oligarchs sought relief from the sanctions. Mikhail Fridman was the co-founder and largest shareholder of Alfa Group, a Russian investment firm. He had been sanctioned in early 2022 by the European Union and the United Kingdom.[94] He was said to have offered to transfer $1 billion into Alfa Bank-Ukraine to be used for projects in the country including health, energy, and food, seemingly to have sanctions against him lifted.[95] He had previously reportedly sought a deal with the acting US ambassador to Ukraine to avoid sanctions, and argued that he did not have the ability to affect Putin's actions.[96] He also obtained letters from Russian opposition leaders attesting to his character or supporting him in seeking to have the sanctions on him removed.[97]

Oligarchs also challenged the sanctions against them. A number of them, including Roman Abramovich, brought suit in the Court of Justice of the European Union to remove the sanctions against them. Their cases were argued on such grounds as the infringement of the principles of proportionality, equal treatment, and fundamental rights.[98] Relatives of sanctioned oligarchs who had themselves been sanctioned also appealed their designations. Challenges at the Court of Justice resulted in the removal of some EU sanctions designations, like that of Russian-Uzbek billionaire Alisher Usmanov's sister and Mikhail Fridman's former wife.[99] A US court of appeals in March 2022[100] ruled against Oleg Deripaska's challenge to OFAC's 2018 designation of him as an SDN.[101]

The sanctions placed financial pressures on the oligarchs that provided them with incentives to speak out against the invasion of Ukraine. But the risks of doing so might be steep. An unusual number of oligarchs died mysterious deaths during 2022. The deaths could have been coincidental; but of course, other critics of and opponents to Putin's regime had been poisoned, like Navalny or Yushchenko.[102] In a few instances, the oligarchs who died had publicly opposed or criticized Putin. Lukoil chairman Ravil Maganov, for instance, fell out of a hospital window in the beginning of September.[103] In March, Lukoil's board of directors had publicly opposed the Russian invasion of Ukraine.[104] But many of the oligarchs who died had not criticized the invasion, nor had been personally sanctioned.[105] In any case, while the sanctions might have provided an impetus for oligarchs to speak out against the invasion, the slew of recent deaths of wealthy Russians might influence them to do otherwise.

RUSSIAN SANCTIONS AGAINST INDIVIDUALS

Russia responded with its own sanctions on individuals from the coalition of sanctioning nations. Some were government officials and clear targets for individual sanctions, such as US President Joe Biden, Secretary of State Antony Blinken, and Defense Secretary Lloyd Austin.[106] Some were high-profile celebrities, like Sean Penn and Ben Stiller, who had publicly supported Ukraine and criticized Russia.[107] Russia sanctioned journalists, academics, politicians, executives, and others from a host of nations, most often those within the coalition of sanctioning powers.

Certainly, the Russian sanctions against individuals from the coalition of nations had much less of a financial effect than did the sanctions against Russian individuals imposed by those same countries. Russian individuals held much more wealth abroad, in the currencies and banking systems of those sanctioning nations. The sanctions imposed by Russia against individuals were more likely to be purely symbolic in nature, as those individuals were much less likely to hold rouble-denominated wealth or hold assets in the Russian banking system. The sanctions against individuals thus reflected the relative importance of nations' financial systems and resembled the relative importance of the sanctions against financial entities in this way.

CONCLUSION

As described in this chapter, the sanctions on individuals had several purposes. They were intended to undermine political support for Putin among influential, wealthy Russians. They also sought to weaken the oligarchs, thus diminishing the resources of key Putin supporters. Asset and property seizures siphoned off funds that had a connection to criminal acts, reducing the gains from those activities. Enforcement actions against individuals raised the cost of attempting to evade those sanctions.

By no means would the sanctions against individuals have been effective had they not been accompanied by sanctions against Russian entities and institutions. The importance of sanctions against individuals was dwarfed by the importance of sanctions against Russian financial institutions. But the sanctions against individuals had important symbolic value. A new barrier was now erected to help stem the easy flow of dirty money across the globe. Seizures of oligarchs' assets represented a long-overdue step against corruption.

Whether the sanctions against the oligarchs would significantly reduce their support of Putin in the long term would remain to be seen. Bruce Jentleson has described how sanctions placed on elites can function either as "circuit breakers" or "transmission belts," respectively dampening or amplifying those sanctions' impact on the government depending on the extent to which the sanctions on those elites harm their own interests.[108] While the sanctions harmed the Russian oligarchs personally, the oligarchs had benefited immensely from their connection to Putin's regime. Stringent enforcement, and uncovering the hidden locations of the oligarchs' wealth, would be important to cutting into the oligarchs' support for Putin. In the longer term, the need for greater financial transparency remained, both to reduce sanctions evasion and for the broader purpose of reducing corruption and stemming illegal flows of funds around the world.

9

Escalation

We will never recognize these purported annexations, nor the sham "referenda" conducted at gunpoint.

—G7 Foreign Ministers Statement[1]

In September, Ukraine launched a counteroffensive in the Kherson region in the south, and the Kharkiv region in the northeast.[2] The Ukrainians gained territory quickly in Kherson. Russian troops abandoned military equipment – like tanks – as they retreated.[3] By mid-November, Russia stated that it had completed its retreat from the region.[4] In Kharkiv, Ukraine's progress was slower. The Russian retreat was hard-fought in some areas of that region.[5] Zelensky commented in late September that about fifty Ukrainian soldiers or more were being killed each day.[6]

Putin responded to Ukraine's military gains, calling up reserves to serve in the military. Russia, he vowed, would use "all available means" to protect itself. Its resources, he noted, included nuclear weapons.[7]

The rapid Ukrainian progress seemed to lead Putin to announce that votes on annexation would be held in four Ukrainian territories: Donetsk and Luhansk (the so-called DNR and LNR regions recognized by Russia in the immediate prelude to the broader Ukrainian invasion), as well as Zaporizhzhia and Kherson. These referenda were reminiscent of the 2014 Crimea referendum under the purported authority of which Putin had annexed Crimea after the vote reflected over 95 percent in favor of annexation. The four 2022 referenda returned similarly unbelievable figures of alleged pro-Russian sentiment: 87 percent in Kherson, 93 percent in Zaporizhzhia, 98 percent in Luhansk, and 99 percent in Donetsk.[8] Shortly thereafter, on September 30, Putin held a ceremony to mark the annexation. Once again, he said, Russia would use all available means in its defense; Russia now included the four annexed territories.[9]

Much of the international community swiftly condemned the sham votes. The G7 foreign ministers issued a statement: "President Putin's efforts to incorporate [the four] regions into the territory of the Russian Federation constitute a new low point in Russia's blatant flouting of international law, and yet another example of Russia's unacceptable violations of Ukraine's sovereignty, the UN Charter, and the commonly agreed principles and commitments of the Helsinki Final Act and the Paris Charter."[10] The G7 nations would turn once again to an economic response.

The United States, rather than announcing entirely new legal provisions, instead unveiled a slew of new designations. These were made under existing authorities, and imposed blocking sanctions on Russian military suppliers, family members of Russian officials, and 278 members of the Russian legislature for enabling the annexation attempt.[11] OFAC and BIS also noted that they would "more aggressively" target those providing support to Russia as described in sanctions-related executive orders. Retaliatory US measures would include imposing blocking sanctions under existing legal authorities and adding such parties to BIS's Entity List. Exports, re-exports, and other relevant activities with these Entity List parties would thereafter require a license from the government; applications for such licenses would be reviewed with a presumption of denial.

The European Union adopted a proposed new sanctions package on October 6, the eighth so far.[12] It also sanctioned additional parties, and took further actions as well. It extended the more comprehensive sanctions covering the Donetsk and Luhansk regions to include Zaporizhizhia and Kherson as well. Additional export bans were implemented, including a ban on the export of coal to Russia, certain electronic components that could be used in weaponry, small arms, and other items. New bans on imports of specific products from Russia were also established, including ones on finished and semi-finished steel products, machinery, plastics, textiles, footwear, non-gold jewelry, and more. All crypto-asset wallet services to Russia were banned, eliminating a previous exemption for crypto-wallet services for wallet accounts below €10,000. The package also included a mechanism by which individuals could be subject to sanctions for facilitating the circumvention of sanctions by others.

As these sanctions were put in place, Ukraine continued to tally military gains. An explosion collapsed a portion of the Kerch Strait Bridge that connected Russia with Crimea and which had been a key supply line for Russia to the southern Ukrainian front.[13] Putin blamed Ukraine and termed the event "an act of terrorism."[14]

But while these Ukrainian successes were dramatic, they did not signal an end to the war. Toward the end of 2022, Russia still controlled significant areas of territory in the south and east of Ukraine, the Donetsk and Luhansk regions occupied just prior to the general invasion, as well as the Crimea peninsula, which had been occupied since 2014.[15] The war, and the sanctions, would continue on.

10

Enforcement

[W]ith respect to the assets of the Russian Central Bank ... the United States and our partners ... [have] blocked around $300 billion of those assets. And I think it's very natural that given the enormous destruction in Ukraine, and huge rebuilding costs that they will face that we will look to Russia to help pay at least a portion of the price that will be involved. That said ... it would not be legal now, in the United States, for the government to seize those [assets].[1]

—US Treasury Secretary Janet Yellen, May 18, 2022

Designing new sanctions was one prong of the response to Russia. But to carry real weight, they had to be enforced. In practice, this presented considerable difficulties. Authorities had to detect attempts to evade sanctions; link opaque asset ownership information to blocked individuals and entities; and uncover secretive illegal activity around the globe.

Enforcement was carried out through national authorities, as was typically done for other sanctions regimes. The sanctioning powers also launched new initiatives to coordinate their enforcement efforts multilaterally. The 2022 sanctions thus created the possibility for sanctions to be enforced on a broader basis in the future. Yet these sanctions also illustrated the shortcomings of sanctions as a whole; when enforcement was imperfect, or when significant economies were not part of the sanctioning coalition, sanctions evasion and the substitution of economic partners could dampen the sanctions' effect.

COORDINATING AND IMPROVING SANCTIONS ENFORCEMENT

The sanctions against Russia were imposed by many nations. A successful enforcement strategy required robust enforcement by each jurisdiction. An efficient enforcement response would involve coordination of those efforts across jurisdictions. The year 2022 saw the creation of new legal frameworks and enforcement protocols to do so. Throughout the year, some individual jurisdictions also took steps to strengthen their own sanctions enforcement powers.

In March, the EU and the G7 created the Russian Elites, Proxies, and Oligarchs (REPO) Task Force.[2] The REPO Task Force committed to "tak[ing] all available legal steps to find, restrain, freeze, seize, and, where appropriate, confiscate or forfeit the assets" of parties sanctioned in connection with the Russian invasion of Ukraine.[3] It also coordinated with the private sector, including with financial institutions subject to sanctions and anti-money-laundering requirements, to "identify and immobilize assets subject to sanctions and work[] to prevent Russia from evading sanctions."[4]

The European Union faced challenges in enforcing its sanctions because the union lacked a centralized enforcement authority, even though the imposition of sanctions were coordinated at the union level. Instead, national authorities were responsible for enforcement.[5] In order to address the issue of coordinating EU sanctions among national authorities, the European Union implemented the Freeze and Seize Task Force in March.[6] The group coordinated sanctions enforcement among European Union Member States by, for example, obtaining information about Russian assets frozen in each country.[7] It also worked with the REPO Task Force on the confiscation of oligarch assets.[8]

Some thought that EU sanctions enforcement could be further strengthened by creating a centralized body with legal enforcement authority. Mairead McGuinness, EU Commissioner for Financial Stability, Financial Services and the Capital Markets Union, publicly discussed the possibility of creating an EU enforcement body like the United States' OFAC, or alternatively giving the forthcoming EU Anti-Money Laundering Authority sanctions enforcement authority by legislative amendment.[9]

The European Union also worked to coordinate with sanctions enforcement efforts outside its own borders. At the end of the year, the European Commission appointed Ambassador David O'Sullivan (former Secretary-General of the European Commission) as EU Sanctions Envoy, to promote greater sanctions compliance. He took office in January of 2023.[10] The envoy was charged with coordinating enforcement outside the union as well in countries thought to be sites of sanctions evasion, like Turkey.

In the United States, Ambassador James O'Brien was confirmed in April as Head of the Office of Sanctions Coordination.[11] The office had been re-created by way of legislation passed in late 2020 (after having been established in 2013 and dissolved in 2017).[12] In Congressional testimony in September 2022, he stressed the importance of coordinating sanctions enforcement with allies and working to combat sanctions evasion elsewhere: "International partnerships are key to maintaining our impact," he said.[13]

Other resources for coordinating sanctions enforcement were Financial Intelligence Units (FIUs), which had been created on a national level to combat money laundering activities and were expanded to handle terrorist finance issues.

They analyzed Suspicious Activity Reports (SARs) from financial institutions and referred their results to domestic law enforcement authorities, as well as to foreign FIUs in some instances.[14] But the FIUs recognized that their structure and functioning could be modified to enforce sanctions and detect crime more effectively. In March, the FIUs of Australia, Canada, France, Germany, Italy, Japan, the Netherlands, New Zealand, the United Kingdom, and the United States issued a statement of intent highlighting the need for those nations to take "concrete actions" including "enhanc[ing] financial intelligence on sanction-related matters," "increas[ing] sharing of financial intelligence," and coordinating with the private sector.[15] The statement noted that "under the current international, EU and national legal frameworks, FIUs do not have a uniform and comprehensive legal basis and mandate to receive, analyse and share information on financial sanctions and related measures." The concrete actions called for by the FIUs were designed to improve sanctions enforcement through the increased availability of information.

Germany's Sanctions Enforcement Act I became effective in May, which allowed for increased sharing of information between enforcement authorities within Germany, introduced a requirement to declare assets frozen by sanctions, and created greater investigatory powers relative to sanctions enforcement.[16] It was followed by a Sanctions Enforcement Act II, which among other provisions created a Central Office for Sanctions Enforcement.[17]

In addition to multilateral coordination, there was a role for bilateral joint enforcement efforts. In October, the United Kingdom and the United States announced a new level of enforcement coordination.[18] According to the press release, the two authorities would "exchang[e] best practices," "strengthen[] working relationships at all levels," "identify opportunities to pool expertise," "explore opportunities to align the way we implement sanctions," and "assist . . . stakeholders either through joint products or by providing guidance resulting from collaboration behind the scenes," among others.[19]

SANCTIONS EVASION

As the initial wave and successive rounds of sanctions were implemented, parties subject to those sanctions took action to evade the restrictions targeting them. Some third-party nations were the site of efforts to evade sanctions. Sanctions violations also occurred within Russia and in Belarus, and even within the sanctioning nations themselves.

The United States viewed countries already subject to other US sanctions regimes as probable sites for attempts to evade sanctions. To understand the nature of strategies used in these areas to skirt sanctions, new reporting requirements were implemented in the US National Defense Authorization Act for Fiscal Year 2023, which was enacted at the end of 2022. Namely, Section 6807 required semi-annual reports from the Director of National Intelligence of sanctions evasion and circumvention efforts by Russia through direct or indirect engagement or assistance from Cuba, Nicaragua, Venezuela, China, Iran, and any other country considered appropriate.[20] The report was also required to detail evasion techniques, including through the use of cryptocurrency.

Other third-party nations more closely allied with the sanctioning powers were also seen as potential or suspected sites of sanctions evasion. The sanctioning powers were concerned about sanctions evasion occurring through Turkey, both with respect to the Russia sanctions and for other sanctions including those against Iran. These concerns were heightened when Ukrainian intelligence intercepted a Russian document detailing potential means for Turkey to aid Russia in evading sanctions, such as allowing correspondent accounts for Russian entities at Turkish banks and allowing Russia to buy stakes in Turkish energy companies to hide the origin of Russian oil.[21]

The UAE was another site of concern regarding sanctions evasion activities.[22] The country was grey-listed by the FATF in March, subjecting it to increased monitoring by the organization. In response, UAE representatives promised that the country would "continue its ongoing efforts to identify, disrupt and punish criminals and illicit financial networks."[23] They also highlighted actions the UAE had already taken in this area, including establishing a database containing beneficial ownership information and entering into extradition agreements with other nations.[24] Elizabeth Rosenberg, the US Assistant Secretary for Terrorist Financing and Financial Crimes, publicly noted in October the presence of Russian money laundering in the Middle East, "[u]sing unusually pointed language that US officials sa[id] was intended as a warning."[25]

The documentation required to show compliance with the crude oil price cap was intended to reduce the incidence of sanctions evasion with respect to energy supplies. Oil refineries in India, for example, now had to compile shipping and contract documentation to show that they were buying Russian crude oil only below the price cap.[26] Even so, data of sales from the month after the price cap showed that Russian oil was still being sold in certain areas above the price cap. The average price was $74 per barrel, with the price cap having been set at $60, demonstrating a high level of sanctions evasion and noncompliance.[27]

Dramatic increases in trade volumes with Russia and certain third-party nations pointed to probable evasive actions with respect to sanctions and export controls. For example, smartphone imports to Armenia greatly increased during 2022; in turn, Armenian exports of smartphones to Russia rose as well.[28] New trade patterns such as these pointed to the likely use of transshipment and product diversion to evade sanctions.

The US export control authority, BIS, issued a list of red flags that might indicate that a product ordered for one destination or user was actually intended for a sanctioned party, and that the true destination of the product was hidden for the purpose of evading US sanctions and/or export controls. These red flags included, for example:

Transactions involving entities with little or no web presence.

Transactions involving a change in shipments or payments that were previously scheduled to go to Russia or Belarus, or a company located in Russia or Belarus, but that are now going to a different country/company...

Last-minute changes to transactions associated with an originator or beneficiary located in Russia or Belarus...

Transactions associated with atypical shipping routes for a product and destination...

Transactions connected with Russian petroleum-related firms or firms that resell electronics and other similar items to Russian firms.

Where red flags such as these existed, exporters subject to US export requirements had a duty to inquire further into the nature of the transaction.[29] BIS also identified "several countries as transshipment points through which restricted or controlled exports have been known to pass before reaching destinations in Russia or Belarus." Included were Armenia, Brazil, China, Georgia, India, Israel, Kazakhstan, Kyrgyzstan, Mexico, Nicaragua, Serbia, Singapore, South Africa, Taiwan, Tajikistan, Turkey, the UAE, and Uzbekistan.

Other bodies also issued warnings about likely methods used to evade sanctions. In March, FinCEN issued an alert to financial institutions, advising them to exercise increased vigilance against attempts to evade Russian sanctions. The alert also included details about potential "red flag indicators" that might be associated with such attempts.[30] These included the use of legal structures and arrangements, along with the use of third parties to obscure the ownership and source of funds. The alert also reminded financial institutions of their Suspicious Activity Reporting (SAR) requirements where a transaction was suspected to be linked to illegal activities.

Likewise, in July the UK National Crime Agency and OFSI published a Red Alert on financial sanctions evasion typologies.[31] They detailed the strategies that designated persons were likely to take to achieve sanctions evasion. These included moving funds to non-sanctioned jurisdictions like the UAE, Turkey, China, Brazil, India, and states of the former Soviet Union (with the exception of Ukraine and Latvia, Lithuania, and Estonia).[32] The document cautioned that Designated Persons would attempt to evade sanctions by use of "alternative payment methods, including the use of crypto-assets," though the public transparency of blockchain lessened its attractiveness as a medium of exchange in this situation.

ENFORCEMENT ACTIONS

To combat evasion of sanctions and export controls, the sanctioning nations pursued enforcement actions. A number of successful actions were announced in 2022, in addition to those against the individual Russian oligarchs described in Chapter 6.[33]

Many of these actions focused on identifying and eliminating networks that illicitly shipped products to Russian destinations and end-users.

One such action was made public at the end of March, when OFAC designated as SDNs various parties involved in the sanctions evasions network centered around Serniya Engineering and Sertal.[34] These were Russian companies that worked with entities located in Russia, the United Kingdom, Spain, and Singapore to procure dual-use equipment and technology for Russian defense. In coordination, the European Union and Japan placed export controls on Serniya and other sanctioned entities, as did the United Kingdom for those entities subject to UK law. In December, certain parties and individuals associated with Serniya and Sertal were made subject to a Temporary Denial Order, which prohibited them from exporting from the United States or receiving exports from the United States or reexports subject to the US Export Administration Regulations.[35] That same month, the United States indicted five Russian and two American individuals for their dealings with Serniya and Sertal.[36]

In October, five Russian nationals and two oil traders acting for the benefit of PdVSA were indicted in the United States. The allegations described a global procurement network that obtained export-controlled US technology. As the press release noted, "[s]ome of the same electronic components obtained through the criminal scheme [were] found in Russian weapons platforms seized on the battlefield in Ukraine."

Aircraft were a particular focus of enforcement activities following the Russian invasion. In March and again in August, BIS released a list of aircraft it had been tracking as having flown into Russia, violating the US export controls.[37] These aircraft were either of US origin or were foreign-produced but contained over 25 percent by value of US-origin content and thus were subject to the US Export Administration Regulations. This had the effect of prohibiting actions with respect to the aircraft listed by BIS that included "refueling, maintenance, repair, or the provision of spare parts or services," according to General Prohibition Ten of the EAR.[38] BIS also issued Temporary Denial Orders on numerous Russian airlines as well as the Belarusian airline Belavia, which prevented those airlines for an initial 180 days from engaging in transactions governed by the EAR, which included receiving exports from the United States or reexports from other countries of items subject to the EAR.[39] In August, the Task Force KleptoCapture coordinated the seizure of a $45 million airplane owned by Lukoil, the Russian oil and gas company.[40] The plane had flown a Lukoil official from Dubai in the UAE to Moscow on March 12, without the required licenses to reexport the US-origin (and therefore US export-controlled) Boeing 737 into Russia.[41]

By September 2022, German prosecutors were investigating more than one hundred potential cases of sanctions violations, largely alleged to have been committed by German companies and individuals.[42] Some allegations involved the potential supply of Bosch- and ZF-branded electronic items to the Russian military.

French authorities carried out a targeted investigation of real estate agencies in the Alpes-Maritimes department, which included Nice and other cities and towns on the French Riviera. They found that about 60 percent of the entities investigated either were not aware of or were deliberately neglecting to carry out their legal obligations, such as checking the names of their clients against the national registry of parties whose assets had been frozen.[43]

A focus on sanctions enforcement would continue into 2023, with a number of actions announced that penalized sanctions evasion activities that had occurred in the prior year. In February 2023, for example, OFAC sanctioned Igor Zimenkov and his son Jonatan, who worked to enable sales of Russian defense products to third-party nations; Igor also aided a sanctioned Belarusian defense organization in attempting to sell to Latin America.[44] Also designated were shell organizations designed to hide the Zimenkovs' unlawful activities.

SEIZING AND FORFEITING ASSETS

The various sanctions put in place beginning in March 2022 had the effect of freezing large sums of money held by the Russian government, Russian banks, and others. A debate soon arose about the legality of possibly seizing these frozen assets. By February 2023, the World Bank estimated that the cost of an eventual Ukrainian recovery and rebuilding had by that point reached $411 billion. Direct damage to the country had reached over $135 billion.[45] Some called for the seizure of Russian assets already frozen by sanctions in order to help pay for the reconstruction of Ukraine.[46]

Within the United States, much of the debate focused on whether IEEPA already provided the authority to seize assets. US Treasury officials concluded that it did not, and took no action to seize assets under the existing legal regime. As discussed in Chapter 8, sanctioning nations were able to seize some assets from oligarchs where a nexus existed to link those funds with criminal activity. No such link existed to authorize the seizure of assets from Russian banks. Some parties proposed novel legislative measures to create that authority, though none were passed in the United States during 2022.

Laurence Tribe posited that the presidential declaration of an emergency authorized the president to confiscate Russian assets, based on language in IEEPA that the president could "transfer" "any right, power or privilege" with respect to the property interest of a foreign country.[47] This assertion, however, was disputed by many other legal experts.[48] As Paul Stephan noted, "the seizure of assets belonging to the Russian state outside of normal criminal and regulatory processes would violate international law," when not used to satisfy legal judgments rendered against Russia by international investment tribunals.[49] Such seizures without compensation in return could not be justified under the international law of countermeasures, as the imposition of economic sanctions often were.[50] Under international law, countermeasures are "responses to an internationally wrongful act," which are "intrinsically unlawful, but are justified by the alleged initial failing to which they were a response."[51] Lawful countermeasures are generally limited to ones that are proportional in nature to the allegedly wrongful act.[52] Asset seizures in response to the Russian invasion of Ukraine would likely lack this proportional nature.[53] They would also be nonreversible, which was required of countermeasures to the extent possible.[54]

The US statutes pursuant to whose authority Russian assets in the United States were frozen, IEEPA and TWEA, did not allow for the seizure of assets frozen under those authorities in peacetime, absent an attack on the United States or US engagement in armed hostilities.[55] Nor would US civil forfeiture statutes permit such seizure absent some evidence of criminality.[56] The US Supreme Court had not yet ruled on the issue, but it also seemed possible that the Foreign Sovereign Immunities Act would bar criminal prosecution of foreign sovereigns and their instrumentalities, including state-owned corporations.[57]

The Due Process Clause of the Fifth Amendment of the US Constitution also provided protection from the seizure of at least those Russian assets owned by corporations and individuals with "substantial connections" to the US.[58] This standard was likely to be met by the presence of significant assets in the US. Thus such assets could not be seized without notice to the asset holders and the opportunity to be heard to contest their seizure.[59] Seizure without compensation might also violate the Takings Clause of the Fifth Amendment of the US Constitution, which requires just compensation upon the taking of private property for public use.[60]

US enforcement authorities themselves did not attempt to apply any seizure authority on the grounds of any pre-2022 legal authority. US Treasury Secretary Janet Yellen, as she commented in the quote at the beginning of this chapter, stated that the United States did not have the authority at that time to seize assets frozen by the sanctions against Russia. And, while Russian bank assets were frozen, they were not seized or otherwise forfeited given the absence of a demonstrated link to criminal activity. Nor could they be used to satisfy judgments. Ingrid Brunk noted that customary international law required central bank assets be immune from the execution of judgments, and that it likely did the same for all other types of central bank assets as well.[61]

Additional legal authority was sought by enforcement authorities in the United States to create the potential for additional types of forfeitures beyond those currently available. Andrew Adams, Director of Task Force KleptoCapture, testified before a US Senate committee to request increased legislative tools including the amendment of IEEPA to allow for the forfeiture of property used to facilitate sanctions violations.[62] A bipartisan group of senators filed legislation to provide authority to seek forfeiture of seized Russian assets, the proceeds of which were to be used for humanitarian purposes in Ukraine.[63] Adams had called for such authority when he testified before the Senate Committee on Banking, Housing, and Urban Affairs in September.[64] The bill passed the Senate, but it required a link to criminal activity for such assets to be seized.[65]

Similar debates were occurring in Europe around whether legislation should be passed to confer this type of seizure authority. The EU freezing and confiscating of assets is governed by Article 83(1) of the Treaty on the Functioning of the European Union (TFEU). In May, the European Commission proposed a Directive on asset recovery and confiscation that would extend the crimes listed under this Article to include the violation of restrictive measures imposed by the European Union.[66] The measure was adopted in November.[67] Also in November, the European Commission proposed that certain Russian funds be used for the reconstruction of Ukraine. This would be done by way of investing frozen funds of the Central Bank of Russia and applying gains on those investments to Ukraine. The plan envisioned that in the longer term, a peace agreement would be entered into, under the terms of which Russia would agree to compensate Ukraine. The Central Bank assets would be returned when the sanctions on it were lifted, less the compensatory amounts promised for Ukraine.[68] The European Commission would not seize the principal of the frozen assets themselves, due to the legal immunity of the Russian state.[69]

Forfeiture authority was created in Canada in June, when the country enacted Bill C-19. It amended the Special Economic Measures Act (SEMA) and the Sergei Magnitsky Law to provide legal authority for the forfeiture of property seized under those sanctions authorities.[70] In December, Canadian Foreign Affairs Minister Melanie Joly announced that she would use this new legal authority to seek the forfeiture of assets held in Citco Bank Canada belonging to Granite Capital Holdings, a company owned by Roman Abramovich.[71] In May, Ukraine passed a law allowing for the seizure of assets of those supporting the Russian invasion of Ukraine in various ways, thus creating offenses that would allow for the seizure of funds, including funds already frozen by way of Ukrainian sanctions.[72]

In February 2023, a working group led by the Swiss Federal Office of Justice provided the Swiss Federal Council with conclusions that the seizure of frozen Russian assets that had been lawfully obtained would be "inconsistent" with the Swiss Constitution, as well as with "the prevailing legal order," and would "violate[] Switzerland's international commitments."[73]

The potential seizure of Russian assets raised concerns with respect to maintaining the rule of law. Under international investment law, such seizures would be expropriations.[74] Unlawful expropriations not connected to a civil or criminal proceeding must be compensated in a prompt, adequate, and effective manner. To uphold the rule of law and the interests of its own investors, the United States and other sanctioning powers had an incentive to not seize Russian assets in a way that would undermine the international investment framework of law.[75]

So too did the sanctioning nations have an interest in respecting national constitutional protections and upholding customary international law. The economic sanctions were enacted in response to Russia's invasion of Ukraine and violations of international law in doing so. The economic response had to address the Russian aggression, but also had to respect domestic and international law as well.[76]

CONCLUSION

While implementation of the sanctions in early 2022 was the first step in the economic response to Russia, they would ultimately have been ineffective without sufficient accompanying enforcement. The latter portion of 2022 heralded new trends in the economic response to Russia: increased coordination of enforcement across jurisdictions; heightened focus on sanctions evasion attempts, especially those occurring within third-party nations; and even the consideration of new potential mechanisms to achieve the seizure of assets, rather than merely their freezing. Whether the sanctions would ultimately be successful in the long run depended in large part on the success of these enforcement efforts.

11

Assessing the Sanctions

[T]he costs are accumulating every single day, because the impact of the sanctions is both immediate but then it grows over time. And what we're seeing is Russia having an inability to replace the weapons it's using, in large part because of the export controls that we put in place ... And in particular, if you're looking at Russia's efforts to modernize its economy ... whether it's energy technology, whether it's basic telecommunications infrastructure, whether it's its defense and aerospace industry, every single day that goes by with these sanctions in place the burden on Russia gets heavier and heavier, its ability to prosecute these kinds of wars gets weaker and weaker.

—US Secretary of State Antony J. Blinken[1]

At the end of 2022, the coalition of sanctioning nations faced a question: Were the historic set of sanctions against Russia working? Assessing the sanctions, of course, required defining the specific goals of the various sanctions regimes, as well as balancing those goals with the economic fallout and unintended third-party effects of the sanctions.[2] The sanctions' effects on the trade in food, fuel, and fertilizer were some of the most notable costs.

Whether the sanctions were "effective" was too broad a question to be answered with a clear yes or no. The long-term impact of the sanctions could not be fully understood in the months immediately following their imposition. Moreover, understanding the effectiveness of the sanctions against Russia required understanding the various goals of the sanctions; dividing the sanctions and other measures by discrete type and understanding the effects of each, which could vary drastically; and comparing the costs of the sanctions against the effects those sanctions achieved.[3]

And regardless of their potential long-term effects, Russia still waged war against Ukraine as 2022 came to a close. This fact alone led some to call into question the effectiveness of the sanctions. Whether the sanctions would be maintained or strengthened in the coming months and years ahead, and whether Russia would draw back from its invasion of Ukraine, would remain to be seen in the coming years.

BALANCING COSTS AGAINST IMPACT

Evaluating the effectiveness of any sanctions program necessarily includes reckoning the cost of those sanctions, both on the target country and on third-party nations. As described in Chapter 7, the use of sanctions has been linked to the worsening of humanitarian crises in multiple instances. The demonstrated humanitarian impacts have been widely recognized as a significant and sometimes enormously tragic cost of imposing sanctions.[4]

Smart sanctions have arisen in recent years in an attempt to minimize the economic harm done to a populace, by targeting key individuals, entities, or sectors rather than an entire country.[5] Such targeted sanctions, however, generally do not fully achieve the goal of limiting economic harm from sanctions to only the targets themselves. When smart sanctions are deployed against a large number of targets in one country, including systemically important entities, the impetus for overcompliance is greater.[6]

The Russian invasion and the subsequent sanctions triggered profound third-party effects, including with respect to the prices of food and energy. In Congressional testimony in September, Elizabeth Rosenberg, the US Treasury's Assistant Secretary for Terrorist Financing and Financial Crimes, highlighted the measures that the department had taken in response to concerns of significant third-party effects that had arisen after the imposition of sanctions. These "real time adjustment[s]" included the issuance of multiple fact sheets designed to clarify the nature of sanctions prohibitions, including "that agricultural and medical products are not the targets of US sanctions."[7]

Sanctions can also introduce costs for parties in sanctioning nations themselves.[8] Entities in sender states may lose customers who previously purchased their exports; can lose affordable sources for inputs; and might incur costs in the administration necessary to ensure that they are complying with new sanctions as they are enacted.[9] Enforcement efforts also cost governments money to carry out. Parties in large sender states, however, can in some instances adjust by finding alternative markets and trading partners.[10] As discussed in earlier chapters, the costs of the 2022 sanctions were greatest for sanctioning nations most notably in the energy sector, where energy supplies are fairly fungible and Russia plays a key role in supplying the world's energy.

ECONOMIC EFFECTS

As was anticipated and intended by sender nations at the time of the sanctions' enactment, the sanctions caused notable economic effects to Russia.

Analysis by the World Bank, the IMF, and the OECD estimated that Russia's GDP declined by 2.1 percent in 2022.[11] By May 2023, there were conflicting estimates as to whether Russian GDP would further decrease by the end of 2023 or not.[12] Russa's budget deficit reached a record 1.8 trillion rubles in January 2023, from a January 2022 budget surplus of about 125 billion rubles.[13] The deficit grew sharply as the price cap took effect and cut into revenue from energy sales.[14]

Russia's trade patterns shifted. Trade volumes grew markedly with India, China, Turkey, and Brazil, to name a few; they fell between Russia and the United States, the United Kingdom, and South Korea, among others.[15] Trade volumes grew with even some sanctioning states, like Japan and the European Union Member States of Spain, Belgium, and the Netherlands.[16] According to Russia's central bank, Russia's trade surplus rose to a record $227.4 billion in 2022, up 86 percent from the prior year.[17] This increased surplus was caused by a fall in imports from sanctioning nations, paired with higher energy prices and increased trade with non-sanctioning nations.

As described earlier, inbound foreign direct investment into Russia declined sharply in 2022.[18] This resulted both from the prohibitions of the sanctions and due to private action not mandated by sanctions. Over 1,000 companies withdrew from Russia in the first few months following the invasion, as public pressure grew on private companies to voluntarily halt business with Russia even when they were still permitted to do so under the new sanctions.[19] (Conflicting research concluded that by the end of November 2022, only about 120 companies had divested from Russia.)[20] Some companies from sanctioning nations retained operations or sales in Russia, like Auchan, the French supermarket, and Heineken, the Dutch brewing company.[21]

Russian consumers reported some observable developments after the imposition of sanctions and as private entities withdrew from Russia following the invasion. Job vacancies declined.[22] Stores in Russia operated by brands from the sanctioning nations closed, though consumers still had some access to certain foreign goods through parallel import channels.[23] Prices in Russia spiked immediately after the invasion, with the country reporting 17 percent inflation in April[24] and an 11.9 percent inflation rate for 2022 as a whole.[25] However, the inflation rate had dropped sharply by the end of March 2023, when the annual inflation rate had fallen back below 5 percent.[26]

These numbers suggested that the sanctions were having a significant impact on the Russian economy. A clear picture of Russia's economy, however, was difficult to determine. Sonnenfeld and Tian noted the unreliability of data about the Russian economy, given that its source was the Russian government itself. In some instances, economic data was withheld entirely.[27] The United States created legislation that attempted to obtain a more accurate picture as to the economic effects of the sanctions. Specifically, in addition to requiring reports of sanctions evasions efforts, the US National Defense Authorization Act for 2023 also mandated semi-annual reporting on "the material effects of the sanctions" imposed in response to the Ukrainian invasion, including "a discussion of those sanctions that had significant effects, as well as those that had no observed effects."[28] The report would include a description of the methodologies used, "including with respect to specific industries, entities, individuals, and transactions."

The immediate data available suggested significant economic effects on Russia, though trade restrictions on the part of sender states were offset by Russia's moving to alternative trading partners like India and China. The needs of the war itself, like the conscription of Russians to fight in the conflict, were also diverting economic resources within Russia. The level of industrial output in Russia was hardly affected during 2022, due in part to increased government spending on military outputs.[29]

In the long term, it seemed that the economic measures implemented in 2022 had the potential to further wreak economic harm on Russia. Indeed, though the level of industrial output remained high, a report of the US government detailed the pressures the sanctions were placing on the Russian economy, industry, and the defense sector. It noted the decline of Russian defense exports (with arms export revenues estimated to drop 25 percent in 2022) because of sanctions and other factors.[30] About thirteen months after the first rounds of sanctions were imposed, it seemed that the sanctions were seeding future long-term effects within Russia.[31] Increased military production masked more systemic economic issues. The IMF projected a 7 percent reduction in Russian economic output from prewar estimates.[32]

Export controls seemed likely to inflict long-term harm, as they had the potential to degrade Russian technological capability as the country ran out of semiconductors and access to the technological know-how from sender nations. As Edward Fishman commented on the sanctions: "They're not trying to make Putin … wake up in the morning and decide that Ukraine was not worth … the effort. What they are really trying to do is just create attrition in Russia's military industrial complex and its economy writ large."[33]

Indeed, export controls were already causing noticeable effects within Russia by the end of 2022. Particularly concerning was the inability of Russian airlines to obtain spare parts for their airplanes after the imposition of sanctions. Instead, they salvaged parts from other planes, even from functional aircraft.[34] This raised concerns that at some point these aircraft would become unsafe to fly.[35] Export controls on semiconductors jeopardized Russia's ongoing ability to consistently source reliable chips. This was especially true because the United States had restricted China's access to the most advanced semiconductor manufacturing production capabilities and technology, in turn reducing Russia's access to the most sophisticated chips.[36] This had the potential to affect Russia's production of both military and civilian items.[37]

NONECONOMIC EFFECTS

The response to Russia was intended primarily to inflict damage on the Russian economy and limit its ability to wage war. But the coalition of sanctioning nations also took actions with primarily symbolic importance, signaling that the world community was condemning the Russian invasion of Ukraine, based upon the norms of international law and upon moral grounds. Such symbolism was apparent when, for example, the European Parliament adopted a resolution to designate Russia as a state sponsor of terrorism. While there was no existing EU framework to trigger consequences as a result of that designation, the Parliament urged that such legal provisions be created.[38] The broad international condemnation of Russia's invasion was also apparent in actions like suspending Russia from sports.[39] For instance, immediately after the invasion commenced, the International Olympic Committee recommended that Russian and Belarusian athletes and officials be prohibited from participating in international competitions.[40] The soccer governing bodies FIFA and UEFA likewise banned Russian teams from international competition, including the 2022 World Cup.[41]

The sanctions themselves had symbolic value as well. Beyond their strictly economic effects, they represented a statement that Russia's violation of Ukraine's territorial integrity was contrary to the rule of law. The language used by world leaders when the sanctions were introduced, strongly condemning the Russian invasion, highlighted this. In the context of both Russia specifically and other sanctioned nations more generally, sanctions were useful for demonstrating that sender states would take action against violations of the norms of the international community.[42]

Targeted sanctions directed against particular parties were also seen as having symbolic value in naming specific individuals and entities to be made subject to penalties.[43] As Kimberly Ann Elliott has commented: "[T]argeted sanctions . . . are quite useful in signaling displeasure and as tangible signs of support for international norms."

Beyond affirming the international community's support for and adherence to the rule of law, the symbolic value of sanctions was important for Ukraine, in the midst of fighting for its survival as a nation. Pre-2022 research noted the importance of morale to the Ukrainian opposition to Russia in the Donbas region.[44] So too was support from the sender nations, by way of the economic sanctions, seen by many as an important symbol of support for Ukraine and condemnation of Russia.

POLITICAL RAMIFICATIONS

Beyond quantifying the immediate economic effects, examining the effectiveness of the sanctions required consideration of a larger question: What impact would these economic and other actions have on Russia's behavior, either in the short or long term? Would the sanctions and other measures persuade Russia to withdraw from Ukraine? Would they deter Russia from other expansionist moves? Even if Russia were not deterred, could the sanctions serve as an effective warning to third-party nations to respect to the territorial integrity of other nations?

The sanctions already imposed against Russia after its invasion of Crimea in 2014 did not prevent the greater Russian invasion of Ukraine in 2022. But evidence suggested that those 2014 sanctions were not wholly ineffective. Stanislav Secrieru's analysis concluded that those sanctions did not change Russia's strategic goals in Ukraine; were partially successful in stymieing Russia's operational goals in that they prevented at the time further Russian military advancement into Ukraine, and made the annexation of Crimea more expensive; and were most effective as a military tactic in that they stalled the Russian invasion, allowing Ukraine time to build its military capacity.[45] Those earlier sanctions targeted specific sectors such as defense and energy, and imposed significant economic costs on Russia. Effects were also apparent in finance and agriculture.[46] An October 2022 analysis found that the impact of sanctions on the Russian government's fiscal balance – while not enough to hasten the end of the war – would reduce its expenditure capacity in the future.[47]

Sanctions were generally most effective in other contexts where the goals of sanctions were clearly defined and where criteria for their removal were clearly communicated by the sender to the target state.[48] Sanctions that sought a change in leadership rarely effected that result, given the ambitious nature of the attempted goal.[49] One objective of the 2022 sanctions against Russia was clear: to halt the Russian invasion of Ukraine. Whether these sanctions against Russia could eventually achieve that purpose, however, depended in part on how integral Ukraine was to Putin's own conception for a newly imperialist Russia. His mentions of nuclear weapons suggested that the conquest of Ukraine was integral to his vision of an expansionist Russia.[50] The sanctions may have been tailored to achieve a specified result. But they seemed perhaps unlikely to affect the behavior of a ruler who would incur great losses and ignore any rational cost–benefit analysis in pursuit of his aims.

Beyond Russia's invasion of Ukraine, some questioned whether such sanctions could deter future violations of self-determination and territorial integrity in other contexts. Global tensions had been growing in recent years over the possibility of a Chinese invasion of Taiwan.[51] The disparate response of these two nations to the Russian invasion of Ukraine was perhaps telling of the disagreement between them concerning the political status of Taiwan. Specifically, Taiwan joined with the sanctioning powers in the response to Russia, "call[ing] for Ukraine's sovereignty and territorial integrity to be respected."[52] China, meanwhile, refused to join in the sanctions response, criticizing the sanctions against Russia as "illegal."[53]

As described elsewhere in this book, targeted sanctions and export controls had already been implemented against selected Chinese parties for a variety of reasons. A future invasion of Taiwan would almost certainly trigger some sort of sanctions response by the United States and perhaps other nations. It was, in fact, reported in

September that US authorities were considering possible sanctions against China to deter an invasion of Taiwan.[54] But sanctions against China in that eventuality might look quite different than the 2022 sanctions against Russia. China held a much more central role in the world economy than had Russia even pre-sanctions. It was clear that the sort of broad-based sanctions that had been imposed against Russia, were they someday to be levied against China, had the potential to be deeply disruptive for sender and target alike.[55]

OPPOSITION TO THE SANCTIONS

The complex sanctions analysis of first- and second-order effects led various parties in the sender states to different conclusions about their effectiveness. Some opposition to the sanctions existed in the sender states even from the time the earliest rounds of sanctions were imposed. In the United States, Representative Ilhan Omar issued a statement at the commencement of Russia's invasion, on February 24. She stated that while she supported "sanctions that are targeted at Putin, his oligarchs, and the Russian military," she "oppose[d] broad-based sanctions that would amount to a collective punishment of a Russian population that did not choose this."[56]

Other voices of opposition in the sender states joined in as the year progressed without an immediate Russian withdrawal from Ukraine. This questioning increased as volatile food and energy prices increasingly affected consumers. Certain members of both the Republican and Democratic political parties in the United States questioned both the sanctions and aid to Ukraine.[57] By early 2023, support by the American public for the economic measures had dropped from 71 percent in May 2022, but the sanctions were still favored by 63 percent.[58]

The voices opposing sanctions were counterbalanced by those who favored maintaining them, or even expanding them. Indeed, one year after the invasion, the sanctioning nations enacted a new tranche of sanctions.[59] The European Commission announced: "This package is turning up the pressure in response to Putin's brutal war."[60]

CONCLUSION

The sanctions did not cause the immediate collapse of the Russian economy; but then, there had been no reasonable expectation at the time of their imposition that they would do so.[61] Sanctions are an inherently limited tool. Though powerful, they could not stop the Russian war machine from its onslaught in Ukraine. As Nicholas Mulder noted, they would ultimately be less important than the provision of direct financial aid to support and rebuild Ukraine's economy, which was profoundly damaged by the invasion.[62] The sanctions, however, sought to first address the existential threat to Ukraine posed by Russia that would have to be overcome were rebuilding to ever occur.

But of greater near-term consequence than sanctions to Ukraine's survival was the provision of military aid and supplies to the embattled nation. Such aid gave Ukrainians the resources to continue to hold at bay the Russian army and the Wagner Group of mercenaries. By the end of the year, the invading Russian army fought on, even as Ukrainians regained territory. And the sanctions remained in place.

Conclusion

By the end of 2022, the sanctions were voluminous. But the economic and other measures deployed against Russia were not as comprehensive as other sanctions regimes had been. Technically, the sanctions remained targeted. There was no comprehensive trade embargo, for example, against Russia by the United States or the European Union. Regulated parties, however, tended toward overcompliance; companies also ceased to do business with Russia for reputational reasons. These trends meant that the implementation of targeted sanctions often resembled comprehensive ones in practice. But the Russia sanctions were not so sweeping as those imposed upon Cuba, Iran, North Korea, or Syria, for instance.

Nor, by the end of 2022, had the United States designated Russia as a state sponsor of terrorism, though the European Parliament had already voted to do so in November.[1] At that time, state sponsors of terrorism designated by the United States were Cuba, North Korea, Iran, and Syria. The move by the European Union was "largely symbolic," as no framework of EU law triggered penalties as a result of the designation.[2] A US designation would result in sanctions overlapping to a large extent restrictions already in place, including limitations on foreign assistance to Russia from the United States, and export bans on defense and dual-use items.[3] While various measures had been introduced in Congress to designate Russia a state sponsor of terrorism, at the close of 2022 the country had not yet been so named.[4]

As the continuing debate over designating Russia a state sponsor of terrorism illustrated, by the end of 2022 the economic response to Russia was by no means over. Additional parties supporting the Russian war effort continued to be made subject to sanctions. At the beginning of 2023, the United States designated the Wagner Group as a significant transnational criminal organization, supplementing its already-existing designation of the mercenary group as a sanctioned entity with further condemnation at least symbolic in nature.[5]

More significantly, the one-year anniversary of the Russian invasion brought a coordinated round of new sanctions. The United States imposed sanctions on over

200 individuals and entities; announced tariffs on Russian imports including metals, minerals, and chemicals; created new sectoral sanctions, including on the Russian metals and mining sector; and listed nearly ninety companies in Russia and elsewhere for "engaging in sanctions evasion and backfill activities in support of Russia's defense sector."[6] The United Kingdom announced that it was "committing to prohibit the export to Russia of every item Russia has been found using on the battlefield."[7] Among other measures, it sanctioned four additional banks and sanctioned individuals associated with Russia's military-industrial complex and the Russian state-owned nuclear power company Rosatom. The United Kingdom also introduced new trade measures including import bans on iron and steel products from Russia processed in third countries.[8] The European Union also issued a tenth package of sanctions.[9] This package included export bans worth over €11 billion, bringing the European Union to sanctioning or banning nearly half of its preinvasion 2021 exports. EU import bans on bitumen, asphalt, synthetic rubber, and carbon blacks announced in the tenth package were worth over €1.3 billion and along with the import bans in previous rounds encompassed over half of the EU's 2021 imports from Russia. Coordinated measures were issued by Australia, Canada, Japan, South Korea, New Zealand, and Norway as well.[10] The G7 nations issued a statement: "We reaffirm our commitment to strengthening the unprecedented and coordinated sanctions and other economic measures the G7 and partner countries have taken to date to further counter Russia's capacity to wage its illegal aggression."[11]

The Russian military action against Ukraine continued on. Beyond the scope of this book, but certainly a key part of the sanctioning nations' support of Ukraine, was the military aid sent to the country. The United States committed more than $31 billion in security assistance in the year since the Russian invasion in February 2022.[12] The United Kingdom was the second-largest provider of military aid, committing £2.3 billion between February 2022 and March 2023.[13] At the beginning of 2023, Germany and the United States announced their intent to send tanks to support Ukrainian forces.[14]

Beyond the economic arena, Ukraine continued to fight on the battlefield to preserve its integrity as an independent nation. It had already sacrificed a great deal in 2022 to do so. By the end of the year, at least 13,000 soldiers had been killed. Around 3,500 Ukrainian soldiers were being held as prisoners of war.[15] Ukrainians had been the victims of war crimes on a staggering scale. Ukrainian children were stolen and relocated to Russia.[16] Nearly a year after the invasion, over 7,000 civilians had been killed, and over 11,000 had been injured.[17]

The economic response to Russia was the weapon chosen by the sanctioning nations to respond to the Russian invasion of Ukraine. It was selected to assert the value of territorial sovereignty, and most importantly, to try to protect the lives of the Ukrainian people and to respond to the atrocities committed against them. They sought to diminish Russia's ability to wage war, to diminish its future imperialist ambitions, and to defend a shared understanding among nations that law matters.

On December 21, 2022, President Zelensky addressed the US Congress. "You can strengthen sanctions to make Russia feel how ruinous its aggression truly is. It is in your power, really, to help us bring to justice everyone who started this unprovoked and criminal war. Let us do it . . . [L]et the terrorist state be held responsible for its terror and aggression and compensate all losses done by this war."[18]

Selected Jurisdictions/Countries Joining in the 2022 Sanctions Response to Russia

The European Union (composed of Member States Austria, Belgium, Bulgaria, Croatia, Cyprus, Czechia, Denmark, Estonia, Finland, France, Germany, Greece, Hungary, Ireland, Italy, Latvia, Lithuania, Luxembourg, Malta, the Netherlands, Poland, Portugal, Romania, Slovakia, Slovenia, Spain, Sweden); Albania; Andorra; Antigua and Barbuda; Australia; the Bahamas; Canada; Iceland; Japan; Kosovo; Liechtenstein; Moldova (only after initial sanctions response); Monaco; Montenegro; New Zealand; North Macedonia; Norway; San Marino; Singapore; South Korea; St. Kitts and Nevis; Switzerland; Taiwan; Ukraine; the United Kingdom; and the United States.

Notes

CHAPTER 1 BEFORE THE INVASION

1 Timothy Gardner, *Analysis: With Record Pump Prices, Biden Hard-Pressed to Ramp up Russia Sanctions*, Reuters (June 17, 2022), www.reuters.com/world/with-record-pump-prices-biden-hard-pressed-ramp-up-russia-sanctions-2022-06-17/.

2 David Sherfinski, *Ukraine Crisis Highlights Big Tech's Potential to Disrupt Daily Life*, Reuters (Mar. 4, 2022), www.reuters.com/legal/litigation/ukraine-crisis-highlights-big-techs-potential-disrupt-daily-life-2022-03-04/.

3 Jonathan Saul, Stine Jacobsen, and Jacob Gronholt-pedersen, *World's Largest Container Lines Suspend Shipping to Russia*, Reuters (Mar. 1, 2022), www.reuters.com/business/worlds-biggest-container-lines-suspend-shipping-russia-2022-03-01/; Liz Alderman and Jenny Gross, *Russia Sanctions Snarl Shipping Even as Pandemic Pressure Eases*, New York Times (Mar. 11, 2022), www.nytimes.com/2022/03/11/business/russia-ukraine-shipping-cargo.html.

4 Ellen Francis, *Berlin's Landmarks Go Dark as Germany Races to Save Energy for Winter*, Washington Post (July 29, 2022), www.washingtonpost.com/world/2022/07/29/germany-russia-energy-berlin-lights-hanover-showers/.

5 Barry Levy et al., *Russia's War in Ukraine – The Devastation of Health and Human Rights*, 387 New England J. Med. 102, 104 (July 14, 2022), www.nejm.org/doi/full/10.1056/NEJMp2207415; *Nearly Half of Mariupol Has Suffered Grave Damage*, The Economist (Apr. 23, 2022), www.economist.com/graphic-detail/2022/04/23/nearly-half-of-mariupol-has-suffered-grave-damage; *The "Devastating Truth" about What Happened in Mariupol, Ukraine, from Those Who Lived through the Destruction*, CBC (Nov. 24, 2022), www.cbc.ca/documentaries/the-passionate-eye/the-devastating-truth-about-what-happened-in-mariupol-ukraine-from-those-who-lived-through-the-destruction-1.6662949; *Ukraine: Russian Forces' Trail of Death in Bucha*, Human Rights Watch (Apr. 21, 2022), www.hrw.org/news/2022/04/21/ukraine-russian-forces-trail-death-bucha; Joscha Weber and Kathrin Wesolowski, *Fact Check: Atrocities in Bucha Were Not "Staged*,*"* DW (Apr. 5, 2022), www.dw.com/en/fact-check-atrocities-in-bucha-not-staged/a-61366129; *Evidence of Russian War Crimes Mounts as Invasion of Ukraine Drags On*, Associated Press (Dec. 30, 2022),

www.pbs.org/newshour/world/evidence-of-russian-war-crimes-mounts-as-invasion-of-ukraine-drags-on; www.csce.gov/international-impact/events/russian-war-crimes-ukraine.

6 Georgi Kantchev, Caitlin Ostroff, and Matthew Luxmoore, *The West's Sanctions Barrage Severs Russia's Economy from Much of the World*, Wall Street Journal (Feb. 28, 2022), www.wsj.com/articles/russias-ruble-financial-markets-are-hammered-by-sanctions-11646038133.

7 Barry E. Carter, *Economic Sanctions*, Max Planck Encyclopedia of Public Int'l Law (Apr. 2011), https://opil.ouplaw.com/display/10.1093/law:epil/9780199231690/law-9780199231690-e1521?prd=OPIL.

8 Benjamin Coates, *A Century of Sanctions*, Origins (Dec. 2019), https://origins.osu.edu/article/economic-sanctions-history-trump-global?language_content_entity=en.

9 Elizabeth Clark Hersey, *No Universal Target: Distinguishing between Terrorism and Human Rights Violations in Targeted Sanctions Regimes*, 38 Brook. J. Int'l. L. 1231, 1234 n.16 (2013), citing Gary Clyde Hufbauer and Barbara Oegg, *Reconciling Political Sanctions with Globalization and Free Trade: Economic Sanctions: Public Goals and Private Compensation*, 4 Chi. J. Int'l L. 305, 305 n.2 (2003).

10 David S. Cohen and Zachary K. Goldman, *Like It or Not, Unilateral Sanctions Are Here to Stay*, 113 Am. J. In'tl L. 146 (2019).

11 Jean-Marc Thouvenin, *Articulating UN Sanctions with Unilateral Restrictive Measures*, Research Handbook on Unilateral and Extraterritorial Sanctions (2021), www.elgaronline.com/display/edcoll/9781839107849/9781839107849.00017.xml.

12 Iryna Bogdanova, *The Legality of Unilateral Economic Sanctions under Public International Law*, Unilateral Sanctions in International Law and the Enforcement of Human Rights (June 2022), https://brill.com/display/book/9789004507890/BP000004.xml.

13 15 C.F.R. § 772.1 ("[t]*echnology* means: [i]nformation necessary for the 'development,' 'production,' 'use,' operation, installation, maintenance, repair, overhaul, or refurbishing ... of an item ... '[t]echnology' may be in any tangible or intangible form such as written or oral communications").

14 15 C.F.R. § 730.5(a) ("[c]ommodities, software, and technology that have been exported from the United States are generally subject to the EAR [US Export Administration Regulations] with respect to reexport").

15 Bert Chapman, *Export Controls: A Contemporary History* (2013); *Entity List*, Bureau of Industry and Security (2020), www.bis.doc.gov/index.php/policy-guidance/lists-of-parties-of-concern/entity-list.

16 *Quantitative Restrictions*, World Trade Organization (2023), www.wto.org/english/tratop_e/markacc_e/qr_e.htm.

17 *About OFAC*, U.S. Department of the Treasury (last accessed 2023), https://ofac.treasury.gov/about-ofac.

18 Ian F. Fergusson and Paul K. Kerr, *The U.S. Export Control System and the Export Control Reform Initiative*, Congressional Research Service, at 2 (last updated Jan. 28, 2020), https://crsreports.congress.gov/product/pdf/R/R41916/58.

19 10 United States Code of Federal Regulations (C.F.R.) Part 810 (2023).

20 Christopher Casey et al., *The International Emergency Economic Powers Act: Origins, Evolution, and Use*, Congressional Research Service (last updated July 14, 2020), https://sgp.fas.org/crs/natsec/R45618.pdf.

21 Paul K. Kerr and Christopher A. Casey, *The U.S. Export Control System and the Export Control Reform Act of 2018*, Congressional Research Service (last updated June 7, 2021), https://crsreports.congress.gov/product/pdf/R/R46814.

22 *Basic Information on OFAC and Sanctions*, U.S. Department of the Treasury (last updated 2023), https://ofac.treasury.gov/faqs/topic/1501.

23 *Id.*

24 Nicholas Mulder, The Economic Weapon: The Rise of Sanctions as a Tool of Modern War (2022).

25 Kimberly Ann Elliott and Gary Clyde Hufbauer, *Same Song, Same Refrain? Economic Sanctions in the 1990's*, 89 Am. Econ. Rev. 403 (1999), www.aeaweb.org/articles?id=10.1257/aer.89.2.403; Samuel Kern Alexander III, *The Origins and Use of Economic Sanctions*, Economic Sanctions (2009), https://link.springer.com/chapter/10.1057/9780230227286_2.

26 Harold J. Berman and John R. Garson, *United States Export Controls – Past, Present, and Future*, 67 Columbia L. Rev. 791 (1967), www.jstor.org/stable/1120967; Mitchel B. Wallerstein with William W. Snyder, Jr., *Appendix G*, Finding Common Ground: U.S. Export Controls in a Changed Global Environment (1991), https://nap.nationalacademies.org/read/1617/chapter/21.

27 *New Body to Support Financial Sanctions Implementation Launched*, HM Treasury (Mar. 31, 2016), www.gov.uk/government/news/new-body-to-support-financial-sanctions-implementation-launched.

28 *Stronger OFAC Style Sanctions Enforcement Comes to the UK*, Financier Worldwide Magazine (Aug. 2017), www.financierworldwide.com/stronger-ofac-style-sanctions-enforcement-comes-to-the-uk.

29 Viktor Szép and Peter Van Elsuwege, *EU Sanctions Policy and the Alignment of Third Countries: Relevant Experiences for the UK?* Routledge Handbook on the Int'l Dimension of Brexit (2020), www.taylorfrancis.com/chapters/edit/10.4324/9781003002970-16/eu-sanctions-policy-alignment-third-countries-viktor-sz%C3%A9p-peter-van-elsuwege.

30 *Current Sanctions Imposed by Canada*, Government of Canada (last updated May 31, 2023), www.international.gc.ca/world-monde/international_relations-relations_internatio nales/sanctions/current-actuelles.aspx?lang=eng.

31 Leah Ferris, *Sanctions Imposed on Russia in Response to Aggression against Ukraine – How Are They Imposed under Australi's Sanctions Laws?*, Parliament of Australia (Feb. 28, 2022), www.aph.gov.au/About_Parliament/Parliamentary_Departments/Parliamentary_Library/FlagPost/2022/February/Sanctions_on_Russia.

32 *Five Things You Need to Know about the Maastricht Treaty*, European Central Bank (2023), www.ecb.europa.eu/ecb/educational/explainers/tell-me-more/html/25_years_maastricht.en .html; Francesco Giumelli et al., *The When, What, Where and Why of European Union Sanctions*, 30 European Security 1, 1 (2021), www.tandfonline.com/doi/full/10.1080/09662839.2020.1797685.

33 *Overview of Sanctions and Related Tools*, European Commission (last updated July 26, 2023), https://finance.ec.europa.eu/eu-and-world/sanctions-restrictive-measures/overview-sanctions-and-related-tools_en; *EU Sanctions Policy and Procedure*, UK Parliament (2017), https://publications.parliament.uk/pa/ld201617/ldselect/ldeucom/102/10205.htm.

34 *Policy Dutch Government on International Sanctions*, Government of the Netherlands (Nov. 19, 2019), www.government.nl/topics/international-sanctions/policy-international-sanctions.

35 *Dispositif national de gel des avoirs à but de lutter contre le terrorisme*, Ministère de l'Économie, des Finances et de la Souveraineté Industrielle et Numérique (Jan. 7, 2022), www.tresor.economie.gouv.fr/services-aux-entreprises/sanctions-economiques/dispositif-national-de-gel-des-avoirs.

36 Wesley Pydiamah and Léonor d'Albiousse, *France*, Eversheds Sutherland (Aug. 18, 2021), https://ezine.eversheds-sutherland.com/global-sanctions-guide/france.

37 *United Nations Sanctions*, Council of Europe Committee of Legal Advisers on Public Int'l Law, www.coe.int/en/web/cahdi/united-nations-sanctions; Masahiko Asada, *Definition and Legal Justification of Sanctions*, Economic Sanctions in International Law and Practice (2019).

38 *Permanent and Non-Permanent Members*, U.N. Security Council, www.un.org/securitycouncil/content/current-members.

39 *United Nations: Sanctions against Rhodesia*, Time (Dec. 23, 1996), https://content.time.com/time/subscriber/article/0,33009,840760,00.html; *Democratic People's Republic of Korea (North Korea) Sanctions Regime*, Australian Government (Mar. 20, 2020), www.dfat.gov.au/international-relations/security/sanctions/sanctions-regimes/democratic-peoples-republic-korea-sanctions-regime; *Sanctions*, U.N. Security Council (Dec. 28, 2018), www.un.org/securitycouncil/sanctions/information.

40 See, e.g., Jamil Jaffer, *Strengthening the Wassenaar Export Control Regime*, 3 Chicago J. Int'l L. 519, 520 (2002), https://chicagounbound.uchicago.edu/cjil/vol3/iss2/22/.

41 15 C.F.R. § 730.3 ("[a] 'dual-use' item is one that has civil applications as well as terrorism and military or weapons of mass destruction (WMD)-related applications").

42 15 C.F.R. Part 774.

43 Michael Beck and Seema Gahlaut, *Creating a New Multilateral Export Control Regime*, 33 Arms Control Today 12, 13 (Apr. 2003), www.armscontrol.org/act/2003-04/features/creating-new-multilateral-export-control-regime.

44 See, e.g., *Implementation of Australia Group Decisions from 2021 and 2022 Virtual Meetings: Controls on Marine Toxins, Pathogens and Biological Equipment*, 88 Fed. Reg. 2507 (Jan. 17, 2023), www.federalregister.gov/documents/2023/01/17/2023-00397/implementation-of-australia-group-decisions-from-2021-and-2022-virtual-meetings-controls-on-marine.

45 Barry E. Carter, *Int'l Econ. Sanctions: Improving the Haphazard U.S. Legal Regime*, 75 Cal. L. Rev. 1162 (1987), www.jstor.org/stable/3480594.

46 *Sanctions Programs and Country Information*, U.S. Department of the Treasury (last updated 2023), https://ofac.treasury.gov/sanctions-programs-and-country-information.

47 Daniel W. Drezner, *Sanctions Sometimes Smart: Targeted Sanctions in Theory and Practice*, 13 Int'l Studies Rev. 96 (2011), www.jstor.org/stable/23016144; James Pattinson, The Alternatives to War: From Sanctions to Nonviolence (2018), at 42.

48 Drezner, note 47.

49 Ashish Kumar Sen, *A Brief History of Sanctions on Iran*, Atlantic Council (May 8, 2018), www.atlanticcouncil.org/blogs/new-atlanticist/a-brief-history-of-sanctions-on-iran/.

50 Meaghan McCurdy, *Unilateral Sanctions with a Twist: The Iran and Libya Sanctions Act of 1996*, 13 Am. U. Int'l L. Rev. 397 (1997), https://digitalcommons.wcl.american.edu/auilr/vol13/iss2/4/.

51 Nicholas Davidson, *U.S. Secondary Sanctions: The U.K. and E.U. Response*, 27 Stetson L. Rev. 1425 (1998).

52 Cornelius Adebahr, *Easing EU Sanctions on Iran*, Carnegie Europe (June 16, 2014), https://carnegieeurope.eu/2014/06/16/easing-eu-sanctions-on-iran-pub-55955.

53 Decision 2010/413/CFSP and Regulation (EU) No. 267/2012.

54 Michael Jacobson, *Sanctions against Iran: A Promising Struggle*, Washington Quarterly (2008), http://csis-website-prod.s3.amazonaws.com/s3fs-public/legacy_files/files/publication/twq08summerjacobson.pdf.

55 Paul K. Kerr et al., *Possible U.S. Return to Iran Nuclear Agreement: Frequently Asked Questions*, Congressional Research Service (Jan. 29, 2021), https://crsreports.congress.gov/product/pdf/R/R46663.

56 *Joint Comprehensive Plan of Action and Restrictive Measures*, European Council (last accessed Oct. 24, 2022), www.consilium.europa.eu/en/policies/sanctions/iran/jcpoa-restrictive-measures/.

57 Eytan J. Fisch et al., *"Implementation Day": Key Aspects of US and EU Implementation of Iran Sanctions Relief*, Skadden, Aprs, Slate, Meagher & Flom LLP (Jan. 28, 2016), www.skadden.com/insights/publications/2016/01/implementation-day–key-aspects-of-us-and-eu-imple ("[n]on-U.S. persons are the primary beneficiaries of U.S. sanctions relief on Implementation Day, as the vast majority of U.S. sanctions relief provided under the JCPOA affects secondary sanctions").

58 Cyril T. Brennan, *U.S. Withdrawal from Iran Nuclear Deal to Trigger Additional Sanctions*, Greenberg Traurig (May 9, 2018), www.gtlaw.com/en/insights/2018/5/us-withdrawal-from-iran-nuclear-deal-to-trigger-additional-sanctions ("[f]or practical purposes, the effect of the JCPOA on 'primary' sanctions imposed by the United States on Iran was relatively minor").

59 Mark Landler, *Trump Abandons Iran Nuclear Deal He Long Scorned*, New York Times (May 8, 2018), www.nytimes.com/2018/05/08/world/middleeast/trump-iran-nuclear-deal.html.

60 *Iran's Breaches of the Nuclear Deal*, US Institute of Peace (July 7, 2021), https://iranprimer.usip.org/blog/2019/oct/02/iran%E2%80%99s-breaches-nuclear-deal.

61 *Joint Statement by the Foreign Ministers of France, Germany, and the United Kingdom on the Joint Comprehensive Plan of Action*, France Diplomacy (Jan. 14, 2020), www.diplomatie.gouv.fr/en/country-files/iran/news/article/joint-statement-by-the-foreign-ministers-of-france-germany-and-the-united.

62 Suzanne Maloney, *After the Iran Deal: A Plan B to Contain the Islamic Republic*, Foreign Affairs (Feb. 28, 2023), www.foreignaffairs.com/middle-east/iran-nuclear-deal-plan-b-contain-islamic-republic.

63 *The US Embargo against Cuba: Its Impact on Economic and Social Rights*, Amnesty Int'l (2009), www.amnesty.org/en/wp-content/uploads/2021/08/amr250072009en.pdf.

64 *Cuba Sanctions*, U.S. Department of State (July 23, 2021), www.state.gov/cuba-sanctions/.

65 Jonathan C. Poling, Wynn H. Segall, and Christian C. Davis, *Obama Administration Loosens Restrictions on Cuba Travel and Commerce*, Akin (Jan. 16, 2015), www.akingump.com/en/insights/alerts/obama-administration-loosens-restrictions-on-cuba-travel-and.

66 Matthew Lee and Joshua Goodman, *Trump Hits Cuba with New Sanctions in Waning Days*, PBS (Jan. 11, 2021), www.pbs.org/newshour/politics/trump-hits-cuba-with-new-terror ism-sanctions-in-waning-days.

67 *Biden Administration Measures to Support the Cuban People*, U.S. Department of State (May 16, 2022), www.state.gov/biden-administration-measures-to-support-the-cuban-people/.

68 Christopher Sabatini and Lauren Cornwall, *Boxing Cuba in Benefits No One*, Foreign Policy (Feb. 6, 2022), https://foreignpolicy.com/2022/02/06/cuba-us-relations-isolation-sanc tions/.

69 *UN General Assembly Calls for US to End Cuba Embargo for 29th Consecutive Years*, UN News (June 23, 2021), https://news.un.org/en/story/2021/06/1094612.

70 Zachary Laub, *Syria's Civil War: The Descent into Horror*, Council on Foreign Relations (Mar. 17, 2021), www.cfr.org/article/syrias-civil-war.

71 *Syria Sanctions*, U.S. Department of State (June 14, 2023), www.state.gov/syria-sanctions/.

72 Alexander Orakhelashvili, *The Impact of Unilateral EU Economic Sanctions on the UN Collective Security Framework: The Cases of Iran and Syria*, Economic Sanctions under International Law (2015), at 3–21, https://doi.org/10.1007/978-94-6265-051-0_1.

73 *Syria War: Russia and China Veto Sanctions*, BBC (Feb. 28, 2017), www.bbc.com/news/world-middle-east-39116854.

74 *UN Security Council Resolutions on North Korea*, Arms Control Ass'n (last updated Jan. 2022), www.armscontrol.org/factsheets/UN-Security-Council-Resolutions-on-North-Korea.

75 Seung-Ho Jung, *Effects of Economic Sanctions on North Korea-China Trade: A Dynamic Panel Analysis*, 29 Seoul Journal of Economics 481 (2016), http://sje.ac.kr/xml/26523/26523 .pdf.

76 Stephan Haggard and Marcus Noland, *North Korea's Foreign Economic Relations*, 8 Int'l Relations of the Asia-Pacific 219 (2008), www.jstor.org/stable/26159484.

77 Samantha Beech, *China and Russia Veto New UN Sanctions against North Korea for First Time since 2006*, CNN (May 27, 2022), www.cnn.com/2022/05/26/asia/us-north-korea-united-nations-intl-hnk/index.html.

78 *Publication of a Fact Sheet on the Provision of Humanitarian Assistance and Trade to Combat COVID-19*, U.S. Department of the Treasury (Apr. 16, 2020), https://home .treasury.gov/policy-issues/financial-sanctions/recent-actions/20200416.

79 *Trade Sanctions Reform and Enhancement Act of 2000 (TSRA) Program Information*, U.S. Department of the Treasury (Dec. 22, 2016), https://ofac.treasury.gov/ofac-license-applica tion-page/trade-sanctions-reform-and-export-enhancement-act-of-2000-tsra-program/trade-sanctions-reform-and-export-enhancement-act-of-2000-tsra-program-information.

80 Kenneth Katzman, *Iran Sanctions*, Congressional Research Service (last updated Feb. 2, 2022), https://sgp.fas.org/crs/mideast/RS20871.pdf.

81 *NIAC and 42 Other Organizations Urge Biden to Provide Humanitarian Relief to Iran*, National Iranian American Council Action (Apr. 21, 2022), www.niacouncil.org/news/ joint-humanitarian-letter/?locale=en.

82 *April 28 Letter to President Biden*, National Iranian American Council (Apr. 28, 2022), www.niacouncil.org/news/panel-asses-civilian-impact-of-broad-sanctions/; *Parties to*

Yemen Conflict Must Set Differences aside, Move towards Lasting Political Settlement, Special Envoy, Other Officials Tell Security Council, UN Security Council 8525th Meeting (AM), Meetings Coverage (May 15, 2019), https://press.un.org/en/2019/sc13809 .doc.htm.

83 Mona Yacoubin, *How Will New U.S. Sanctions Impact Syria's Conflict?* U.S. Institute of Peace (June 17, 2020), www.usip.org/publications/2020/06/how-will-new-us-sanctions-impact-syrias-conflict.

84 Mary Ellen O'Connell, *Debating the Law of Sanctions,* 13 European Journal of International Law 63, 69–70 (2002), https://academic.oup.com/ejil/article/13/1/63/417876.

85 Paolo Spadoni, Failed Sanctions: Why the U.S. Embargo against Cuba Could Never Work (2010).

86 Bruce D. McDonald III and Vincent Reitano, *Sanction Failure: Economic Growth, Defense Expenditures, and the Islamic Republic of Iran,* 42 Armed Forces & Society 635, 636 (2016), www.jstor.org/stable/48669897.

87 Richard Haas, *Economic Sanctions: Too Much of a Bad Thing,* Brookings (June 1, 1998), www.brookings.edu/research/economic-sanctions-too-much-of-a-bad-thing/.

88 Gary Clyde Hufbauer et al., Economic Sanctions Reconsidered (3rd ed. 2009), at 6.

89 Ioana M. Petrescu, *Rethinking Economic Sanction Success: Sanctions as Deterrents,* Working Paper, American Enterprise Institute (2010), at 1, www.semanticscholar.org/ paper/Rethinking-Economic-Sanction-Success%3A-Sanctions-as-Petrescu/8e6aad96d c3ae5cb77c3ff1670e68fe92d3ad281, citing J. Galtung, *On the Effects of Int'l Economic Sanctions: With Examples from the Case of Rhodesia,* 19 World Politics 378 (1967).

90 Joseph Hanlon, *Successes and Future Prospects of Sanctions against South Africa,* 47 Rev. Afr. Pol. Econ. 84 (1990), www.tandfonline.com/doi/abs/10.1080/03056249008703849.

91 Dursun Peksen, *Better or Worse? The Effect of Economic Sanctions on Human Rights,* 46 J. Peace Research 59 (2009), www.jstor.org/stable/27640799.

92 Daniel Treisman, *Why Putin Took Crimea: The Gambler in the Kremlin,* 95 Foreign Affairs 47 (2016), www.foreignaffairs.com/articles/ukraine/2016-04-18/why-russian-presi dent-putin-took-crimea-from-ukraine.

93 *Blocking Property of Certain Persons and Prohibiting Certain Transactions with Respect to the Crimea Region of Ukraine,* Executive Order 13,685, 79 Fed. Reg. 77,357(Dec. 19, 2014), www.federalregister.gov/documents/2014/12/24/2014-30323/blocking-property-of-cer tain-persons-and-prohibiting-certain-transactions-with-respect-to-the-crimea.

94 Dianne E. Rennack and Cory Welt, *U.S. Sanctions on Russia: An Overview,* Congressional Research Service (last updated Sept. 1, 2021), https://sgp.fas.org/crs/row/ IF10779.pdf.

95 Claire Mills, *Sanctions against Russia,* UK Parliament House of Commons Library (Apr. 28, 2022), https://commonslibrary.parliament.uk/research-briefings/cbp-9481/.

96 *MH17 Crash: Passengers Were Unlawfully Killed, Coroner Concludes,* BBC (July 1, 2022), www.bbc.com/news/uk-england-62014068.

97 *MH17 Crash: MEPs Call for Solidarity with Ukraine and Sanctions against Russia,* European Parliament Press Release (July 22, 2014), www.europarl.europa.eu/news/en/ press-room/20140722IPR53223/mh17-crash-meps-call-for-solidarity-with-ukraine-and-sanc tions-against-russia.

98 Rowena Mason, *MH17 Crash: Sanctions against Russia Are Illegal, Ambassador Claims*, The Guardian (July 24, 2014), www.theguardian.com/world/2014/jul/24/malaysia-airlines-flight-mh17-russia.

99 Alex Horton, *The Magnitsky Act, Explained*, Washington Post (July 14, 2017), www .washingtonpost.com/news/the-fix/wp/2017/07/14/the-magnitsky-act-explained/.

100 *Magnitsky v. Russia*, Open Society Justice Initiative (Feb. 12, 2014), www.justiceinitiative .org/litigation/magnitsky-v-russia.

101 *Russia and Moldova Jackson-Vanik Repeal and Sergei Magnitsky Rule of Law Accountability Act of 2012*, Public Law 112-208, 112th Congress (2012), www.govinfo.gov/content/pkg/PLAW-112publ208/html/PLAW-112publ208.htm.

102 Committee on Legal Affairs and Human Rights, *Refusing Impunity for the Killers of Sergei Magnitsky*, Parliamentary Assembly of the Council of Europe (Nov. 18, 2013), https://assembly.coe.int/nw/xml/XRef/Xref-XML2HTML-en.asp?fileid=20084& lang=en.

103 Bill Browder, Red Notice: A True Story of High Finance, Murder, and One Man's Fight for Justice (2015); Bill Browder, Freezing Order: A True Story of Money Laundering, Murder, and Surviving Vladimir Putin's Wrath (2022).

104 The US Global Magnitsky Act, passed in 2016, would allow sanctions on human rights abusers around the world.

105 All Things Considered, *Russian Ban on U.S. Adoptions Becomes Embroiled in Trump Controversy*, NPR (July 20, 2017), www.npr.org/2017/07/20/538370632/russian-ban-on-u-s-adoptions-becomes-embroiled-in-trump-controversy.

106 Abigail Abrams, *Here's What We Know So Far about Russia's 2016 Meddling*, Time (Apr. 18, 2019), https://time.com/5565991/russia-influence-2016-election/.

107 *Exposing Russia's Effort to Sow Discord Online: The Internet Research Agency and Advertisements*, U.S. House of Representatives Permanent Select Committee on Intelligence, https://intelligence.house.gov/social-media-content/.

108 Countering America's Adversaries through Sanctions Act, P.L. 115-44, www.congress.gov/bill/115th-congress/house-bill/3364/text; Summary: H.R. 3364 – 115th Congress (2017–18), www.congress.gov/bill/115th-congress/house-bill/3364; Part 2, Peter Jeydel et al., *A Detailed Look at the Countering America's Adversaries through Sanctions Act*, Steptoe (Aug. 10, 2017), www.steptoe.com/en/news-publications/a-detailed-look-at-the-countering-america-s-adversaries-through-sanctions-act.html.

109 Directives 1 and 2 under Exec. Order 13,662 (Sept. 12, 2014), U.S. Department of the Treasury, https://ofac.treasury.gov/media/8686/download?inline and https://ofac.treasury .gov/media/8701/download?inline.

110 FAQ 370, U.S. Department of the Treasury (Nov. 28, 2017), https://ofac.treasury.gov/faqs/370.

111 *Treasury Sanctions Russian Cyber Actors for Interference with the 2016 U.S. Elections and Malicious Cyber-Attacks*, U.S. Department of the Treasury (Mar. 15, 2018), https://home .treasury.gov/news/press-releases/sm0312.

112 Josephine Wolff, *How the NotPetya Attack Is Reshaping Cyber Insurance*, Brookings Tech Stream (Dec. 1, 2021), www.brookings.edu/techstream/how-the-notpetya-attack-is-reshaping-cyber-insurance/; Aparna Banarjea, *NotPetya: How a Russian Malware Created the World's Worst Cyberattack Ever*, Business Standard (Aug. 27, 2018), www.business-

standard.com/article/technology/notpetya-how-a-russian-malware-created-the-world-s-worst-cyberattack-ever-118082700261_1.html.

113 *Treasury Sanctions Russia with Sweeping New Sanctions Authority*, U.S. Department of the Treasury (Apr. 15, 2021), https://home.treasury.gov/news/press-releases/jy0127; Christine Abely, Ransomware, Cyber Sanctions, and the Problem of Timing, 63 B.C. L. Rev. E.Supp. I. 47 (2022), https://lira.bc.edu/work/ns/cc2cbdac-1528-41ae-b9ed-192d9f2a454b.

114 *Imposing Sanctions on Russia for the Poisoning and Imprisonment of Alexei Navalny*, U.S. Department of State (Mar. 2, 2021), www.state.gov/imposing-sanctions-on-russia-for-the-poisoning-and-imprisonment-of-aleksey-navalny/; Global Human Rights Sanctions Regime: EU Sanctions Four People Responsible for Serious Human Rights Violations in Russia, Council of the European Union (Mar. 2, 2021), www.consilium.europa.eu/en/press/press-releases/2021/03/02/global-human-rights-sanctions-regime-eu-sanctions-four-people-responsible-for-serious-human-rights-violations-in-russia/.

115 *Russian Spy: What Happened to Sergei and Yulia Skripal?*, BBC (Sept. 27, 2018), www.bbc.com/news/uk-43643025; Michael Schwirtz and Ellen Barry, A *Spy Story: Sergei Skripal Was a Little Fish. He Had a Big Enemy*, New York Times (Sept. 9, 2018), www.nytimes.com/2018/09/09/world/europe/sergei-skripal-russian-spy-poisoning.html.

116 *Russia Responsible for Navalny Poisoning, Rights Experts Say*, UN News (Mar. 2021), https://news.un.org/en/story/2021/03/1086012; *Second Anniversary of the Poisoning of Aleksey Navalny*, U.S. Department of State (Aug. 20, 2022), www.state.gov/second-anniversary-of-the-poisoning-of-aleksey-navalny/.

117 Dianne E. Rennack and Cory Welt, *Russia: The Navalny Poisoning, Chemical Weapons Use, and U.S. Sanctions*, Congressional Research Service (Apr. 26, 2021), https://crsreports.congress.gov/product/pdf/IF/IF11872.

118 *Russia: Implementation of Chemical and Biological Weapon Control and Warfare Elimination Act of 1991 (CBW Act) Sanctions*, 86 Fed. Reg. 14,689 (Mar. 18, 2021), www.federalregister.gov/documents/2021/03/18/2021-05488/russia-implementation-of-chemical-and-biological-weapons-control-and-warfare-elimination-act-of-1991; *Imposition of Additional Sanctions on Russia Under the Chemical and Biological Weapons Control and Warfare Elimination Act of 1991*, 86 Fed. Reg. 50,203 (Sept. 7, 2021), www.federalregister.gov/documents/2021/09/07/2021-19117/imposition-of-additional-sanctions-on-russia-under-the-chemical-and-biological-weapons-control-and.

119 Jarrett Blanc and Andrew S. Weiss, *US Sanctions on Russia: Congress Should Go Back to Fundamentals*, Carnegie Endowment for International Peace (Apr. 2019), https://carnegieendowment.org/files/Blanc_and_Weiss_Russia_Sanctions_v2.pdf.

120 Daniel P. Ahn and Rodney Ludema, *Measuring Smartness: Understanding the Economic Impact of Targeted Sanctions*, U.S. Department of State Working Paper 2017-01, 8, www.state.gov/wp-content/uploads/2018/12/Measuring-Smartness-Understanding-the-Economic-Impact-of-Targeted-Sanctions-1.pdf.

121 31 C.F.R. Part 589.

122 31 C.F.R. § 589.215.

123 Andrew Dornbierer, *Working Paper 42: From Sanctions to Confiscation while Upholding the Rule of Law*, Basel Institute on Governance (Feb. 2023), https://baselgovernance.org/sites/default/files/2023–03/230309%20Working%20Paper%2042.pdf.

124 *UK Financial Sanctions: General Guidance for Financial Sanctions under the Sanctions and Anti-Money Laundering Act 2018*, Office of Financial Sanctions Implementation HM Treasury, at 9 (Aug. 2022), https://assets.publishing.service.gov.uk/government/uploads/system/uploads/attachment_data/file/1144893/General_Guidance_-_UK_Financial_Sanctions__Aug_2022_.pdf.

125 *Russia Extended Food Import Ban through End 2021*, U.S. Department of Agriculture (Dec. 21, 2020), www.fas.usda.gov/data/russia-russia-extended-food-import-ban-through-end-2021.

126 Viljar Veebel, *The Bust, the Boom and the Sanctions in Trade Relations with Russia*, 11 J. of Int'l Studies 9 (2018), www.jois.eu/?394,en_the-bust-the-boom-and-the-sanctions-in-trade-relations-with-russia.

127 Edward Fishman, *Even Smarter Sanctions: How to Fight in the Era of Economic Warfare*, 96 For. Aff. 102, 104 (2017), www.foreignaffairs.com/united-states/even-smarter-sanctions.

128 Roman Solchanyk, *Ukraine, The (Former) Center, Russia, and "Russia,"* 25 Stud. in Comp. Communism 31 (Mar. 1992).

129 *The December 1, 1991 Referendum/Presidential Election in Ukraine*, Commission on Security and Cooperation in Europe (1992), www.csce.gov/sites/helsinkicommission.house.gov/files/120191UkraineReferendum.pdf.

130 *The Golden Age of Kyvian Rus´*, Harvard University Ukrainian Research Institute (Dec. 25, 2021), https://gis.huri.harvard.edu/golden-age-kyivan-rus.

131 Fiona Hill and Angela Stent, *The World Putin Wants: How Distortions about the Past Feed Delusions about the Future*, 101 Foreign Affairs 108, 111 (2022), www.foreignaffairs.com/russian-federation/world-putin-wants-fiona-hill-angela-stent.

132 Vladimir Putin, On the Historical Unity of Russians and Ukrainians (Jul. 12, 2021).

133 Timothy Snyder, *Ukraine Holds the Future: The War between Democracy and Nihilism*, 101 Foreign Affairs 124, 135 (2022), www.foreignaffairs.com/ukraine/ukraine-war-democracy-nihilism-timothy-snyder.

134 *1991–2022: Ukraine's Struggle for Independence in Russia's Shadow*, Council on Foreign Relations, Council of Foreign Relations (last updated Apr. 12, 2023), www.cfr.org/timeline/ukraines-struggle-independence-russias-shadow.

135 Rajan Menon and Eugene Rumer, Conflict in Ukraine (2015), at 34.

136 Peter Dickinson, *How Ukraine's Orange Revolution Shaped Twenty-First Century Geopolitics*, Atlantic Council (Nov. 22, 2020), www.atlanticcouncil.org/blogs/ukrainealert/how-ukraines-orange-revolution-shaped-twenty-first-century-geopolitics/.

137 Leon Gussow, *Yushchenko, Victim of Dioxin Poisoning, Faces Years of Treatment*, Emergency Medicine News (Feb. 2005), https://journals.lww.com/em-news/fulltext/2005/02000/yushchenko,_victim_of_dioxin_poisoning,_faces.22.aspx; *2,3,7,8-Tetracholorodibenzo-p-dioxin (TCDD) Poisoning in Victor Yushchenko: Identification and Measurement of TCDD Metabolites*, The Lancet (Aug. 5, 2009), www.thelancet.com/journals/lancet/article/PIIS0140-6736(09)60912-0/fulltext.

138 Stuart Ramsay, *Poisoned Ex-Ukrainian President: "I Know What Putin Fears,"* Sky News (Mar. 28, 2018), https://news.sky.com/story/ex-ukraine-leader-do-not-rule-out-military-action-against-russia-11306185.

139 Nathaniel Copsey and Natalia Shapovalova, *The Ukrainian Presidential Election of 2010*, 46 J. Representative Democracy 211, www.tandfonline.com/doi/abs/10.1080/00344893.2010.485842?journalCode=rrep20.

140 Romain Houeix, *From the Maidan Protests to Russia's Invasion: Eight Years of Conflict in Ukraine*, France24 (Feb. 28, 2022), www.france24.com/en/europe/20220228-from-the-maidan-protests-to-russia-s-invasion-eight-years-of-conflict-in-ukraine; *Analysis: Russia's Carrot-and-Stick Battle for Ukraine*, BBC (Dec. 17, 2013), www.bbc.com/news/world-europe-25401179.

141 *Ukraine Protests after Yanukovych EU Deal Rejection*, BBC (Nov. 30, 2013), www.bbc.com/news/world-europe-25162563.

142 *What Did Ukraine's Revolution in 2014 Achieve?*, Economist (Feb. 16, 2022), www.economist.com/the-economist-explains/2022/02/16/what-did-ukraines-revolution-in-2014-achieve; Andrey Kurkov, *Ukraine's Revolution: Making Sense of a Year of Chaos*, BBC (Nov. 21, 2014), www.bbc.com/news/world-europe-30131108.

143 Andrew Higgins and Andrew E. Kramer, *Ukraine Leader Was Defeated Even before He Was Ousted*, New York Times (Jan. 3, 2015), www.nytimes.com/2015/01/04/world/europe/ukraine-leader-was-defeated-even-before-he-was-ousted.html.

144 Alan Taylor, *Ukraine's President Voted Out, Flees Kiev*, The Atlantic (Feb. 22, 2014), www.theatlantic.com/photo/2014/02/ukraines-president-voted-out-flees-kiev/100686/.

145 *Ukraine Crimea: Rival Rallies Confront One Another*, BBC (Feb. 26, 2014), www.bbc.com/news/world-europe-26354705; Andrew Higgins and Steven Lee Myers, *As Putin Orders Drills in Crimea, Protestors' Clash Shows Region's Divide*, The New York Times (Feb. 26, 2014), www.nytimes.com/2014/02/27/world/europe/russia.html.

146 Harriet Salem et al., *Crimean Parliament Seized by Unknown Pro-Russian Gunmen*, The Guardian (Feb. 27, 2014), www.theguardian.com/world/2014/feb/27/crimean-parliament-seized-by-unknown-pro-russian-gunmen.

147 Alissa de Carbonnel and Alessandra Prentice, *Armed Men Seize Two Airports in Ukraine's Crimea, Yanukovich Reappears*, Reuters (Feb. 27, 2014), www.reuters.com/article/cnews-us-ukraine-crisis-idCABREA1Q1E820140228.

148 Wojchiech Kononczuk, *Russia's Real Aims in Crimea*, Carnegie Endowment for International Peace (Mar. 13, 2014), https://carnegieendowment.org/2014/03/13/russia-s-real-aims-in-crimea-pub-54914.

149 Bill Chappell and Mark Memmott, *Putin Says Those Are Not Russian Forces in Crimea*, NPR (Mar. 4, 2014), www.npr.org/sections/thetwo-way/2014/03/04/285653335/putin-says-those-arent-russian-forces-in-crimea; *Putin Admits Russian Forces Were Deployed to Crimea*, Reuters (Apr. 17, 2014), www.reuters.com/article/russia-putin-crimea/putin-admits-russian-forces-were-deployed-to-crimea-idUSL6N0N921H20140417; Carl Schreck, *From 'Not Us' to 'Why Hide It?': How Russia Denied Its Crimea Invasion, Then Admitted It*, RadioFreeEurope RadioLiberty (Feb. 26, 2019), www.rferl.org/a/from-not-us-to-why-hide-it-how-russia-denied-its-crimea-invasion-then-admitted-it/29791806.html.

150 *Crimea Overwhelmingly Supports Split from Ukraine to Join Russia*, NPR (Mar. 16, 2014), www.npr.org/sections/thetwo-way/2014/03/16/290525623/crimeans-vote-on-splitting-from-ukraine-to-join-russia.

151 Steven Pifer, *Five Years after Crimea's Illegal Annexation, the Issue Is No Closer to Resolution*, Brookings (Mar. 18, 2019), www.brookings.edu/blog/order-from-chaos/2019/03/18/five-years-after-crimeas-illegal-annexation-the-issue-is-no-closer-to-resolution/.

152 *Crimea Referendum: Voters "Back Russia Union"*, BBC (Mar. 16, 2014), www.bbc.com/news/world-europe-26606097.

153 Treisman, note 92.

154 Steven Lee Myers and Ellen Barry, *Putin Reclaims Crimea for Russia and Bitterly Denounces the West*, New York Times (Mar. 18, 2014), www.nytimes.com/2014/03/19/world/europe/ukraine.html.

155 *Where Is the G7 Headed?*, Council on Foreign Relations (last updated June 28, 2022), www.cfr.org/backgrounder/where-g7-headed; Jim Acosta, *U.S., Other Powers Kick Russia out of G8*, CNN (Mar. 24, 2014), www.cnn.com/2014/03/24/politics/obama-europe-trip/index.html.

156 *The Illegal Annexation of Crimea Has No Legal Effect and Is Not Recognized by the Council of Europe*, Parliamentary Assembly (Apr. 9, 2014), https://pace.coe.int/en/news/4975/the-illegal-annexation-of-crimea-has-no-legal-effect-and-is-not-recognised-by-the-council-of-europe.

157 *Statement by the Press Secretary on Ukraine* The White House (Mar. 16, 2014), https://obamawhitehouse.archives.gov/the-press-office/2014/03/16/statement-press-secretary-ukraine.

158 Nicole Beland Aandahl, *The Struggle for Ukrainian Self-Determination and Identity*, Center for Strategic and International Studies (Mar. 2, 2022), www.csis.org/analysis/struggle-ukrainian-self-determination-and-identity.

159 Joe Hernandez, *Why Luhansk and Donetsk Are Key to Understanding the Latest Escalation in Ukraine*, NPR (Feb. 22, 2022), www.npr.org/2022/02/22/1082345068/why-luhansk-and-donetsk-are-key-to-understanding-the-latest-escalation-in-ukrain; Sammy Westfall and Claire Parker, *What Is Ukraine's Donbas Region a Target for Russian Forces?*, Washington Post (Apr. 20, 2022), www.washingtonpost.com/world/2022/02/21/what-is-donbas-donetsk-luhansk-conflict/; Vladimir Isachenkov, *EXPLAINER: The Story behind Ukraine's Separatist Regions*, AP News (Feb. 21, 2022), https://apnews.com/article/russia-ukraine-europe-russia-vladimir-putin-moscow-bcdoc04a2aa146e76b7e757f482f27bb.

160 Neuman, Scott, *Ukraine Approves EU Pact and Temporary Self-Rule for Rebels*, NPR (Sept. 16, 2014), www.npr.org/sections/thetwo-way/2014/09/16/348943657/ukraine-approves-eu-pact-and-temporary-self-rule-for-rebels.

161 *NATO-Ukraine Relations*, NATO (Feb. 2022), www.nato.int/nato_static_fl2014/assets/pdf/2022/2/pdf/220214-factsheet_NATO-Ukraine_Relations_.pdf.

162 Cory Welt, *Ukraine: Background, Conflict with Russia, and U.S. Policy*, Congressional Research Service (last updated Oct. 5, 2021), https://crsreports.congress.gov/product/pdf/R/R45008/14; *Ukraine President Signs Constitutional Amendment on NATO, EU Membership*, RadioFreeEurope RadioLiberty (Feb. 19, 2019), www.rferl.org/a/ukraine-president-signs-constitutional-amendment-on-nato-eu-membership/29779430.html.

163 Steven Pifer, *One. More. Time. It's Not about NATO*, Brookings (July 26, 2022), www.brookings.edu/opinions/one-more-time-its-not-about-nato/.

164 *Ukraine Election: Comedian Zelensky Wins Presidency by Landslide*, BBC (Apr. 22, 2019), www.bbc.com/news/world-europe-48007487.

165 Isabelle Khurshudyan et al., *On Ukraine's Doorstep, Russia Boosts Military and Sends Message of Regional Clout to Biden*, Washington Post (Apr. 10, 2021), www.washingtonpost.com/world/europe/russia-ukraine-military-biden-donbas/2021/04/09/99859490-96d3-11eb-8f0a-3384cf4fb399_story.html.

166 Paul Sonne et al., *Russian Troop Movements on Ukraine Border Prompt Concern in U.S., Europe*, Washington Post (Oct. 30, 2021), www.washingtonpost.com/world/russian-troop-movements-near-ukraine-border-prompt-concern-in-us-europe/2021/10/30/c122e57c-3983-11ec-9662-399cfa75efee_story.html.

167 Frank Gardner, *Ukraine: Satellite Images Show Russian Military Activity*, BBC (Feb. 17, 2022), www.bbc.com/news/world-europe-60421378.

168 Michael R. Gordon et al., *Putin's 20-Year March to War in Ukraine – and How the West Mishandled It*, WSJ (Apr. 1, 2022), www.wsj.com/articles/vladimir-putins-20-year-march-to-war-in-ukraineand-how-the-west-mishandled-it-11648826461.

169 *Background Press Call by Senior Administration Officials on Russia Ukraine Economic Deterrence Measures*, The White House (Jan. 25, 2022), www.whitehouse.gov/briefing-room/statements-releases/2022/01/25/background-press-call-by-senior-administration-officials-on-russia-ukraine-economic-deterrence-measures/; *Remarks by Vice President Harris at the Munich Security Conference*, The White House (Feb. 19, 2022), www.whitehouse.gov/briefing-room/speeches-remarks/2022/02/19/remarks-by-vice-president-harris-at-the-munich-security-conference/.

170 *Scholz Stresses Ukraine Support, but No Weapons*, DW (Feb. 14, 2022), www.dw.com/en/germanys-scholz-stresses-ukraine-support-but-no-weapons-during-kyiv-visit/a-60771248; *"We Do Not Want War in Europe" Putin Tells Germany's Scholz*, DW (Feb. 15, 2022), www.dw.com/en/ukraine-crisis-we-dont-want-war-in-europe-putin-says-in-talks-with-scholz/a-60785295.

CHAPTER 2 INVASION: THE FIRST WEEK

1 *Extracts from Putin's Speech on Ukraine*, Reuters (Feb. 21, 2022), www.reuters.com/world/europe/extracts-putins-speech-ukraine-2022-02-21.

2 Chad P. Bown, *Russia's War on Ukraine: A Sanctions Timeline*, PIIE (Mar. 23, 2023), www.piie.com/blogs/realtime-economics/russias-war-ukraine-sanctions-timeline.

3 Andrew Roth, *Putin Orders Troops into Eastern Ukraine on "Peacekeeping Duties,"* The Guardian (Feb. 21, 2022), www.theguardian.com/world/2022/feb/21/ukraine-putin-decide-recognition-breakaway-states-today.

4 Edward Wong and Julian E. Barnes, *China Asked Russia to Delay Ukraine War Until after the Olympics, U.S. Officials Say*, New York Times (Mar. 2, 2022), www.nytimes.com/2022/03/02/us/politics/russia-ukraine-china.html.

5 *Putin Orders Troops to Separatist Regions and Recognizes Their Independence*, New York Times (Feb. 21, 2022), www.nytimes.com/live/2022/02/21/world/ukraine-russia-putin-biden#moscow-orders-troops-to-ukraines-breakaway-regions-for-peacekeeping-functions.

6 Valerie Hopkins, *Highlights from Putin's Address on Breakaway Regions in Ukraine*, New York Times (Feb. 21, 2022), www.nytimes.com/2022/02/21/world/europe/putin-speech-transcript.html.

7 Michael D. Shear and David E. Sanger, *U.S. Offers Limited Initial Response to Russia as It Weighs Stiffer Sanctions*, New York Times (Feb. 21, 2022), www.nytimes.com/2022/02/21/us/politics/russia-ukraine-biden-response.html.

8 *Blocking Property of Certain Persons and Prohibiting Certain Transactions With Respect to Continued Russian Efforts to Undermine the Sovereignty and Territorial Integrity of Ukraine*, Exec. Order 14,065, 87 Fed. Reg. 10,293 (Feb. 21, 2022), www.federalregister.gov/documents/2022/02/23/2022-04020/blocking-property-of-certain-persons-and-prohibiting-certain-transactions-with-respect-to-continued.

9 Sywia A. Lis et al., *US Government Imposes Comprehensive Sanctions on So-Called Donetsk People's Republic and Luhansk People's Republic and EU and UK Announce Plans to*

Impose New Sanctions Related to Same Regions, Baker McKenzie Sanctions & Export Controls Update (Feb. 22, 2022), https://sanctionsnews.bakermckenzie.com/us-government-imposes-comprehensive-sanctions-on-so-called-donetsk-peoples-republic-and-luhansk-peoples-republic-and-eu-and-uk-announce-plans-to-impose-new-sanctions-related-to-same/.

10 *FACT SHEET: Executive Order to Impose Costs for President Putin's Action to Recognize So-Called Donetsk and Luhansk People's Republics*, The White House (Feb. 21, 2022), www.whitehouse.gov/briefing-room/statements-releases/2022/02/21/fact-sheet-execu tive-order-to-impose-costs-for-president-putins-action-to-recognize-so-called-donetsk-and-lu hansk-peoples-republics/.

11 *Ukraine's Territorial Integrity: EU Sanctions Five Persons Involved in the Russian State Duma Elections of September 2021 in Illegally-Annexed Crimea*, Council of the E.U. (Feb. 21, 2022), www.consilium.europa.eu/en/press/press-releases/2022/02/21/ukraine-s-terri torial-integrity-eu-targets-five-more-individuals-with-restrictive-measures/.

12 William James and Alistair Smout, *Britain Prepares Russia Sanctions, Says Ukraine Invasion Could Be Imminent*, Reuters (Feb. 21, 2022), www.reuters.com/world/europe/putins-recogni tion-breakaway-ukraine-regions-is-clear-break-international-law-2022-02-21/.

13 *Conflict in Ukraine Must Be Averted "at All Costs", Political Affairs Chief Tells Security Council as Delegates Reject Moscow's Recognition of Donetsk, Luhansk*, United Nations Meetings Coverage and Press Releases (Feb. 21, 2022), https://press.un.org/en/2022/sc14798 .doc.htm.

14 *Remarks by President Biden Announcing Response to Russian Actions in Ukraine*, The White House (Feb. 22, 2022), www.whitehouse.gov/briefing-room/speeches-remarks/2022/02/22/ remarks-by-president-biden-announcing-response-to-russian-actions-in-ukraine/.

15 Maureen Chowdhury et al., *February 22, 2022 Ukraine-Russia Crisis News*, CNN (Feb. 23, 2022), www.cnn.com/europe/live-news/ukraine-russia-news-02-22-22/index.html; Joseph Choi, *Australia, Canada, Japan, Impose Sanctions on Russia over Ukraine Crisis*, The Hill (Feb. 22, 2022), https://thehill.com/policy/international/595427-australia-canada-and-japan-impose-sanctions-on-russia-over-ukraine/. Morrison spoke on Wednesday in Australia; the news was reported in other parts of the world when it was still Tuesday in some time zones.

16 *PM Statement on the Situation in Ukraine: 22 February 2022*, Government of the United Kingdom (Feb. 22, 2022), www.gov.uk/government/speeches/pm-statement-on-the-situ ation-in-ukraine-22-february-2022.

17 David McHugh, *EXPLAINER: What Is the Russia-Europe Nord Stream 2 Pipeline?*, ABC (Feb. 22, 2022), https://abcnews.go.com/Business/wireStory/explainer-nord-stream-pipe line-83039880.

18 Zia Weise, *Germany Shelves Nord Stream 2 Pipeline*, Politico (Feb. 22, 2022), www.politico .eu/article/germany-to-stop-nord-stream-2/; *Nord Stream 2: How Does the Pipeline Fit into the Ukraine-Russia Crisis?*, BBC (Feb. 22, 2022), www.bbc.com/news/world-europe-60131520.

19 Paul Belkin, Michael Ratner, and Cory Welt, *Russia's Nord Stream 2 Natural Gas Pipeline to Germany Halted*, Congressional Research Service (last updated Mar. 10, 2022), https:// crsreports.congress.gov/product/pdf/IF/IF11138.

20 Holly Ellyat, *Germany Halts Approval of Gas Pipeline Nord Stream 2 after Russia's Actions*, CNBC (Feb. 22, 2022), www.cnbc.com/2022/02/22/germany-halts-certification-of-nord-stream-2-amid-russia-ukraine-crisis.html.

21 Mari Dugas, *Early Edition: February 23, 2022*, Just Security (Feb. 23, 2022), www
.justsecurity.org/80336/early-edition-february-23-2022/.

22 OFAC, *U.S. Treasury Imposes Immediate Economic Costs in Response to Actions in the Donetsk and Luhansk Regions*, U.S. Department of the Treasury (Feb. 22, 2022), https://
home.treasury.gov/news/press-releases/jy0602.

23 *Id.*

24 *Id.*

25 *UK Hits Russian Oligarchs and Bank with Targeted Sanctions: Foreign Secretary's Statement*, Government of the United Kingdom (Feb. 22, 2022), www.gov.uk/government/news/uk-hits-russian-oligarchs-and-banks-with-targeted-sanctions-foreign-secretary-statement.

26 *Prohibitions Related to Certain Sovereign Debt of the Russian Federation*, Directive 1A under Executive Order 14,024 (Feb. 22, 2022), https://ofac.treasury.gov/media/918731/down
load?inline.

27 *Id.*

28 *Remarks by President Biden Announcing Response to Russian Actions in Ukraine*, The White House (Feb. 22, 2022), www.whitehouse.gov/briefing-room/speeches-remarks/2022/
02/22/remarks-by-president-biden-announcing-response-to-russian-actions-in-ukraine/.

29 *Zelensky's Last-Ditch Plea for Peace*, Foreign Policy (Feb. 23, 2022), https://foreignpolicy
.com/2022/02/23/zelenskys-desperate-plea-for-peace.

30 *Ukraine's Parliament Votes to Declare a State of Emergency after Russia Recognized Two Separatist Regions as Independent*, Reuters (Feb. 23, 2022), https://apnews.com/article/
russia-ukraine-ap-news-alert-europe-russia-6abe535bed46f82a3683d9450c89279c.

31 Emiko Terazono, *Us Wheat Futures in Chicago Hit 10-Year High on Escalating Ukraine Tensions*, The Financial Times (Feb. 23, 2022), www.ft.com/content/e1b56151-1dbb-46od-
90eb-2f55e9e44214.

32 Lauren Feiner, *Cyberattack Hits Ukrainian Banks and Government Websites*, CNBC (Feb. 23, 2022), www.cnbc.com/2022/02/23/cyberattack-hits-ukrainian-banks-and-govern
ment-websites.html; *Update: Destructive Malware Targeting Organizations in Ukraine*, CISA (Apr. 28, 2022), www.cisa.gov/news-events/cybersecurity-advisories/aa22-057a; Dustin Volz, *Malware Detected in Ukraine as Invasion Threat Looms*, Wall Street Journal (Feb. 23, 2022), www.wsj.com/livecoverage/russia-ukraine-latest-news/card/malware-
detected-in-ukraine-as-invasion-threat-looms-NaVfMTy8xov41PyZNuzo.

33 *Statement by President Biden on Nord Stream 2*, The White House (Feb. 23, 2022), www
.whitehouse.gov/briefing-room/statements-releases/2022/02/23/statement-by-president-
biden-on-nord-stream-2/.

34 *Eu Adopts Package of Sanctions in Response to Russian Recognition of the Non-government Controlled Areas of the Donetsk and Luhansk Oblasts of Ukraine and Sending of Troops into the Region*, Council of the European Union (Feb. 23, 2022), www.consilium.europa.eu/en/
press/press-releases/2022/02/23/russian-recognition-of-the-non-government-controlled-areas-
of-the-donetsk-and-luhansk-oblasts-of-ukraine-as-independent-entities-eu-adopts-package-of-
sanctions/.

35 65 Official Journal of the European Union 1, 74 (Feb. 23, 2022), https://eur-lex.europa.eu/
legal-content/EN/TXT/PDF/?uri=OJ:L:2022:042I:FULL&from=EN.

36 *Australia's Response to Russia's Aggression against Ukraine*, Minister for Foreign Affairs (Feb. 23, 2022), www.foreignminister.gov.au/minister/marise-payne/media-release/austra

lias-response-russias-aggression-against-ukraine; these sanctions were announced during Feb. 23 Australia time/Feb. 22 in other time zones

37 Kyodo News, *Japan Imposes Sanctions on Russia and Separatist Regions of Ukraine after Actions by Moscow*, Japan Times (Feb. 23, 2022), www.japantimes.co.jp/news/2022/02/23/national/japan-russia-sanctions/.

38 Vala Hafstað, *Iceland Will Participate in the EU's Sanctions*, Iceland Monitor (Feb. 23, 2022), https://icelandmonitor.mbl.is/news/politics_and_society/2022/02/23/iceland_will_participate_in_the_eu_s_sanctions/.

39 Jill Lawless, *Critics Say Mild UK Sanctions on Russia Do Not Match Promises*, Associated Press News (Feb. 23, 2022), https://apnews.com/article/russia-ukraine-boris-johnson-business-europe-iain-duncan-smith-7015b0b3aa1f94600f64ecf57e5d385f.

40 Liz Truss, *Nothing Is off the Table in Our Response to Putin's Aggression*, The Times (Feb. 23, 2022), www.thetimes.co.uk/article/ukraine-crisis-nothing-is-off-the-table-in-our-response-to-putins-aggression-says-liz-truss-73xwjk8nh.

41 Paul Sonne, *Ukraine's Zelensky to Russians: "What Are You Fighting for and with Whom?"*, Washington Post (Feb. 23, 2022), www.washingtonpost.com/national-security/2022/02/23/ukraine-zelensky-russia-address/; NBC News, *Zelenskyy Makes Plea to Russians in Address on Telegram*, YouTube (Feb. 23, 2022), www.youtube.com/watch?v=OMTeSsnNCwo.

42 *Full Transcript of Zelenskyy's Emotional Appeal to Russians*, Reuters (Feb. 23, 2022), www.nbcnews.com/news/world/full-transcript-zelenskyys-emotional-appeal-russians-rcna17485.

43 *Ukraine: Marital Law Introduced in Response to Russian Invasion*, Library of Congress (Feb. 24, 2022), www.loc.gov/item/global-legal-monitor/2022-03-03/ukraine-martial-law-introduced-in-response-to-russian-invasion/.

44 Sudarsan Raghavan et al., *Explosions Heard in Kyiv as Ukrainian President Says "Enemy Sabotage Groups" Have Entered Capital*, Washington Post (Feb. 24, 2022), www.washingtonpost.com/world/2022/02/24/russia-ukraine-attack-news/.

45 *Full Text: Putin's Declaration of War on Ukraine*, The Spectator (Feb. 24, 2022), www.spectator.co.uk/article/full-text-putin-s-declaration-of-war-on-ukraine/.

46 *President Niinistö: Finland Strongly Condemns Russia's Actions and Warfare*, President of the Republic of Finland (Feb. 24, 2022), www.presidentti.fi/en/news/president-niinisto-finland-strongly-condemns-russias-actions-and-warfare/.

47 *European Council Conclusions on Russia's Unprovoked and Unjustified Military Aggression against Ukraine*, European Council (Feb. 24, 2022), www.consilium.europa.eu/media/54495/st00018-en22.pdf.

48 Henry Smith, *Managing Risks from Russia Sanctions*, 69 Risk Management 4 (2022) ("one of the most striking aspects of the sanctions regimes is the speed at which governments reached clear consensus about imposing the measures, surprising many observers"); Elena Chachko and J. Benton Heath, *A Watershed Moment for Sanctions? Russia, Ukraine, and the Economic Battlefield*, 116 AJIL Unbound 135 (May 23, 2022), www.cambridge.org/core/journals/american-journal-of-international-law/article/watershed-moment-for-sanctions-russia-ukraine-and-the-economic-battlefield/E2220ACE5A008F30C0716796A2198D9A (discussing "the sheer scope, speed, and coordination" of the economic response to Russia's 2022 invasion of Ukraine).

49 Paul James Cardwell and Erica Moret, *The EU, Sanctions and Regional Leadership*, 32 European Security 1, 1, 5 (2023), www.tandfonline.com/doi/pdf/10.1080/09662839.2022.2085997.

50 FACT SHEET: *Joined by Allies and Partners, the United States Imposes Devastating Costs on Russia*, The White House (Feb. 24, 2022), www.whitehouse.gov/briefing-room/state ments-releases/2022/02/24/fact-sheet-joined-by-allies-and-partners-the-united-states-imposes -devastating-costs-on-russia/.

51 Jamie L. Boucher et al., *US, UK and EU Impose Significant Sanctions and Export Controls in Response to Russia's Invasion of Ukraine*, Skadden, Arps, Slate, Meagher & Flom (Feb. 26, 2022), www.skadden.com/insights/publications/2022/02/us-uk-and-eu-impose-significant-sanc tions. *See also* OFAC, *U.S. Treasury Announces Unprecedented & Expansive Sanctions against Russia, Imposing Swift and Severe Economic Costs*, U.S. Department of the Treasury (Feb. 24, 2022), https://home.treasury.gov/news/press-releases/jy0608.

52 *Id.*

53 *Foreign Secretary Imposes UK's Most Punishing Sanctions to Inflict Maximum and Lasting Pain on Russia*, Government of the United Kingdom (Feb. 24, 2022), www.gov.uk/ government/news/foreign-secretary-imposes-uks-most-punishing-sanctions-to-inflict-max imum-and-lasting-pain-on-russia.

54 *U.S. Treasury Announces Unprecedented & Expansive Sanctions Against Russia, Imposing Swift and Severe Economic Costs*, U.S. Department of the Treasury (Feb. 24, 2022), https:// home.treasury.gov/news/press-releases/jy0608.

55 William P. Osterberg and James B. Thomson, *Banking Consolidation and Correspondent Banking*, 1 Economic Review 9–20 (1999), www.researchgate.net/publication/5028936_ Banking_consolidation_and_correspondent_banking; Rena S. Miller, *Overview of Correspondent Banking and "De-Risking,"* Congressional Research Service (Apr. 8, 2022), https://crsreports.congress.gov/product/pdf/IF/IF10873.

56 Committee on Payments and Market Infrastructures, *Correspondent Banking*, Bank for International Settlements (July 2016), www.bis.org/cpmi/publ/d147.pdf.

57 31 C.F.R. § 561.307.

58 *Prohibitions Related to Correspondent or Payable-Through Accounts and Processing of Transactions Involving Certain Foreign Financial Institutions*, Directive 2 under Executive Order 14024 (Feb. 24, 2022), https://ofac.treasury.gov/media/918471/download? inline.

59 Compare Barry E. Carter and Ryan M. Farha, *Overview and Operation of U.S. Financial Sanctions, Including the Example of Iran*, 44 Geo. J. Int'l L. 903, 910 (2012), https:// scholarship.law.georgetown.edu/facpub/1257/.

60 *Id.*

61 *UK Prohibits Russia's Sberbank from Sterling Clearance*, Reuters (Mar. 1, 2022), www .reuters.com/business/finance/uk-prohibits-russias-sberbank-sterling-clearance-2022-03-01/.

62 *U.S. Treasury Announces Unprecedented & Expansive Sanctions Against Russia, Imposing Swift and Severe Economic Costs*, U.S. Department of the Treasury (Feb. 24, 2022), https:// home.treasury.gov/news/press-releases/jy0608; *Prohibitions Related to New Debt and Equity of Certain Russia-Related Entities*, Directive 3 under Executive Order 14024 (Feb. 24, 2022), https://ofac.treasury.gov/media/918476/download?inline.

63 *Commerce Implements Sweeping Restrictions on Exports to Russia in Response to Further Invasion of Ukraine*, U.S. Department of Commerce (Feb. 24, 2022), www.bis.doc.gov/ index.php/documents/about-bis/newsroom/press-releases/2914-2022-02-24-bis-russia-rule-press- release-and-tweets-final/file.

64 *U.S. Treasury Targets Belarusian Support for Russian Invasion of Ukraine*, U.S. Department of the Treasury (Feb. 24, 2022), https://home.treasury.gov/news/press-releases/jy0607.

65 *Canada Denounces Lukashenko's Inauguration in Belarus, Preparing Sanctions over Human Rights Violations*, CBC (Sep. 24, 2020), www.cbc.ca/news/politics/canada-denounces-lukashenko-inauguration-belarus-1.5736840.

66 Council Implementing Regulation (EU) 2020/2129 of 17 Dec. 2020 (Dec. 17, 2020), https://eur-lex.europa.eu/legal-content/EN/TXT/HTML/?uri=OJ:L:2020:426I:FULL&from=EN; *Treasury Expands Sanctions against Belarusian Regime with Partners and Allies*, U.S. Department of the Treasury (Dec. 2, 2021), https://home.treasury.gov/news/press-releases/jy0512; The Republic of Belarus (Sanctions) (EU Exit) (Amendment) (No. 2) Regulations 2021, 2021 No. 1146, www.legislation.gov.uk/uksi/2021/1146/contents/made.

67 Aliaksandr Kudrytski, *Why Belarus Is Backing Russia in Its War in Ukraine*, Bloomberg (Dec. 30, 2022), www.washingtonpost.com/business/energy/why-belarus-is-backing-russia-in-its-war-in-ukraine/2022/12/30/63a74b5a-885a-11ed-b5ac-41128ob122ef_story.html.

68 *UK Imposes Sanctions on Belarus for Its Role in the Russian Invasion of Ukraine*, Government of the United Kingdom (Mar. 1, 2022), www.gov.uk/government/news/uk-imposes-sanctions-on-belarus-for-its-role-in-the-russian-invasion-of-ukraine.

69 *Commerce Imposes Sweeping Export Restrictions on Belarus for Enabling Russia's Further Invasion of Ukraine*, U.S. Department of Commerce (Mar. 2, 2022), www.commerce.gov/news/press-releases/2022/03/commerce-imposes-sweeping-export-restrictions-belarus-enabling-russias.

70 *What Is a License?*, U.S. Department of the Treasury (June 16, 2016), https://ofac.treasury.gov/faqs/topic/1506.

71 Cortney O'Toole Morgan and Grant D. Leach, *New U.S. Sanctions and Export Controls Aim to Impose "Devastating Costs" on Russia*, Husch Blackwell (Feb. 25, 2022), www.huschblackwell.com/newsandinsights/new-us-sanctions-and-export-controls-aim-to-impose-devastating-costs-on-russia.

72 Sofia Diogo Mateus, *Ukrainians Google "How to Make a Molotov Cocktail" after Defense Minister's Call to Arms*, Washington Post (Feb. 25, 2022), www.washingtonpost.com/world/2022/02/25/ukraine-google-molotov-cocktails-resistance-russia/.

73 Sébastian Seibt, *Key Battles in the Ukraine War: From Kyiv's Stand to the Kharkiv Counterattack*, France24 (Feb. 21, 2023), www.france24.com/en/europe/20230221-key-battles-in-the-ukraine-war-from-kyiv-s-stand-to-the-kharkiv-counter-attack; Michael Druckman, *It Is Time for the West to Welcome Ukraine Home*, Atlantic Council (Mar. 5, 2023), www.atlanticcouncil.org/blogs/ukrainealert/it-is-time-for-the-west-to-welcome-ukraine-home/.

74 *Ukraine President Orders General Mobilization*, DW (Feb. 25, 2022), www.dw.com/en/ukraine-president-orders-general-mobilization/a-60908996.

75 *Foreign Affairs Council: Press Remarks by High Representative/Vice-President Josep Borrell upon arrival*, Delegation of the European Union to Serbia (Feb. 25, 2022), www.eeas.europa.eu/eeas/foreign-affairs-council-press-remarks-high-representativevice-president-josep-borrell-upon_en?s=227.

76 Roman Olearchyk, John Reed, Henry Foy, and Demetri Sevastopulo, *Zelensky Urges Ukrainians to Resist as Russian Forces Battle for Kyiv*, Financial Times (Feb. 25, 2022), www.ft.com/content/60170757-2fad-4db9-b959-2fc088cc4bc6.

77 *Explosions Heard in Kyiv, Official Says Enemy Aircraft Downed*, Reuters (Feb. 25, 2022), www.reuters.com/world/europe/explosions-heard-kyiv-official-says-enemy-aircraft-downed-2022-02-25/; Nathan Hodge et al., *Battle for Ukrainian Capital Underway As Explosions Seen and Heard in Kyiv*, CNN (Feb. 25, 2022), www.cnn.com/2022/02/24/europe/ukraine-russia-invasion-friday-intl-hnk/index.html.

78 *Satellite Imagery Shows Queues of Traffic as People Flee Ukraine*, CNN (Feb. 25, 2022), www.cnn.com/europe/live-news/ukraine-russia-news-02-25-22/index.html; *Increased Traffic Observed at Polish Border as Ukrainians Flee*, CNN (Feb. 25, 2022), www.cnn.com/europe/live-news/ukraine-russia-news-02-25-22/h_24945ba0a7b104035a4bb801d6d54d89.

79 *Ukrainian MP: When the Russians Come, "That's When You Get a Gun and You Learn How to Shoot It,"* CNN (Feb. 25, 2022), www.cnn.com/europe/live-news/ukraine-russia-news-02-25-22/index.html.

80 Council Decision (CFSP) 2022/307 of 24 February 2022 (Feb. 24, 2022), https://eur-lex.europa.eu/legal-content/EN/TXT/PDF/?uri=CELEX:32022D0307&qid=1647426657418&from=EN.

81 *Sanctions Adopted Following Russia's Military Aggression against Ukraine*, European Commission (last updated 2023), https://finance.ec.europa.eu/eu-and-world/sanctions-restrictive-measures/sanctions-adopted-following-russias-military-aggression-against-ukraine_en.

82 *U.S. Treasury Imposes Sanctions on Russian President Vladimir Putin and Minister of Foreign Affairs Sergei Lavrov*, U.S. Department of the Treasury (Feb. 25, 2022), https://home.treasury.gov/news/press-releases/jy0610.

83 Leah Ferris, *Sanctions Imposed on Russia in Response to Aggression against Ukraine – How Are They Imposed under Australia's Sanctions Laws?*, Parliament of Australia (Feb. 28, 2022), www.aph.gov.au/About_Parliament/Parliamentary_Departments/Parliamentary_Library/FlagPost/2022/February/Sanctions_on_Russia.

84 Helen Davidson, *"Of Course I Worry": Shock Waves from Ukraine Reach Taiwan*, The Guardian (Feb. 25, 2022), www.theguardian.com/world/2022/feb/25/of-course-i-worry-shockwaves-from-ukraine-reach-taiwan.

85 *China Refrains from Condemning Russia Despite Intensifying Ukraine Attack*, Reuters (Feb. 25, 2022), www.reuters.com/world/china/china-hits-back-biden-assertion-stain-over-ukraine-2022-02-25/.

86 Paul Sonne et al., *Battle for Kyiv: Ukrainian Valor, Russian Blunders Combined to Save The Capital*, Washington Post (Aug. 24, 2022), www.washingtonpost.com/national-security/interactive/2022/kyiv-battle-ukraine-survival/.

87 *Security Council Fails to Adopt Draft Resolution on Ending Ukraine Crisis, as Russian Federation Wields Veto*, United Nations Security Council (Feb. 25, 2022), www.un.org/press/en/2022/sc14808.doc.htm.

88 *Joint Statement Following a Vote on a UN Security Council Resolution on Russia's Aggression*, United States Mission to the United Nations (Feb. 25, 2022), https://usun.usmission.gov/joint-statement-following-a-vote-on-a-un-security-council-resolution-on-russias-aggression-toward-ukraine/.

89 *Secretary-General's Press Remarks Following Security Council Meeting on Ukraine*, UN Secretary-General (Feb. 25, 2022), www.un.org/sg/en/content/sg/press-encounter/2022-02-25/secretary-generals-press-remarks-following-security-council-meeting-ukraine.

90 *Russia's Invasion of Ukraine: List of Key Moments from Day 3*, Aljazeera (Feb. 26, 2022), www.aljazeera.com/news/2022/2/26/russias-invasion-of-ukraine-key-moments-by-day.

91 Josh Campbell and Jonny Hallam, *UK Defense Ministry: Russia's Force "Suffering from Logistical Challenges and Strong Ukrainian Resistance,"* CNN (Feb. 26, 2022), www.cnn .com/europe/live-news/ukraine-russia-news-02-26-22/index.html.

92 Ivana Kottasová, Simone McCarthy, Tara John, and Tim Lister, *Kyiv on Heightened Alert as Russian Forces Close in on All Sides,* CNN (Feb. 26, 2022), www.cnn.com/2022/02/26/ europe/ukraine-russia-invasion-saturday-intl-hnk/index.html.

93 *Id.; Joint Statement on Further Restrictive Economic Measures,* The White House (Feb. 26, 2022), www.whitehouse.gov/briefing-room/statements-releases/2022/02/26/joint-statement-on-further-restrictive-economic-measures/; *Joint Statement on Further Restrictive Economic Measures,* European Commission (Feb. 26, 2022), https://ec .europa.eu/commission/presscorner/detail/en/statement_22_1423.

94 Ramishah Maruf, *Meta and Youtube Block Russian State Media from Monetizing on Its Platforms,* CNN (Feb. 26, 2022), www.cnn.com/2022/02/26/tech/meta-youtube-facebook-rt-demonetize/index.html; Paresh Dave, *Google Blocks Rt, Other Russian Channels from Earning Ad Dollars,* Reuters (Feb. 26, 2022), www.reuters.com/technology/youtube-blocks-rt-other-russian-channels-generating-revenue-2022-02-26/.

95 Shannon Bond, *Facebook and Tiktok Block Russian State Media in Europe,* NPR (Feb. 28, 2022), www.npr.org/2022/02/28/1083633239/facebook-and-tiktok-block-russian-state-media-in-europe; *Youtube Blocks Russian State-Funded Media, Including Rt and Sputnik, around the World,* France24 (Mar. 12, 2022), www.france24.com/en/europe/20220312-youtube-blocks-russian-state-funded-media-including-rt-and-sputnik-around-the-world.

96 *Governor Sununu Bans Sale of Russian Spirits at State Liquor Outlets, Grocery Stores,* WMUR (Feb. 27, 2022), www.wmur.com/article/sununu-executive-order-remove-russian-liquor-liquor-wine-outlets/39239875#.

97 Joseph Pisani, *More U.S. States Say No to Russian Vodka Amid Ukraine Invasion,* Wall Street Journal (Mar. 1, 2022), www.wsj.com/articles/more-u-s-states-say-no-to-russian-vodka-amid-ukraine-invasion-11646147015.

98 *Russia Blocks Security Council Action on Ukraine,* UN News (Feb. 26, 2022), https://news .un.org/en/story/2022/02/1112802.

99 *Security Council Calls Emergency Special Session of General Assembly on Ukraine Crisis, Adopting Resolution 2623 (2022) by 11 Votes in Favour, 1 against, 3 Abstentions,* United Nations Meetings Coverage and Press Releases (Feb. 27, 2022), https://press.un.org/en/ 2022/sc14809.doc.htm.

100 *General Assembly Overwhelmingly Adopts Resolution Demanding Russian Federation Immediately End Illegal Use of Force in Ukraine, Withdraw All Troops,* UN Meetings Coverage and Press Releases (Mar. 2, 2022), https://press.un.org/en/2022/ga12407 .doc.htm.

101 *Draft Resolution: Aggression against Ukraine,* United Nations General Assembly (Mar. 1, 2022), www.eeas.europa.eu/sites/default/files/a_es-11_l.1_e.pdf.

102 *General Assembly Resolution Demands End to Russian Offensive in Ukraine,* UN News (Mar. 2, 2022), https://news.un.org/en/story/2023/02/1133847.

103 *Norway to Increase Support to Ukraine and Provide Military Equipment,* Norwegian Government (Feb. 27, 2022), www.regjeringen.no/en/aktuelt/norway-to-increase-support-to-ukraine-and-provide-military-equipment/id2902406/.

104 OCHA Ukraine, *Ukraine: Humanitarian Impact Situation Report No. 1(As of 5:00 p.m. on 26 February 2022)*, reliefweb (Feb. 26, 2022), https://reliefweb.int/report/ukraine/ukraine-humanitarian-impact-situation-report-no-1-500-pm-26-february-2022.

105 *Separate Blasts at Oil Facilities in Kharkiv and Vasylkiv Risk Causing Environmental Catastrophes*, CNBC (Feb. 26, 2022), www.cnbc.com/2022/02/26/ukraine-russia-news-fighting-in-kyiv-zelenskyy-defiant.html.

106 *Statement by President Von Der Leyen on Further Measures to Respond to the Russian Invasion of Ukraine*, European Commission (Feb. 27, 2022), https://ec.europa.eu/commission/presscorner/detail/en/statement_22_1441.

107 *Eu Chief Says Bloc Wants Ukraine – As Member*, Reuters (Feb. 27, 2022), www.reuters.com/world/europe/eu-chief-says-bloc-wants-ukraine-member-they-are-one-us-2022-02-28/.

108 Allison Lampert and David Shepardson, *Europe and Canada Move to Close Skies to Russian Planes*, Reuters (Feb. 27, 2022), www.reuters.com/business/aerospace-defense/europe-moves-close-its-skies-russian-planes-2022-02-27/.

109 Joe Sutton, *Canada to Investigate Russian Flight's Violation of Airspace Ban*, CNN (Feb. 27, 2022), www.cnn.com/europe/live-news/ukraine-russia-news-02-27-22/index.html; *Canada Says Russian Airline Aeroflot Violated Its Airspace*, Reuters (Feb. 28, 2022), www.reuters.com/world/americas/canada-shut-its-airspace-russian-operators-immediately-2022-02-27/.

110 Inke Kappeler, *Russian Aircraft Banned from German Airspace*, CNN (Feb. 26, 2022), www.cnn.com/europe/live-news/ukraine-russia-news-02-26-22/index.html.

111 *Japan to Join U.S., EU in Swift Ban on Russian Banks*, Nikkei Asia (Feb. 28, 2022), https://asia.nikkei.com/Politics/Ukraine-war/Japan-to-join-U.S.-EU-in-SWIFT-ban-on-Russian-banks.

112 Reuters, *Norway Says Its Sovereign Fund Will Divest from Russia*, CNN Business (Feb. 27, 2022), www.cnn.com/2022/02/27/intl_business/norway-sovereign-fund-russia/index.html.

113 *Norway to Send Weapons to Ukraine, in Change of Policy*, Reuters (Feb. 28, 2022), www.reuters.com/markets/europe/norway-send-weapons-ukraine-change-policy-2022-02-28/.

114 *Germany Decides to Send Weapons to Ukraine – As It Happened*, DW (Feb. 26, 2022), www.dw.com/en/germany-reverses-ban-on-weapon-sales-to-ukraine-as-it-happened/a-60924798; Tetyana Klug, *Does Germany Send Weapons to Crisis Regions?*, DW (Feb. 8, 2022), www.dw.com/en/fact-check-does-germany-send-weapons-to-crisis-regions/a-60701220.

115 Elizabeth Culliford, *Google Temporarily Disables Google Maps Live Traffic Data in Ukraine*, Reuters (Feb. 27, 2022), www.reuters.com/technology/google-temporarily-disables-google-maps-live-traffic-data-ukraine-2022-02-28/; Brian Fung, *Google Maps Suspends Live Traffic Layer in Ukraine*, CNN (Feb. 27, 2022), www.cnn.com/europe/live-news/ukraine-russia-news-02-27-22/index.html.

116 *Bp's Position in Russia*, bp (Dec. 9, 2022), www.bp.com/en/global/corporate/news-and-insights/press-releases/bps-position-in-russia.html.

117 Rupert Neate, *Rosneft Takes over Tnk-Bp in $55bn Deal*, The Guardian (Mar. 21, 2013), www.theguardian.com/business/2013/mar/21/rosneft-takes-over-tnk-bp; *Rosneft and Bp Complete Tnk-Bp Sale and Purchase Transaction*, bp (Mar. 20, 2013), www.bp.com/en/global/corporate/news-and-insights/press-releases/rosneft-and-bp-complete-tnk-bp-sale-and-purchase-transaction.html.

118 Marcia Reverdosa, *Brazil's Bolsonaro Refuses to Sanction Russia, Says Ukrainians "Trusted a Comedian with the Fate of a Nation,"* CNN (Feb. 27, 2022), www.cnn.com/europe/live-news/ukraine-russia-news-02-27-22/index.html.

119 *Treasury Prohibits Transactions with Central Bank of Russia and Imposes Sanctions on Key Sources of Russia's Wealth,* U.S. Department of the Treasury (Feb. 28, 2022), https://home.treasury.gov/news/press-releases/jy0612; Alan Rappeport, *U.S. Escalates Sanctions with a Freeze on Russian Central Bank Assets,* New York Times (Feb. 28, 2022), www.nytimes.com/2022/02/28/us/politics/us-sanctions-russia-central-bank.html.

120 Fjori Sinoruka, *Albania Unveils Sanctions on Russia over Attack on Ukraine,* BalkanInsight (Feb. 28, 2022), https://balkaninsight.com/2022/02/28/albania-unveils-sanctions-on-russia-over-attack-on-ukraine/.

121 Richard Oscar, *The War in Ukraine: A New Paradigm of Sanctions Practice,* Lawfare (Aug. 1, 2022), www.lawfaremedia.org/article/war-ukraine-new-paradigm-sanctions-practice.

122 Antony Blinken, *Commending New Zealand's New Sanctions Regime,* U.S. Department of State (Mar. 14, 2022), www.state.gov/commending-new-zealands-new-sanctions-regime/; Stephen Wright, *New Zealand, Which Lacks Own Sanctions Law, Joins Condemnation of Russia,* Wall Street Journal (Feb. 24, 2022), www.wsj.com/livecoverage/russia-ukraine-latest-news/card/new-zealand-which-lacks-own-sanctions-law-joins-condemnation-of-russia-geXTLJoJnJkrAJ5Djpz2; Geoffrey Miller, *How Significant Is New Zealand's New Russia Sanctions Law?,* Diplomat (Mar. 9, 2022), https://thediplomat.com/2022/03/how-significant-is-new-zealands-new-russia-sanctions-law/.

123 Joseph Cotterill, *South Africa's Support Underscores Moscow's Propaganda Success,* Financial Times (Jan. 27, 2023), www.ft.com/content/2b7ee958-5f70-4da8-9695-2f17238dc61a.

124 Pavel Tarasenko, *Will Brazil's New President Back Russia's Dream of Multipolarity?,* Carnegie Endowment for International Peace (Nov. 14, 2022), https://carnegieendowment.org/politika/88331.

125 Isabel Debre, *Israel's Balancing Act between Russia and the West Complicated by Russia's Use of Iranian Drones,* PBS (Oct. 19, 2022), www.pbs.org/newshour/world/israels-balancing-act-between-russia-and-the-west-complicated-by-russias-use-of-iranian-drones.

126 *Mexico's President Not Planning Sanctions on Russia for War in Ukraine,* Reuters (May 4, 2022), www.reuters.com/world/mexicos-president-not-planning-sanctions-russia-war-with-ukraine-2022-05-04/.

127 Marton Duani, *Serbia's President Aleksandar Vucic Rejects Sanctions on Russia,* Financial Times (Apr. 21, 2022), www.ft.com/content/0041d1a9-7fbd-4ea3-8176-e8b7d99e4a92.

128 *Venezuela's Maduro Slams Sanctions against Russia As "Madness,"* France24 (Mar. 3, 2023), www.france24.com/en/live-news/20220303-venezuela-s-maduro-slams-sanctions-against-russia-as-madness.

129 Ailsa Chang, Ashish Valentine, and Amy Isackson, *Many African Countries Are Staying Neutral on Russia's Invasion of Ukraine,* NPR (Mar. 15, 2022), www.npr.org/2022/03/15/1086733882/why-many-african-countries-are-staying-neutral-on-russias-invasion-of-ukraine; Shivshankar Menon, *The Fantasy of the Free World,* Foreign Affairs (Apr. 4, 2022), www.foreignaffairs.com/articles/united-states/2022-04-04/fantasy-free-world.

130 Mark A. Green, *Russia can count on support from many developing countries*, Economist Intelligence Unit (Mar. 30, 2022), www.eiu.com/n/russia-can-count-on-support-from-many-developing-countries/.

131 *Largest Economies Worldwide in 2022, by Gross Domestic Product*, Statista (Jan. 12, 2023), www.statista.com/statistics/1356755/share-global-economy-country/.

CHAPTER 3 THE FINANCIAL SANCTIONS AND IMPACT ON THE GLOBAL FINANCIAL SYSTEM

1 *French Finance Minister Le Maire: We Want to Isolate Russia Financially*, Reuters (Feb. 25, 2022), www.reuters.com/world/europe/french-finance-minister-le-maire-we-want-isolate-russia-financially-2022-02-25/.

2 Henry Farrell and Abraham Newman, *Weaponized Interdependence: How Global Economic Networks Shape State Coercion*, 44 Int'l Security 42, 45 (2019), https://direct .mit.edu/isec/article/44/1/42/12237/Weaponized-Interdependence-How-Global-Economic.

3 Daniel W. Drezner, *The Uses and Abuses of Weaponized Interdependence*, The Uses and Abuses of Weaponized Interdependence (2021).

4 Farrell and Newman, note 2, at 46.

5 *Id.* at 58.

6 *See, e.g.,* Pierre-Hugues Verdier, Global Banks on Trial: U.S. Prosecutions and the Remaking of Int'l Finance, at 111 (2020).

7 Gary Clyde Hufbauer and Barbara Oegg, *Targeted Sanctions: A Policy Alternative?*, PIIE (Feb. 23, 2000), www.piie.com/commentary/speeches-papers/targeted-sanctions-policy-alternative; Claudia Girardone, *Russian Sanctions and the Banking Sector*, 33 British J. Mgmt. 1682–88 (2022), https://onlinelibrary.wiley.com/doi/pdf/10.1111/ 1467–8551.12656.

8 Farid Makhlouf and Refk Selmi, *Do Sanctions Work in a Crypto World? The Impact of the Removal of Russian Banks from Swift on Remittances*, Hal Open Science (2022), https://hal .science/hal-03599089/document.

9 Robert Greene, *How Sanctions on Russia Will Alter Global Payment Flows*, Carnegie Endowment for International Peace (Mar. 4, 2022), https://carnegieendowment.org/2022/ 03/04/how-sanctions-on-russia-will-alter-global-payments-flows-pub-86575.

10 *Swift and Sanctions*, Swift (2023), www.swift.com/about-us/legal/compliance-0/swift-and-sanctions.

11 Sanctions Européennes (UE), Service Public Fédéral Finances (2023), https://finances .belgium.be/fr/tresorerie/sanctions-financieres/sanctions-europ%C3%A9ennes-ue.

12 *Swift Oversight*, Swift, www.swift.com/about-us/organisation-governance/swift-oversight; Juan C. Zarate, Treasury's War, at 49 (2013).

13 Agence France-Presse, *SWIFT, the Global Finance Arm that the West Can Twist*, France24, (Feb. 25, 2022), www.france24.com/en/live-news/20220225-swift-the-global-finance-arm-that-the-west-can-twist; *Iranian Banks Reconnected to SWIFT Network after Four-Year Hiatus*, Reuters (Feb. 17, 2016), www.reuters.com/article/us-iran-banks-swift/iranian-banks-reconnected-to-swift-network-after-four-year-hiatus-idUSKCN0VQ1FD.

14 Council Regulation (EU) No. 267/2012 of 23 March 2012 Concerning Restrictive Measures against Iran and Repealing Regulation (EU) No. 961/2010, https://eur-lex.europa.eu/legal-content/EN/TXT/?uri=celex%3A32012R0267.

15 Section 220, P.L. 112-158 (Aug. 10, 2012) (Iran Threat Reduction and Syria Human Rights Act of 2012); Rachelle Younglai and Roberta Rampton, *U.S. Pushes EU, Swift to Eject Iran Banks*, Reuters (Feb. 15, 2012), www.reuters.com/article/us-iran-usa-swift/u-s-pushes-eu-swift-to-eject-iran-banks-idUSTRE81F00I20120216; Ellie Geranmayeh and Manuel Lafont Rapnouil, *Meeting the Challenge of Secondary Sanctions*, 289 ECFR 1, 3 (June 2019).

16 *Sanctions Statement*, Swift (Oct. 6, 2014), www.swift.com/insights/press-releases/swift-sanctions-statement-0.

17 Russell Hotten, *Ukraine Conflict: What Is Swift and Why Is Banning Russia So Significant?*, BBC News (May 4, 2022), www.bbc.com/news/business-60521822.

18 Ananya Kumar and Josh Lipsky, *The Dollar Has Some Would-Be Rivals. Meet The Challengers*, Atlantic Council New Atlanticist (Sept. 22, 2022), www.atlanticcouncil.org/blogs/new-atlanticist/the-dollar-has-some-would-be-rivals-meet-the-challengers/; Charles Riley, *What Is Swift and How Is It Being Used against Russia?*, CNN (Feb. 28, 2022), www.cnn.com/2022/02/28/business/swift-sanctions-explainer/index.html.

19 Farrell and Newman, note 2, at 67.

20 Joanna Caytas, *Weaponizing Finance: U.S. and European Options, Tools, and Policies*, 23 Columbia J. of European L. 441, 449 (2017), https://papers.ssrn.com/sol3/papers.cfm?abstract_id=2988373.

21 Gary Robinson, Sabine Dörry, and Ben Derudder, *Global Networks of Money and Information at the Crossroads: Correspondent Banking and SWIFT*, 23 Global Networks 478 (2022), www.researchgate.net/publication/364352189_Global_networks_of_money_and_information_at_the_crossroads_Correspondent_banking_and_SWIFT.

22 Alexandra Brzozowski and János Allenbach-Ammann, *Russia Ban from Swift on the Table As Germany Drops Opposition*, Euractiv (Feb. 26, 2022), www.euractiv.com/section/europe-s-east/news/russia-ban-from-swift-on-the-table-as-germany-drops-opposition/.

23 Council Regulation (EU) 2022/345 of 1 March 2022 Amending Regulation (Eu) No. 833/2014 Concerning Restrictive Measures in View of Russia's Actions Destabilizing the Situation in Ukraine, https://eur-lex.europa.eu/legal-content/EN/TXT/?uri=uriserv%3AOJ.L_.2022.063.01.0001.01.ENG&toc=OJ%3AL%3A2022%3A063%3ATOC.

24 Laurence Norman, *EU to Remove Russia's Biggest Bank from Swift Network*, Wall Street Journal (June 2, 2022), www.wsj.com/livecoverage/russia-ukraine-latest-news-2022-06-02/card/eu-to-remove-russia-s-biggest-bank-from-swift-network-MaOJ54J37GOZ6f96v507.

25 *Russia's War on Ukraine: EU Adopts Sixth Package of Sanctions against Russia*, European Commission (June 3, 2022), https://ec.europa.eu/commission/presscorner/detail/en/IP_22_2802.

26 *Russia's Aggression against Ukraine: EU Adopts Sixth Package of Sanctions*, Council of the EU Press Release (June 3, 2022), www.consilium.europa.eu/en/press/press-releases/2022/06/03/russia-s-aggression-against-ukraine-eu-adopts-sixth-package-of-sanctions/.

27 Alexander Marrow, *Russia's Swift Alternative Expanding Quickly This Year, Central Bank Says*, Reuters (Sept. 23, 2022), www.reuters.com/business/finance/russias-swift-alternative-expanding-quickly-this-year-says-cbank-2022-09-23/.

28 Maziar Motamedi, *What's behind Iran and Russia's Efforts to Link Banking Systems?*, Al Jazeera (Feb. 8, 2023), www.aljazeera.com/news/2023/2/8/whats-behind-iran-and-russias-efforts-to-link-banking-systems.

29 Andrew R. Johnson, *5 Things on Dollar Clearing and BNP Paribas*, Wall Street Journal (June 30, 2014), www.wsj.com/articles/BL-263B-880; *Unpacking Clearing and Settlement*, The Federal Reserve (Oct. 8, 2020), www.frbservices.org/financial-services/fednow/instant-payments-education/unpacking-clearing-and-settlement.html.

30 *Prohibitions Related to Correspondent or Payable-Through Accounts and Processing of Transactions Involving Certain Foreign Financial Institutions*, Directive 2 under Executive Order 14,024, U.S. Department of the Treasury (Feb. 24, 2022), https://ofac.treasury.gov/media/918471/download?inline.

31 *List of Foreign Financial Institutions Subject to Correspondent Account or Payable-Through Account Sanctions (CAPTA List)*, U.S. Department of the Treasury (last updated Apr. 6, 2022), https://ofac.treasury.gov/consolidated-sanctions-list-non-sdn-lists/list-of-foreign-financial-institutions-subject-to-correspondent-account-or-payable-through-account-sanctions-capta-list.

32 Rena S. Miller, *Overview of Correspondent Banking and "De-Risking" Issues*, Congressional Research Service (last updated Apr. 8, 2022), https://crsreports.congress.gov/product/pdf/IF/IF10873/3.

33 *About CHIPS*, The Clearing House (Feb. 2, 2023), www.theclearinghouse.org/payment-systems/chips.

34 83 Fed. Reg. 31,391 (July 5, 2018).

35 *CHIPS ISO 2022 Migration Remains on Schedule for 2023*, The Clearing House (May 26, 2022), www.theclearinghouse.org/payment-systems/Articles/2022/05/CHIPS_ISO_20022_Migration_05-26-2022.

36 Robinson et al., note 21.

37 Susan Emmenegger and Florence Zuber, *To Infinity and Beyond: U.S. Dollar-Based Jurisdiction in the U.S. Sanctions Context*, 2 SZW/RSDA 114 (2022); Meredith Rathbone and Peter Jeydel, *OFAC's Case against British Arab Commercial Bank and Offshore Use of the U.S. Dollar*, Steptoe (Oct. 7, 2019), www.steptoe.com/en/news-publications/ofacs-case-against-british-arab-commercial-bank-and-offshore-use-of-the-us-dollar.html; Christine Abely, *Causing a Sanctions Violation with U.S. Dollars; Differences in Regulatory Language across OFAC Sanctions Programs*, 48 Ga. J. Int'l & Comp. L. 29 (2019), https://papers.ssrn.com/sol3/papers.cfm?abstract_id=3535212.

38 *Prohibitions Related to Certain Sovereign Debt of the Russian Federation*, Directive 4 under Executive Order 14,024 (Feb. 28, 2022).

39 *Treasury Prohibits Transactions with Central Bank of Russia and Imposes Sanctions on Key Sources of Russia's Wealth*, U.S. Department of the Treasury (Feb. 28, 2022), https://home.treasury.gov/news/press-releases/jy0612.

40 *UK Statement on Further Economic Sanctions Targeted at the Central Bank of the Russian Federation*, UK Government (Feb. 28, 2022), www.gov.uk/government/news/uk-statement-on-further-economic-sanctions-targeted-at-the-central-bank-of-the-russian-federation.

41 *Russia's Military Aggression against Ukraine Imposes Sanctions on 26 Persons and One Entity*, European Council (Feb. 28, 2022), www.consilium.europa.eu/en/press/press-releases/2022/02/28/russia-s-military-aggression-against-ukraine-council-imposes-sanctions-on-26-persons-and-one-entity/.

42 Jasper Ward, *Bahamas Orders Halt to Financial Operations with Sanctioned Russian Entities*, Reuters (Mar. 13, 2022), www.reuters.com/world/americas/bahamas-orders-halt-financial-operations-with-sanctioned-russian-entities-2022-03-13/.

43 *Singapore to Impose Sanctions on Russia, Including Bank Transactions*, Reuters (Feb. 28, 2022), www.reuters.com/world/asia-pacific/singapore-impose-appropriate-sanctions-restric tions-russia-2022-02-28/.

44 Antony J. Blinken, *Japan's Financial Sanctions against Russia*, U.S. Department of State (Feb. 27, 2022), www.state.gov/japans-financial-sanctions-against-russia/.

45 Sohee Kim, *South Korea Joins Financial Sanctions against Russian Banks*, Bloomberg (Mar. 1, 2022), www.bloomberg.com/news/articles/2022-03-01/south-korea-joins-financial-sanctions-against-russian-banks.

46 *Treasury Prohibits Transactions with Central Bank of Russia and Imposes Sanctions on Key Sources of Russia's Wealth*, U.S. Department of the Treasury (Feb. 28, 2022), https://home.treasury.gov/news/press-releases/jy0612.

47 *U.S. Treasury Announces Unprecedented & Expansive Sanctions against Russia, Imposing Swift and Severe Economic Costs*, U.S. Department of the Treasury (Feb. 24, 2022), https://home.treasury.gov/news/press-releases/jy0608; *U.S. Treasury Escalates Sanctions on Russia for Its Atrocities in Ukraine*, U.S. Department of the Treasury (Apr. 6, 2022), https://home.treasury.gov/news/press-releases/jy0705.

48 *EU's 7th Package of Russia Sanctions Targets Gold, Sberbank and Fine-Tunes Existing Sanctions*, White & Case (Aug. 17, 2022), www.whitecase.com/insight-alert/e^{us}-7th-pack age-russia-sanctions-targets-gold-sberbank-and-fine-tunes-existing.

49 *Id.*

50 *U.S. Designates Facilitators of Russian Sanctions Evasion*, U.S. Department of the Treasury (Apr. 20, 2022), https://home.treasury.gov/news/press-releases/jy0731.

51 Joshua Kirschenbaum and Nicolas Véron, *The EU Has Sanctioned Fewer Russian Banks than the US and Could Do More*, PIIE (Apr. 15, 2022), www.piie.com/research/piie-charts/eu-has-sanctioned-fewer-russian-banks-us-and-could-do-more.

52 Max Seddon and Henry Foy, *Russia Plans to Sue over Frozen Currency Reserves, Central Bank Says*, Financial Times (Apr. 19, 2022), www.ft.com/content/055231b1-e3bc-44fe-a7fb-6eaaa0933f72.

53 *Brussels Says about $24 Bln of Russian Central Bank Assets Frozen in EU, Less Than Expected*, Reuters (May 25, 2022), www.reuters.com/world/europe/brussels-says-about-24-bln-russian-central-bank-assets-frozen-eu-less-than-2022-05-25/.

54 Alfons J Weichenrieder, *Russia Today: The Russian Invasion of Ukraine and Russia's Public Finances*, SAFE Policy Letter, No. 96, Leibniz Institute for Financial Research (2022), https://publikationen.ub.uni-frankfurt.de/frontdoor/index/index/docId/63482.

55 Anastasia Stognei, *Russia Embraces China's Renminbi in Face of Western Sanctions*, Financial Times (Mar. 26, 2023), www.ft.com/content/65681143-c6af-4b64-827d-a7ca6171937a.

56 Darya Korsunskaya and Alexander Marrow, *Russian Rainy Day Fund to Get Out of All U.S. Dollar Assets*, Reuters (June 3, 2021), www.reuters.com/article/us-russia-reserves-idUSKCN2DF1R9.

57 Richard Berner, Stephen Cecchetti, and Kim Schoenholtz, *Russian Sanctions: Some Questions and Answers*, VoxEU (Mar. 21, 2022), https://cepr.org/voxeu/columns/russian-sanctions-some-questions-and-answers.

58 Council Regulation (EU) 2022/328, Feb. 25, 2022, https://eur-lex.europa.eu/legal-content/EN/TXT/PDF/?uri=CELEX:32022R0328&from=EN; Council Decision (CFSP) 2022/327 of 25 Feb. 2022 amending Decision 2014/512/CFSP Concerning Restrictive Measures in View of Russia's Actions Destabilizthethe Situation in Ukraine, https://eur-lex.europa.eu/eli/dec/2022/327.

59 *Sanctions in Response to Putin's Illegal Annexation of Ukrainian Regions*, UK Government (Sept. 30, 2022), www.gov.uk/government/news/sanctions-in-response-to-putins-illegal-annexation-of-ukrainian-regions.

60 *FAQ 1028*, U.S. Department of the Treasury (Mar. 11, 2022), https://home.treasury.gov/policy-issues/financial-sanctions/faqs/1028; *General License 18: Authorizing U.S. Dollar-Denominated Banknote Noncommercial, Personal Remittances Prohibited by Executive Order of Mar. 11, 2022*, U.S. Department of the Treasury (Mar. 11, 2022), https://ofac.treasury.gov/media/919081/download?inline.

61 *European Commission Welcomes Joint Statement to Provide Affordable, Accessible and Transparent Remittance Services to Ukraine*, Delegation of the EU to Ukraine (Sept. 27, 2022), www.eeas.europa.eu/delegations/ukraine/european-commission-welcomes-joint-statement-provide-affordable-accessible-and_en?s=232.

62 *Remittances to Reach $630 billion in 2022 with Record Flows into Ukraine*, World Bank (May 11, 2022), www.worldbank.org/en/news/press-release/2022/05/11/remittances-to-reach-630-billion-in-2022-with-record-flows-into-ukraine.

63 *Central Asian Governments Fret over Shrinking Remittances from Russia*, Economist (June 23, 2022), www.economist.com/asia/2022/06/23/central-asian-governments-fret-over-shrinking-remittances-from-russia.

64 Ayzirek Imanaliyeva, *Kyrgyzstan Nat'l Bank Predicts 20% Decline in Remittances*, Eurasianet (June 10, 2022), https://eurasianet.org/kyrgyzstan-national-bank-predicts-20-decline-in-remittances.

65 Armine Avestisyan, *Russian Migration Shakes up Armenian Economy, Society*, Moscow Times (Oct. 2, 2022), www.themoscowtimes.com/2022/10/02/russian-migration-shakes-up-armenian-economy-society-a78935.

66 Georgios Georgiadis et al., *Fundamentals vs. Policies: Can the US Dollar's Dominance in Global Trade Be Dented?*, European Central Bank (July 2021), www.ecb.europa.eu/pub/pdf/scpwps/ecb.wp2574~664b8e9249.en.pdf.

67 Mrugank Bhusari and Maia Nikoladze, *Russia and China: Partners in Dedollarization*, Atlantic Council (Feb. 18, 2022), www.atlanticcouncil.org/blogs/econographics/russia-and-china-partners-in-dedollarization/.

68 Dimitri Simes, *China and Russia Ditch Dollar in Move towadrs "Financial Alliance,"* Nikkei Asia (Aug. 6, 2020), https://asia.nikkei.com/Politics/International-relations/China-and-Russia-ditch-dollar-in-move-toward-financial-alliance; Vladimir Soldatkin, *Russia Signs Deals with China to Help Weather Sanctions*, Reuters (Oct. 13, 2014), www.reuters.com/article/uk-russia-china-banks/russia-signs-deals-with-china-to-help-weather-sanctions-idUKKCN0I21D420141013.

69 Emily Jin, *Why China's CIPS Matters (and Not for the Reasons You Think)*, Lawfare (Apr. 5, 2022), www.lawfaremedia.org/article/why-chinas-cips-matters-and-not-reasons-you-think.

70 Barry Eichengreen, *Sanctions, SWIFT, and China's Cross-Border Interbank Payments System*, CSIS (May 20, 2022), www.csis.org/analysis/sanctions-swift-and-chinas-cross-border-interbank-payments-system; Daniel McDowell, Bucking the Buck (2023).

71 *Amid Western Sanctions, China's Yuan Has Its Moment in Russia*, Al Jazeera (Sept. 20, 2022), www.aljazeera.com/news/2022/9/20/amid-western-sanctions-chinas-yuan-has-its-moment-in-russia.

72 Swati Bhat and Nupur Anand, *Rupee Settlement Will Help India Trade with Russia, Iran and South Asian Neighbors, Experts Say*, Reuters (July 12, 2022), www.reuters.com/world/india/rupee-settlement-will-help-india-trade-with-russia-iran-sasian-neighbours-2022-07-12/.

73 *Russia's Sberbank Opens "Vostro" Rupee Accounts at India Branches*, Reuters (Oct. 24, 2022), www.reuters.com/markets/currencies/russias-sberbank-opens-vostro-rupee-accounts-india-branches-2022-10-24/.

74 *Visa and Mastercard Suspend Russian Operations*, BBC (Mar. 6, 2022), www.bbc.com/news/business-60637429.

75 Megumi Fujikawa, *Japanese Credit Card Issuer JCB to Suspend Russian Operations*, Wall Street Journal (Mar. 8, 2022), www.wsj.com/livecoverage/russia-ukraine-latest-news-2022-03-08/card/japanese-credit-card-issuer-jcb-to-suspend-russian-operations-SYPeeEnIopT2onNK6f7w.

76 *Discover Statement on Russian Banks and Payments Acceptance*, Discover (Mar. 7, 2022), https://investorrelations.discover.com/newsroom/press-releases/press-release-details/2022/Discover-Statement-on-Russian-Banks-and-Payments-Acceptance/default.aspx.

77 Farangis Najibullah, *Credit Card Tourism: Russians Avoid Sanctions by Flying to Uzbekistan for VISA, Mastercards*, RadioFreeEurope RadioLiberty (Mar. 31, 2022), www.rferl.org/a/russia-credit-card-tourism-sanctions-uzbekistan/31780174.html.

78 *Apple Closes Russian Mir Card Loophole for Apple Pay, Says Sberbank*, Reuters (Mar. 25, 2022), www.reuters.com/technology/apple-closes-russian-mir-card-loophole-apple-pay-says-sberbank-2022-03-25/.

79 Nicholas Gordon, *Visa and Mastercard Have Already Cut Ties with Russian Banks. Now China's Largest Credit Card Brand Might Be Pulling out Too*, Fortune (Apr. 22, 2022), https://fortune.com/2022/04/22/unionpay-china-credit-card-sberbank-secondary-sanctions-russia/.

80 *Sanctions Compliance Guidance for Instant Payment Systems*, U.S. Department of the Treasury (Sept. 2022), https://ofac.treasury.gov/media/928316/download?inline.

81 Paresh Dave, *PayPal Shuts down Its Services in Russia Citing Ukraine Aggression*, Reuters (Mar. 5, 2022), www.reuters.com/business/paypal-shuts-down-its-services-russia-citing-ukraine-aggression-2022-03-05/.

82 *Settlement Agreement between the U.S. Dep't of the Treasury's Office of Foreign Assets Control and PayPal, Inc.; OFAC Has Also Releases Additional Enforcement Information*, U.S. Department of the Treasury (Mar. 25, 2015), https://home.treasury.gov/policy-issues/financial-sanctions/recent-actions/20150325_33#.

83 Kochergin Mitry and Yangirova Alsu, *Modern Development of the National Payment Card System in Russia*, 104 Advances in Economics, Business and Management Research (2018), www.atlantis-press.com/article/125924767.pdf.

84 Matthew Humphries, *Desperate for Bank Card Microchips, Russia Looks to China*, PCMag (Apr. 5, 2022), www.pcmag.com/news/desperate-for-bank-card-microchips-russia-looks-to-china.

85 *Russia's Sberbank Re-uses Bank Card Chips to Combat Shortage*, Reuters (July 7, 2022), www.reuters.com/technology/russias-sberbank-re-uses-bank-card-chips-combat-shortage-2022-07-07/.

86 *FAQ 1082*, U.S. Department of the Treasury (Sept. 15, 2022), https://home.treasury.gov/policy-issues/financial-sanctions/faqs/1082.

87 Angelika Hellweger, *Turkey, Mir and the Threat of Secondary Sanctions*, Rahman Ravelli (Sept. 26, 2022), www.rahmanravelli.co.uk/articles/turkey-mir-and-the-threat-of-secondary-sanctions/.

88 *Treasury Targets Additional Facilitators of Russia's Aggression in Ukraine*, U.S. Department of the Treasury (Sept. 15, 2022), https://home.treasury.gov/news/press-releases/jy0954.

89 *Treasury Imposes Swift and Severe Costs on Russia for Putin's Purported Annexation of Regions of Ukraine*, U.S. Department of the Treasury (Sept. 30, 2022), https://home.treasury.gov/news/press-releases/jy0981.

90 *Major Turkish Banks Halt Use of Russia's Mir Payment System*, Moscow Times (Sept. 20, 2022), www.themoscowtimes.com/2022/09/20/major-turkish-banks-halt-use-of-russias-mir-payment-system-a78837; *All Turkish Banks Halt Russia's Mir Payment System*, Moscow Times (Sept. 29, 2022), www.themoscowtimes.com/2022/09/28/all-turkish-banks-halt-russias-mir-payment-system-reports-a78916.

91 *Dushanbe City Bank Suspends Russia's Mir Payment System*, RadioFreeEurope RadioLiberty (Sept. 27, 2022), www.rferl.org/a/tajikistan-bank-russia-mir-payments/32054393.html.

92 *Major Tajik Bank Halts Use of Russia's Mir Cards*, Reuters (Sept. 26, 2022), www.reuters.com/article/ukraine-crisis-mir-tajikistan/major-tajik-bank-halts-use-of-russias-mir-cards-idUSL1N30X0T6.

93 *Prohibiting Certain Imports and New Investments With Respect to Continued Russian Federation Efforts to Undermine the Sovereignty and Territorial Integrity of Ukraine*, Executive Order 14,066 of Mar. 8, 2022, 87 Fed. Reg. 13,625 (Mar. 10, 2022), www.federalregister.gov/documents/2022/03/10/2022-05232/prohibiting-certain-imports-and-new-investments-with-respect-to-continued-russian-federation-efforts.

94 *Prohibiting Certain Imports, Exports, and New Investment With Respect to Continued Russian Federation Aggression*, Executive Order 14,068 of Mar. 11, 2022, 87 Fed. Reg. 14,381 (Mar. 15, 2022), www.federalregister.gov/documents/2022/03/15/2022-05554/prohibiting-certain-imports-exports-and-new-investment-with-respect-to-continued-russian-federation.

95 *Prohibiting New Investment in and Certain Services to the Russian Federation in Response to Continued Russian Federation Aggression*, White House (Apr. 6, 2022), www.whitehouse.gov/briefing-room/presidential-actions/2022/04/06/prohibiting-new-investment-in-and-certain-services-to-the-russian-federation-in-response-to-continued-russian-federation-aggression/.

96 *UK Imposes Sweeping New Sanctions to Starve Putin's War Machine*, UK Government (Apr. 6, 2022), www.gov.uk/government/news/uk-imposes-sweeping-new-sanctions-to-starve-putins-war-machine.

97 *Japan: Phases out Imports of Russian Coal and Prohibits New Japanese Investment in the Russian Federation*, UNCTAD Investment Policy Hub (Apr. 8, 2022), https://investmentpolicy.unctad.org/investment-policy-monitor/measures/3867/phases-out-imports-of-russian-coal-and-prohibits-new-japanese-investment-in-the-russian-federation.

98 *Russia's Military Aggression against Ukraine: Fourth EU Package of Sectoral and Individual Measures*, European Council (Mar. 15, 2022), www.consilium.europa.eu/en/press/press-releases/2022/03/15/russia-s-military-aggression-against-ukraine-fourth-eu-package-of-sectoral-and-individual-measures/.

99 *Ukraine: EU Agrees Ninth Package of Sanctions against Russia*, European Commission (Dec. 16, 2022), https://ec.europa.eu/commission/presscorner/detail/en/IP_22_7652.

100 31 CFR § 589.326.

101 31 CFR § 589.324.

102 *FAQ 1054*, U.S. Department of the Treasury (June 6, 2022), https://ofac.treasury.gov/faqs/1054.

103 *FAQ 1049*, U.S. Department of the Treasury (June 6, 2022), https://ofac.treasury.gov/faqs/1049.

104 *Covid-19 Hits Foreign Investment Flows to Transition Economies Harder than Other Regions, Says UN Report*, United Nations Conference on Trade and Development (June 21, 2021), https://unctad.org/press-material/covid-19-hits-foreign-investment-flows-transition-economies-harder-other-regions; *United Nations Conference on Trade and Development*, World Investment Report (2021) https://unctad.org/system/files/official-document/wir2021_en.pdf.

105 Heli Simola, *What Effects Have Sanction Had on the Russian Economy?*, World Economic Forum (Dec. 22, 2022), www.weforum.org/agenda/2022/12/sanctions-russian-economy-effects/.

106 Michael Bradley, Irving de Lira Salvatierra, W. Mark, C. Weidemaier, and Mitu Gulati, *A Silver Lining to Russia's Sanctions-Busting Clause?*, 108 Va. L. Rev. Online 326 (Dec. 7, 2022), https://virginialawreview.org/articles/a-silver-lining-to-russias-sanctions-busting-clause/.

107 Giulia Morpurgo and Libby Cherry, *Russia Slips into Historic Default as Sanctions Muddy Next Steps*, Bloomberg (June 26, 2022), www.bloomberg.com/news/articles/2022-06-26/russia-defaults-on-foreign-debt-for-first-time-since-1918; Eshe Nelson, Alan Rappeport, and Lauren Hirsch, *Dollars or Rubles? Russian Debt Payments Are Due, and Uncertain*, New York Times (Mar. 15, 2022), www.nytimes.com/2022/03/15/business/russia-debt-bonds-default.html.

108 *La Russie fait défaut sur sa dette souveraine en devises étrangères, le Kremlin dement*, Euronews (June 27, 2022), https://fr.euronews.com/2022/06/27/la-russie-fait-defaut-sur-sa-dette-souveraine-en-devises-etrangeres-une-premiere-en-un-sie; Caitlin Ostroff and Ann M. Simmons, *Kremlin Says Russia Didn't Default on Debt after Missed Payments*, Wall Street Journal (June 27, 2022), www.wsj.com/livecoverage/ukraine-russia-war-g7-summit-germany/card/russia-says-it-will-redirect-gold-in-response-to-ban-disputes-debt-default-7rkQowbVwdmGgHyG5vgh.

109 Grigory Marinichev, Sabine Konrad, and Yaroslav Smorodin, *Update: New Mechanism Established for Repayment of Russian Sovereign Debt*, Morgan Lewis (June 30, 2022), www.morganlewis.com/pubs/2022/06/update-new-mechanism-established-for-repayment-of-russian-sovereign-debt.

110 Rebecca M. Nelson, *Russia's War on Ukraine: The Economic Impact*, Congressional Research Service (May 3, 2022), https://crsreports.congress.gov/product/pdf/IF/IF12092.

111 Tommy Stubbington and Polina Ivanova, *Russia Steadies Rouble with Harsh Capital Controls and Investment Curbs*, Financial Times (Apr. 1, 2022), www.ft.com/content/4ebde1bf-674c-468d-a8f0-2b306496962d.

112 Georgi Kantchev, *Russia Eases Capital Controls as Ruble's Strength Threatens Economy*, Wall Street Journal (May 24, 2022), www.wsj.com/livecoverage/russia-ukraine-latest-news-2022-05-24/card/russia-eases-capital-controls-as-ruble-s-strength-threatens-economy-EkUBEKHFw3wWHAGHHOD8.

113 Irina Ivanova, *Russia's Ruble Is the Strongest Currency in the World This Year*, CBS (June 28, 2022), www.cnbc.com/2022/06/23/russias-ruble-is-at-strongest-level-in-7-years-des pite-sanctions.html; Natasha Turak, *Russia's Ruble Hit Its Strongest Level in 7 Years Despite Massive Sanctions*, CNBC (June 23, 2022), www.cnbc.com/2022/06/23/russias-ruble-is-at-strongest-level-in-7-years-despite-sanctions.html.

114 *The Artificial Strength of the Russian Ruble*, NPR (July 7, 2022), www.npr.org/transcripts/1110354162.

115 Associated Press, *What Does It Mean That the Euro Has Fallen below Parity with the Dollar?*, PBS (Aug. 23, 2022), www.pbs.org/newshour/economy/ask-the-headhunter/what-does-it-mean-that-the-euro-has-fallen-below-parity-with-the-dollar.

116 Ashutosh Pandey, *Why the Euro's Weakness Is a Big Deal*, DW (Sept. 5, 2022), www.dw.com/en/why-the-euros-weakness-is-a-big-deal/a-62909600#.

117 Suzuki Shunichi, *Statement by the Honorable Suzuki Shunichi*, Ministry of Finance, Japan (Oct. 14, 2022), www.mof.go.jp/english/policy/international_policy/imf/imfc/imfc_20221014_2.pdf.

118 Shinji Kitamura and Yoshifumi Takemoto, *Japan Intervened, Buying Yen in Foreign Exchange Market Friday*, Bloomberg (Oct. 22, 2022), www.bloomberg.com/news/articles/2022-10-14/japan-voices-deep-concerns-over-volatility-in-currency-market.

119 Marijn Bolhuis and Peter Kovacs, *Africa's Inflation among Region's Most Urgent Challenges*, IMF Blog (Oct. 20, 2022), www.imf.org/en/Blogs/Articles/2022/10/20/africas-inflation-among-regions-most-urgent-challenges.

120 *Russian Inflation at 0.24% in First Nine Days of 2023*, Reuters (Jan. 11, 2023), www.reuters.com/world/europe/russian-inflation-024-first-nine-days-2023-2023-01-11.

121 *G7 Finance Ministers and Central Bank Governors' Statement on the Global Economic Impact of Russia's Ware of Aggression against Ukraine and G7 Support to Ukraine*, U.S. Department of the Treasury (Oct. 12, 2022), https://home.treasury.gov/news/press-releases/jy1016.

122 *About the FSB*, Financial Stability Board (last updated Nov. 16, 2020), www.fsb.org/about/; *Work of the FSB*, Financial Stability Board (last updated Mar. 30, 2023), www.fsb.org/work-of-the-fsb/.

123 FX Global Code, Global Foreign Exchange Committee (July 2021), www.globalfxc.org/docs/fx_global.pdf.

124 *Id.*

125 Kevin Roose, *Bitcoin Was Made for This Moment. So Why Isn't It Booming?*, New York Times (Mar. 11, 2022), www.nytimes.com/2022/03/11/technology/bitcoin-ukraine-russia-roose.html; David Yaffe-Bellany, Erin Griffith, and Ephrat Livni, *Cryptocurrencies Melt down in a "Perfect Storm" of Fear and Panic*, New York Times (May 12, 2022), www.nytimes.com/2022/05/12/technology/cryptocurrencies-crash-bitcoin.html.

126 Emily Flitter and David Yaffe-Bellany, *Russia Could Use Cryptocurrency to Blunt the Force of U.S. Sanctions*, New York Times (Feb. 23, 2022), www.nytimes.com/2022/02/23/business/russia-sanctions-cryptocurrency.html.

127 *Sanctions-Dodgers Hoping to Use Crypto to Evade Detection Are Likely to Be Disappointed*, Economist (Mar. 19, 2022), www.economist.com/finance-and-eco nomics/why-crypto-is-unlikely-to-be-useful-for-sanctions-dodgers/21808188.

128 *Cryptocurrency Markets Are Not Liquid Enough for Mass Russian Sanctions Evasion*, Chainalysis (Apr. 13, 2022), https://blog.chainalysis.com/reports/cryptocurrency-liquidity-russia-sanctions/.

129 *Crypto*-Assets, European Commission (last updated Mar. 21, 2023), https://finance.ec
.europa.eu/system/files/2023-03/faqs-sanctions-russia-crypto_en.pdf; *Ukraine: EU Agrees
on Eighth Package of Sanctions against Russia*, European Commission (Oct. 6, 2022),
https://ec.europa.eu/commission/presscorner/detail/en/ip_22_5989; *Question and Answers
on the Fifth Package of Restrictive Measures against Russia*, European Commission
(Apr. 8, 2022), https://ec.europa.eu/commission/presscorner/detail/en/QANDA_22_2333;
U.S. Treasury Designates Faciliators of Russian Sanctions Evasion, U.S. Department of
the Treasury (Apr. 20, 2022), https://home.treasury.gov/news/press-releases/jy0731.

130 *U.S. Treasury Designates Facilitators of Russian Sanctions Evasion*, U.S. Department of
the Treasury (Apr. 20, 2022), https://home.treasury.gov/news/press-releases/jy0731.

131 *Publication of Sanctions Compliance Guidance for the Virtual Currency Industry and
Updated Frequently Asked Questions*, U.S. Department of the Treasury (Oct. 15,
2021), https://home.treasury.gov/policy-issues/financial-sanctions/recent-actions/20211015.

132 *History of the FATF*, Financial Action Task Force (Jan. 18, 2023), www.fatf-gafi.org/en/
the-fatf/history-of-the-fatf.html; *Economic Declaration*, G7 (July 16, 1989), www.g8
.utoronto.ca/summit/1989paris/communique/index.html.

133 *Who We Are*, Financial Action Task Force (Apr. 26, 2023), www.fatf-gafi.org/en/the-fatf/
who-we-are.html.

134 *FATF Steps Up Money Laundering Battle: Admits Russia and South Africa*, 238 OECD
Observer 1, 4 (July 2003).

135 *Anti-money Laundering and Counter-Terrorist Financing Measures: Russian Federation*,
FATF (Dec. 2019), www.fatf-gafi.org/media/fatf/documents/reports/mer4/Mutual-
Evaluation-Russian-Federation-2019.pdf.

136 *FATF Public Statement on the Situation in Ukraine*, Financial Action Task Force
(Mar. 5, 2022), www.fatf-gafi.org/en/publications/Fatfgeneral/Ukraine-2022.html.

137 *Id.*

138 *Strengthening Financial Sanctions against the Russian Federation*, International Working
Group on Russian Sanctions (June 22, 2022), https://fsi.stanford.edu/working-group-sanctions.

139 *FATF Statement on the Russian Federation*, Financial Action Task Force (June 2022), www
.fatf-gafi.org/publications/fatfgeneral/documents/ukraine-june-2022.html.

140 AFP, *Myanmar Blacklisted, Russia Sidelined by Money-Laundering Watchdog*, Barron's
(Oct. 21, 2022), www.barrons.com/news/myanmar-blacklisted-russia-sidelined-by-money-laun
dering-watchdog-01666378206; *Russian Federation*, Financial Action Task Force
(Feb. 24, 2023), www.fatf-gafi.org/en/countries/detail/Russian-Federation.html.

CHAPTER 4 EXTRATERRITORIALITY

1 *Treasury Targets Actors Involved in Production and Transfer of Iranian Unmanned Aerial
Vehicles to Russia for Use in Ukraine*, U.S. Department of the Treasury (Nov. 15,
2022), https://home.treasury.gov/news/press-releases/jy1104.

2 Mark N. Katz, *Why US Allies in the Middle East Aren't Taking Sides in the Ukraine War*,
Atlantic Council (Sept. 8, 2022), www.atlanticcouncil.org/blogs/new-atlanticist/why-us-
allies-in-the-middle-east-arent-taking-sides-in-the-ukraine-war/; Alan Crawford, Jenni
Marsh, and Antony Sguazzin, *The U.S. Drive to Isolate Russia and China Is Falling*

Short, Bloomberg (Aug. 5, 2022), www.bloomberg.com/news/articles/2022-08-05/the-us-led-drive-to-isolate-russia-and-china-is-falling-short.

3 Mark Daniel Jaeger, *Circumventing Sovereignty: Extraterritorial Sanctions Leveraging the Technologies of the Financial System*, 27 Swiss Political Science Rev. 180, 183 (2021), https://onlinelibrary.wiley.com/doi/full/10.1111/spsr.12436.

4 *Id.*; Julia Schmidt, *The Legality of Unilateral Extra-territorial Sanctions under International Law*, 27 J. Conflict & Security L. 53, 57 n.20 (2022), https://academic.oup .com/jcsl/article/27/1/53/6528963.

5 Susan Emmenegger, *Extraterritorial Economic Sanctions and Their Foundation in International Law*, 33 Ariz. J. Int'l & Comp. L. 631 (2016), http://arizonajournal.org/ wp-content/uploads/2017/01/02_EMMENEGGER_EICFinal.pdf.

6 See, e.g., Expert Consultation on "The Notion, Characteristics, Legal Status and Targets of Unilateral Sanctions" convened on April 26, 2021, United Nations High Commissioner for Human Rights (May. 14, 2021), www.ohchr.org/sites/default/files/ Documents/Issues/UCM/expert-consultation-26April2021.pdf (see statements of Dr. Kazazi and Prof. de Zayas; see also statement of Prof. Emmenegger, "not[ing] that extraterritorial measures are problematic, as when the United States used the US dollar to justify applying its jurisdiction abroad while calling its own measures 'territorial' when they may in fact be extraterritorial"; "[w]ith regard to extraterritoriality, Prof. Emmenegger said she would consider it illegal under customary international law for US primary sanctions to be imposed against a Turkish company that trades with Iran, which is the subject of comprehensive US sanctions").

7 Mortimer Sellers, *Why States Are Bound by Customary International Law*, 4 Int'l Legal Theory 22 (1998), https://scholarworks.law.ubalt.edu/cgi/viewcontent.cgi?article=2167& context=all_fac.

8 Menno Kamminga, *Extraterritoriality*, Max Planck Encyclopedias of International Law (2020), https://opil.ouplaw.com/display/10.1093/law:epil/9780199231690/law-9780199231690-e1040?prd=MPIL.

9 Restatement (Fourth) of Foreign Relations Law of the U.S. § 407 (2022). See also William S. Dodge, *Reasonableness in the Restatement (Fourth) of Foreign Relations Law*, 55 Willamette L. Rev. 521 (2019), https://papers.ssrn.com/sol3/papers.cfm?abstract_id= 3373370 (describing how the genuine-connection requirement rejects the case-by-case balancing approach of old Section 403 in the Restatement [Third] of Foreign Relations Law).

10 Restatement, Note 9, § 408; *see also* Patrick C. R. Terry, *Enforcing U.S. Foreign Policy by Imposing Unilateral Secondary Sanctions: Is Might Right in Public International Law?*, 30 Wash. Int'l L.J. 1, 11 (2020), https://digitalcommons.law.uw.edu/wilj/vol30/iss1/4/.

11 Restatement, Note 9, § 409.

12 *Id.*, § 410.

13 *Id.*, § 411.

14 *Id.*, § 412; *see U.S. v. Zehe*, 601 F.Supp. 196 (D. Mass. 1985); Monika Krizek, *The Protective Principle of Extraterritorial Jurisdiction*, 6 B.U. In't. L. J. 337 (1988)

15 Restatement, Note 9, § 413.

16 Emmenegger, note 5, , 654–56.

17 Samuel Hatcher, *Circuit Board Jurisdiction: Electronic Payment and the Presumption against Extraterritoriality*, 48 Ga. J. Int'l & Comp. L. 591, 608 (2020), https://digitalcommons.law.uga.edu/gjicl/vol48/iss2/8/.

18 Daniel Jaeger, note 3, at 183.

19 Tom Ruys and Cedric Ryngaert, *Secondary Sanctions: A Weapon Out of Control? The International Legality of, and European Responses to, US Secondary Sanctions*, British Yearbook of International Law (2020), https://doi.org/10.1093/bybil/braa007.

20 Yann Kerbrat, *Unilateral/Extraterritorial Sanctions as a Challenge to the Theory of Jurisdiction*, Research Handbook on Unilateral and Extraterritorial Sanctions (2021), at 171–72, www.elgaronline.com/configurable/content/edcoll$002f9781839107849$002f9781839107849.00018.xml?t:ac=edcoll%24002f9781839107849%24002f9781839107849.00018.xml.

21 *Barcelona Traction, Light & Power Co., Ltd. (Belgium v. Spain)*, International Court of Justice (1970).

22 Schmidt, note 4, at 69, n. 89, citing C. Ryngaert, *Extraterritorial Export Controls (Secondary Boycotts)* (2008) 7 Chinese J. Int'l L. 625, 628; C. Staker, *Jurisdiction*, International Law (5th ed. 2008).

23 Tom Ruys and Cedric Ryngaert, *Secondary Sanctions: A Weapon Out of Out of Control? Part I: Permissibility of the Sanctions under the Law of Jurisdiction*, EJIL:Talk! (Blog of the European Jouranl of International Law) (Sept. 30, 2020), https://dspace.library.uu.nl/bitstream/handle/1874/415681/ejiltalk.org_Secondary_Sanctions_A_Weapon_Out_of_Control_Part_I_Permissibility_of_the_sanctions_under_the_law_of_j.pdf?sequence=1.

24 *Id.*

25 Emmenegger, note 5, 648–49.

26 *Id.*, at 652.

27 Kristina Larsson, United States Extraterritorial Application of Economic Sanctions and the New International Sanctions against Iran, Lund University (2011), https://lup.lub.lu.se/luur/download?fileOId=1975926&func=downloadFile&recordOId=1969940, at 22, citing Kern Alexander, Economic Sanctions Law and Public Policy (2009), at 56–67.

28 Jeffrey Meyer, *Secondary Thoughts on Secondary Sanctions*, 30 U. Pa. L. Rev. 905 (2008).

29 Jonathan M. Epstein, *Iran Sanctions: U.S. Bans Foreign Subsidiaries of U.S. Companies from Doing Business with Iran*, Holland & Knight, (Oct. 11, 2022), www.hklaw.com/en/insights/publications/2012/10/iran-sanctions-us-bans-foreign-subsidiaries-of-us; Harry L. Clark, *Dealing with U.S. Extraterritorial Sanctions and Foreign Countermeasures*, 25 U. Pa. J. Int'l Econ. L. 455, 467 (2004), https://scholarship.law.upenn.edu/jil/vol20/iss1/2/.

30 31 C.F.R. 598.201.

31 32 C.F.R. 598.207.

32 31 C.F.R. 589.215.

33 Christine Abely, *Causing a Sanctions Violation with U.S. Dollars*, 48 Ga. J. Int'l & Comp. L. 29 (2019), https://papers.ssrn.com/sol3/papers.cfm?abstract_id=3535212.

34 Susan Emmenegger and Thirza Döbeli, *Extraterritorial Application of U.S. Sanctions Law*, US Litigation Today: Still a Threat for European Businesses or Just a Paper Tiger?, Conference Proceedings from the 29th Journée de droit international privée of 23 June 2017 (2018), www.ziv.unibe.ch/e7688/e50302/e150986/e196606/e248813/e728442/e770815/2018_Emmenegger_Doebeli_USSanctions_ger.pdf; see also Pierre-Hugues

Verdier, *The New Financial Extraterritoriality*, 87 Geo. Wash. L. Rev. 239 (2019), www
.gwlr.org/wp-content/uploads/2019/04/87-Geo.-Wash.-L.-Rev.-239.pdf (analyzing U.S.
extraterritorial criminal cases involving banks).

35 *U.S. v. Zarrab*, Case 1:15-cr-00867-RMB, Decision & Order (S.D.N.Y. Oct. 17, 2016).

36 *See RJR Nabisco v. E.C.*, 579 U.S. 325 (2016), outlining a two-step test for determining
whether a particular statute should be applied extraterritorially. Under the first step, the
court determines "whether the statute gives a clear, affirmative indication that it applies
extraterritorially"; if there is no such indication, the court then "determine[s] whether the
case involves a domestic application of the statute," doing so "by looking to the
statute's 'focus.'"

37 But see commentary arguing that *U.S. v. Hoskins*, 902 F.3d 69 (2d Cir. 2018), which
applied the presumption against extraterritoriality to limit conspiracy and complicity
statutes to their terms and "barr[ed] the government from using the conspiracy and
complicity statutes to charge [defendant] with any offense that is not punishable under
the FCPA itself because of the statute's territorial limitations," similarly applies with
respect to the extraterritorial application of conspiracy statute for underlying violation of
IEEPA; Kevin McCart, *Hoskins May Limit Extraterritorial Enforcement of U.S. Sanctions*,
Squire Patton Boggs Global Investigations & Compliance Review (Sept. 13, 2018), www
.globalinvestigations.blog/anti-corruption/hoskins-may-limit-extraterritorial-enforcement-
of-u-s-sanctions/.

38 Anupreet Amole et al., *Extraterritoriality: The UK Perspective*, Global Investigations
Review (2022), https://globalinvestigationsreview.com/guide/the-practitioners-guide-
global-investigations/2022/article/extraterritoriality-the-uk-perspective#footnote-031-back
link; *OFSI Enforcement and Monetary Penalties for Breaches of Financial Sanctions*, HM
Treasury (2022), https://assets.publishing.service.gov.uk/government/uploads/system/
uploads/attachment_data/file/1083297/15.06.22_OFSI_enforcement_guidance.pdf.

39 *About Sanctions*, Australian Government Department of Foreign Affairs and Trade
(Feb. 15, 2021), www.dfat.gov.au/international-relations/security/sanctions/about-
sanctions.

40 Joop Voetelink, *Limits on the Extraterritoriality of United States Export Control and
Sanctions Legislation*, Netherlands Annual Review of Military Studies 187 (2021),https://
link.springer.com/chapter/10.1007/978-94-6265-471-6_11.

41 Bryan Early and Keith Preble, *Enforcing Economic Sanctions; Analyzing How OFAC
Punishes Violators of U.S. Sanctions*, SSRN (2018), https://papers.ssrn.com/sol3/papers
.cfm?abstract_id=3306653.

42 Jacques Delors Institute, *Remarks by HR/Josep Borell at Seminar on Extra-Territorial
Sanctions* (July 10, 2021), www.eeas.europa.eu/eeas/jacques-delors-institute-remarks-hrvp-
josep-borrell-seminar-extra-territorial-sanctions_en.

43 George Ball, *The Case against Sanctions*, New York Times (Sept. 12, 1982), www.nytimes
.com/1982/09/12/magazine/the-case-against-sanctions.html.

44 Patrizio Merciai, *The Euro-Siberian Gas Pipeline Dispute – A Compelling Case for the
Adoption of Jurisdictional Codes of Conduct*, 8 Md. J. Int'l L. 12 (1984), https://
digitalcommons.law.umaryland.edu/mjil/vol8/iss1/3/.

45 *Extraterritorial Application of U.S. Law: The Case of Export Controls*, 132 U. Penn.
L. Rev. 355, 365–66 (1984).

46 Schmidt, note 4, at 61.

47 George-Dian Balan, *The Latest United States Sanctions against Iran: What Role to the WTO Security Exceptions?*, 18 J. Conflict & Sec. L. 365, 373 (2013), www.jstor.org/stable/26296265. *But see* Meredith Rathbone et al., *Sanctions, Sanctions Everywhere: Forging a Path through Complex Transnational Sanctions Laws*, 44 Geo. J. Int'l L. 1055, 1071 n. 105 (2013) (noting characterization of CISADA and other statutes as non-extraterritorial, since "[w]hile their effect may be aimed at foreign companies, the sanctions only impose legal duties on U.S. entities").

48 Ashish Kumar Sen, *A Brief History of Sanctions on Iran*, Atlantic Council New Atlanticist (May 8, 2018), www.atlanticcouncil.org/blogs/new-atlanticist/a-brief-history-of-sanctions-on-iran/.

49 Kali Robinson, *What Is the Iran Nuclear Deal?*, Council on Foreign Relations (July 20, 2022), www.cfr.org/backgrounder/what-iran-nuclear-deal; https://2009-2017 .state.gov/e/eb/tfs/spi/iran/jcpoa/index.htm; Kenneth Katzman, *Iran Sanctions*, Congressional Research Service (last updated Feb. 2, 2022), https://sgp.fas.org/crs/ mideast/RS20871.pdf; *The Rise and Fall of U.S. Secondary Sanctions: The Iran Outcasting and Re-Outcasting Regime*, https://digitalcommons.law.uga.edu/cgi/ viewcontent.cgi?article=2540&context=gjicl.

50 Luis Gutierrez, *Title III of the* Libertad *Act: Proceeding in the Absence of True Liberty*, 22 Marquette Benefits & Social Welfare L. Rev. 127, 127–28 (2020), https://scholarship.law .marquette.edu/cgi/viewcontent.cgi?article=1069&context=benefits.

51 John Bellinger and Sean Mirski, *Suits under Title III of the Helms-Burton Act Suffer Their First Significant Setback*, Lawfare (June 11, 2020), www.lawfaremedia.org/article/suits-under-title-iii-helms-burton-act-suffer-their-first-significant-setback.

52 *DS38: United States – The Cuban Liberty and Democratic Solidarity Act*, World Trade Organization (last reviewed Dec. 3, 2020), www.wto.org/english/tratop_e/dispu_e/cases_e/ ds38_e.htm; Elizabeth Wise, *EU to Continue Attack on Helms Burton Law*, Politico (Oct. 16, 1996), www.politico.eu/article/eu-to-continue-attack-on-helms-burton-law/.

53 Joy Gordon, *Extraterritoriality: Issues of Overbreadth and the Chilling Effect in the Cases of Cuba and Iran*, 57 Harvard J. Int'l L. Online (Jan. 2016) at 3, https://harvardilj.org/wp-content/uploads/sites/15/January-2016_Vol-57_Gordon.pdf; Natalia Maniaci, *The Helms-Burton Act: Is the U.S. Shooting Itself in the Foot?*, 35 San Diego L. Rev. 897, 909 (1998), https://digital.sandiego.edu/cgi/viewcontent.cgi?article=3235&context=sdlr.

54 *Declaration by the High Representative on Behalf of the EU on the Full Activation of the Helms-Burton (LIBERTAD) Act by the United States*, Council of the European Union (May 2, 2019), www.consilium.europa.eu/en/press/press-releases/2019/05/02/declaration-by-the-high-representative-on-behalf-of-the-eu-on-the-full-activation-of-the-helms-burton-liber tad-act-by-the-united-states/.

55 *What Is the Blocking Statute?*, European Commission, https://finance.ec.europa.eu/eu-and-world/open-strategic-autonomy/extraterritoriality-blocking-statute_en.

56 *Bank Melli Iran* (C-124/20), InfoCuria (May 12, 2021), https://curia.europa.eu/juris/docu ment/document.jsf?text=&docid=241168&pageIndex=0&doclang=en&mode=lst&dir=& occ=first&part=1&cid=3640369.

57 Lena Hornkohl, The Extraterritorial Application of Statutes and Regulations in EU Law (2022), at 28, https://papers.ssrn.com/sol3/papers.cfm?abstract_id=4036688.

58 *Foreign Extraterritorial Measures Act*, Government of Canada (Mar. 31, 2011), https://laws-lois.justice.gc.ca/eng/acts/f-29/index.html.

59 David Mortlock, *The "Blocking Statute": China's New Attempt to Subvert US Sanctions*, Atlantic Council (Feb. 8, 2021), www.atlanticcouncil.org/blogs/new-atlanticist/the-blocking-statute-chinas-new-attempt-to-subvert-us-sanctions/.

60 *The 10 INSTEX Shareholder States Have Agreed to Liquidate INSTEX due to Continued Obstruction from Iran*, Ministère de L'Europe et Des Affaire Étrangères (Mar. 9, 2023), www.diplomatie.gouv.fr/en/country-files/iran/news/article/the-10-instex-shareholder-states-have-decided-to-liquidate-instex-due-to.

61 Tytti Erästö, *European Non-Proliferation Diplomacy in the Shadow of Secondary Sanctions*, SIPRI (Aug. 2020), www.sipri.org/sites/default/files/2020–08/pb_2008_instex.pdf.

62 Marie Aftalion, *INSTEX, a Game Changer?*, VCDNP, www.nonproliferation.eu/wp-content/uploads/2020/04/Marie-Aftalion-INSTEX-Paper_Final-1.pdf.

63 *China's Ambition of Extraterritorial Jurisdiction and the American Response*, Columbia J. Transnat'l L. Bulletin (Mar. 4, 2021), www.jtl.columbia.edu/bulletin-blog/chinas-ambition-of-extraterritorial-jurisdiction-and-the-american-response.

64 Bernadette Zelger, *EU Competition Law and Extraterritorial Jurisdiction – A Critical Analysis of the ECJ's Judgment in* Intel, 16 European Competition Journal 613, www.tandfonline.com/doi/full/10.1080/17441056.2020.1840844.

65 Jeannette Chu, *The New Arms Race: Sanctions, Export Control Policy, and China*, CSIS (Mar. 25, 2022), www.csis.org/analysis/new-arms-race-sanctions-export-control-policy-and-china; Bruce Jentleson, Sanctions: What Everyone Needs to Know® (2022), at 146.

66 Bethany Allen-Ebrahimian, *The Rise of China's Secondary Sanctions*, Axios (Jan. 25, 2022), www.axios.com/2022/01/25/china-secondary-sanctions-lithuania-dispute-taiwan.

67 Tristan Kohl, *Unilateral and Extraterritorial Sanctions Symposium: Extraterritorial Sanctions – Overcompliance and Globalization*, Opinio Juris (Feb. 3, 2022), https://opiniojuris.org/2022/03/02/unilateral-and-extraterritorial-sanctions-symposium-extraterritorial-sanctions-overcompliance-and-globalization/.

68 Jason Bartlett and Megan Ophel, *Sanctions by the Numbers: U.S. Secondary Sanctions*, CNAS (Aug. 26, 2021), www.cnas.org/publications/reports/sanctions-by-the-numbers-u-s-secondary-sanctions.

69 Daniel Drezner, *How Not to Sanction*, 98 Int'l Affairs 1533 (2022), https://academic.oup.com/ia/article/98/5/1533/6686647; *"Maximum Pressure": US Economic Sanctions Harm Iranians' Right to Health*, Human Rights Watch (Oct. 29, 2019), www.hrw.org/report/2019/10/29/maximum-pressure/us-economic-sanctions-harm-iranians-right-health.

70 Amir Abdoli, *Iran, Sanctions, and the COVID-19 Crisis*, 23 Journal of Medical Economics 1461 (Dec. 16, 2020), www.tandfonline.com/doi/full/10.1080/13696998.2020.1856855; Djaved Salehi Isfahani, *Iran: The Double Jeopardy of Sanctions and COVID-19*, Brookings (2020), www.brookings.edu/opinions/iran-the-double-jeopardy-of-sanctions-and-covid-19/; Gordon, note 53, at 9.

71 *High Commissioner to Human Rights Council: Sanctions Can Create Severe and Undue Suffering for Individuals Who Have Neither Perpetrated Crimes nor Otherwise Borne Responsibility for Improper Conduct*, United Nations Human Rights (Sept. 16, 2021), www.ohchr.org/en/press-releases/2021/09/high-commissioner-human-rights-coun

cil-sanctions-can-create-severe-and-undue ("[t]he negative humanitarian effects of [unilateral] sanctions were exacerbated enormously by their extraterritorial application, the expanding use of secondary sanctions, and civil and criminal penalties against those who cooperated with States, companies and individuals targeted by primary sanctions").

72 *CAATSA Section 231 "Imposition of Sanctions on Turkish Presidency of Defense Industries"*, U.S. Department of State (Dec. 14, 2020), https://2017-2021.state.gov/caatsa-section-231-imposition-of-sanctions-on-turkish-presidency-of-defense-industries/index.html.

73 Agathe Demarais, Backfire (2022), at 73; Samantha Sultoon and Justine Walker, *Secondary Sanctions' Implications and the Transatlantic Relationship*, Atlantic Council Economic Sanctions Initiative and UK Finance (2019), www.atlanticcouncil.org/wp-content/uploads/2019/09/SecondarySanctions_Final.pdf.

74 Kerbrat, note 28, 181–82; PEESA (Sec. 7503 of FY2020 NDAA), as amended by FY2021 NDAA Sec. 1242; Olivier Malherbe, *U.S. Economic Sanctions against Nord Stream 2 under International Jurisdiction Principles*, 53 N.Y.U. J. Int'l L. & Pol. 1017 (2021), www.nyujilp.org/wp-content/uploads/2021/08/NYUJILP_53.3_Olivier-Malherbe_US-Sanctions-Nord-Stream-2.pdf.

75 22 U.S.C. 9526; Paul Belkin, Michael Ratner, and Cory Welt, *Russia's Nord Stream 2 Natural Gas Pipeline to Germany Halted*, Congressional Research Service (last updated Mar. 10, 2022), https://crsreports.congress.gov/product/pdf/IF/IF11138.

76 *FAQ 1082*, U.S. Department of the Treasury (Sept. 15, 2022), https://home.treasury.gov/policy-issues/financial-sanctions/faqs/1082.

77 *US Sanctions Threat Zaps Russia's Homegrown Mir Cards in Setback*, Bloomberg (Nov. 22, 2022), www.bloomberg.com/news/articles/2022-11-22/us-sanctions-threat-zaps-russia-s-homegrown-mir-cards-in-setback.

78 Suhasini Haidar, *U.S. Deputy NSA Cautions India against Trade Deals with Russia*, The Hindu (Mar. 31, 2022), www.thehindu.com/news/national/us-deputy-nsa-daleep-singh-cautions-india-against-trade-deals-with-russia/article65277933.ece.

79 Joop Voetelink, *Limits on the Extraterritoriality of United States Export Control and Sanctions Legislation*, Netherlands Annual Review of Military Studies, at 187 (2021), https://link.springer.com/chapter/10.1007/978-94-6265-471-6_11..

80 *Treasury Targets Actors*, note 1,.

81 *Treasury Imposes Swift and Severe Costs on Russia for Putin's Purported Annexation of Regions of Ukraine*, U.S. Department of the Treasury (Sept. 30, 2022), https://home.treasury.gov/news/press-releases/jy0981; Marcin Szczepański, *Briefing: Russia's War on Ukraine: US Sanctions*, European Parliamentary Research Service, at 2 (Feb. 2023), www.europarl.europa.eu/RegData/etudes/BRIE/2023/739358/EPRS_BRI(2023)739358_EN.pdf.

82 James Politi and Derek Brower, *US Warns of Sanctions for Buyers that Flout Price Cap on Russian Oil*, Financial Times (Sept. 9, 2022), www.ft.com/content/e5b63797-1aad-46cd-ab30-c1b5d014b140.

83 *Toomey, Van Hollen Comment on G7 Price Cap*, United States Senate Committee on Banking, Housing, and Urban Affairs (Dec. 5, 2022), www.banking.senate.gov/newsroom/minority/toomey-van-hollen-comment-on-g7-price-cap-agreement.

84 Alan Rappeport, *The U.S. Accused Chinese Companies of Supporting Russia's Military*, New York Times (June 29, 2022), www.nytimes.com/2022/06/29/business/chinese-com panies-russia-sanctions.html.

85 *Addition of Entities, Revision and Correction of Entries, and Removal of Entities from the Entity List*, Bureau of Industry and Security (June 30, 2022), https://public-inspection .federalregister.gov/2022-14069.pdf.

86 *Extraterritorial application*, New Zealand Russia Sanctions Act 2022, Public Act 2022 No. 6 (date of assent Mar. 11, 2022), www.legislation.govt.nz/act/public/2022/0006/latest/ whole.html#LMS652967.

87 *Questions and Answers on the eighth package of restrictive measures against Russia*, European Commission (Oct. 6, 2022), https://ec.europa.eu/commission/presscorner/ detail/en/qanda_22_5990.

88 Decisions (CFSP) 2022/1907, amending Decision 2014/145/CFSP.

89 Kerbrat, note 28; Simon Henseler and Aurelia Tamò-Larrieux, *Reaching beyond Its Territory – An Analysis of the Extraterritorial Scope of European Data Protection Law*, Research Handbook on EU Data Protection Law (2022).

90 Erica Moret, *Sanctions and the Costs of Russia's War in Ukraine*, Reliefweb (May 12, 2022), https://reliefweb.int/report/ukraine/sanctions-and-costs-russia-s-war-ukraine.

CHAPTER 5 THE ENERGY PROBLEM

1 Silvia Amaro, *"Russia Is Blackmailing Us": EU Asks Member States to Ration Energy as Putin Tightens Grip on Gas Supplies*, CNBC (July 20, 2022), www.cnbc.com/2022/07/20/ europe-to-ask-countries-to-reduce-energy-usage-as-putin-tightens-grip-on-gas.html.

2 Alejandro de la Garza, *John Kerry: "We Have to Push Back Hard" on Efforts to Build New Fossil Fuel Infrastructure in Response to Rising Gas Prices*, Time (June 7, 2022), https://time .com/6184946/john-kerry-2022-time100-summit/.

3 Edward C. Chow, *Smart Oil Sanctions against Russia*, CSIS (June 14, 2022), www.csis.org/ analysis/smart-oil-sanctions-against-russia.

4 *1850–2022: Oil Dependence and U.S. Foreign Policy*, Council on Foreign Relations (Apr. 12, 2023), www.cfr.org/timeline/oil-dependence-and-us-foreign-policy.

5 *Oil Embargo against South Africa*, United Nations General Assembly (Jan. 24, 1979), https://digitallibrary.un.org/record/618859?ln=en.

6 Comprehensive Anti-Apartheid Act of 1986, 99th Congress (1986), www.congress.gov/bill/ 99th-congress/house-bill/4868.

7 Bernard Gwertzman, *U.S. Decision to Embargo Libyan Oil Is Reported*, New York Times (Feb. 26, 1982), www.nytimes.com/1982/02/26/world/us-decision-to-embargo-libyan-oil-is-reported.html; *The U.S. Tightened Its Sanctions against Libya*, Los Angeles Times (June 23, 1986), www.latimes.com/ archives/la-xpm-1986-06-23-fi-20027-story.html; Agathe Demarais, Backfire (2022), at 36–37.

8 Office of the Historian, *Oil Embargo, 1973–1974*, U.S. Department of State (last reviewed 2016), https://history.state.gov/milestones/1969-1976/oil-embargo.

9 *Effects of the Repeal of the Crude Oil Export Ban*, U.S. Government Accountability Office (Oct. 2020), www.gao.gov/assets/gao-21-118.pdf.

10 *Id.*

11 Sharon Otterman, *IRAQ: Oil for Food Scandal*, Council on Foreign Relations (Oct. 28, 2005), www.cfr.org/backgrounder/iraq-oil-food-scandal/.

12 *Treasury Sanctions Venezuela's State-Owned Oil Company Petroleos de Venezuela, S.A.*, U.S. Department of the Treasury (Jan. 28, 2019), https://home.treasury.gov/news/press-releases/sm594; D. J. Wolff and Eduardo Mathison, *All or Nothing? OFAC Adds PDVSA to the SDN List*, Crowell (Jan. 30, 2019), www.crowell.com/NewsEvents/AlertsNewsletters/all/All-or-Nothing-OFAC-Adds-PDVSA-to-the-SDN-List.

13 Demarais, note 7, at 36–37.

14 Directive 4 (as amended on Oct. 31, 2017) under Executive Order 13,662, https://ofac.treasury.gov/media/8716/download?inline.

15 Eugene Rumer et al., *Russia in the Arctic: A Critical Examination*, Carnegie Endowment for International Peace (Mar. 29, 2021), https://carnegieendowment.org/2021/03/29/russia-in-arctic-critical-examination-pub-84181.

16 Ella Koeze and Clifford Krauss, *Why Gas Prices Are So High*, New York Times (June 14, 2022), www.nytimes.com/interactive/2022/06/14/business/gas-prices.html.

17 Marc Stocker, John Baffes and Dana Vorisek, *What Triggered the Oil Price Plunge of 2014–2016 and Why It Failed to Deliver an Economic Impetus in Eight Charts*, Let's Talk Development (World Bank Blogs) (Jan. 18, 2018), https://blogs.worldbank.org/developmenttalk/what-triggered-oil-price-plunge-2014-2016-and-why-it-failed-deliver-economic-impetus-eight-charts/.

18 Rebecca Engebretsen and Catherine Anderson, *The Impact of Coronavirus (COVID-19) and the Global Oil Price Shock on the Fiscal Position of Oil-Exporting Developing Countries*, OECD (Sept. 30, 2020), www.oecd.org/coronavirus/policy-responses/the-impact-of-coronavirus-covid-19-and-the-global-oil-price-shock-on-the-fiscal-position-of-oil-exporting-developing-countries-8bafbd95//, citing *Oil Market Report – April 2020*, International Energy Agency (Apr. 15, 2020), www.iea.org/reports/oil-market-report-april-2020.

19 David Gaffen, *Analysis: Oil's Journey from Worthless in the Pandemic to $100 a Barrel*, Reuters (Feb. 24, 2022), www.reuters.com/business/energy/oils-journey-worthless-pandemic-100-barrel-2022-02-24/.

20 *Crude Petroleum in Russia*, Observatory of Economic Complexity (May 6, 2023), https://oec.world/en/profile/bilateral-product/crude-petroleum/reporter/rus.

21 *Id.*

22 *Energy Fact Sheet: Why Does Russian Oil and Gas Matter?*, International Energy Agency (Mar. 21, 2022), www.iea.org/articles/energy-fact-sheet-why-does-russian-oil-and-gas-matter.

23 Kim Mackrael, *In Symbolic Move, Canada Bans Russian Oil Imports*, Wall Street Journal (Feb. 28, 2022), www.wsj.com/livecoverage/russia-ukraine-latest-news-2022-02-28/card/in-symbolic-move-canada-bans-russian-oil-imports-9rZUk6fmTPxRoBgSEIai; *Government of Canada Moves to Prohibit Import of Russian Oil*, Government of Canada (Feb. 28, 2022), www.canada.ca/en/natural-resources-canada/news/2022/02/government-of-canada-moves-to-prohibit-import-of-russian-oil.html.

24 *Id.*

25 *Oil Supply and Demand*, Governement of Canada (last updated Dec. 16, 2019), www.nrcan.gc.ca/our-natural-resources/energy-sources-distribution/fossil-fuels/crude-oil/oil-supply-demand/18086.

26 S.3757 – *Ban Russian Energy Imports Act*, 117th Congress (introduced Mar. 3, 2022), www
.congress.gov/bill/117th-congress/senate-bill/3757.

27 *Press Briefing by Press Secretary Jen Psaki*, The White House (Mar. 3, 2022), www
.whitehouse.gov/briefing-room/press-briefings/2022/03/03/press-briefing-by-press-secretary-
jen-psaki-march-3rd-2022/.

28 Tom Wilson, Ji Pickard and Harriet Agnew, *BP Under Pressure over Ties to Rosneft and
Fuel Supplies to Russian Army*, Financial Times (Feb. 25, 2022), www.ft.com/content/
24ee9fcb-0ee5-4487-9185-0bc12b6fde0c.

29 Bernard Looney, *A Message to All bp Staff on Our Relationship with Rosneft*, bp (Feb. 27,
2022), www.bp.com/en/global/corporate/news-and-insights/reimagining-energy/a-message-
to-all-bp-staff-on-our-relationship-with-rosneft.html; Darya Korsunskaya, *Exclusive: Russian
State Gave up Majority Stake in Rosneft in Venezuela Deal*, Reuters (Mar. 30, 2020), www
.reuters.com/article/us-russia-rosneft-venezuela-exclusive/exclusive-russian-state-gave-up-maj
ority-stake-in-rosneft-in-venezuela-deal-idUSKBN21H1HL.

30 Joe Hoppe, *Shell, BP to Withdraw from Russian Oil, Gas*, Wall Street Journal (Mar. 8,
2022), www.wsj.com/articles/shell-to-withdraw-from-russian-oil-and-gas-amid-ukraine-war-
11646737271.

31 *FACT SHEET: United States Bans Imports of Russian Oil, Liquefied Natural Gas, and
Coal*, The White House (Mar. 8, 2022), www.whitehouse.gov/briefing-room/statements-
releases/2022/03/08/fact-sheet-united-states-bans-imports-of-russian-oil-liquefied-natural-gas
-and-coal/; *Executive Order on Prohibiting Certain Imports and New Investments with
Respect to Continued Russian Federation Efforts to Undermine the Sovereignty and
Territorial Integrity of Ukraine*, The White House (Mar 8, 2022), www.whitehouse.gov/
briefing-room/presidential-actions/2022/03/08/executive-order-on-prohibiting-certain-imp
orts-and-new-investments-with-respect-to-continued-russian-federation-efforts-to-undermi
ne-the-sovereignty-and-territorial-integrity-of-ukraine/.

32 *UK to Phase Out Russian Oil Imports*, Government of the United Kingdom
(Mar. 8, 2022), www.gov.uk/government/news/uk-to-phase-out-russian-oil-imports.

33 *Id.*

34 *Russia – Extension of Sanctions on Russia to Prohibit the Import into Australia of Russian Oil
and Other Energy Products*, Department of Foreign Affairs and Trade (Mar. 11, 2022), www
.dfat.gov.au/news/news/russia-extension-sanctions-russia-prohibit-import-australia-russian-oil-
and-other-energy-products.

35 Jack Revell, *Australia Does Not Buy Petrol from Russia, So Why Are We Paying So Much
for Fuel?*, The Latch (Mar. 14, 2022), https://thelatch.com.au/where-does-australia-get-its-
petrol-from/.

36 *The EU Imported 58% of Its Energy in 2020*, Eurostat (Mar. 28, 2022), https://ec.europa.eu/
eurostat/web/products-eurostat-news/-/ddn-20220328-2.

37 *Infographic – Where Does the EU's Gas Come From?*, Council of the European Union
(last reviewed Feb. 7, 2023) www.consilium.europa.eu/en/infographics/eu-gas-supply; Oil
and petroleum products – a statistical overview, Eurostat (Mar. 15, 2023), https://ec.europa
.eu/eurostat/statistics-explained/index.php?title=Oil_and_petroleum_products_-_a_statisti
cal_overview&oldid=315177.

38 *Gas Factsheet*, European Union Agency for the Cooperation of Energy Regulators
(July 25, 2021), www.acer.europa.eu/gas-factsheet.

39 *Oil Dependency in the EU*, Cambridge Econometrics, at 8 (May 2020), www
.transportenvironment.org/wp-content/uploads/2021/07/2020_CE_Oil_Dependency_in_
EU_report.pdf.

40 *Oil and Petroleum at Record Low in 2020*, European Union (Feb. 18, 2022), https://ec
.europa.eu/eurostat/web/products-eurostat-news/-/ddn-20220218-1.

41 *The EU Imported 58% of Its Energy in 2020*, Eurostat (Mar. 28, 2022), https://ec.europa.eu/
eurostat/web/products-eurostat-news/-/ddn-20220328-2.

42 *Infographic: Where Does the EU's Energy Come From?*, Council of the European Union
(Sept. 27, 2022), www.consilium.europa.eu/en/infographics/where-does-the-eu-s-energy-
come-from/; John Psaropoulos, *Europe Leaps towards Energy Autonomy as Sanctions
undercut Russia*, Al Jazeera (Feb. 28, 2023), www.aljazeera.com/news/2023/2/28/europe-
leaps-towards-energy-autonomy-as-sanctions-undercut-russia.

43 Niamh Kennedy, *EU Agrees on a Partial Ban of Russian Oil Imports*, CNN Business
(May 31, 2022), www.cnn.com/2022/05/30/energy/eu-russian-oil/index.html; Victoria Kim,
Hungary's Oil Embargo Exemption is the Latest Sign of Its Leader's Affinity for Russia,
New York Times (May 31, 2022), www.nytimes.com/2022/05/31/world/europe/hungary-oil-
embargo-russia.html; *Russia's War on Ukraine: EU Adopts Sixth Package of Sanctions
against Russia*, European Commission (June 3, 2022), https://ec.europa.eu/commission/
presscorner/detail/en/IP_22_2802.

44 Ben Cahill, *European Union Imposes Partial Ban on Russian Oil*, CSIS (June 8,
2022), www.csis.org/analysis/european-union-imposes-partial-ban-russian-oil.

45 Kim, note 43.

46 *Key Facts about Gas in the EU*, European Union Agency for the Cooperation of Energy
Regulators (July 25, 2021), www.acer.europa.eu/gas-factsheet.

47 *Id.*

48 Chris Isidore, *Average US Gas Price Hits $5 for First Time*, CNN Business (June 13,
2022), www.cnn.com/2022/06/11/business/gas-prices-five-dollars-national-june/index.html.

49 Chris Isidore, *Inflation Rises at Fastest Pace in 40 Years, Pushed up by Record Gas Prices*,
CNN Business (June 10, 2022), www.cnn.com/2022/06/10/economy/may-inflation-gas-
prices/index.html; *Consumer Price Index Summary*, U.S. Bureau of Labor Statistics
(Aug. 10, 2023), www.bls.gov/news.release/cpi.nr0.htm; *Consumer Prices up 9.1 Percent
over the Year Ended June 2022, Largest Increase in 40 Years*, U.S. Bureau of Labor
Statistics (July 18, 2022), www.bls.gov/opub/ted/2022/consumer-prices-up-9-1-percent-
over-the-year-ended-june-2022-largest-increase-in-40-years.htm; *Consumer Price Index
Unchanged over the Month, up 8.5 Percent over the Year, in July 2022*, U.S. Bureau of
Labor Statistics (Aug. 15, 2022), www.bls.gov/opub/ted/2022/consumer-price-index-
unchanged-over-the-month-up-8-5-percent-over-the-year-in-july-2022.htm.

50 *Measuring Price Change in the CPI: Motor Fuel*, U.S. Bureau of Labor Statistics (last
modified Feb. 10, 2023), www.bls.gov/cpi/factsheets/motor-fuel.htm.

51 *Measuring Price Change in the CPI: Household Energy*, U.S. Bureau of Labor
Statistics (last modified Feb. 10, 2023), www.bls.gov/cpi/factsheets/household-energy
.htm.

52 François de Soyres et al., *Fiscal Policy and Excess Inflation during Covid-19: A Cross-
country view*, FEDS Notes (July 15, 2022), www.federalreserve.gov/econres/notes/feds-

notes/fiscal-policy-and-excess-inflation-during-covid-19-a-cross-country-view-20220715
.html.

53 Scott Horsley, *Inflation is Cooling Thanks to Gas Prices, but Many Things Still Cost More*,
NPR (Aug. 10, 2022), www.npr.org/2022/08/10/1116481885/gas-prices-inflation-interest-rates-
federal-reserve.

54 Yangyang Chen, Jiexin Jiang, Lei Wang, and Ruisong Wang, *Impact Assessment of Energy
Sanctions in Geo-conflict: Russian-Ukrainian War*, 9 Energy Reports 3082 (2023), www
.sciencedirect.com/science/article/pii/S2352484723001324.

55 *Press Conference by Secretary-General António Guterres at United Nations Headquarters*,
United Nations Meetings Coverage and Press Releases (Aug. 3, 2022), https://press.un.org/
en/2022/sgsm21397.doc.htm.

56 Peter Baker and Clifford Krauss, *Biden Slaps Oil Companies for Profiteering at the Pump*,
New York Times (June 15, 2022), www.nytimes.com/2022/06/15/business/biden-oil-com
panies-gas-prices.html.

57 *ExxonMobil Statement Regarding President Biden's Letter to Oil Industry*, ExxonMobil
(June 15, 2022), https://corporate.exxonmobil.com/News/Newsroom/News-releases/2022/
0615_ExxonMobil-statement-regarding-President-Biden-Letter-to-Oil-Industry/.

58 *Id.*

59 John Frittelli, *Shipping under the Jones Act: Legislative and Regulatory Background*,
Congressional Research Service (Nov. 21, 2019), https://sgp.fas.org/crs/misc/R45725.pdf.

60 Vincent H. Smith and Philip G. Hoxie, *Oil and the Jones Act*, American Enterprise
Institute (Apr. 17, 2020), www.aei.org/american-boondoggle/oil-and-the-jones-act/.

61 Colin Grabow, *New England Governors Seek Jones Act Relief as Spike in Winter Heating
Bills Looms*, Cato Institute (Aug. 26, 2022), www.cato.org/blog/new-england-governors-
seek-jones-act-relief-spike-winter-heating-bills-looms; *Letter from Charles Baker et al. to
Secretary of Energy Jennifer Granholm*, U.S. Department of Energy (July 27, 2022), www
.energy.gov/sites/default/files/2022-09/incoming%20-%20Baker%20Lamont%20Mills%20
Sununu%20McKee%20and%20Scott.pdf.

62 Reuters, *China's Imports of Russian Crude Oil Hit Record High*, CNN Business (June 20,
2022), www.cnn.com/2022/06/20/energy/china-russia-oil-imports-record/index.html.

63 Krutika Pathi and Elaine Kurtenbach, *India and China Increasingly Welcome Shunned
Russian Oil*, PBS NewsHour (June 13, 2022), www.pbs.org/newshour/world/india-and-
china-increasingly-welcome-shunned-russian-oil.

64 *Id.*

65 George Glover, *Iran Is Cutting Its Oil Prices to Compete with Crude for Chinese Buyers:
Report*, Market Insider (July 4, 2022), https://markets.businessinsider.com/news/commod
ities/oil-price-outlook-iran-russia-china-brent-urals-western-sanctions-2022-7.

66 *Iran and Russia's Gazprom Sign Primary Deal for Energy Cooperation*, Reuters (July 19,
2022), www.reuters.com/business/energy/iran-russias-gazprom-sign-primary-deal-energy-cooper
ation-2022-07-19/.

67 Stanley Reed, *With Russia's Exit, Norway Becomes Europe's Energy Champion*, New York
Times (Apr. 6, 2023), www.nytimes.com/2023/04/06/business/energy-environment/
ukraine-russia-war-europe-energy.html.

68 Matthew Kohlman et al., *Mexico Sending Record High Fuel Oil to the US as Refinery
Runs Rise*, S&P Global Commodity Insights (July 22, 2022), www.spglobal.com/commo

dityinsights/en/market-insights/latest-news/oil/072222-mexico-sending-record-high-fuel-oil-to-the-us-as-refinery-runs-rise; Arathy Somasekhar, *U.S. Imports of Latam Oil Soar as Refiners Replace Russian Barrels*, Reuters (May 19, 2022), www.reuters.com/markets/commodities/us-imports-latam-oil-soar-refiners-replace-russian-barrels-2022-05-19/.

69 *Qatar Signs Gas Export Deal with Germany*, DW (Nov. 29, 2022), www.dw.com/en/qatar-signs-gas-export-deal-with-germany/a-63923323.

70 *Dutch Gas Grid Operator Gasunie Says Brunsbuettel LNG Hub to Be Ready in 2026*, Reuters (Oct. 13, 2021), www.reuters.com/business/energy/dutch-gas-grid-operator-gasunie-says-brunsbuettel-lng-hub-be-ready-2026-2022-10-13/.

71 Vera Eckert, *Germany Completes Wilhemlshaven Floating LNG Terminal, More to Come*, Reuters (Nov. 15, 2022), www.reuters.com/business/energy/germany-completes-construction-wilhelmshaven-floating-lng-terminal-2022-11-15/.

72 *Member Countries*, Organization of the Petroleum Exporting Countries (Dec. 18, 2013), www.opec.org/opec_web/en/about_us/25.htm.

73 *Declaration of Cooperation*, Organization of the Petroleum Exporting Countries (Dec. 16, 2020), www.opec.org/opec_web/en/publications/4580.htm.

74 Jacob Bogage and Evan Halper, *OPEC Boosts Oil Production as Gas Prices Soar*, Washington Post (June 2, 2022), www.washingtonpost.com/business/2022/06/02/opec-oil-production-prices/.

75 Stanley Reed, *OPEC Plus Considering Major Production Cut to Prop Up Oil Prices*, New York Times (Oct. 22, 2022), www.nytimes.com/2022/10/02/business/opec-plus-production-cut.html.

76 Chen Aizhu, *Russia, China Agree to 30-Year Gas Deal via New Pipeline, to Settle in Euros*, Reuters (Feb. 4, 2022), www.reuters.com/world/asia-pacific/exclusive-russia-china-agree-30-year-gas-deal-using-new-pipeline-source-2022-02-04/.

77 David Sheppard, Neil Hume, and Tom Mitchell, *Mongolia Says Russia-China Gas Pipeline Will Break Ground in 2024*, Financial Times (July 17, 2022), www.ft.com/content/f0080bf6-5e7d-44be-871f-a5d44dccf5c5.

78 Heba Saleh, *Algeria Struggles to Meet Rising Demand for Its Gas after Russian Invasion of Ukraine*, Financial Times (Apr. 20, 2022), www.ft.com/content/3236fa97-e041-425b-a2a8-4b9c66d3e39b.

79 *Italy Signs Energy Deals with Algeria in Bid to Sidestep Russia*, Al Jazeera (July 19, 2022), www.aljazeera.com/news/2022/7/19/italy-signs-energy-deals-with-algeria-in-bid-to-sidestep-russia.

80 Gabriel Di Bella et al., *Natural Gas in Europe: The Potential Impact of Disruptions to Supply*, International Monetary Fund (July 19, 2022), www.imf.org/en/Publications/WP/Issues/2022/07/18/Natural-Gas-in-Europe-The-Potential-Impact-of-Disruptions-to-Supply-520934.

81 *Council Adopts Regulation on Gas Storage*, Council of the European Union (June 27, 2022), www.consilium.europa.eu/en/press/press-releases/2022/06/27/council-adopts-regulation-gas-storage/.

82 Matina Stevis-Gridneff, *With Russian Cutoff Feared, Europeans Are Told to Curb Natural Gas Use*, New York Times (July 20, 2022), www.nytimes.com/2022/07/20/world/europe/eu-russia-gas-rationing.html.

83 Sabine Kinkartz, *Gas Shortage: Will Heating Become a Luxury in Germany?*, DW (July 31, 2022), www.dw.com/en/gas-shortage-will-heating-become-a-luxury-in-germany/a-62657502; Richard Connor, *Hanover Turns Off Hot Water with Eye to Winter Gas Shortages*, DW (July 29, 2022), www.dw.com/en/hanover-turns-off-hot-water-with-eye-to-winter-gas-short ages/a-62638434.

84 Beth Timmins, *Germany Approves Energy-Saving Measures for Winter*, BBC (Aug. 25, 2022), www.bbc.com/news/business-62659247.

85 *G7 Finance Ministers' Statement on the United Response to Russia's War of Aggression against Ukraine*, G7 Finance Ministers' Statement (Sept. 2, 2022), www .bundesfinanzministerium.de/Content/EN/Downloads/G7-G20/2022-09-02-g7-ministers-statement.pdf?__blob=publicationFile&v=7.

86 *Preliminary Guidance on Implementation of a Maritime Services Policy and Related Price Exception for Seaborne Russian Oil*, U.S. Department of the Treasury (Sept. 9, 2022), https://ofac.treasury.gov/media/925551/download?inline.

87 Muyu Xu, *APPEC U.S. Official Rules Out Secondary Sanctions for Russian Oil Price Cap*, Reuters (Sept. 26, 2022), www.reuters.com/business/energy/appec-us-official-rules-out-secondary-sanctions-russian-oil-price-cap-2022-09-26/.

88 Andrew Duehren and Laurence Norman, *Biden Administration Resists Call to Broaden Russia Oil-Price Cap*, Wall Street Journal (Sept. 26, 2022), www.wsj.com/articles/biden-administration-resists-call-to-broaden-plan-for-russia-oil-price-cap-11664136499.

89 Elisabetta Cornago, *EU Energy Ministers Reach Deal on Gas Price Cap*, Financial Times (Dec. 19, 2022), www.ft.com/content/5b2ffae4-04d1-4e09-89ce-b85f575d8422.

90 *The Energy Crisis and Europe's Astonishing Luck*, Economist (Jan. 11, 2023), www .economist.com/finance-and-economics/2023/01/11/the-energy-crisis-and-europes-astonish ing-luck.

91 Stanley Reed and Melissa Eddy, *Europe Has Weathered an Energy Crisis, for Now*, New York Times (Feb. 24, 2023), www.nytimes.com/2023/02/24/business/europe-energy-crisis .html.

92 Anna Hirtenstein and Benoit Faucon, *Russian Oil Producers Stay One Step Ahead of Sanctions*, Wall Street Journal (June 1, 2022), www.wsj.com/articles/russian-oil-producers-stay-one-step-ahead-of-sanctions-11654076614.

93 *Id.*; Tim de Chant, *Russian Oil Tankers Go Dark, Evading Name-and-Shame Twitter Bot*, Ars Technica (Mar. 28, 2022), https://arstechnica.com/tech-policy/2022/03/twitter-bot-tracks-russian-oil-tankers-in-advance-of-sanctions/. Hannah Towey, *Russian Tankers Turned Off Their Tracking Signals at More than Double the Normal Rate in March, as "Dark Activity" Skyrockets Following the Invasion of Ukraine*, Business Insider (Apr. 6, 2022), www.businessinsider.com/russian-tankers-turned-off-tracking-systems-sanctions-eva sion-2022-3.

94 Anna Hirtenstein, *The West Is Still Buying Russian Oil, but It's Now Harder to Track*, Wall Street Journal (Apr. 21, 2022), www.wsj.com/articles/russian-oil-flows-but-increasingly-under-the-radar-11650541684.

95 Anna Hirtenstein, *U.S. Releases Oil Tanker That Sailed From Russian Port*, Wall Street Journal (July 1, 2022), www.wsj.com/articles/u-s-releases-vitol-oil-tanker-that-sailed-from-russian-port-11656686403.

96 Barbara Moens, Leonie Kijewski and Jacopo Barigazzi, *EU Agrees Oil Price Cap in New Russia Sanctions Plan*, Politico (Oct. 4, 2022), www.politico.eu/article/eu-agrees-oil-price-cap-plan-in-new-russia-sanctions/.

97 *Id.*

98 Daniel Gros, *Will Europe's Embargo on Russian Oil Succeed?*, Project Syndicate (June 6, 2022), www.project-syndicate.org/commentary/eu-embargo-on-russian-oil-limited-impact-by-daniel-gros-2022-06.

99 Amy Myers Jaffe, *Can Wealthy Nations Stop Buying Russian Oil?*, The Conversation (Mar. 1, 2022), https://theconversation.com/can-wealthy-nations-stop-buying-russian-oil-178008.

100 Sergei Vakulenko, *A Big Bang? Anticipating the Impact of Europe's Sanctions on Russian Energy*, Carnegie Endowment for International Peace (June 14, 2022), https://carnegieendowment.org/eurasiainsight/87318.

101 Hiroko Tabuchi, *Russia's Oil Revenue Soars Despite Sanctions, Study Finds*, New York Times (June 13, 2022), www.nytimes.com/2022/06/13/climate/russia-oil-gas-record-revenue.html, citing Centre for Research on Energy and Clean Air, *Financing Putin's War: Fossil Fuel Imports from Russia in the First 100 Days of the Invasion* (June 13, 2022), https://energyandcleanair.org/wp/wp-content/uploads/2022/06/Financing-Putins-war-100-days_20220613.pdf.

102 Victoria Kim, Clifford Krauss, and Anton Torianovski, *Western Move to Choke Russia's Oil Exports Boomerangs, for Now*, New York Times (June 21, 2022), www.nytimes.com/2022/06/21/world/europe/ukraine-russian-oil-embargo.html.

103 Oleg Ustenko, *The West's Phantom Energy Sanctions Fuel Russia's War Machine*, Financial Times (Aug. 7, 2022), www.ft.com/content/e593ae2f-62c5-4d8a-8011-b18b6cdee5d0.

104 Georgi Kantchev, *Sanctions Threaten Russia's Next Huge Oil Field*, Wall Street Journal (July 5, 2022), www.wsj.com/articles/sanctions-threaten-russias-next-huge-oil-field-1167018190.

105 Georgi Kantchev, *Gazprom Claims Force Majeure in Its Halt of Gas Deliveries to Europe*, Wall Street Journal (July 18, 2022), www.wsj.com/articles/gazprom-claims-force-majeure-in-its-halt-of-gas-deliveries-to-europe-11658165893.

106 *Uniper Has Received Gazprom's Force majeure Letter on Gas Supplies*, Reuters (July 18, 2022), www.reuters.com/article/ukraine-crisis-gazprom-uniper/uniper-has-received-gazproms-force-majeure-letter-on-gas-supplies-idUSL8N2YZ3VA.

107 *Nord Stream 1: Why Is Russia Cutting Gas Supplies to Europe?*, BBC (July 27, 2022), www.bbc.com/news/world-europe-60131520.

108 *Nord Stream 1 Gas Flows Stop as Maintenance Begins*, Reuters (July 11, 2022), www.reuters.com/business/energy/nord-stream-1-gas-flows-dwindle-maintenance-begins-2022-07-11/.

109 Cassandra Vinograd, *Canada Will Return a Sanctioned Nord Stream 1 Turbine to Ease Germany's Gas Crisis*, New York Times (July 10, 2022), www.nytimes.com/2022/07/10/world/europe/germany-gas-crisis-canada.html.

110 *Comment of the Ministry of Foreign Affairs of Ukraine in Connection with the Decision by the Government of Canada to Return the Repaired Nord Stream 1 Turbines to Germany*, Ministry of Foreign Affairs of Ukraine (July 10, 2022), www.kmu.gov.ua/en/news/zaiava-

mzs-ukrainy-u-zviazku-iz-rishenniam-kanady-povernuty-do-nimechchyny-vidremonto
vani-turbiny-pivnichnoho-potoku-1.

111 Darren Major, *Ottowa Revokes Sanctions Waiver on Nord Stream Gas Turbines*, CBC
(Dec. 14, 2022), www.cbc.ca/news/politics/sanctions-waiver-nord-stream-revoked-1
.6686306.

112 Irene Nasser and Yong Xiong, *Russian Gas Is Flowing to Europe Again over the Crucial
Nord Stream 1 Pipeline*, CNN Business (July 21, 2022), www.cnn.com/2022/07/21/energy/
nord-stream-1-gas/index.html.

113 *Russia to Further Slash Gas Deliveries to Germany via Nord Stream Pipeline*, DW (July 25,
2022), www.dw.com/en/russia-to-further-slash-gas-deliveries-to-germany-via-nord-stream-
pipeline/a-62588620.

114 Geoff Brumfiel and Rob Schmitz, *Seismologists Suspect Explosions Damaged Undersea
Pipelines that Carry Russian Gas*, NPR (Sept. 27, 2022), www.npr.org/2022/09/27/
1125401980/nord-stream-leaks-explosions-russia-natural-gas-sabotage.

115 Laura Benshoff, *The Nord Stream Pipelines Have Stopped Leaking. But the Methane
Emitted Broke Records*, NPR (Oct. 4, 2022), www.npr.org/2022/10/04/1126562195/the-nord-
stream-pipelines-have-stopped-leaking-but-the-methane-emitted-broke-rec.

116 Shane Harris et al., *No Conclusive Evidence Russia Is Behind the Nord Stream Attack*,
The Washington Post (Dec. 21, 2022), www.washingtonpost.com/national-security/2022/
12/21/russia-nord-stream-explosions/.

117 Mauro Orro and Jenny Strasburg, *Russia Takes Control of International LNG Project*,
Wall Street Journal (July 1, 2022), www.wsj.com/articles/russia-takes-control-of-inter
national-lng-project-11656678678?mod=article_inline; *Putin Orders Transfer of
Sakhalin-2 Gas Project to Russian Entity*, Financial Times (July 1, 2022), www.ft.com/
content/787d185a-d64b-4568-a181-93229e17d266.

118 Uka Obayashi, *Japan's JERA Signs New LNG Deal with Russia's Sakhalin-2*, Reuters
(Aug. 26, 2022), www.reuters.com/business/energy/jera-signs-deal-with-new-operator-
russias-sakhalin-2-keep-lng-contract-2022-08-26/.

119 *Russia Allows $1.2 bln Sakhalin-2 Payment to Shell – Kommersant*, Reuters (Apr. 4,
2023), www.reuters.com/markets/deals/russia-allows-12-bln-sakhalin-2-payment-shell-kom
mersant-2023-04-04/.

120 Andrew E. Kramer, *Russia Raises Pressure on Sakhalin-2 Project*, New York Times
(Oct. 25, 2006), www.nytimes.com/2006/10/25/business/worldbusiness/25iht-shell.3285227
.html; Andrew E. Kramer, *Moscow Gets Further Concession on Sakhalin-2*, New York
Times (Dec. 28, 2006), www.nytimes.com/2006/12/28/business/worldbusiness/28iht-shell
.4042726.html.

121 Sabrina Valle, *Exclusive: Exxon Exits Russia Empty-Handed with Oil Project "Unilaterally
Rerminated"*, Reuters (Oct. 17, 2022), www.reuters.com/business/energy/exclusive-exxon-
exits-russia-empty-handed-with-oil-project-unilaterally-2022-10-17/.

122 Colin Eaton, *Russia Wipes Out Exxon's Stake in Sakhalin Oil-and-Gas Project*, Wall
Street Journal (Oct. 17, 2022), www.wsj.com/articles/russia-wipes-out-exxons-stake-in-sakh
alin-oil-and-gas-project-11666040367; Justin Jacobs, *ExxonMobil Accuses Russia of
"Expropriation" as It Exits Oil Project*, Financial Times (Oct. 17, 2022), www.ft.com/
content/3f46cfb0-68d2-4d29-b98e-1d7628d4638a.

123 *Japan to Maintain Stake in Russia's Sakhalin 1 Oil Project*, Nikkei Asia (Nov. 4, 2022), https://asia.nikkei.com/Business/Energy/Japan-to-maintain-stake-in-Russia-s-Sakhalin-1-oil-project; *Japan Government Decides to Retain Stake in New Sakhalin-1 Operator*, Reuters (Oct. 31, 2022), www.reuters.com/business/energy/japan-govt-says-it-asked-firms-apply-stake-new-sakhalin-1-operator-2022-11-01/.

124 *EU and Azerbaijan Enhance Bilateral Relations, Including Energy Cooperation*, European Union (July 18, 2022), https://ec.europa.eu/commission/presscorner/detail/en/IP_22_4550.

125 Jennifer Rankin, *Human Rights Groups Criticise EU's Azerbaijan Gas Deal*, The Guardian (July 19, 2022), www.theguardian.com/world/2022/jul/19/human-rights-groups-criticise-eus-azerbaijan-gas-deal.

126 Melissa Eddy and Stanley Reed, *Germany Counts on Chilled Gas to Keep Warm Over Winter*, New York Times (July 27, 2022), www.nytimes.com/2022/07/27/world/europe/germany-lng-energy-gas.html.

127 Lisa Friedman, *Biden Administration Offers an Offshore Drilling Plan. Likely Backers: Very Few*, New York Times (July 1, 2022), www.nytimes.com/2022/07/01/climate/biden-oil-gas-drilling-alaska.html.

128 *Causes and Effects of Climate Change*, United Nations (Mar. 21, 2022), www.un.org/en/climatechange/science/causes-effects-climate-change.

129 *Future of Climate Change*, City of Chicago, United States Environmental Protection Agency (Dec. 20, 2019), https://climatechange.chicago.gov/climate-change-science/future-climate-change#ref2, citing T.F. Stocker et al., eds., Climate Change 2013: The Physical Science Basis (2014).

130 *IPC Report: "Code Red" for Human Driven Global Heating, Warns UN Chief*, United Nations (Aug. 9, 2021), https://news.un.org/en/story/2021/08/1097362.

131 *Vital Signs*, NASA (last updated Aug. 24, 2022) https://climate.nasa.gov/vital-signs/sea-level/.

132 Rebecca Lindsey, *Climate Change: Global Sea Level*, NOAA (Apr. 19, 2022), www.climate.gov/news-features/understanding-climate/climate-change-global-sea-level.

133 Somini Sengupta and Melissa Eddy, *War and Warming Upend Global Energy Supplies and Amplify Suffering*, New York Times (July 20, 2022), www.nytimes.com/2022/07/20/climate/global-energy-crisis-climate-war.html.

134 *Climate Target Plan*, European Commission (Mar. 15, 2020), https://ec.europa.eu/clima/eu-action/european-green-deal/2030-climate-target-plan_en.

135 *Gas Supply Security in the EU*, European Union (Oct. 31, 2022), https://eur-lex.europa.eu/EN/legal-content/summary/gas-supply-security-in-the-eu.html.

136 *Secure Gas Supplies*, European Commission (Mar. 30, 2023), https://energy.ec.europa.eu/topics/energy-security/secure-gas-supplies_en.

137 *UN Climate Change Conference UK 2021*, UK National Archives (last accessed Apr. 1, 2023), https://ukcop26.org/.

138 Kate Abnett and Simon Jessop, *U.S., Canada among 20 Countries to Commit to Stop Financing Fossil Fuels Abroad*, Reuters (Nov. 4, 2021), www.reuters.com/business/cop/19-countries-plan-cop26-deal-end-financing-fossil-fuels-abroad-sources-2021-11-03/.

139 Adie Tomer, *The Russian Oil Embargo Proves We Need a Clean Energy Revolution*, Brookings (Mar. 16, 2022), www.brookings.edu/blog/the-avenue/2022/03/16/the-russian-oil-embargo-proves-we-a-need-a-clean-energy-revolution/.

140 Evan Halper, *Why an Energy Crisis and $5 Gas Aren't Spurring a Green Revolution*, Washington Post (June 14, 2022), www.washingtonpost.com/business/2022/06/14/gas-prices-energy-climate/.

141 John Kerry: *"We have to Push Back Hard" on Efforts to Build New Fossil Fuel Infrastructure in Response to Rising Gas Prices*, Time (June 7, 2022), https://time.com/6184946/john-kerry-2022-time100-summit/; www.youtube.com/watch?v=QXma_uVutBk.

142 *China Tells Europe Not to Backslide on Climate Commitments*, Al Jazeera (Sept. 22, 2022), www.aljazeera.com/news/2022/9/22/china-tells-europe-dont-backslide-on-climate-commitments.

143 Paul Hockenos, *How Russia's War Is Putting Green Tech Progress in Jeopardy*, Yale Environment (June 16, 2022), https://e360.yale.edu/features/russia-ukraine-war-metals-electric-vehicles-renewables.

144 Ashutosh Pandey, *How Russia's Invasion of Ukraine Rocked Commodity Markets*, DW (Mar. 23, 2022), www.dw.com/en/how-russias-invasion-of-ukraine-rocked-commodity-markets/a-61235041.

145 Fred Bever and Eric McDaniel, *Solar Projects Are on Hold as U.S. Investigates whether China Is Skirting Trade Rules*, NPR (May 11, 2022), www.npr.org/2022/05/11/1097644931/solar-panels-solar-power-u-s-investigates-china-trade-rules.

146 Sarah Hurtes and Weiyi Cai, *Europe Is Sacrificing Its Ancient Forests for Energy*, New York Times (Sept. 7, 2022), www.nytimes.com/interactive/2022/09/07/world/europe/eu-logging-wood-pellets.html.

147 *Letter from Scientists to the EU Parliament Regarding Forest Biomass*, Partnership for Policy Integrity (last updated Jan. 14, 2018), www.pfpi.net/wp-content/uploads/2018/04/UPDATE-800-signatures_Scientist-Letter-on-EU-Forest-Biomass.pdf.

148 *Germany to Extend Last 2 Nuclear Power Plant Lifespans by a Few Weeks*, DW (May 9, 2022), www.dw.com/en/germany-to-extend-last-2-nuclear-power-plant-lifespans-by-a-few-weeks/a-63023953; Erika Solomon and Melissa Eddy, *Breaking Taboo, Germany Extends Life of 2 Nuclear Reactors*, New York Times (Sept. 5, 2022), www.nytimes.com/2022/09/05/world/europe/germany-extend-life-nuclear-reactors.html.

149 *Fact Sheet: President Biden Takes Bold Executive Action to Spur Domestic Clean Energy Manufacturing*, The White House (June 6, 2022), www.whitehouse.gov/briefing-room/statements-releases/2022/06/06/fact-sheet-president-biden-takes-bold-executive-action-to-spur-domestic-clean-energy-manufacturing/.

150 *BY THE NUMBERS: The Inflation Reduction Act*, The White House (Aug. 15, 2022), www.whitehouse.gov/briefing-room/statements-releases/2022/08/15/by-the-numbers-the-inflation-reduction-act/.

CHAPTER 6 TRADE AS A WEAPON

1 *Six Months into Russian Invasion, Commerce Actions Making a Difference in Support of Ukrainian People*, Bureau of Industry and Security (Aug. 25, 2022), www.bis.doc.gov/index.php/documents/about-bis/newsroom/press-releases/3123-2022-08-24-press-release-commerce-actions-in-support-of-ukraine/file.

2 *Western Sanctions Will Eventually Impair Russia's Economy*, Economist (Aug. 24, 2022), www.economist.com/finance-and-economics/2022/08/24/western-sanctions-will-eventually-impair-russias-economy.

3 *Russia*, Observatory of Economic Complexity (May 6, 2023), https://oec.world/en/profile/country/rus.

4 Douglas Broom, *What Else Does Russia Export, beyond Oil and Gas?*, World Economic Forum (Mar. 18, 2022), www.weforum.org/agenda/2022/03/russia-gas-oil-exports-sanctions/.

5 *FACT SHEET: United States, European Union, and G7 to Announce Further Economic Costs on Russia*, White House (Mar. 11, 2022), www.whitehouse.gov/briefing-room/statements-releases/2022/03/11/fact-sheet-united-states-european-union-and-g7-to-announce-further-economic-costs-on-russia/.

6 Sebastian Whale, *UK Bans Imports of Russian Caviar, Silver, and Other High-End Products*, Politico (Apr. 21, 2022), www.politico.eu/article/uk-russia-import-ban-silver-caviar-wood-boris-johnson/.

7 *Russia*, Observatory of Economic Complexity (last updated 2023), https://oec.world/en/profile/country/rus.

8 *Factbox: Western Ban on Russian Gold Imports Is Largely Symbolic*, Reuters (June 27, 2022), www.reuters.com/markets/commodities/western-ban-russian-gold-imports-is-largely-symbolic-2022-06-27/.

9 Martha Mendoza, *Six Months into War, Russian Goods Still Flowing to US*, AP News (Aug. 25, 2022), https://apnews.com/article/russia-ukraine-putin-biden-baltimore-only-on-ap-81a34ce2eecebe491f52ace380ce87fb.

10 *Id.*

11 Reuters, *Biden Administration May Block Russian Aluminum Imports*, CNBC (Oct. 12, 2022), www.cnbc.com/2022/10/13/biden-administration-may-block-russian-aluminum-imports.html; *Business Groups Say Bans on Russian Aluminum Will Decimate European Industry*, Reuters (Oct. 24, 2022), www.reuters.com/markets/commodities/business-groups-say-bans-russian-aluminium-will-decimate-european-industry-2022-10-24/.

12 *Treasury Designates Russian Oligarchs, Officials, and Entities in Response to Worldwide Malign Activity*, U.S. Department of the Treasury (Apr. 6, 2018), https://home.treasury.gov/news/press-releases/sm0338.

13 Margaret Taylor, *Lifting of Treasury Sanctions on Deripaska Highlights Role of Congress in Foreign Affairs Decisions*, Lawfare (Dec. 21, 2018), www.lawfaremedia.org/article/lifting-treasury-sanctions-deripaska-highlights-role-congress-foreign-affairs-decisions.

14 *Business Groups Say Bans on Russian Aluminum Will decimate European Industry*, Reuters (Oct. 24, 2022), www.reuters.com/markets/commodities/business-groups-say-bans-russian-aluminium-will-decimate-european-industry-2022-10-24/.

15 *A Proclamation on Adjusting Imports of Aluminum into the United States*, The White House (Feb. 24, 2023), www.whitehouse.gov/briefing-room/presidential-actions/2023/02/24/a-proclamation-on-adjusting-imports-of-aluminum-into-the-united-states-4/.

16 *Canada Bans Russian Aluminum and Steel Imports*, Department of Finance Canada (Mar. 10, 2023), www.canada.ca/en/department-finance/news/2023/03/canada-bans-russian-aluminum-and-steel-imports.html.

17 Laurence Norman, *Russian Titanium Maker Is Pulled Off Sanctions List*, Wall Street Journal (July 21, 2022), www.wsj.com/articles/russian-titanium-maker-is-pulled-off-sanctions-list-11658425381.

18 Aishwarya Nair and Tim Hepher, *Boeing Suspends Russian Titanium as Airbus Keeps Buying*, Reuters (Mar. 7, 2022), www.reuters.com/business/aerospace-defense/boeing-sus pends-part-its-business-russia-wsj-2022-03-07/.

19 Tim Hepher, *Airbus Says to Decouple from Russian Titanium "in Months,"* Reuters (Dec. 1, 2022), www.reuters.com/business/aerospace-defense/airbus-says-decouple-russian-titanium-in-months-2022-12-01/.

20 Vivian C. Jones and Liana Wong, *International Trade: Rules of Origin*, Congressional Research Service (Mar. 3, 2020), https://sgp.fas.org/crs/row/RL34524.pdf.

21 Joshua Goodman and Helen Wieffering, *How Leaks in U.S. Ban on Russian Seafood Are Undermining Efforts to Stop Putin's War Machine*, PBS News Hour (Apr. 15, 2022), www .pbs.org/newshour/economy/how-leaks-in-a-u-s-ban-on-russian-seafood-is-undermining-efforts-to-stop-putins-war-machine.

22 Sally Yozell, *Hearing on "Russian Seafood Ban Implementation and Seafood Traceability,"* Stimson (Apr. 7, 2022), www.stimson.org/2022/hearing-on-russian-seafood-ban-implementa tion-and-seafood-traceability/.

23 *Russia Hits Back at Western Sanctions with Export Bans*, BBC (Mar. 10, 2022), www.bbc .com/news/business-60689279.

24 *From the GATT to the WTO: A Brief Overview*, Georgetown Law Library (last updated Mar. 15, 2023), https://guides.ll.georgetown.edu/c.php?g=363556&p=4108235.

25 Roy Santana, *70th Anniversary of the GATT: Stalin, the Marshall Plan, and the Provisional Application of the GATT 1947*, 9 Trade, Law & Development 118, 121 (2017), www .tradelawdevelopment.com/index.php/tld/article/view/74.

26 Liana Wong, *Russia's Trade Status, Tariffs, and WTO Issues*, Congressional Research Service (Apr. 11, 2022) https://crsreports.congress.gov/product/pdf/IF/IF12071.

27 *Principles of the Trading System*, World Trade Organization (2023), www.wto.org/english/ thewto_e/whatis_e/tif_e/fact2_e.htm.

28 *Id.*

29 *Id.*

30 A *Unique Contribution*, World Trade Organization (2023), www.wto.org/english/thewto_ e/whatis_e/tif_e/disp1_e.htm; *Members Continue Push to Commence Appellate Body Appointment Process*, World Trade Organization (Mar. 28, 2022), www.wto.org/english/ news_e/news22_e/dsb_28mar22_e.htm; Yuka Hayashi, *U.S. Seeks to Fix WTO's Broken Trade Dispute Process*, Wall Street Journal (July 11, 2022), www.wsj.com/articles/u-s-seeks-to-fix-wtos-broken-trade-dispute-process-11657540800.

31 *Request for Comments and Notice of Public Hearing Concerning Russia's Implementation of Its WTO Commitments*, 87 Fed. Reg. 52,102 (Aug. 24, 2022), www.federalregister.gov/ documents/2022/08/24/2022–18253/request-for-comments-and-notice-of-public-hearing-con cerning-russias-implementation-of-its-wto.

32 *Accession of the Republic of Ukraine to the World Trade Org.*, United States Trade Representative (June 3, 2009), https://ustr.gov/trade-agreements/wto-multilateral-affairs/ wto-accessions/accession-republic-ukraine-world-trade-orga.

33 *Joint Statement Regarding the Application from Belarus for Accession to the World Trade Organization*, Government of Canada (Mar. 24, 2022), www.international.gc.ca/world-monde/international_relations-relations_internationales/wto-omc/news-nouvelles/2022-03-28-statement-belarus-declaration.aspx?lang=eng.

34 Cathleen D. Cimino-Isaacs, Nina M. Hart, Brandon J. Murrill, and Liana Wong, *Russia's Trade Status, Tariffs, and WTO Issues*, Congressional Research Service (last updated Apr. 11, 2022), https://crsreports.congress.gov/product/pdf/IF/IF12071.

35 Thomas Franck, *Congress Votes to Revoke Russia's "Most Favored Nation" Trade Status, Sends Bill to Biden*, CNBC (Apr. 7, 2022), www.cnbc.com/2022/04/07/senate-votes-to-strip-russia-of-most-favored-nation-trade-status.html; *H.R.7108 – Suspending Normal Trade Relations with Russia and Belarus Act*, 117th Congress (introduced Mar. 17, 2022), www.congress.gov/bill/117th-congress/house-bill/7108.

36 *Japan Formally Revokes Russia's "Most Favored Nation" Status*, Bloomberg (Apr. 20, 2022), www.bloomberg.com/news/articles/2022-04-20/japan-formally-revokes-russia-s-most-favored-nation-status; *Allies Join G7's WTO Stance towards Russia – EU Trade Chief*, Reuters (Mar. 15, 2022), www.reuters.com/business/allies-join-g7s-wto-stance-towards-russia-eu-trade-chief-2022-03-15/.

37 *Canada Cuts Russia and Belarus from Most-Favoured-Nation treatment*, Government of Canada (Mar. 3, 2022), www.canada.ca/en/department-finance/news/2022/03/canada-cuts-russia-and-belarus-from-most-favoured-nation-tariff-treatment.html.

38 *Russia Plans to Exit World Trade Organization and Other Global Bodies*, International Institute for Sustainable Development, (June 6, 2022), www.iisd.org/articles/news/russia-plans-exit-world-trade-organization; Sarah Anne Aarup and Ashleigh Furlong, *Russia Takes First Steps to withdraw from WTO, WHO*, Politico (May 18, 2022), www.politico.eu/article/russia-takes-first-steps-to-withdraw-from-wto-who/.

39 *U.S., EU, Allies Block Belarus' Bid to Join WTO*, Reuters (Mar. 24, 2022), www.reuters.com/business/us-eu-allies-block-belarus-bid-join-wto-2022-03-24/; *Joint Statement Regarding the Application from Belarus for Accession to the World Trade Organization*, World Trade Organization (Mar. 24, 2022), https://docs.wto.org/dol2fe/Pages/SS/directdoc.aspx?filename=q:/WT/GC/246.pdf&Open=True.

40 *Import Tariffs Overview and Resources*, International Trade Administration (Jan. 24, 2020), www.trade.gov/import-tariffs-fees-overview-and-resources.

41 Csilla Lakatos, *Back to the 1930s: Do US Tariffs Signal a Shift to Smoot-Hawley-Type Protectionism?*, Brookings (July 26, 2018), www.brookings.edu/blog/future-development/2018/07/26/back-to-the-1930s-do-us-tariffs-signal-a-shift-to-smoot-hawley-type-protectionism/.

42 *Id.*

43 Ed Gresser, *Trade Fact of the Week: America's "Non-MFN" Tariffs on Natural Resources Are Usually Low*, PPI (Mar. 9, 2022), www.progressivepolicy.org/blogs/trade-fact-of-the-week-americas-non-mfn-tariffs-on-natural-resources-are-usually-low/.

44 Cimino-Isaacs et al., note 34.

45 *Canada Cuts Russia and Belarus from Most-Favoured-Nation Tariff Treatment*, Government of Canada (Mar. 3, 2022), www.canada.ca/en/department-finance/news/2022/03/canada-cuts-russia-and-belarus-from-most-favoured-nation-tariff-treatment.html.

46 Sarah Anne Aarup and Barbara Moens, *Removing Russia's Trade Privileges – What You Need to Know*, Politico (Mar. 11, 2022), www.politico.eu/article/remove-russia-trade-privilege-what-need-know/; Eric Emerson et al., *Major Global Economies Take Aim at Trade with Russia Following Military Invasion of Ukraine*, Steptoe Global Trade Policy Blog (Mar. 21, 2022), www.steptoeglobaltradeblog.com/2022/03/major-global-economies-take-aim-at-trade-with-russia-following-military-invasion-of-ukraine/.

47 *Countries Currently Designated by Commerce as Non-Market Economy Countries,* International Trade Administration (July 1, 2020), www.trade.gov/nme-countries-list.

48 *U.S. Department of Commerce Revokes Russia's Market Economy Status in Antidumping Proceedings,* International Trade Administration (Nov. 10, 2022), www .trade.gov/press-release/us-department-commerce-revokes-russias-market-economy-status -antidumping-proceedings; *Antidumping Margin Calculation Programs,* International Trade Administration (last updated Dec. 30, 2022), https://access.trade.gov/resources/ sas/programs/amcp.html.

49 *Technical Information on Anti-dumping,* World Trade Organization (2023), www.wto.org/ english/tratop_e/adp_e/adp_info_e.htm.

50 *Countervailing duties,* European Commission (2023), https://trade.ec.europa.eu/access-to-markets/en/glossary/countervailing-duties.

51 Yuka Hayashi, *U.S. Downgrades Russia to Nonmarket Economy,* Wall Street Journal (Nov. 10, 2022) www.wsj.com/articles/u-s-downgrades-russia-to-nonmarket-economy-11668122071.

52 Gary Clyde Hufbauer et al., Economic Sanctions Reconsidered, 3rd ed., at 93 (2019).

53 Yevheniia Filipenko, *Letter to H.E. Mr. Didier Chambovey,* Chairman, WTO General Council, Permanent Mission of Ukraine, posted on the International Economic Law and Policy Blog (Mar. 2, 2022), https://worldtradelaw.typepad.com/files/ukraine-wto-1.pdf; Ahan Gadkari, *Legality of Extraterritorial Coercive Economic Measures Taken against Russia from the Lens of Int'l Trade Law,* Opinio Juris (Sept. 13, 2022), http://opiniojuris .org/2022/09/13/legality-of-extraterritorial-coercive-economic-measures-taken-against-russia-from-the-lens-of-international-trade-law/.

54 *Article XXI: Security Exceptions,* Analytical Index of the GATT (Apr. 20, 2009), www.wto .org/english/res_e/booksp_e/gatt_ai_e/art21_e.pdf.

55 *Id.*

56 *Russia – Measures Concerning Traffic in Transit of Ukrainian Products, Request for Consultations by Ukraine,* World Trade Organization (Sept. 14, 2016).

57 *Russia – Measures Concerning Traffic in Transit,* DS512, World Trade Organization (panel report adopted Apr. 26, 2019), www.wto.org/english/tratop_e/dispu_e/cases_e/ ds512_e.htm.

58 Prabhash Ranjan, *Russia-Ukraine War and WTO's National Security Exception,* Sage Journals (July 17, 2022), https://journals.sagepub.com/doi/full/10.1177/00157325221114586.

59 James Bacchus, *The Black Hole of National Security,* CATO Institute (Nov. 9, 2022), www.cato.org/policy-analysis/black-hole-national-security#recent-wto-dispute-settle ment-national-security-exception; *The WTO's First Ruling on National Security: What Does It Mean for the United States?,* CSIS (Apr. 5, 2019), www.csis.org/analysis/wtos-first-ruling-national-security-what-does-it-mean-united-states.

60 *The General Agreement on Trade in Services (GATS),* European Commission (2023), https://trade.ec.europa.eu/access-to-markets/en/content/general-agreement-trade-services-gats.

61 *Communication from the Russian Federation,* World Trade Organization (Mar. 16, 2022), https://docs.wto.org/dol2fe/Pages/SS/directdoc.aspx?filename=q:/WT/GC/245.pdf& Open=True/.

62 *The Wassenaar Arrangment at a Glance*, Arms Control Association (last reviewed Feb. 2022), www.armscontrol.org/factsheets/wassenaar.

63 *U.S. Export Policy toward the PRC*, Select Committee on U.S. National Security and Military/Commercial Concerns with the People's Republic of China (May 25, 1999), www.govinfo.gov/content/pkg/GPO-CRPT-105hrpt851/html/ch9b0d .html#anchor5563742; John H. Henshaw, *The Origins of CoCom: Lessons for Contemporary Proliferation Control Regimes*, The Henry L. Stimson Center (1993), www.stimson.org/wp-content/files/file-attachments/Report7_1.pdf.

64 Chad P. Bown, *The Return of Export Controls*, Foreign Affairs (Jan. 24, 2023), www .foreignaffairs.com/united-states/return-export-controls.

65 *Taiwan Says Chip Companies Complying with Russia Export Controls*, Reuters (Feb. 27, 2022), www.reuters.com/technology/taiwan-says-chip-companies-complying-with-russia-export-controls-2022-02-27/.

66 Tobias Gehrke and Julian Ringhof, *Caught in the Crossfire: Why EU States Should Discuss Strategic Export Controls*, European Council on Foreign Relations (Jan. 11, 2023), https://ecfr.eu/article/caught-in-the-crossfire-why-eu-states-should-discuss-strategic-export-controls/; Chad Bown, *The Return of Export Controls*, Foreign Affairs (Jan. 24, 2023) www.foreignaffairs.com/united-states/return-export-controls.

67 Kolja Brockmann, *The Missile Technology Control Regime at a Crossroads*, SIPRI (Oct. 1, 2021), www.sipri.org/commentary/topical-backgrounder/2021/missile-technology-control-regime-crossroads; *Switzerland Replaces Russia as Chair of Ballistic Missile Body*, swissinfo (Oct. 19, 2022), www.swissinfo.ch/eng/politics/switzerland-replaces-russia-as-chair-of-ballistic-missile-body/47991758.

68 *The Australia Group at a Glance*, Arms Control Association (last reviewed Mar. 2021), www.armscontrol.org/factsheets/australiagroup.

69 15 CFR § 772.1.

70 15 CFR § 734.9.

71 James Mulvenon, *Seagate Technology and the Case of the Missing Huawei FDPR Enforcement*, Lawfare (June 6, 2022), www.lawfaremedia.org/article/seagate-technology-and-case-missing-huawei-fdpr-enforcement.

72 *U.S. Department of Commerce & Bureau of Industry and Security Russia and Belarus Rule Fact Sheet*, U.S. Department of Commerce (Feb. 24, 2022), www.commerce.gov/news/fact-sheets/2022/02/us-department-commerce-bureau-industry-and-security-russia-and-belarus.

73 Paresh Dave and Jeffrey Dastin, *Explainer: The New U.S. Export Rules Designed to Freeze Russian Tech*, Reuters (Feb. 25, 2022), www.reuters.com/technology/new-us-export-rules-designed-freeze-russian-tech-2022-02-25/.

74 Zhanna Malekos Smith, *Make Haste Slowly for Quantum*, CSIS (Feb. 11, 2022), www.csis .org/analysis/make-haste-slowly-quantum.

75 *Id.*

76 Felicia Schwartz, *US Accuses North Korea of Arming Kremlin-Linked Wagner Group*, Financial Times (Dec. 22, 2022), www.ft.com/content/0257f550-ada2-4771-a554-b0c5a2e75528.

77 *What Is Russia's Wagner Group of Mercenaries in Ukraine?*, BBC (Oct. 3, 2022), www.bbc .com/news/world-60947877.

78 András Rácz, *Band of Brothers: The Wagner Group and the Russian State*, CSIS (Sept. 21, 2020), www.csis.org/blogs/post-soviet-post/band-brothers-wagner-group-and-russian-state.

79 Felicia Schwartz, *US Accuses North Korea of Arming Kremlin-Linked Wagner Group*, Financial Times (Dec. 22, 2022), www.ft.com/content/0257f550-ada2-4771-a554-b0c5a2e75528.

80 *Commerce Imposes Additional Restrictions on Exports to Wagner Group*, U.S. Department of Commerce (Dec. 21, 2022), www.bis.doc.gov/index.php/documents/about-bis/news room/press-releases/3200-2022-12-21-bis-press-release-wagner-group-entity-listing-modificati on/file.

81 *Canada Imposes Additional Sanctions on Russian Oligarchs in Response to Putin's Continued Aggression*, Government of Canada (May 20, 2022), www.canada.ca/en/global-affairs/news/2022/05/canada-imposes-additional-sanctions-on-russian-oligarchs-in-res ponse-to-putins-continued-aggression-on-ukraine.html.

82 *FACT SHEET: US, European Union, and G7 to Announce Further Economic Costs on Russia*, The White House (Mar 11, 2022), www.whitehouse.gov/briefing-room/statements-releases/2022/03/11/fact-sheet-united-states-european-union-and-g7-to-announce-further-ec onomic-costs-on-russia/.

83 Kantaro Komiya, *Japan to Ban Russia-Bound Exports of Luxury Cars, Goods from April 5*, Reuters (Mar. 29, 2022), www.reuters.com/business/autos-transportation/japan-ban-russia-bound-exports-luxury-cars-goods-april-5-2022-03-29/.

84 Vanessa Friedman, *The U.S. and E.U., Aiming to Punish Oligarchs, Ban Luxury Exports to Russia*, New York Times (Mar. 11, 2022), www.nytimes.com/2022/03/11/business/russia-luxury-exports.html.

85 Jeanne Whalen, *Sanctions Forcing Russia to Use Appliance Parts in Military Gear, U.S. Says*, Washington Post (May 11, 2022), www.washingtonpost.com/technology/2022/05/11/russia-sanctions-effect-military/.

86 *Western Sanctions Will Eventually Impair Russia's Economy*, The Economist (Aug. 24, 2022), www.economist.com/finance-and-economics/2022/08/24/western-sanctions-will-eventually-impair-russias-economy.

87 *Risk of Medical Gear Shortage in Russia Falls as West Restores Exports*, Reuters (Apr. 20, 2022), www.reuters.com/world/europe/risk-medical-gear-shortage-russia-falls-west-restores-exports-2022-04-20/.

88 *Commodity, End-user, and Transshipment Country Red Flag FAQs*, Bureau of Industry and Security (Aug. 16, 2022), www.bis.doc.gov/index.php/documents/policy-guidance/3120-best-practices-faq-draft-8-15-22-final/file.

89 *New Exceptions to Parallel Import Rules in Russia Coming*, DLA Piper (Apr. 7, 2022), www.dlapiper.com/en/insights/publications/2022/04/new-exceptions-to-parallel-import-rules-in-russia-coming.

90 Pelin Bicen and Naveen Gudigantala, *Parallel Imports Debate: Resource Advantage Theory Perspective*, 8 J. of Marketing Development & Competitiveness 25 (2014).

91 *Russia Publishes List of "Parallel Imports" Goods*, Reuters (May 6, 2022), www.reuters.com/business/russia-publishes-list-parallel-imports-goods-2022-05-06/; Morten Buttler, *Lego Ceases Russian Sales, Ends Contract with Store Operator*, Bloomberg (July 12, 2022), www.bloomberg.com/news/articles/2022-07-12/lego-ceases-russian-sales-ends-deal-with-operator-of-81-stores; Alexander Osipovich, *Russia Allows Imports of Apple Watches, Bentleys and*

Xboxes via Third Countries, Wall Street Journal (May 6, 2022), www.wsj.com/livecoverage/russia-ukraine-latest-news-2022-05-06/card/russia-allows-imports-of-apple-watches-bentleys-and-xboxes-via-third-countries-EMeU8oNJEDFuAuhoWlNU.

92 Reuters, *Russia's Wildberries Selling Zara Clothes Online Despite Inditex Halting Operations*, Euronews (June 14, 2022), www.euronews.com/next/2022/06/14/ukraine-crisis-russia-inditex.

93 *Russia Adding IKEA, Lancome and Other Luxury Goods to Parallel Import List*, Reuters (Mar. 13, 2023), www.reuters.com/business/retail-consumer/russia-adding-ikea-lancome-other-luxury-goods-parallel-import-list-2023-03-13/.

94 *Has Russia Legalized Intellectual Property Theft?*, Economist (June 2, 2022), www.economist.com/business/2022/06/02/has-russia-legalised-intellectual-property-theft; *Background Paper on the Zero Remuneration Rate*, World Intellectual Property Organization (Apr. 26, 2022), www.wipo.int/edocs/mdocs/sct/en/sct_45/sct_45_russian_federation_info_paper_2.pdf.

95 Ian Talley and Anthony DeBarros, *China Aids Russia's War in Ukraine, Trade Data Shows*, Wall Street Journal (Feb. 4, 2023), www.wsj.com/articles/china-aids-russias-war-in-ukraine-trade-data-shows-11675466360.

96 Matthew Humphries, *China Is Selling Russia Lots of Faulty Chips*, PC Mag (Oct. 19, 2022), www.pcmag.com/news/china-is-selling-russia-lots-of-faulty-chips.

97 *FACT SHEET: Disrupting and Degrading – One Year of U.S. Sanctions on Russia and Its Enablers*, U.S. Department of the Treasury (Feb. 24, 2023), https://home.treasury.gov/news/press-releases/jy1298.

98 Kylie Atwood, *Iran Is Preparing to Send Additional Weapons Including Ballistic Missiles to Russia to Use in Ukraine, Western Officials Say*, CNN (Nov. 1, 2022), www.cnn.com/2022/11/01/politics/iran-missiles-russia/index.html.

99 *EU Agrees on New Iran Sanctions over Ukraine Drone Strikes*, DW (Oct. 20, 2022), www.dw.com/en/eu-agrees-on-new-iran-sanctions-over-ukraine-drone-strikes/a-63498497.

100 *UK Sanctions Iran over Kamikaze Russian Drones*, Government of the United Kingdom (Oct. 20, 2022), www.gov.uk/government/news/uk-sanctions-iran-over-kami kaze-russian-drones; *Ukraine: EU Sanctions Three Individuals and One Entity in Relation to the Use of Iranian Drones in Russian Aggression*, European Council (Oct. 20, 2022), www.consilium.europa.eu/en/press/press-releases/2022/10/20/ukraine-eu-sanctions-three-individuals-and-one-entity-in-relation-to-the-use-of-iranian-drones-in-rus sian-aggression/; *New UK Sanctions Target Senior Russian Commanders Following Strikes on Ukrainian Civilian Infrastructure*, Government of the United Kingdom (Dec. 13, 2022), www.gov.uk/government/news/new-uk-sanctions-target-senior-russian-commanders-following-strikes-on-ukrainian-civilian-infrastructure; *Treasury Targets Actors Involved in Production and Transfer of Iranian Unmanned Aerial Vehicles to Russia for Use in Ukraine*, U.S. Department of the Treasury (Nov. 15, 2022), https://home.treasury.gov/news/press-releases/jy1104.

101 Golnar Motevalli, *Iran to Get Russian Fighter Jets by March*, Bloomberg (Jan. 15, 2023), www.bloomberg.com/news/articles/2023-01-15/iran-expects-delivery-of-russian-sukhoi-fighter-jets-by-march-tasnim-says.

102 Julian Barnes, *Russia Is Buying North Korean Artillery, according to U.S. Intelligence*, New York Times (Sept. 5, 2022), www.nytimes.com/2022/09/05/us/politics/russia-north-korea-artillery.html.

CHAPTER 7 FOOD INSECURITY

1 *Joint Statement on Global Food Security*, U.S. Department of State (Nov. 14, 2022), www .state.gov/joint-statement-on-global-food-security/.

2 *Russian Attacks "Deliberately Target" Ukrainian Fields, Farms and Food Storage*, France24 (May 27, 2022), https://observers.france24.com/en/tv-shows/the-observers/20220527-russian-attacks-deliberately-target-ukrainian-fields-farms-and-food-storage.

3 Muh Amat Nasir, Agus Dwi Nugroho, and Zoltan Lakner, *Impact of the Russian-Ukrainian Conflict on Global Food Crops*, 11 Foods 2979 (2022), www.mdpi.com/2304-8158/11/19/2979/pdf.

4 Alan Rappeport, *Global Food Crisis Tests Western Resolve to Retain Russia Sanctions*, New York Times (June 27, 2022), www.nytimes.com/2022/06/27/business/russia-food-crisis-sanctions.html.

5 Caitlin Welsh, *Russia, Ukraine, and Global Food Security: A One-Year Assessment*, Center for Strategic and International Studies (Feb. 24, 2023), www.csis.org/analysis/russia-ukraine-and-global-food-security-one-year-assessment.

6 Joseph Glauber and David Laborde, *How Sanctions on Russia and Belarus Are Impacting Exports of Agricultural Products and Fertilizer*, International Food Policy Research Institute (Nov. 9, 2022), www.ifpri.org/blog/how-sanctions-russia-and-belarus-are-impacting-exports-agricultural-products-and-fertilizer.

7 European Council, *Infographic – How the Russian Invasion of Ukraine Has Further Aggravated the Global Food Crisis*, Council of the European Union (last updated Dec. 2, 2022), www.consilium.europa.eu/en/infographics/how-the-russian-invasion-of-ukraine-has-further-aggravated-the-global-food-crisis/.

8 Agathe Demarais, Backfire (2022), at 53–54.

9 Maryam Zamanialaei et al., *Weather or Not? The Role of International Sanctions and Climate on Food Prices in Iran*, 6 Frontiers in Sustainable Food Systems 1 (2023).

10 Mohammad Nasiri, *Beset by Inflation, Iranians Struggle with High Food Prices*, Associated Press (Sept. 30, 2021), https://apnews.com/article/business-lifestyle-iran-nuclear-economy-prices-cbac212486fa405bb16711712ddb278a.

11 *Id.*; Jalal Hejazi and Sara Emamgholipour, *The Effects of the Re-Imposition of US Sanctions on Food Security in Iran*, 11 Int'l J. Health Policy & Management 651 (2022), www.ncbi.nlm.nih.gov/pmc/articles/PMC9309942/.

12 Jane Ferguson and Zeba Warsi, *Afghanistan Sinks Deeper into Crisis as Sanctions Take Heavy Toll on Civilians*, PBS (Aug. 26, 2022), www.pbs.org/newshour/show/afghanistan-sinks-deeper-into-crisis-as-sanctions-take-heavy-toll-on-civilians.

13 Zainab Syyeda Rahmat et al., *Child Malnutrition in Afghanistan amid a Deepening Humanitarian Crisis*, International Health (2022), https://doi.org/10.1093/inthealth/ihac055, citing Rahim Faiez and Lee Keath, *1.1. Million Afghan Children under 5 Could Face Severe Malnutrition This Year, UN Says*, PBS (May 25, 2022), www.pbs.org/news hour/world/1-1-million-afghan-children-under-5-could-face-severe-malnutrition-this-year-u n-says.

14 *Afghanistan: Economic Crisis Underlies Mass Hunger*, Human Rights Watch (Aug. 4, 2022), www.hrw.org/news/2022/08/04/afghanistan-economic-crisis-underlies-mass-hunger.

15 *Id.*

16 *Afghanistan: Economic Roots of the Humanitarian Crisis*, Human Rights Watch (Mar. 1, 2022), www.hrw.org/news/2022/03/01/afghanistan-economic-roots-humanitarian-crisis#_What_should_be.

17 *Id.*

18 Don Melvin et al., *Starvation in Syria "a War Crime," U.N. Chief Says*, CNN (Jan. 15, 2016), www.cnn.com/2016/01/15/middleeast/syria-madaya-starvation/index.html; *Security Council Deems Syria's Chemical Weapon's Declaration Incomplete, Urges Nation to Close Issues, Resolve Gaps, Inconsistencies, Discrepancies*, UN Security Council Meetings Coverage, 9275th Meeting (PM), SC/15220 (Mar. 6, 2023), https://press.un.org/en/2023/sc15220.doc.htm.

19 *WFP Syria Country Brief*, World Food Programme (Jan. 2023), https://docs.wfp.org/api/documents/WFP-0000147289/download/?_ga=2.76624275.769014000.1681088789-1719027826.1681088789.

20 *What to Know about Sanctions on North Korea*, Council on Foreign Relations (last updated July 27, 2022), www.cfr.org/backgrounder/north-korea-sanctions-un-nuclear-weapons.

21 Association for Asian Studies, *North Korea's 1990s Famine in Historical Perspective*, 16 Education About Asia 24 (Winter 2011), www.asianstudies.org/publications/eaa/archives/north-koreas-1990s-famine-in-historical-perspective/.

22 Marcus Noland, *North Korea as a Complex Humanitarian Emergency: Assessing Food Insecurity*, 2 Asia and the Global Economy 100049 (2022), www.sciencedirect.com/science/article/pii/S2667111522000263; Kolja Brockmann, *European Union Sanctions on North Korea: Balancing Non-proliferation with the Humanitarian Impact*, Stockholm International Peace Research Institute (Dec. 11, 2020), www.sipri.org/commentary/topical-backgrounder/2020/european-union-sanctions-north-korea-balancing-non-proliferation-humanitarian-impact.

23 Nazanin Zadeh-Cummings and Lauren Harris, *The Impact of Sanctions against North Korea on Humanitarian Aid*, 2 Hournal of Humanitarian Aid 44, 47–49 (2020).

24 Sylvanus Kwaku Afesorgbor, *Sanctioned to Starve? The Impact of Economic Sanctions on Food Security in Targeted States*, Research Handbook on Economic Sanctions (2021), https://papers.ssrn.com/sol3/papers.cfm?abstract_id=3660536.

25 Rebecca Brubaker and Sophie Huvé, *UN Sanctions and Humanitarian Action*, UN University Centre for Policy Research, at 4 (Jan. 2021), http://collections.unu.edu/eserv/UNU:7895/UNSHA_ScopingPaper_FINAL_WEB.pdf.

26 *Guidance Note on Overcompliance with Unilateral Sanctions and Its Harmful Effects on Human Rights*, UN Human Rights Office of the High Commissioner (2022), www.ohchr.org/en/special-procedures/sr-unilateral-coercive-measures/resources-unilateral-coercive-measures/guidance-note-overcompliance-unilateral-sanctions-and-its-harmful-effects-human-rights; *Financial Sector Overcompliance with Unilateral Sanctions Is Harmful to Human Rights: UN Expert*, UN Human Rights Office of the High Commissioner (June 28, 2022), www.ohchr.org/en/press-releases/2022/06/financial-sector-overcompliance-unilateral-sanctions-harmful-human-rights-un.

27 *Guidance Note*, note 26.

28 Nazanin Zadeh-Cummings and Laurne Harris, *Humanitarian Aid in North Korea: Needs, Sanctions and Future Challenges*, Centre for Humanitarian Leadership (2020), https://

centreforhumanitarianleadership.org/wp-content/uploads/2020/04/CHL_North-Korea-Report_Final.pdf.

29 Alice Debarre, *Making Sanctions Smarter: Safeguarding Humanitarian Action*, International Peace Institute, at 3 (Dec. 2019), www.ipinst.org/2019/12/making-sanc tions-smarter-safeguarding-humanitarian-action; Demarais, note 8, at 62–64.

30 Agathe Demarais, *Why Sanctions Do Not Work against Dictatorships*, Journal of Democracy (Nov. 2022), https://journalofdemocracy.org/why-sanctions-dont-work-against-dictatorships/.

31 Dursun Peksin, *Better or Worse? The Effect of Economic Sanctions on Human Rights*, 46 J. Peace Research 5 (2009).

32 Jerg Gutmann et al., *Precision-Guided or Blunt? The Effects of US Economic Sanctions on Human Rights*, 185 Public Choice 161 (2020), https://link.springer.com/article/10.1007/s11127-019-00746-9.

33 Antonis Adam and Sofia Tsarsitalidou, *Do Sanctions Lead to a Decline in Civil Liberties?*, 180 Public Choice 191 (2015), www.jstor.org/stable/48703927.

34 Ryan Yu-Lin Liou et al., *Revisiting the Causal Links between Economic Sanctions and Human Rights Violations*, 74 Political Research Quarterly 808 (2021), https://journals.sagepub.com/doi/10.1177/1065912920941596.

35 *Food Prices Are Outpacing Wider Inflation across Most of the World*, Economist (Oct. 7, 2022), www.economist.com/graphic-detail/2022/10/07/food-prices-are-outpacing-wider-infla tion-across-most-of-the-world.

36 *Id.*; *African Swine Fever Helps Drive World Food Prices to Two-Year High*, New Scientist (Dec. 5, 2019), www.newscientist.com/article/2226363-african-swine-fever-helps-drive-world-food-prices-to-two-year-high/.

37 *The World's Top Wheat Exporters in 2021*, RadioFreeEurope RadioLiberty, www.rferl.org/a/top-10-wheat-exporters-russia-ukraine/31871594.html, citing U.S. Department of Agriculture (2022).

38 Hannah Ritchie, *How Could the War in Ukraine Impact Global Food Supplies?*, Our World in Data (Mar. 24, 2022), https://ourworldindata.org/ukraine-russia-food; Annia Ciezadlo, *The World Has Plenty of Wheat. Putin Still Uses It as a Weapon*, Washington Post (May 6, 2022), www.washingtonpost.com/outlook/2022/05/06/wheat-weapon-putin-ukraine/.

39 Kashish Rastogi and Carmen Ang, *These Are the 10 Countries that Produce the Most Wheat*, World Economic Forum (Aug. 4, 2022), www.weforum.org/agenda/2022/08/top-10-countries-produce-most-wheat.

40 *Wheat*, Observatory of Economic Complexity (Jan. 15, 2020), https://oec.world/en/profile/hs/wheat.

41 Florin Aliu et al., *Agricultural Commodities in the Context of the Russia-Ukraine War: Evidence from Corn, Wheat, Barley, and Sunflower Oil*, 5 Forecasting 351 (2023), www.mdpi.com/2571-9394/5/1/19.

42 Tarek Ben Hassen and Hamid El Bilali, *Impacts of the Russia-Ukraine War on Global Food Security: Towards More Sustainable and Resilient Food Systems?*, 11 Foods 2301 (2022), www.mdpi.com/2304-8158/11/15/2301, citing Kibrom A. Abay et al., *The Russia-Ukraine Crisis: Implications for Global and Regional Food Security and Potential*

Policy Responses, MENA RP Working Paper (2022), https://doi.org/10.2499/p15738coll2.135913.

43 Isabelle Khurshudyan and Serhiy Morgunov, *Ukraine Grain Farmers Devastated by Russia's Black Sea Blockade*, Washington Post (July 8, 2022), www.washingtonpost.com/world/2022/07/07/ukraine-grain-farmers-black-sea-blockade/.

44 Vittoria Elliott, *Satellite Data Shows How Russia Has Destroyed Ukrainian Grain*, Wired (Sept. 15, 2022), www.wired.com/story/satellites-ukraine-russia-grain/.

45 *Ukrainian Wheat Burns As Food Crisis Looms*, RadioFreeEurope RadioLiberty (July 19, 2022), www.rferl.org/a/ukraine-wheat-fire-war-russia-invasion/31950153.html.

46 *"They're Burning Our Crops on Purpose"; Ukraine Says Russia Deliberately Torching Grain Fields*, France24 (July 20, 2022), www.france24.com/en/europe/20220720-they-re-burning-our-crops-on-purpose-ukraine-says-russia-deliberately-torching-grain-fields; Pariesa Brody, *Russian Attacks on Farms and Silos "Deliberately Trying to Destroy the Ukrainian Economy"*, France24 (May 6, 2022), https://observers.france24.com/en/europe/20220506-russian-attacks-on-farms-and-silos-deliberately-trying-to-destroy-the-ukrainian-economy.

47 *Ukraine Grain Exports Down 29.6% at 18.1 Mln T so far in 2022/23*, Reuters (Dec. 2, 2022), www.reuters.com/article/ukraine-crisis-grain-exports-idAFL1N32S2GN.

48 Nurith Aizenman, *The Impact of the Ukraine War on Food Supplies: "It Could Have Been So Much Worse,"* NPR (Feb. 27, 2023), www.npr.org/sections/goatsandsoda/2023/02/27/1159630215/the-russia-ukraine-wars-impact-on-food-security-1-year-later.

49 *Russia to Suspend Grain Exports to Eurasian Economic Union until Aug. 31*, Reuters (Mar. 10, 2022), www.reuters.com/business/russia-suspend-grain-exports-eurasian-economic-union-until-aug-31-2022-03-10/.

50 Farangis Najibullah, *Central Asian Neighbors to Feel the Pain as Kazakhstan Suspends Wheat, Flour Exports*, RadioFreeEurope RadioLiberty (Apr. 14, 2022), www.rferl.org/a/kazakhstan-suspends-wheat-exports-neighbors-pain/31803803.html.

51 *India Bans Wheat Exports due to Domestic Supply Concerns*, United States Department of Agriculture (May 19, 2022), www.fas.usda.gov/data/india-india-bans-wheat-exports-due-domestic-supply-concerns.

52 *How to Address Agricultural Export Restrictions?*, WTO Forum (Feb. 27, 2015), www.wto.org/english/forums_e/debates_e/debate33_e.htm.

53 Andy Bounds, *WTO Takes Aim at Export Controls in Effort to Stem Rising Food Prices*, Financial Times (June 12, 2022), www.ft.com/content/bc81e1ae-821b-4f9d-8baa-a93c96e0a91a.

54 *Id.*

55 *Joint Statement by the Heads of the Food and Agriculture Organization, International Monetary Fund, World Bank Group, World Food Programme, and World Trade Organization on the Global Food Security Crisis*, International Monetary Fund (July 15, 2022), www.imf.org/en/News/Articles/2022/07/15/pr22259-joint-statement-heads-fao-imf-wbg-wfp-wto-global-food-security-crisis.

56 Almaz Kumenov, *Russia Scraps Ban of Cereals to Eurasian Union*, eurasianet (Apr. 1, 2022), https://eurasianet.org/russia-scraps-ban-of-cereals-to-eurasian-union.

57 Polina Devitt, *Russia's December What Exports Close to Record, Experts Say*, Reuters (Dec. 7, 2022), www.reuters.com/markets/commodities/russias-december-wheat-exports-close-record-experts-say-2022-12-07/.

58 Sybille De La Hamaide, *World Food Prices Hit Record High in 2022*, Reuters (Jan. 6, 2023), www.reuters.com/markets/world-food-prices-hit-record-high-2022-despite-december-fall-2023-01-06/.

59 Lotanna Emediegwu and Sascha Becker, *How Is the War in Ukraine Affecting Global Food Prices?*, Economics Observatory (June 21, 2022), www.economicsobservatory.com/how-is-the-war-in-ukraine-affecting-global-food-prices.

60 *Id.*

61 *Escalating Death, Destitution and Destruction as Yemeni Civilians Left to Bear Brunt of 7-Year War*, Oxfam (Mar. 24, 2022), www.oxfam.org/en/press-releases/escalating-death-destitution-and-destruction-yemeni-civilians-left-bear-brunt-7-year.

62 *Food Prices Are Outpacing Wider Inflation across Most of the World*, The Economist (Oct. 7, 2022), www.economist.com/graphic-detail/2022/10/07/food-prices-are-outpacing-wider-inflation-across-most-of-the-world; Michaël Tanchum, *Lebanon Is Running Out of Time to Avert Starvation*, MEI (Mar. 11, 2022), www.mei.edu/blog/lebanon-running-out-time-avert-starvation; *Overview*, The World Bank (Nov. 2, 2022), www.worldbank.org/en/country/lebanon/overview; Maha El Dahan and Ellen Francis, *Exclusive: Lebanon Navigates Food Challenge with No Grain Silo and Few Stocks*, Reuters (Aug. 7, 2020), www.reuters.com/article/us-lebanon-security-blast-grains-exclusi/exclusive-lebanon-navigates-food-challenge-with-no-grain-silo-and-few-stocks-idUSKCN25317I.

63 Dasl Yoon, *North Korea Suffers One of Its Worst Food Shortages in Decades*, Wall Street Journal (Mar. 2, 2023), www.wsj.com/articles/north-korea-suffers-one-of-its-worst-food-crises-in-decades-ee25aa86; Junnosuke Kobara, *North Korea's Triple Economic Woes Stoke Fears of "Silent" Famine*, Nikkei Asia (Aug. 7, 2022), https://asia.nikkei.com/Spotlight/N-Korea-at-crossroads/North-Korea-s-triple-economic-woes-stoke-fears-of-silent-famine.

64 Alistair MacDonald, *Russian Ministry Recommends Suspending Fertilizer Exports*, Wall Street Journal (Mar. 4, 2022), www.wsj.com/livecoverage/russia-ukraine-latest-news-2022-03-04/card/russian-ministry-recommends-suspending-fertilizer-exports-8gJNAaRR7PBi6HvV4T3o.

65 *The Importance of Ukraine and the Russian Federation for Global Agricultural Markets and the Risks Associated with the War in Ukraine*, Food and Agriculture Organization of the U.N. (June 10, 2022), www.fao.org/3/cb9013en/cb9013en.pdf; Associated Press, *Russia-Ukraine War Worsens Fertilizer Crunch, Risking Food Supplies*, NPR (Apr. 12, 2022), www.npr.org/2022/04/12/1092251401/russia-ukraine-war-worsens-fertilizer-crunch-risking-food-supplies.

66 NPR, note 65.

67 *Russian Tycoon Urges Africa to Press EU on Fertilizer Snarl*, Bloomberg (Dec. 28, 2022), www.bloomberg.com/news/articles/2022-12-28/russia-billionaire-asks-africa-to-lobby-eu-to-help-resolve-fertilizer-impasse.

68 *Wheat Shortage Leads to New Bread Recipes in Togo*, DW (Nov. 18, 2022), www.dw.com/en/wheat-shortage-leads-to-new-bread-recipes-in-togo/video-63814307.

69 Agence France-Presse, *I.Coast Eyes Cassava for Its Bread as Wheat Prices Surge*, Seychelles News Agency (July 5, 2022), http://m.seychellesnewsagency.com/view_news.php?id=17019.

70 *International Year of Millets 2023*, Food and Agriculture Organization of the United Nations (last updated June 13, 2023), www.fao.org/millets-2023/en.

71 Kareem Fahim, *Russia and Ukraine Agree to Release Blockaded Grain Exports*, Washington Post (July 22, 2022), www.washingtonpost.com/world/2022/07/22/ukraine-grain-deal-turkey-russia/; *Ukraine, Russia Agree to Export Grain, Ending a Standoff that Threatened Food Supply*, NPR (July 22, 2022), www.npr.org/2022/07/22/1112880942/ukraine-grain-exports-deal.

72 *Joint Coordination Centre for the Black Sea Grain Initiative*, United Nations (Mar. 19, 2023), www.un.org/en/black-sea-grain-initiative/background; *Beacon on the Black Sea*, United Nations (2023), www.un.org/en/black-sea-grain-initiative.

73 Kirk Maltais, *Wheat Prices Fall after Russia-Ukraine Deal*, Wall Street Journal (July 22, 2022), www.wsj.com/articles/wheat-prices-fall-after-russia-ukraine-deal-11658509561.

74 David Laborde and Joseph Glauber, *Suspension of the Black Sea Grain Initiative: What Has the Deal Achieved, and What Happens Now?*, International Food Policy Research Institute (Oct. 31, 2022), www.ifpri.org/blog/suspension-black-sea-grain-initiative-what-has-deal-achieved-and-what-happens-now.

75 Erin Cunningham, *Russia and Ukraine Have Renewed the U.N. Grain Deal. Is It Working?*, Washington Post (Nov. 17, 2022), www.washingtonpost.com/world/2022/11/17/russia-ukraine-grain-deal-black-sea/.

76 Frank Tang, *As Ukraine Crisis Deepens, China Lifts All Wheat-Import Restrictions on Russia*, South China Morning Post (Feb. 24, 2022), www.scmp.com/economy/china-economy/article/3168278/ukraine-crisis-deepens-china-lifts-all-wheat-import; Laura He, *China Lifts Restrictions on Russian Wheat Imports*, CNN Business (Feb. 25, 2022), www.cnn.com/2022/02/25/business/wheat-russia-china-intl-hnk/index.html.

77 Michael Hogan and Gus Trompiz, *Russian Wheat Sales Climb as Buyers Seek Lower-Cost Options*, Reuters (Apr. 6, 2022), www.reuters.com/article/ukraine-crisis-russia-grains-idAFL5N2W33G8.

78 *Taliban Signs "Preliminary" Deal with Russia for Oil, Gas, Wheat*, Al Jazeera (Sept. 28, 2022), www.aljazeera.com/news/2022/9/28/taliban-signs-preliminary-deal-with-russia-to-buy-gas-wheat.

79 *Russia Slams Sanctions, Seeks to Blame West for Food Crisis*, Al Jazeera (May 26, 2022), www.aljazeera.com/news/2022/5/26/russia-slams-sanctions-seeks-to-blame-west-for-food-crisis.

80 Jeremy W. Peters, *Food Supply Disruption Is Another Front for Russian Falsehoods*, New York Times (Sept. 19, 2022), www.nytimes.com/2022/09/19/business/media/russia-war-food-supply-chain-disinformation.html.

81 Lara Jakes, *U.S. Aid Chief Criticizes China's "Absence" in a Food Crisis Stoked by Russia's Invasion*, New York Times (July 18, 2022), www.nytimes.com/2022/07/18/us/politics/samantha-power-china-food-crisis.html.

82 *China's Position on Russia's Invasion of Ukraine*, U.S.-China Economic and Security Review Commission (Apr. 26, 2023), www.uscc.gov/research/chinas-position-russias-invasion-ukraine; Orange Wang, *As China, US Point Blame over Global Food Crisis, What Role Can Their "Good Interactions" Play?*, South China Morning Post (July 21, 2022), www.scmp.com/economy/china-economy/article/3185966/china-us-point-blame-over-global-food-crisis-what-role-can.

83 *Russia's Disinformation Cannot Hide Its Responsibility for the Global Food Crisis*, U.S. Department of State (June 22, 2022), www.state.gov/disarming-disinformation/russias-disinformation-cannot-hide-its-responsibility-for-the-global-food-crisis/.

84 *Outcome of Proceedings*, Council of the European Union (June 20, 2022), https://data
.consilium.europa.eu/doc/document/ST-10066-2022-INIT/en/pdf.

85 *Id.*

86 *Treasury Releases Fact Sheet on Food and Fertilizer-Related Authorizations Under Russia
Sanctions; Expands General License Authorizing Agricultural Transactions*, U.S. Department
of the Treasury (July 14, 2022), https://home.treasury.gov/news/press-releases/jy0868.

87 *Id.*

88 *Joint Statement on Global Food Security*, U.S. Department of State (Nov. 14, 2022), www
.state.gov/joint-statement-on-global-food-security/.

89 *Publication of Russian Harmful Foreign Activities Sancti ons Regulations General Licenses
6, 6A, 6B, 25C, 30A, and 44*, 87 Fed. Reg. 50,570 (Aug. 17, 2022), www.federalregister
.gov/documents/2022/08/17/2022-17646/publication-of-russian-harmful-foreign-activities-
sanctions-regulations-web-general-licenses-6-6a-6b.

90 *General Licence – Transactions Related to Agricultural Commodities Including
the Provision of Insurance and Other Services: INT/2022/2349952*, HM Treasury
(Nov. 4, 2022; amended June 6, 2023), https://assets.publishing.service.gov.uk/govern
ment/uploads/system/uploads/attachment_data/file/1115733/LICENCE_INT-2022-23499
52_.pdf.

91 *Russia Slams Sanctions, Seeks to Blame West for Food Crisis*, Al Jazeera (May 26, 2022),
www.aljazeera.com/news/2022/5/26/russia-slams-sanctions-seeks-to-blame-west-for-food-
crisis; Missy Ryan, *Diplomats Urge Action as Global Food Crisis Deepens*, Washington
Post (June 24, 2022), www.washingtonpost.com/national-security/2022/06/24/food-security-
ukraine/.

92 Susannah Savage, Bartosz Brzezinski, Barbara Moens and Jacopo Barigazzi, *EU Agrees to
Ease Russia Fertilizer Curbs after Row, Angering Ukraine*, Politico (Dec. 15, 2022), www
.politico.eu/article/fertilizer-row-holds-up-eu-latest-russia-ukraine-war-sanctions-package-
famine-food-supplies/; *Under U.N. Pressure, EU Seeks to Unblock Transit of Russian
Fertilizers*, Wall Street Journal (Dec. 16, 2022), www.wsj.com/articles/under-u-n-pressure-
eu-seeks-to-unblock-transit-of-russian-fertilizers-11671214638.

93 Alexandra Brzozowski, *EU Breaks Fertilizer Deadlock, Approves Ninth Russian Sanctions
Package*, euractiv (Dec. 16, 2022), www.euractiv.com/section/europe-s-east/news/eu-breaks-
fertiliser-deadlock-approves-ninth-russia-sanctions-package/; *EU Countries Have Another
Go at Russia Sanctions amid Polish, Baltic Concerns*, Reuters (Dec. 15, 2022), www
.reuters.com/world/europe/eu-members-fail-reach-agreement-new-russia-sanctions-diplo
mats-2022-12-15/.

94 Laurence Norman and Jared Malsin, *Russia's War of Aggression against Ukraine: EU
Adopts 9th Package of Economic and Individual Sanctions*, European Union (Dec. 16,
2022), www.consilium.europa.eu/en/press/press-releases/2022/12/16/russia-s-war-of-aggres
sion-against-ukraine-eu-adopts-9th-package-of-economic-and-individual-sanctions/;
Laurence Norman and Jared Malsin, *Under U.N. Pressure, EU Seeks to Unblock Transit of
Russian Fertilizers*, Wall Street Journal (last updated Dec. 16, 2022), www.wsj.com/articles/
under-u-n-pressure-eu-seeks-to-unblock-transit-of-russian-fertilizers-11671214638.

95 *What You Need to Know about Food Security and Climate Change*, The World Bank
(Oct. 17, 2022), www.worldbank.org/en/news/feature/2022/10/17/what-you-need-to-know-
about-food-security-and-climate-change.

CHAPTER 8 THE OLIGARCHS, AND OTHERS

1 *Quotation of the Day: Putin Oligarch Finds Himself Pariah in West's Playgrounds*, New York Times (Mar. 12, 2022), www.nytimes.com/2022/03/12/todayspaper/quotation-of-the-day-putin-oligarch-finds-himself-pariah-in-wests-playgrounds.html.

2 OFAC, *Treasury Sanctions Serious Human Rights Abusers on International Human Rights Day*, U.S. Department of the Treasury (Dec. 10, 2020), https://home.treasury.gov/news/press-releases/sm1208.

3 Simon Lewis and Chris Gallagher, *U.S. Issues Sanctions on Alleged Arms Sales for Myanmar Junta*, Reuters (Mar. 25, 2022), www.reuters.com/world/asia-pacific/us-issues-sanctions-alleged-arms-dealers-myanmar-junta-2022-03-25/.

4 Marshall I. Goldman, *Putin and the Oligarchs*, 83 Foreign Affairs 33 (2004), www.jstor.org/stable/20034135.

5 *U.S. Treasury Imposes Sanctions on Russian Federation President Vladimir Putin and Minister of Foreign Affairs Sergei Lavrov*, U.S. Department of the Treasury (Feb. 25, 2022), https://home.treasury.gov/news/press-releases/jy0610.

6 *FACT SHEET: Executive Order Imposing Costs on Alyaksandr Lukashenka and Belarusian Authorities for Ongoing Attacks against Democratic Freedoms, Human Rights, and International Norms*, The White House (Aug. 9, 2021), www.whitehouse.gov/briefing-room/statements-releases/2021/08/09/fact-sheet-executive-order-imposing-costs-on-alyak sandr-lukashenka-and-belarusian-authorities-for-ongoing-attacks-against-democratic-free doms-human-rights-and-international-norms/; *After Rigging an Election, Belarus's Regime Beats Protesters*, The Economist (Aug. 13, 2020), www.economist.com/europe/2020/08/13/after-rigging-an-election-belaruss-regime-beats-protesters.

7 *Blocking Property of Senior Officials of the Government of Syria*, Executive Order 13,573, 76 Fed. Reg. 29,143 (May 18, 2011), www.federalregister.gov/documents/2011/05/20/2011-12645/blocking-property-of-senior-officials-of-the-government-of-syria.

8 Carol Morello, *U.S. Sanctions North Korean Leader Kim Jong Un*, Washington Post (July 6, 2016), www.washingtonpost.com/world/national-security/us-sanctions-north-korean-leader-kim-jong-un/2016/07/06/afoda71c-4390-11e6-bc99-7d269f8719b1_story.html.

9 *Security Council Imposes Sanctions on Libyan Authorities in Bid to Stem Violent Repression*, UN News (Feb. 26, 2011), https://news.un.org/en/story/2011/02/367672.

10 *Treasury Releases CAATSA Reports, Including on Senior Foreign Political Figures and Oligarchs in the Russian Federation*, U.S. Department of the Treasury (Jan. 29, 2018), https://home.treasury.gov/news/press-releases/sm0271.

11 Brian Egan and Peter Jeydel, *More on the Russian Oligarch Report*, Steptoe (Jan. 22, 2018), www.steptoeinternationalcomplianceblog.com/2018/01/more-on-the-russian-oligarch-report/.

12 San Tabahriti and Abby Wallace, *Russian Oligarch's Most Prized Assets, from Superyachts and Jets to Properties Are Being Targeted by Sanctions. Here's What's Been Seized So Far*, Business Insider (Apr. 3, 2022), www.businessinsider.com/russian-oligarchs-roman-abramo vich-superyachts-properties-jets-seized-2022-3?inline-endstory-related-recommendations=.

13 *Attorney General Merrick B. Garland Announces Launch of Task Force KleptoCapture*, U.S. Department of Justice (Mar. 2, 2022), www.justice.gov/opa/pr/attorney-general-mer rick-b-garland-announces-launch-task-force-kleptocapture.

14 Tal Yellin, *From Yachts to Lavish Estates, Tracking Russian Assets Seized So Far*, CNN Business (last updated Apr. 27, 2022), www.cnn.com/interactive/business/russian-oligarchs-yachts-real-estate-seizures/index.html.

15 Dareh Gregorian, *Here Are the Superyachts Seized from Russian Oligarchs*, NBC (Mar. 16, 2022), www.nbcnews.com/politics/politics-news/are-superyachts-seized-russian-oligarchs-rcna20346.

16 Ho-Chun Herbert Chang et al., *Complex Systems of Secrecy: The Offshore Networks of Oligarchs*, 2 PNAS Nexus 1 (2023), https://doi.org/10.1093/pnasnexus/pgad051.

17 *Russian Abramovich: Stealth Oligarch*, PBS Frontline World (2003), www.pbs.org/frontli neworld/stories/moscow/abramovich.html.

18 David D. Kirkpatrick et al., *Roman Abramovich's Fortune Bought Him Good Will, and Made Him a Target*, New York Times (Mar. 11, 2022), www.nytimes.com/2022/03/11/world/europe/roman-abramovich-russian-oligarch-sanctions.html.

19 Vivan Salama et al., *Ukrainian President Asked Biden Not to Sanction Abramovich, to Facilitate Peace Talks*, Wall Street Journal (Mar. 23, 2022), www.wsj.com/articles/ukrainian-president-asked-biden-not-to-sanction-abramovich-to-facilitate-peace-talks-11648053860.

20 *Roman Abramovich Suffered "Suspecting Poisoning" at Talks*, BBC (Mar. 28, 2022), www.bbc.com/news/world-europe-60904676.

21 Tom Porter, *UK Sanctions Daughter of Russia's Foreign Minister, Who Somehow Bought a $5 Million Apartment in London in Cash Aged 21*, Business Insider (Mar. 24, 2022), www.businessinsider.com/uk-sanctions-lavrovs-stepdaughter-who-owns-5m-london-apartment-2022-3.

22 Ryan Smith, *Who Is Polina Kovaleva? Stepdaughter of Russia's Lavrov Hit by Sanctions*, Newsweek (Mar. 24, 2022), www.newsweek.com/polina-kovaleva-stepdaughter-russia-ser gei-lavrov-sanctions-uk-invasion-1691399.

23 Vivian Salama et al., *U.S. Withholds Sanctions on a Very Close Putin Associate: His Reputed Girlfriend*, Wall Street Journal (Apr. 24, 2022), www.wsj.com/articles/u-s-with holds-sanctions-on-a-very-close-putin-associate-his-alleged-girlfriend-11650816894.

24 Bryan Pietsch, *Putin's Alleged Mistress Is Possible U.S. Sanctions Target*, Washington Post (Apr. 26, 2022), www.washingtonpost.com/world/2022/04/26/putin-mistress-alina-kabaeva-russia-sanctions/.

25 Barbara Moens, *EU Sanctions Putin's Alleged Girlfriend Alina Kabaeva*, Politico (June 3, 2022), www.politico.eu/article/eu-sanction-putin-alleged-girlfriend-alina-kabaeva/.

26 *Treasury Sanctions Elites and Companies in Economic Sectors that Generate Substantial Revenue for the Russian Regime*, U.S. Department of the Treasury (Aug. 2, 2022), https://home.treasury.gov/news/press-releases/jy0905.

27 *WATCH: State Department Spokesman Ned Price Calls Navalny Trial Ruling a "Sham"*, PBS (Mar. 22, 2022), www.pbs.org/newshour/politics/watch-state-department-spokesman-ned-price-calls-navalny-trial-ruling-a-sham; *Navalny Sentenced to 9 Years in Prison by Russian Court*, PBS (Mar. 22, 2022), www.pbs.org/newshour/world/navalny-sentenced-to-9-years-in-prison-by-russian-court.

28 AFP, *Navalny Urges Systematic Sanctions against Russian Oligarchs*, The Moscow Times (Aug. 16, 2022), www.themoscowtimes.com/2022/08/16/navalny-urges-systematic-sanctions-against-russian-oligarchs-a78587.

29 Stephanie Baker and Tom Maloney, *Half of Russia's 20 Richest Billionaires Are Not Sanctioned*, Bloomberg (Mar. 30, 2022), www.bloomberg.com/graphics/2022-russian-bil lionaires-sanctioned-ukraine-war/.

30 Cassandra Morgan, *Australian Government "Made Mistakes" in Sanctioning Russian Oligarch, Lawyer Claims*, 9News (Oct. 25, 2022), www.9news.com.au/national/australia-sanctions-russia-oligarch-alexander-abramov-court-case-penny-wong/6db16c7e-0f05-48e3-a4bf-1f7815eacc9c.

31 *Treasury Sanctions*, note 26.

32 Ilya Gridneff and Sarah Anne Aarup, *The Soft Spot in the EU's Steel Sanctions*, Politico (Oct. 3, 2022), www.politico.eu/article/eu-steel-sanctions-soft-spot-ukraine-war-russi/.

33 *Russian Oligarch Oleg Vladimirovich Deripaska and Associates Indicted for Sanctions Evasion and Obstruction of Justice*, U.S. Department of Justice (Sept. 29, 2022), www.justice.gov/opa/pr/russian-oligarch-oleg-vladimirovich-deripaska-and-associates-indicted-sanctions-evasion-and.

34 *OFAC Delists En+, Rusal, and EuroSibEnergo*, U.S. Department of the Treasury (Jan. 27, 2019), https://home.treasury.gov/news/press-releases/sm592; Pratima Desai, *Aluminium Shortages to Deter Blanket Sanctions on Rusal – Analysts*, Reuters (Feb. 21, 2022), www.reuters.com/business/energy/aluminium-shortages-deter-blanket-sanctions-rusal-analysts-2022-02-21/.

35 James Politi, *US Hits Russian Oligarch Vladimir Potanin with Sanctions*, Financial Times (Dec. 15, 2022), www.ft.com/content/e2d063a9-313f-4584-b205-7a2283f13eb5; Alistair MacDonald, *This Russian Metals Giant Might Be Too Big to Sanction*, Wall Street Journal (Mar. 7, 2022), www.wsj.com/articles/this-russian-metals-giant-might-be-too-big-to-sanction-11646559751.

36 *UK Sanctions Russia's Second Richest Man*, Government of the United Kingdom (June 29, 2022), www.gov.uk/government/news/uk-sanctions-russias-second-richest-man; Blake Schmidt, *Russia's Two Richest Tycoons Face First Western Sanctions*, Bloomberg (Apr. 6, 2022), www.bloomberg.com/news/articles/2022-04-06/russia-s-two-richest-men-face-first-western-sanctions-in-canada.

37 *Foreign Secretary Announces Sanctions on Putin's Propaganda*, Government of the United Kingdom (Mar. 31, 2022), www.gov.uk/government/news/foreign-secretary-announces-sanctions-on-putins-propaganda–2.

38 Andrew Rettman, *Next EU Sanctions to Strike at Russia's Pro-war Media*, EUObserver (Dec. 12, 2022), https://euobserver.com/world/156528.

39 *Council Adopts Full Suspension of Visa Facilitation with Russia*, European Council (Sept. 9, 2022), www.consilium.europa.eu/en/press/press-releases/2022/09/09/council-adopts-full-suspension-of-visa-facilitation-with-russia/.

40 Isabelle Khurshudyan, *Zelensky Calls on West to Ban All Russian Travelers*, Washington Post (Aug. 8, 2022), www.washingtonpost.com/world/2022/08/08/ukraine-zelensky-interview-ban-russian-travelers/.

41 *UK Scraps Rich Foreign Investor Visa Scheme*, BBC (Feb. 17, 2022), www.bbc.com/news/uk-politics-60410844.

42 *FATF Moves Forward in Combating Corruption and Illegal Fentanyl Trafficking, Enhancing Financial Transparency*, U.S. Department of the Treasury (Oct. 21, 2022), https://home.treasury.gov/news/press-releases/jy1044; *Outcomes FATF Plenary*, FATF (June 14–17, 2022), www.fatf-gafi.org/en/publications/Fatfgeneral/Outcomes-fatf-plenary-june-2022.html.

43 Josef Federman and Ilan Ben Zion, *Israel Grapples with Fate of Oligarchs as Ukraine War Rages*, PBS (Mar. 14, 2022), www.pbs.org/newshour/world/israel-grapples-with-fate-of-oligarchs-as-ukraine-war-rages; Shira Rubin, *Israel Is Trying to Keep Out Russian Oligarchs Fleeing Sanctions – But Some Have Already Arrived*, Washington Post (Mar. 14, 2022), www.washingtonpost.com/world/2022/03/14/israel-russia-oligarchs-ukraine/.

44 *Russian Billionaire Prokhorov Said to Receive Israeli Citizenship*, Times of Israel (Apr. 4, 2022), www.timesofisrael.com/russian-billionaire-prokhorov-said-to-receive-israeli-citizenship/.

45 *Testimony of Andrew Adams before the U.S. Senate Committee on Banking, Housing, and Urban Affairs*, U.S. Department of Justice (Sept. 20, 2022), www.banking.senate.gov/download/adams-testimony-9-20-22.

46 Catie Edmonson, *House Passes Bill Urging Biden to Sell Seized Russian Yachts and Aid Ukraine*, New York Times (Apr. 27, 2022), www.nytimes.com/2022/04/27/us/politics/biden-russia-sanctions.html; *H.R. 6930 – Asset Seizure for Ukraine Reconstruction Act*, 117th Congress (introduced March 3, 2022), www.congress.gov/bill/117th-congress/house-bill/6930/text.

47 Jeff Stein, *ACLU Helped Defeat Plan to Seize Russian Oligarchs' Funds for Ukraine*, Washington Post (Apr. 8, 2022), www.washingtonpost.com/us-policy/2022/04/08/aclu-ukraine-russia-oligarchs/.

48 Christopher M. Davis, *"Sense of" Resolutions and Provisions*, Congressional Research Service (Oct. 16, 2019), https://sgp.fas.org/crs/misc/98-825.pdf.

49 *FACT SHEET: President Biden's Comprehensive Proposal to Hold Russian Oligarchs and Elites Accountable*, The White House (Apr. 28, 2022) www.whitehouse.gov/briefing-room/statements-releases/2022/04/28/fact-sheet-president-bidens-comprehensive-proposal-to-hold-russian-oligarchs-accountable/. (By the end of 2022, the House bill did not become law, having been referred to the Senate Committee on Foreign Relations but no Senate vote having occurred.)

50 *Readout of Russian Elites, Proxies, and Oligarchs (REPO) Task Force Deputies Meeting*, U.S. Department of Justice (Sept. 30, 2022), www.justice.gov/opa/pr/readout-russian-elites-proxies-and-oligarchs-repo-task-force-deputies-meeting.

51 Mike Eckel, *U.S. Prosecutors Move to Seize $5 Million Tied to Russian Oligarch Malofeyev*, RadioFreeEurope RadioLiberty (Dec. 1, 2022), www.rferl.org/a/us-prosecutors-seize-5-million-russian-oligargh-malofeyev/32157210.html.

52 Sealed Indictment, *U.S. v. Hanick*, 1:21-cr-00676 (S.D.N.Y., filed Nov. 4, 2021), www.justice.gov/usao-sdny/press-release/file/1479811/download.

53 *Russian Oligarch Charged with Violating United States Sanctions*, U.S. Department of Justice (Apr. 6, 2022), www.justice.gov/usao-sdny/pr/russian-oligarch-charged-violating-united-states-sanctions.

54 Luc Cohen, *Russian Oligarch Ordered to Forfeit $5.4 Mln to U.S., Ukraine May Get Funds*, Reuters (Feb. 2, 2023), www.reuters.com/world/europe/russian-oligarch-ordered-forfeit-54-mln-us-ukraine-may-get-funds-2023-02-02/.

55 *FinCEN Alert on Real Estate, Luxury Goods, and Other High-Value Assets Involving Russian Elites, Oligarchs, and Their Family Members*, FinCEN (Mar. 16, 2022), www.fincen.gov/sites/default/files/2022-03/FinCEN%20Alert%20Russian%20Elites%20High%20Value%20Assets_508%20FINAL.pdf.

56 Yasmine Salam and Kenzi Abou-Sabe, *U.S. Trying to Seize $325 Million Superyacht Reportedly Owned by Sanctioned Russian Oligarch Suleiman Kerimov*, CNBC (Apr. 19, 2022), www.cnbc.com/2022/04/19/us-trying-to-seize-325-million-superyacht-reportedly-owned-by-sanctioned-russian-oligarch-suleiman-kerimov.html.

57 Ian Talley, *U.S. Sanctions Target Russian Military Suppliers, Alleged Money Launderers*, Wall Street Journal (Nov. 14, 2022), www.wsj.com/articles/u-s-sanctions-target-russian-military-suppliers-alleged-money-launderers-11668441481.

58 *Russian Oligarch Oleg Vladimirovich Deripaska and Associates Indicted for Sanctions Evasion and Obstruction of Justice*, U.S. Department of Justice (Sept. 29, 2022), www.justice.gov/opa/pr/russian-oligarch-oleg-vladimirovich-deripaska-and-associates-indicted-sanctions-evasion-and.

59 *Canada Starts First Process to Seize and Pursue the Forfeiture of Assets of Sanctioned Russian Oligarch*, Government of Canada (Dec. 19, 2022), www.canada.ca/en/global-affairs/news/2022/12/canada-starts-first-process-to-seize-and-pursue-the-forfeiture-of-assets-of-sanctioned-russian-oligarch.html.

60 Dylan Robertson, *Ottowa to Attempt Seizure of Russian Oligarch's Assets: A First for Sanctions Regime*, CBC (Dec. 19, 2022), www.cbc.ca/news/politics/ottawa-attempting-seize-russian-oligarch-assets-1.6691431; Janyce McGregor, *Canada Can Now Seize, Sell Off Russian Assets. What's Next?*, CBC (June 27, 2022), www.cbc.ca/news/politics/c19-russia-sanctions-asset-seizures-test-case-1.6496047.

61 *Bill C-19: An Act to Implement Certain Provisions of the Parliament on April 7, 2022 and Other Measures*, Government of Canada (last updated June 14, 2022), www.justice.gc.ca/eng/csj-sjc/pl/charter-charte/c19_2.html.

62 Oliver Bullough, *How Britain Let Russia Hide Its Dirty Money*, The Guardian (May 25, 2018), www.theguardian.com/news/2018/may/25/how-britain-let-russia-hide-its-dirty-money.

63 Allison Morrow, *How Much Is Vladimir Putin Worth? Almost No One Knows for Sure*, CNN (Feb. 28, 2022), www.cnn.com/2022/02/28/business/vladimir-putin-wealth-sanctions.

64 *Testimony of William Browder to the Senate Judiciary Committee on FARA Violations Connected to the Anti-Magnitsky Campaign by Russian Government Interests*, U.S. Senate Judiciary Committee (July 26, 2017), www.judiciary.senate.gov/imo/media/doc/07-26-17%20Browder%20Testimony.pdf.

65 Luke Harding, *Revealed: The $2bn Offshore Trail that Leads to Vladimir Putin*, The Guardian (Apr. 3, 2016), www.theguardian.com/news/2016/apr/03/panama-papers-money-hidden-offshore.

66 Paul Radu, *Russia: The Cellist and the Lawyer*, Organized Crime and Corruption Reporting Project (Apr. 26, 2016), www.occrp.org/en/panamapapers/russia-the-cellist-and-the-lawyer/; *The Secret Caretaker*, Organized Crime and Corruption Reporting Project (Apr. 3, 2016), www.occrp.org/en/panamapapers/the-secret-caretaker/.

67 Greg Miller et al., *Billions Hidden beyond Reach*, Washington Post (Oct. 3, 2021), www.washingtonpost.com/business/interactive/2021/pandora-papers-offshore-finance/.

68 *Pandora Papers: A Simple Guide to the Pandora Papers Leak*, BBC (Oct. 5, 2021), www.bbc.com/news/world-58780561.

69 Scilla Alecci, *Russian Bankers Shuffled Personal Wealth Offshore Long before Latest Sanctions, Pandora Papers Show*, International Consortium of Investigative Journalists (Apr. 11, 2022), www.icij.org/investigations/pandora-papers/russian-bankers-wealth-sanctions-offshore/.

70 James Oliver et al., *Banned Russian Oligarchs Exploited UK Secrecy Loophole*, BBC (Aug. 3, 2022), www.bbc.com/news/uk-62410715.

71 Filip Novokmet et al., *From Soviets to Oligarchs; Inequality and Property in Russia, 1905–2016*, National Bureau of Economic Research (Aug. 2017), www.nber.org/system/files/working_papers/w23712/w23712.pdf.

72 Anders Aslund and Julia Friedlander, *Defending the United States against Russian Dark Money*, Atlantic Council (Nov. 17, 2020), www.atlanticcouncil.org/in-depth-research-reports/report/defending-the-united-states-against-russian-dark-money/.

73 *Global Advisory on Russian Sanctions Evasion Issued Jointly by the Multilateral REPO Task Force*, U.S. Department of the Treasury (Mar. 9, 2023), https://home.treasury.gov/system/files/136/REPO_Joint_Advisory.pdf.

74 Elizabeth Warren et al., *Letter to Janet Yellen and Himamauli Das*,Robert Menendez (May 9, 2022), www.menendez.senate.gov/imo/media/doc/letter_on_corporate_transparency_act.pdf.

75 *Grassley Joins Warren, Colleagues on Bipartisan Letter Urging Treasury to Implement Corporate Transparency Act to Support Russian Sanctions*, Chuck Grassley (May 10, 2022), www.grassley.senate.gov/news/news-releases/grassley-joins-warren-colleagues-on-bipartisan-letter-urging-treasury-to-implement-corporate-transparency-act-to-support-russian-sanctions.

76 *FinCEN issues Final Rule for Beneficial Ownership Reporting to Support Law Enforcement Efforts, Counter Illicit Finance, and Increase Transparency*, Financial Crimes Enforcement Network (Sept. 29, 2022), www.fincen.gov/news/news-releases/fincen-issues-final-rule-beneficial-ownership-reporting-support-law-enforcement.

77 *Economic Crime (Transparency and Enforcement) Act 2022*, Originated in the House of Commons, Session 2021-22, UK Parliament (last updated Mar. 28, 2022), https://bills.parliament.uk/bills/3120.

78 *Federal Council Wishes to Increase Transparency of Legal Entities*, The Federal Council (Oct. 12, 2022), www.admin.ch/gov/en/start/documentation/media-releases.msg-id-90662.html.

79 *Sanctions Enforcement II: Making Sure Sanctions Work*, Federal Ministry of Finance (Dec. 16, 2022), www.bundesfinanzministerium.de/Content/EN/Standardartikel/Topics/Priority-Issues/Financial-Crime/sanctions-enforcement-act-II.html.

80 *Key Takeaways from the 5th AML Directive*, Swift (Apr. 2, 2020), www.swift.com/your-needs/financial-crime-cyber-security/anti-money-laundering-aml/5th-aml-directive-5amld; Maíra Martini, *Why Are EU Public Registers Going Offline, and What's Next for Corporate Transparency?*, Transparency International (Nov. 25, 2022), www.transparency.org/en/blog/cjeu-ruling-eu-public-beneficial-ownership-registers-what-next-for-corporate-transparency#beneficial-ownership-registers%20pre-cjeu-ruling.

81 Judgment of the Court (Grand Chamber) of Justice of the European Union, Joined Cases C-37/20 and C-601/20 (Nov. 22, 2022), https://curia.europa.eu/juris/document/document .jsf?text=&docid=268059&pageIndex=0&doclang=EN&mode=req&dir=&occ=first& part=1&cid=410481.

82 Kate Beioley and Cynthia O'Murchu, *European Countries Begin Taking Down Public Company Registers after Ruling*, Financial Times (Nov. 23, 2022), www.ft.com/content/ e4b31a4e-a79d-40f7-8a19-c1e451a95c4b.

83 Matti Kohonen, *Targeting Only Russian Oligarchs, a Historic Mistake*, Financial Transparency Coalition (Mar. 3, 2022), https://financialtransparency.org/targeting-rus sian-oligarchs-historic-mistake/.

84 *A Roadmap for a Global Asset Registry*, Independent Commission for the Reform of International Corporate Taxation (Mar. 2019), https://static1.squarespace.com/static/ 5a0c602bf43b5594845abb81/t/5c988368eef1a1538c2ae7eb/1553498989927/GAR.pdf.

85 Brooke Harrington, *Break the Chain between Russian Oligarchs and Managers, and You Break Everything*, New York Times (Mar. 21, 2023), www.nytimes.com/2023/03/21/opinion/ russian-oligarchs-wealth-managers.html.

86 Jasper Jolly, *UK to Speed Up Sanctions on Russian Oligarchs by Copying Allies' Decisions*, The Guardian (Mar. 4, 2022), www.theguardian.com/politics/2022/mar/04/uk-to-speed-up-sanctions-on-russian-oligarchs-by-copying-allies-decisions.

87 Barbara Moens and Jakob Hanke Vela, *Hungary Demands EU Lift Sanctions on 3 Russian Oligarchs*, Politico (Sept. 6, 2022), www.politico.eu/article/hungary-russia-sanction-list-eu-oligarch/.

88 Barbara Moens and Jacopo Barigazzi, *Hungary Backs Down on Push to Lift EU Sanctions on 3 Russian Oligarchs: For Now*, Politico (Sept. 7, 2022), www.politico.eu/article/hun gary-backs-down-on-delisting-russian-oligarchs-for-now/.

89 Rupert Neate, *Russian Oligarchs Lose $95bn in 2022 amid Sanctions after Ukraine war*, The Guardian (Dec. 30, 2022), www.theguardian.com/world/2022/dec/30/russian-oli garchs-lose-95bn-in-2022-amid-sanctions-after-ukraine-war.

90 *Id.*

91 Franziska Bremus and Pia Hütti, *Sanctions against Russian Oligarchs Also Affect Their Companies*, EconStor (2022), www.econstor.eu/bitstream/10419/260552/1/1807311988.pdf.

92 Alexander Cooley and Brooke Harrington, *The Power of Stigma*, Foreign Affairs (Oct. 27, 2022), www.foreignaffairs.com/russian-federation/power-stigma-shaming-russia-elites-weaken-putin;Brooke Harrington, *Sanctions on Russia Are a Reminder that Shame Works on Oligarchs*, Washington Post (Apr. 4, 2022), www.washingtonpost.com/outlook/ 2022/04/04/oligarchs-sanctions-shame/.

93 *Sanctioned Billionaire Tinkov Slams "Insane War" in Ukraine*, Bloomberg (Apr. 19, 2022), www.bloomberg.com/news/articles/2022-04-19/sanctioned-russian-billionaire-tinkov-slams-insane-ukraine-war?; Brooke Harrington, *Sanctioning Russia's Oligarchs: With Shame*, Bulletin of the Atomic Scientists (Nov. 9, 2022), https://thebulletin.org/premium/2022-11/ sanctioning-russias-oligarchs-with-shame/.

94 Brett Forrest and Ian Talley, *Russian Billionaire Mikhail Fridman Offers $1 Billion to Ukraine in Hope of Sanctions Relief*, Wall Street Journal (Sept. 8, 2022), www.wsj.com/ articles/russian-billionaire-mikhail-fridman-offers-1-billion-to-ukraine-in-hope-of-sanctions-relief-11662659071.

95 *Id.*

96 Max Seddon, *Russia's Melancholy Oligarchs*, Financial Times (Sept. 7, 2022), www.ft.com/content/daee2387-6d96-4f2e-9a80-5cc70cd8cc67.

97 Polina Ivanova and Max Seddon, *The Letter-Writing Campaign in Pursuit of Russian Sanctions Relief*, Financial Times (Mar. 14, 2023), www.ft.com/content/8f1cb299-dc7e-45f3-9fe2-6dad5b68573e.

98 *Abramovich v. Council*, Case T-313/22 (May 25, 2022), https://curia.europa.eu/juris/document/document.jsf?text=&docid=262757&pageIndex=0&doclang=en&mode=req&dir=&occ=first&part=1&cid=49983; Sara Ruberg and Max Colchester, *Roman Abramovich, Other Sanctioned Russian Oligarchs Fight Back in Court*, Wall Street Journal (July 16, 2022), www.wsj.com/articles/roman-abramovich-other-sanctioned-russian-oligarchs-fight-back-in-court-11657978210.

99 Leonie Kijewski, *The Oligarch Sanctions Runaround: Freeze, Lose in Court, and Still Keep the Money*, Politico (Nov. 15, 2022), www.politico.eu/article/russian-oligarch-european-union-sanctions-lose-in-court-still-keep-money/.

100 *Deripaska v. Yellen*, No. 21-5157 (D.C. Cir. Mar. 29, 2022).

101 Jacqueline Thomsen, *Russian Oligarch Deripaska Loses U.S. Court Battle to Lift Sanctions*, Reuters (Mar. 29, 2022), www.reuters.com/legal/government/russian-oligarch-deripaska-loses-us-court-battle-lift-sanctions-2022-03-29/.

102 Elaine Godfrey, *Sudden Russian Death Syndrome*, The Atlantic (Dec. 29, 2022), www.theatlantic.com/ideas/archive/2022/12/russian-tycoon-pavel-antov-dies-putin-ukraine/672601/.

103 Ivana Kottasová, *At least Eight Russian Businessmen Have Died in Apparent Suicide or Accidents in Just Six Months*, CNN (Sept. 2, 2022), www.cnn.com/2022/09/02/business/russian-oligarchs-deaths-intl/index.html.

104 *Lukoil Chairman Critical of Invasion of Ukraine Dies*, DW (Sept. 1, 2022), www.dw.com/en/russia-lukoil-chairman-who-criticized-invasion-of-ukraine-dies/a-62991025.

105 Zoe Strozewski, *Russian Oligarchs Who Died Mysteriously This Year Have Two Things in Common*, Newsweek (May 11, 2022), www.newsweek.com/russian-oligarchs-found-dead-all-have-2-things-common-1705780.

106 *Russia Says It's Sanctioning Hillary Clinton and Top U.S. Officials*, NPR (Mar. 15, 2022), www.npr.org/2022/03/15/1086811273/russia-putin-sanctions-biden-clinton-us-officials.

107 AP, *Russia Sanctions 25 More Americans, Including Sean Penn and Ben Stiller*, NPR (Sept. 5, 2022), www.npr.org/2022/09/05/1121129839/russia-sanctions-25-more-americans-including-sean-penn-and-ben-stiller.

108 Bruce W. Jentleson, *Weaponized Interdependence, the Dynamics of Twenty-First Century Power, and U.S. Grand Strategy*, at 245, The Uses and Abuses of Weaponized Interdependence (2021).

CHAPTER 9 ESCALATION

1 *G7 Foreign Ministers' Statement on the Illegal Annexation of Sovereign Ukrainian Territory*, U.S. Department of State (Sept. 30, 2022), www.state.gov/g7-foreign-ministers-statement-on-the-illegal-annexation-of-sovereign-ukrainian-territory.

2 Julian E. Barnes, Eric Schmitt and Helene Cooper, *The Critical Moment behind Ukraine's Rapid Advance*, New York Times (Sept. 13, 2022), www.nytimes.com/2022/09/13/us/politics/ukraine-russia-pentagon.html.

3 Samuel Oakford and Alex Horton, *Here's What Russian Soldiers Left behind When They Withdrew from Izyum*, Washington Post (Sept. 13, 2022), www.washingtonpost.com/investi gations/2022/09/13/russia-retreat-abandoned-weapons-izyum/.

4 *Russia Says That It Has Completed Retreat from Kherson*, Reuters (Nov. 11, 2022), www.reuters .com/world/europe/russia-says-it-has-completed-kherson-withdrawal-tass-2022-11-11/.

5 Jason Beaubien, *Ukraine's Offensive in Kharkiv Was Hard and Bitter, Says Soldiers Who Did the Fighting*, NPR (Sept. 29, 2022), www.npr.org/2022/09/29/1125278321/ukraine-offen sive-russia-borshchova-kharkiv-oblast.

6 *Guerre en Ukraine. Kiev perd "50 hommes par jour," Annonce Volodymyr Zelensky*, oeust France (Sept. 23, 2022), www.ouest-france.fr/europe/ukraine/volodymyr-zelensky/guerre-en-ukraine-kiev-perd-50-hommes-par-jour-annonce-volodymyr-zelensky-b6aa752a-3b2f-11ed-a6d4-69a981b2a43f.

7 Charles Maynes, *Putin Is Mobilizing Hundreds of Thousands of Russian Reservists to Fight in Ukraine*, NPR (Sept. 21, 2022), www.npr.org/2022/09/21/1124215514/putin-announces-a-partial-military-mobilization-for-russian-citizens.

8 Associated Press, *Kremlin Paves Way to Annexing 4 Regions of Ukraine as It Announces Referendum Results*, CBC (Sept. 27, 2022), www.cbc.ca/news/world/moscow-ukraine-refer endums-1.6597755.

9 Nick Schifrin and Zeba Warsi, *Putin Vows to Defend Illegally Seized Regions in Ukraine by "All Available Means,"* PBS (Sept. 30, 2022), www.pbs.org/newshour/show/putin-vows-to-defend-illegally-seized-regions-in-ukraine-by-all-available-means.

10 *G7 Foreign Ministers' Statement*, note 1.

11 *Treasury Sanctions International Suppliers for Supporting Russia's Defense Sector and Warns of Costs for Those Outside Russia Who Provide Political or Economic Support for Russia's Purported Annexation*, U.S. Department of the Treasury (Sept. 30, 2022), https:// home.treasury.gov/news/press-releases/jy0981.

12 *Ukraine: EU Agrees on Eighth Package of Sanctions against Russia*, European Commission (Oct. 6, 2022), https://ec.europa.eu/commission/presscorner/detail/en/ip_22_5989.

13 Andrew E. Kramer and Michael Schwirtz, *Explosion on 12-Mile Crimea Bridge Kills 3*, New York Times (Oct. 8, 2022), www.nytimes.com/live/2022/10/08/world/russia-ukraine-war-news#a-fireball-erupts-on-a-bridge-linking-crimea-to-russia.

14 Aoife Walsh, *Crimea Bridge: Putin Accuses Ukraine of "Terrorism,"* BBC (Oct. 9, 2022), www.bbc.com/news/world-europe-63195504.

15 Pierre Breteau, *Nine Months of War in Ukraine in One Map: How Much Territory Did Russia Invade and Then Cede?*, Le Monde (last updated Nov. 28, 2022), www.lemonde.fr/ en/les-decodeurs/article/2022/11/25/nine-months-of-war-in-ukraine-in-one-map-how-much-territory-did-russia-invade-and-then-cede_6005655_8.html.

CHAPTER 10 ENFORCEMENT

1 *Transcript of Press Conference from Secretary of the Treasury Janet L. Yellen in Bonn, Germany*, U.S. Department of the Treasury (May. 18, 2022), https://home.treasury.gov/ news/press-releases/jy0793.

2 Kim B. Olsen and Simon Fasterkjær Kjeldsen, *Strict and Uniform: Improving EU Sanctions Enforcement*, German Council on Foreign Relations (Sept. 29, 2022), https://dgap.org/en/ research/publications/strict-and-uniform-improving-eu-sanctions-enforcement.

3 *Russian Elites, Proxies, and Oligarchs Task Force Ministerial Joint Statement*, U.S. Department of Justice (Mar. 17, 2022), www.justice.gov/opa/pr/russian-elites-proxies-and-oligarchs-task-force-ministerial-joint-statement.

4 *Russian Elites, Proxies, and Oligarchs Task Force Joint Statement*, U.S. Department of the Treasury (June 29, 2022), https://home.treasury.gov/news/press-releases/jy0839.

5 Laurence Norman and Patricia Kowsmann, *EU Works to Tighten Russia Sanctions Enforcement*, Wall Street Journal (July 9, 2022), www.wsj.com/articles/eu-works-to-tighten-russia-sanctions-enforcement-11657371600; *Overview of Sanctions and Restrictive Measures*, European Commission (Apr. 6, 2023), https://finance.ec.europa.eu/eu-and-world/sanctions-restrictive-measures/overview-sanctions-and-related-resources_en.

6 *Enforcing Sanctions against Listed Russian and Belarussian Oligarchs: Commission's "Freeze and Seize" Task Force Steps up Work with Internationa Partners*, European Commission (Mar. 17, 2022), https://ec.europa.eu/commission/presscorner/detail/en/IP_22_1828.

7 *"Freeze and Seize Task Force": Almost €30 Billion of Assets of Russian and Belarussian Oligarchs and Entities Frozen by the EU So Far*, European Commission (Apr. 8, 2022), https://ec.europa.eu/commission/presscorner/detail/en/IP_22_2373.

8 *Enforcing Sanctions against Listed Russian and Belarussian Oligarchs*, note 6.

9 Sam Fleming and Andy Bounds, *Brussels Pushes for Tougher Sanctions Enforcement via EU-Wide Body*, Financial Times (July 3, 2022), www.ft.com/content/fe83c67b-5dcc-447e-aba3-34911aa5f39d.

10 Sam Fleming, *EU to Name Sanctions Envoy to Enforce Curbs on Russia*, Financial Times (Dec. 12, 2022), www.ft.com/content/5c423057-61ee-4e64-ae7c-45e4daacfdc1; *EU Appoints David O'Sullivan as International Special Envoy for the Implementation of EU Sanctions*, European Commission (Dec. 13, 2022), https://ireland.representation.ec.europa.eu/news-and-events/news/eu-appoints-david-osullivan-international-special-envoy-implementation-eu-sanctions-2022-12-13_en.

11 *Head of the Office of Sanctions Coordination*, U.S. Department of State (Apr. 14, 2022), www.state.gov/head-of-the-office-of-sanctions-coordination/.

12 Daniel Fried and Edward Fishman, *The Rebirth of the State Department's Office of Sanctions Coordination: Guidelines for Success*, New Atlanticist (Feb. 12, 2021), www.atlanticcouncil.org/blogs/new-atlanticist/the-rebirth-of-the-state-departments-office-of-sanctions-coordination-guidelines-for-success/.

13 *Keeping the Pressure on Russia and Its Enablers: Examining the Reach of and Next Steps for U.S. Sanctions*, Testimony of Ambassador James C. O'Brien, Coordinator for Sanctions Policy, U.S. Department of State before the State Foreign Relations Committee (Sept. 28, 2022), www.foreign.senate.gov/imo/media/doc/6d41b4b3-08bf-c9c9-07d1-456a63bf0067/092822_OBrien_Testimony.pdf.

14 *Financial Intelligence Units: An Overview*, IMF (2004), at 4, www.imf.org/external/pubs/ft/fiu/fiu.pdf; *Suspicious Activity Reports*, NCA (2023), www.nationalcrimeagency.gov.uk/what-we-do/crime-threats/money-laundering-and-illicit-finance/suspicious-activity-reports.

15 *Russia-Related Illicit Finance and Sanctions FIU Working Group Statement of Intent*, Financial Crimes Enforcement Network (Mar. 16, 2022), www.fincen.gov/news/news-releases/russia-related-illicit-finance-and-sanctions-fiu-working-group-statement-intent.

16 *Federal Cabinet Approves Tool to Help Formulate the Sanctions Enforcement* Act, Federal Ministry for Economic Affairs and Climate Action (Oct. 5, 2022), www.bmwk.de/

Redaktion/EN/Pressemitteilungen/2022/05/20220510-federal-cabinet-approves-tool-to-help-formulate-the-sanctions-enforcement-act.html.

17 Sanctions *Enforcement Act II: Making Sure Sanctions Work*, Federal Ministry of Finance (Oct. 26, 2022), www.bundesfinanzministerium.de/Content/EN/Standardartikel/Topics/Priority-Issues/Financial-Crime/sanctions-enforcement-act-II.html.

18 *Enhancing the US-UK Sanctions Partnership*, U.S. Department of the Treasury (Oct. 17, 2022), https://home.treasury.gov/news/featured-stories/enhancing-the-us-uk-sanctions-partnership.

19 *Id.*

20 P.L. 117-263, www.intelligence.senate.gov/sites/default/files/legislation/BILLS-117hr7776enr.pdf; Kerry Contini and Bruce Linskens, *US President Signs Two Bills with Implications for Sanctions, Export Controls, and Related Subjects*, Baker McKenzie (Jan. 16, 2023), https://sanctionsnews.bakermckenzie.com/us-president-signs-two-bills-with-implications-for-sanctions-export-controls-and-related-subjects/.

21 Catherine Belton and Kareem Fahim, *Russia Turns to Turkey, Other Trading Partners to Blunt Sanctions' Impact*, Washington Post (Aug. 5, 2022), www.washingtonpost.com/world/2022/08/05/russia-turkey-war-sanctions-trade/; Laura Pitel et al., *Alarm Mounts in Western Capitals over Turkey's Deepening Ties with Russia*, Financial Times (Aug. 7, 2022), www.ft.com/content/00badf9e-f0d9-417f-9aec-9ac1c2207835.

22 Jonathan Guyer, *Where in the World Are Russians Going to Avoid Sanctions?*, Vox (Aug. 9, 2022), www.vox.com/world/23283965/russia-sanctions-united-arab-emirates-dubai-emirates-finance-money-yachts.

23 *UAE Placed on Money-Laundering Grey List, Promises "Robust" Response*, France24 (May 3, 2022), www.france24.com/en/live-news/20220305-uae-placed-on-money-laundering-grey-list-promises-robust-response.

24 Andrew England, *Financial Crimes Watchdog Puts UAE on "Gray List,"* Financial Times (Mar. 4, 2022), www.ft.com/content/7b93180f-c4ae-442d-bf71-60e340b736f0.

25 Ian Talley, *U.S. Presses Allies to Tighten Up Sanctions Enforcement on Russia*, Wall Street Journal (Nov. 21, 2022), www.wsj.com/articles/u-s-presses-allies-to-tighten-up-sanctions-enforcement-on-russia-11668878641.

26 Zinya Salfiti, *Indian Buyers for Russia's Oil Are Drowning in Price-Cap Paperwork and That Could Hit Moscow's Sales, Report Says*, Business Insider (Feb. 28, 2023), https://markets.businessinsider.com/news/commodities/russia-oil-india-exports-ukraine-sanctions-price-cap-paperwork-sales-2023-2.

27 Tania Babina et al., *Assessing the Impact of International Sanctions on Russian Oil Exports*, SSRN (Mar. 1, 2023), https://papers.ssrn.com/sol3/papers.cfm?abstract_id=4366337; *Russia Sold Oil Far above Price Cap, Researchers Say*, Bloomberg (Feb. 24, 2023), www.bloomberg.com/news/articles/2023-02-24/researchers-say-russia-is-selling-oil-far-above-the-price-cap.

28 Ana Swanson, *Russia Sidesteps Western Punishments, with Help From Friends*, New York Times (Jan. 31, 2023), www.nytimes.com/2023/01/31/business/economy/russia-sanctions-trade-china-turkey.html.

29 *Commodity, End-User, and Transshipment Country Red Flag FAQs*, Bureau of Industry and Security (Aug. 16, 2022), www.bis.doc.gov/index.php/documents/policy-guidance/3120-best-practices-faq-draft-8-15-22-final/file; 15 C.F.R. Appendix Supp. No. 3 to Part 732.

30 *FinCEN Advises Increased Vigilance for Potential Russian Sanctions Evasion Attempts,* Financial Crimes Enforcement Network (Mar. 7, 2022), www.fincen.gov/sites/default/ files/2022–03/FinCEN%20Alert%20Russian%20Sanctions%20Evasion%20FINAL%20508 .pdf.

31 *Financial Sanctions Evasion Typologies: Russian Elites and Enablers,* National Crime Agency (July 2022), https://nationalcrimeagency.gov.uk/who-we-are/publications/605-necc- financial-sanctions-evasion-russian-elites-and-enablers/file.

32 *Id.,* at 4.

33 *Five Russian Nationals and Two Oil Traders Charged in Global Sanctions Evasion and Money Laundering Scheme,* U.S. Department of Justice (Oct. 19, 2022), www.justice.gov/ usao-edny/pr/five-russian-nationals-and-two-oil-traders-charged-global-sanctions-evasion- and-money.

34 *Treasury Targets Sanctions Evasion Networks and Russian Technology Companies Enabling Putin's War,* U.S. Department of the Treasury (Mar. 31, 2022), https://home .treasury.gov/news/press-releases/jy0692.

35 *Commerce Cuts Off Russian Procurement Network Evading Export Controls,* U.S. Department of Commerce (Dec. 13, 2022), www.bis.doc.gov/index.php/documents/ about-bis/newsroom/press-releases/3194-2022-12-13-bis-press-release-russian-network-tdo/file.

36 Masood Farivar, *US Charges 7 with Running Procurement Network for Russia Military,* VOA (Dec. 13, 2022), www.voanews.com/a/us-charges-7-with-running-procurement-net work-for-russia-military-/6875119.html; *Five Russian Nationals and Two Oil Traders Charged in Global Sanctions Evasion and Money Laundering Scheme,* U.S. Department of Justice (Oct. 19, 2022), www.justice.gov/usao-edny/pr/five-russian-nation als-and-two-oil-traders-charged-global-sanctions-evasion-and-money.

37 *Commerce Department Identifies Commercial and Private Aircraft Exported to Russia in Apparent Violation of U.S. Export Controls,* U.S. Department of Commerce (Mar. 18, 2022), www.commerce.gov/news/press-releases/2022/03/commerce-department-identifies- commercial-and-private-aircraft-exported; *Commerce Department Updates List of Aircraft Exported to Russia in Apparent Violation of U.S. Export Controls; Removes Planes Returned from Russia,* U.S. Department of Commerce (Mar. 30, 2022), www.bis.doc .gov/index.php/documents/about-bis/newsroom/press-releases/2942-2022-03-30-bis-list-of-air craft-violating-the-ear-press-release-final/file.

38 *Commerce Department Identifies First Foreign-Produced Commercial Aircraft Exported to Russia in Apparent Violation of U.S. Export Controls,* U.S. Department of Commerce (Aug. 2, 2022), www.bis.doc.gov/index.php/documents/about-bis/newsroom/press-releases/ 3108-2022-08-02-bis-press-release-gp10-list-foreign-produced-de-minimis-additions/file.

39 *Id.; BIS Takes Enforcement Actions against Three Russian Airlines Operating Aircraft in Violation of U.S. Export Controls,* U.S. Department of Commerce (Apr. 7, 2022), www .commerce.gov/news/press-releases/2022/04/bis-takes-enforcement-actions-against-three- russian-airlines-operating.

40 *BIS Takes Enforcement Action against PJSC Lukoil for Violation of U.S. Export Controls,* U.S. Department of Commerce (Aug. 31, 2022), www.bis.doc.gov/index.php/documents/ about-bis/newsroom/press-releases/3126-2022-08-31-bis-press-release-lukoil-charging-letter/ file.

41 *Id.*

42 Erice Beres, *Many Procedures for Violating Sanctions*, tagesschau (Sept. 23, 2022), www.tagesschau.de/investigativ/swr/sanktionen-russland-ermittlungen-101.html.

43 *Lutte contre le blanchiment des capitaux et le financement du terrorisme: la DGCCRF mène une action coup de point dans les Alpes-Maritimes*, Ministry of Finance (Jan. 12, 2023), www.economie.gouv.fr/dgccrf/lutte-contre-le-blanchiment-des-capitaux-et-le-financement-du-terrorisme-la-dgccrf-mene-o; Giorgio Leali, *French Riviera Real Estate Firms Ignoring Russia Sanctions, Authority Says*, Politico (Jan. 12, 2023), www.politico.eu/article/french-riviera-estate-agencies-neglect-russia-sanctions/.

44 *Treasury Targets Global Sanctions Evasion Network Supporting Russia's Military-Industrial Complex*, U.S. Department of the Treasury (Feb. 4, 2023), https://home.treasury.gov/news/press-releases/jy1241.

45 *Ukraine Rapid Damage and Needs Assessment: February 2022–February 2023*, World Bank (Mar. 2023), at 9, https://documents.worldbank.org/en/publication/documents-reports/documentdetail/099184503212328877.

46 Alan Rappeport and David E. Sanger, *Seizing Russian Assets to Help Ukraine Sets Off White House Debate*, New York Times (May 31, 2022), www.nytimes.com/2022/05/31/us/politics/russia-sanctions-central-bank-assets.html.

47 Laurence Tribe, *Does American Law Currently Authorize the President to Seize Sovereign Russian Assets?*, Lawfare (May 23, 2022), www.lawfaremedia.org/article/does-american-law-currently-authorize-president-seize-sovereign-russian-assets; Laurence H. Tribe and Jeremy Lewin, *$100 Billion. Russia's Treasure in the U.S. Should Be Turned against Putin*, New York Times (Apr. 15, 2022), www.nytimes.com/2022/04/15/opinion/russia-war-currency-reserves.html.

48 Paul Stephan, *Seizing Russian Assets*, 17 Capital Markets L. J. 13pp. (2022), https://papers.ssrn.com/sol3/papers.cfm?abstract_id=4129862; Paul Stephan, *Giving Russian Assets to Ukraine – Freezing Is Not Seizing*, Lawfare (Apr. 26, 2022), www.lawfaremedia.org/article/giving-russian-assets-ukraine-freezing-not-seizing; *Statement of Paul B. Stephan*, Senate Judiciary Committee (July 19, 2022), at 5–16, www.judiciary.senate.gov/imo/media/doc/Testimony%20-%20Stephan%20-%202022-07-19.pdf; Scott R. Anderson and Chimène Keitner, *The Legal Challenges Presented by Seizing Frozen Russian Assets*, Lawfare (May 26, 2022), www.lawfaremedia.org/article/legal-challenges-presented-seizing-frozen-russian-assets.

49 Stephan, *Seizing Russian Assets*, note 48.

50 *Proposals to Seize – Russian Assets to Rebuild Ukraine: Session 22 of the Congressional Study Group*, Brookings (Dec. 29, 2022), www.brookings.edu/research/proposals-to-seize-russian-assets-to-rebuild-ukraine/.

51 Denis Alland, *Countermeasures of General Interest*, 13 European J. Int'l L. 1221, 1221 (2002), www.researchgate.net/publication/228228057_Countermeasures_of_General_Interest.

52 Enzo Cannizzaro, *The Role of Proportionality in the Law of International Countermeasures*, 12 European J. Int'l L. 889, 889–890, (2001), https://academic.oup.com/ejil/article/12/5/889/422270.

53 *Proposals to Seize Russian Assets to Rebuild Ukraine: Session 22 of the Congressional Study Group*, Brookings (Dec. 29, 2022), www.brookings.edu/research/proposals-to-seize-russian-assets-to-rebuild-ukraine/.

54 Scott R. Anderson and Chimène Keitner, *The Legal Challenges Presented by Seizing Frozen Russian Assets*, Lawfare (May 26, 2022), www.lawfaremedia.org/article/legal-chal lenges-presented-seizing-frozen-russian-assets; Paul Stephan, *Response to Philip Zelikow: Confiscating Russian Assets and the Law*, Lawfare (May 13, 2022), www.lawfaremedia.org/article/response-philip-zelikow-confiscating-russian-assets-and-law.

55 Andrew Boyle, *Why Proposals for U.S. to Liquidate and Use Russian Central Bank Assets Are Legally Unavailable*, Just Security (Apr. 18, 2022), www.justsecurity.org/81165/why-proposals-for-u-s-to-liquidate-and-use-russian-central-bank-assets-are-legally-unavailable/.

56 *Id.*

57 Paul Stephan, *Justice and the Confiscation of Russian State Assets*, Lawfare (Mar. 13, 2023), www.lawfaremedia.org/article/response-philip-zelikow-confiscating-russian-assets-and-law, citing Curtis Bradley and Jack Goldsmith, *Turkiye Halk Bankasi A.S. v. United States, Part 1: The FSIA and Criminal Prosecutions*, Lawfare (Jan. 11, 2023), www.lawfaremedia.org/article/turkiye-halk-bankasi-v-united-states-part-1-fsia-and-criminal-prosecutions.

58 Anderson and Keitner, note 48, citing *US v. Verdugo-Urquidez*, 494 US 259 (1990).

59 *Fuentes v. Shevin*, 407 US 67 (1972).

60 Evan J. Criddle, *Turning Sanctions into Reparations: Lessons for Russia/Ukraine*, Harvard Int'l L. J. Online (2023), https://scholarship.law.wm.edu/facpubs/2123/.

61 Ingrid (Wuerth) Brunk, *Immunity from Execution of Central Bank Assets*, Cambridge Handbook of Immunities and International Law (2019), https://papers.ssrn.com/sol3/papers.cfm?abstract_id=3125048; Ingrid (Wuerth) Brunk, *Sovereign Immunity of Foreign Central Bank Assets*, Lawfare (Feb. 23, 2018), www.lawfaremedia.org/article/sovereign-immunity-foreign-central-bank-assets.

62 *Testimony of Andrew Adams before the U.S. Senate Committee on the Judiciary*, U.S. Senate Committee on the Judiciary (July 19, 2022), www.judiciary.senate.gov/imo/media/doc/Testimony%20-%20Adams%20-%202022-07-19.pdf.

63 *Senators Offer Russian Asset Seizure Legislation*, Foreign Relations Committee (Oct. 4, 2022), www.foreign.senate.gov/press/rep/release/senators-offer-russian-asset-seizure-legislation.

64 *Statement of Andrew Adams, Director Task Force KleptoCapture, before the Committee on Banking, Housing, and Urban Affairs of the United States Senate, at a Hearing Entitled "Tightening the Screws on Russia: Smart Sanctions, Economic Statecraft and Next Steps"*, U.S. Senate (Sept. 20, 2022), www.banking.senate.gov/imo/media/doc/Adams%20Testimony%209-20-22.pdf.

65 Elisabeth Braw, *Freeze – Do not Seize – Russian Assets*, Foreign Policy (Jan. 13, 2023), https://foreignpolicy.com/2023/01/13/putin-sanctions-oligarchs-freeze-seize-assets/.

66 *Ukraine: The Commission Proposes Rules on Freezing and Confiscating Assets of Oligarchs Violating Restrictive Measures and of Criminals*, European Council (May 25, 2022), www.consilium.europa.eu/en/press/press-releases/2022/11/28/sanctions-council-adds-the-viola tion-of-restrictive-measures-to-the-list-of-eu-crimes.

67 *Sanctions: Council Adds the Violation of Restrictive Measures to the List of EU Crimes*, European Council (Nov. 28, 2022), www.consilium.europa.eu/en/press/press-releases/2022/11/28/sanctions-council-adds-the-violation-of-restrictive-measures-to-the-list-of-eu-crimes.

68 *Ukraine: Commission Presents Options to Make Sure that Russia Pays for Its Crimes*, European Commission (Nov. 30, 2022), https://ec.europa.eu/commission/presscorner/detail/en/ip_22_7311.

69 Laurence Norman, *EU Says It Cannot Seize Frozen Russian Central-Bank Assets for Ukraine*, Wall Street Journal (Nov. 30, 2022), www.wsj.com/articles/eu-says-it-cant-seize-frozen-russian-central-bank-assets-for-ukraine-11669827828.

70 John W. Boscariol, Martha Harrison, and Ljiljana Stanic, *New Seizure and Forfeiture Mechanism Enters into Force*, McCarthy Tetrault (July 5, 2022), www.mccarthy.ca/en/insights/blogs/terms-trade/canada-imposes-further-sanctions-against-russia-and-belarus-unprecedented-asset-forfeiture-mechanism-comes-force; Janyce McGregor, *Canada Can Now Seize, Sell Off Russian Assets. What's Next?*, CBC (June 27, 2022), www.cbc.ca/news/politics/c19-russia-sanctions-asset-seizures-test-case-1.6496047.

71 Dylan Robertson, *Canada's Move to Seize Assets from Russian Oligarch Roman Abramovich Could Test Charter, Trade Lawyer Says*, The Globe and Mail (Dec. 22, 2022), www.theglobeandmail.com/canada/article-canadas-move-to-seize-assets-from-russian-oligarch-roman-abramovich/.

72 Bill Chappell, *Ukraine's New Law Will Let It Fund the War Effort by Selling Russian Assets*, NPR (May 23, 2022), www.npr.org/2022/05/23/1100767629/ukraine-law-fund-war-selling-russian-assets.

73 *Federal Council Has Received Legal Clarifications on Frozen Russian Assets*, Federal Council of Switzerland (Feb. 15, 2023), www.admin.ch/gov/en/start/documentation/media-releases.msg-id-93089.html.

74 *Proposals to Seize*, note 50.

75 Chimène Keitner, *Expert Q&A on Asset Seizure in Russia's War on Ukraine*, Just Security (Apr. 3, 2023), www.justsecurity.org/85299/expert-qa-on-asset-seizure-in-russias-war-in-ukraine/.

76 *Russian Asset Seizures Must Follow the Law*, Financial Times (June 5, 2022), www.ft.com/content/30d3a780-633e-4b06-b9bc-ed3fc608ff98.

CHAPTER 11 ASSESSING THE SANCTIONS

1 *Secretary Antony J. Blinken with Jake Tapper of CNN State of the Union*, U.S. Department of State (Dec. 4, 2022), www.state.gov/secretary-antony-j-blinken-with-jake-tapper-of-cnn-state-of-the-union-2/.

2 Michael P. Malloy, *Human Rights and Unintended Consequences: Empirical Analysis of International Economic Sanctions in Contemporary Practice*, 31 B.U. Int'l L.J. 75, 78 (2013), www.bu.edu/ilj/files/2014/05/Malloy_JCI-2.pdf.

3 *See, e.g.*, David Baldwin, *Evaluating Economic Sanctions*, 23 Int. Sec. 13 (1998), www.jstor.org/stable/2539384 (arguing that "only the combined analysis of costs and effectiveness allows one to make judgments about the efficiency of economic sanctions").

4 Daniel W. Drezner, *The United States of Sanctions: The Use and Abuse of Economic Coercion*, 100 Foreign Affairs 142 (2021), https://heinonline.org/HOL/Page?handle=hein.journals/fora100&div=124&g_sent=1&casa_token=&collection=journals.

5 Gary Clyde Hufbauer and Barbara Oegg, *Targeted Sanctions: A Policy Alternative?*, Peterson Institute for International Economics (Feb. 23, 2000), www.piie.com/commentary/speeches-papers/targeted-sanctions-policy-alternative.

6 Joy Gordon, *The Not So Targeted Instrument of Asset Freezes*, 33 Ethics & Int'l Affairs 303 (2019), https://philpapers.org/rec/GORTNS-2.

7 *Keeping the Pressure on Russia and Its Enablers: Examining the Reach of and Next Steps for U.S. Sanctions*, Testimony of Elizabeth Rosbenberg, Asisstant Secretary for Terrorist Financing and Financial Crimes, U.S. Department of the Treasury, before the U.S. Senate Committee on Foreign Relations, U.S. Senate (Sept. 28, 2022), www.foreign.senate.gov/imo/media/doc/6d41b4b3-08bf-c9c9-07d1-456a63bf0067/092822_Rosenberg_%20Testimony.pdf.

8 Richard W. Parker, *The Cost Effectiveness of Economic Sanctions*, 32 Law & Poly'l Int'l Business 21, 23 (2000), https://digitalcommons.lib.uconn.edu/law_papers/428/, citing Gary C. Hufbauer et al., *U.S. Economic Sanctions: Their Impact on Trade, Jobs, and Wages*, PIIE Working Papers (Apr. 1997), www.piie.com/publications/working-papers/us-economic-sanctions-their-impact-trade-jobs-and-wages.

9 Özgur Özdamar and Evgeniia Shahin, *Consequences of Economic Sanctions: The State of the Art and Paths Forward*, 23 Int'l Studies Review 1646, 1650–51 (2021), https://academic.oup.com/isr/article/23/4/1646/6309628.

10 *Id.*, at 5, citing R. D. Farmer, *Costs of Economic Sanctions to the Sender*, 23(1) World Economy 93–117 (2000), www.researchgate.net/publication/4792191_Costs_of_Economic_Sanctions_to_the_Sender.

11 *Infographic – Impact of Sanctions on the Russia Economy*, European Council (last updatedd Mar. 17, 2023), www.consilium.europa.eu/en/infographics/impact-sanctions-russian-economy/.

12 *Id.*

13 Alexandra Prokopenko, *Does a Record Budget Deficit Herald the Collapse of the Russian Economy?*, Carnegie Endowment for International Peace (Feb. 10, 2023), https://carnegieendowment.org/politika/89009.

14 Max Seddon and Anastasia Stognei, *Russia's Budget Deficit Soars as Energy Revenues Slump by Almost Half*, Financial Times (Feb. 6, 2023), www.ft.com/content/3def31b3-ca3d-4d6b-8add-3008ac6dfb44.

15 Lazaro Gamio and Ana Swanson, *How Russia Pays for War*, New York Times (Oct. 30, 2022), www.nytimes.com/interactive/2022/10/30/business/economy/russia-trade-ukraine-war.html.

16 *Id.*

17 *Russia Posts Record Current Account Surplus of $227 Bln in 2022*, Reuters (Jan. 17, 2023), www.reuters.com/world/europe/russias-current-account-surplus-almost-doubled-2022-central-bank-2023-01-17/.

18 Heli Simola, *What Effects Have Sanctions Had on the Russian Economy?*, World Economic Forum (Dec. 22, 2022), www.weforum.org/agenda/2022/12/sanctions-russian-economy-effects/.

19 Jeffrey Sonnenfeld et al., *Over 1,000 Companies Have Curtailed Operations in Russia – But Some Remain*, Yale School of Management (last updated Aug. 7, 2023), https://som.yale.edu/story/2022/over-1000-companies-have-curtailed-operations-russia-some-remain.

20 Simon Evenett and Niccolò Pisani, *Less than Nine Percent of Western Firms Have Divested from Russia*, SSRN (2022), at 5, https://papers.ssrn.com/sol3/papers.cfm?abstract_id=4322502; Douglas Busvine, *Western Firms Say They Are Quitting from Russia. Where's the Proof?*, Politico (Feb. 28, 2023), www.politico.eu/article/western-firm-quit-russia-proof-sanctions-war-ukraine/.

21 Liz Alderman, *Leave Russia? A Year Later Many Companies Cannot, or Won't*, New York Times (Mar. 2, 2023), www.nytimes.com/2023/03/02/business/russia-companies-exit.html.

22 Polina Ivanova, *Russia's Fraying Economy: Consumers Start to Feel the Sanctions*, Financial Times (May 31, 2022), www.ft.com/content/7df9b453-509b-41c4-8957-ac170a ca61aa; Kira Sokolova, *As Western Companies Disappear from Russia, So Do Jobs*, DW (May 5, 2022), www.dw.com/en/western-companies-leave-russia-taking-russian-jobs-with-them/a-61697175.

23 Polina Ivanova, *"The End of an Era": Ikea, Russia's Middle Class and the New Cold War*, Financial Times (Mar. 11, 2022) www.ft.com/content/eb927a3d-f4dd-43af-bc8b-815b8ea14e92; Pjotr Sauer and Andrew Roth, *The Grey Zara Market: How "Parallel Imports" Give Comfort to Russian Consumers*, The Guardian (Aug. 12, 2022), www .theguardian.com/world/2022/aug/12/russia-grey-market-parallel-imports-consumers-west ern-brands-zara.

24 *Inflation in Russia Hits Highest in More than 20 Years*, Reuters (Apr. 13, 2022), www.reuters .com/world/europe/inflation-russia-hits-highest-more-than-20-years-2022-04-13/.

25 *Russian Economy Minister Says Inflation 11.9% in 2022, Will Be Lower in 2023*, Reuters (Jan. 11, 2023), www.reuters.com/article/ukraine-crisis-russia-economy/russian-economy-minister-says-inflation-11-9-in-2022-will-be-lower-in-2023-idINS8N32Z03E.

26 *Russia Consumer Inflation Drops below 4% Target for the First Time in a Year*, Reuters (Apr. 12, 2023), www.reuters.com/markets/europe/russian-consumer-inflation-drops-below-4-target-first-time-year-2023-04-12/.

27 Jeffrey Sonnenfeld and Steven Tian, *Actually, the Russian Economy Is Imploding*, Foreign Policy (July 22, 2022), https://foreignpolicy.com/2022/07/22/russia-economy-sanctions-myths-ruble-business/.

28 *H.R. 7776 – James M. Inhofe National Defense Authorization Act for Fiscal Year 2023*, 117th Congress (introduced May 16, 2022) (became P.L. 117-263), www.congress.gov/bill/117th-congress/house-bill/7776/text.

29 *Putin's War Machine Helps Keep Russian Industry Humming*, Bloomberg (Feb. 1, 2023), www.bloomberg.com/news/articles/2023-02-01/putin-s-war-machine-helps-keep-rus sian-industry-humming.

30 *FACT SHEET: Disrupting and Degrading – One Year of U.S. Sanctions on Russia and Its Enablers*, U.S. Department of the Treasury (Feb. 24, 2023), https://home.treasury.gov/ news/press-releases/jy1298.

31 Georgi Kantchev and Evan Gershkovich, *Russia's Economy Is Starting to Come Undone*, Wall Street Journal (Mar. 28, 2023), www.wsj.com/articles/russias-economy-is-starting-to-come-undone-431a2878.

32 Mike Eckel, *Standard Deviations: How an IMF Forecast for Russia Kicked up a Storm*, RadioFreeEurope RadioLiberty (Mar. 20, 2023), www.rferl.org/a/russia-economy-imf-fore cast-controversy/32326741.html.

33 Jackie Northam, *Russia's Economy Is Still Working but Sanctions Are Starting to Have an Effect*, NPR (Dec. 27, 2022), www.npr.org/2022/12/27/1144226139/russia-sanctions-ukraine-war.

34 FACT SHEET: *Disrupting and Degrading – One Year of U.S. Sanctions on Russia and Its Enablers*, U.S. Department of the Treasury (Feb. 24, 2023), https://home.treasury.gov/news/press-releases/jy1298; *Exclusive: Russia Starts Stripping Jetliners for Parts as Sanctions Bite*, Reuters (Aug. 9, 2022), www.reuters.com/business/aerospace-defense/exclusive-russia-starts-stripping-jetliners-parts-sanctions-bite-2022-08-08/.

35 Luanna Muniz, *European Official Worried about Russia Flying Western-Made Planes*, Politico (June 15, 2022), www.politico.eu/article/patrick-ky-concern-russia-fly-western-plane/.

36 *Commerce Implements New Export Controls on Advanced Computing and Semiconductor Manufacturing Items to the People's Republic of China (PRC)*, U.S. Department of Commerce (Oct. 7, 2022), www.bis.doc.gov/index.php/documents/about-bis/newsroom/press-releases/3158-2022-10-07-bis-press-release-advanced-computing-and-semiconductor-manufacturing-controls-final/file.

37 Don Graves, *America's Hidden Tool Is Hobbling Russia's War Machine with Multilateral Impact*, War on the Rocks (Feb. 1, 2023), https://warontherocks.com/2023/02/americas-hidden-tool-is-hobbling-russias-war-machine-with-multilateral-impact/.

38 Jamie Dettmer and Tristan Fiedler, *European Parliament Declares Russia a "State Sponsor of Terrorism" as Putin Launches Fresh Attacks on Ukraine*, Politico (Nov. 23, 2022), www.politico.eu/article/eu-declares-russia-a-state-sponsor-of-terrorism/.

39 William Allen Reinsch, *Evaluating the Russia Sanctions*, CSIS (Apr. 11, 2022), www.csis.org/analysis/evaluating-russia-sanctions; Leo Goretti, *The Sporting Sanctions against Russia: Debunking the Myth of the Sport's Neutrality*, IAI (May 17, 2022), www.iai.it/en/pubblicazioni/sporting-sanctions-against-russia-debunking-myth-sports-neutrality.

40 *IOC EB Recommends No Participation of Russian Belarusian Athletes and Officials*, IOC (Feb. 28, 2022), https://olympics.com/ioc/news/ioc-eb-recommends-no-participation-of-russian-and-belarusian-athletes-and-officials.

41 Andrew Moore, *Putin's Invasion of Ukraine Will Impact Russian Sports for Decades*, NC State University (Mar. 15, 2022), https://cnr.ncsu.edu/news/2022/03/ukraine-invasion-russian-sports/; *Former Host Russia Frozen Out as World Cup Begins in Qatar*, AP (Nov. 14, 2022), https://apnews.com/article/putin-world-cup-soccer-sports-uzbekistan-8c0ad177a1172e54657331d2d848cf63.

42 Hufbauer et al., note 8, at 5.

43 Adam Taylor, *13 Times that Economic Sanctions Really Worked*, Washington Post (Apr. 28, 2014), www.washingtonpost.com/news/worldviews/wp/2014/04/28/13-times-that-economic-sanctions-really-worked/.

44 Jokull Johannesson, *The Critical Role of Morale in Ukraine's Fight against the Russian Invasion*, Open Journal of Social Sciences (2020), www.scirp.org/journal/paperinformation.aspx?paperid=100903.

45 Stanislav Secrieru, *Have EU Sanctions Changed Russia's Behaviour in Ukraine?* (Sept. 2015), EU Institute for Security Studies, https://repository.graduateinstitute.ch/record/293855/files/Biersteker-EU_Sanctions_2015.pdf.

46 Richard Connolly, *The Impact of EU Economic Sanctions on Russia*, On Target?: EU Sanctions as Security Policy Tools, European Union Institute for Security Studies (2015), at 29–38, www.jstor.org/stable/resrep07074.7.

47 Maria Demertzis et al., *How Have Sanctions Impacted Russia?*, Policy Contribution (Oct. 2022), www.bruegel.org/sites/default/files/2022–10/PC%2018%202022_1.pdf.

48 Agathe Demarais, Backfire, at 41 (2022).

49 *Id.*, citing Gary Hufbauer et al., Economic Sanctions Reconsidered, 3rd ed. (2009).

50 Peter Clement, *Putin's Risk Spiral: The Logic of Escalation in an Unraveling War*, Foreign Affairs (Oct. 26, 2022), www.foreignaffairs.com/ukraine/putin-risk-spiral-logic-of-escalation-in-war.

51 Josh Chin, *China and Taiwan Relations Divide Explained: What's behind the Divide*, Wall Street Journal (Mar. 10, 2023), www.wsj.com/articles/china-taiwan-relations-tensions-explained-11653322751.

52 *The Republic of China (Taiwan) Government Strongly Condemns Russia's Invasion of Ukraine in Ciolation of the UN Charter, Joins International Economic Sanctions against Russia*, Ministry of Foreign Affairs, Republic of China (Taiwan) (Feb. 25, 2022), www.roc-taiwan.org/th_en/post/4629.html.

53 Orange Wang, *China Opposes "Illegal" Sanctions against Russia by United States and Its Allies*, South China Morning Post (Mar. 2, 2022), www.scmp.com/economy/china-economy/article/3168972/china-opposes-illegal-sanctions-against-russia-united-states; *China, Russia Slam "Illegal" International Sanctions Targeting Putin over Ukraine*, Radio Free Asia (Mar. 30, 2022), www.rfa.org/english/news/china/russia-ukraine-03302022094602.html.

54 *Exclusive: U.S. Weighs China Sanctions to Deter Taiwan Action, Taiwan Presses EU*, Reuters (Sept. 14, 2022), www.reuters.com/world/asia-pacific/exclusive-us-considers-china-sanctions-deter-taiwan-action-taiwan-presses-eu-2022-09-13/.

55 David Brunnstrom and Michael Martina, *Explainer: How Could the U.S. Sanction China to Deter a Taiwan Attack?*, Reuters (Sept. 14, 2022), www.reuters.com/world/how-could-us-sanction-china-deter-taiwan-attack-2022-09-14/.

56 *Rep. Omar's Statement on Russian Invasion of Ukraine*, Ilhan Omar (Feb. 24, 2022), https://omar.house.gov/media/press-releases/rep-omars-statement-russian-invasion-ukraine.

57 Gabriel Schoenfeld, *Moral Equivalence and Ukraine*, Lawfare (Apr. 20, 2022), www.lawfaremedia.org/article/moral-equivalence-and-ukraine.

58 Aamer Madhani and Emily Swanson, *Support for Ukraine Aid Softens in U.S. Public, Poll Says*, AP (Feb. 15, 2023), www.pbs.org/newshour/politics/support-for-ukraine-aid-softens-in-u-s-public-poll-says.

59 Anthony J. Blinken, *The United States Imposes Additional Sweeping Costs on Russia*, U.S. Department of State (Feb. 24, 2023), www.state.gov/the-united-states-imposes-additional-sweeping-costs-on-russia/; Gabriela Baczynska, *EU Approves 10th Package of Russia Sanctions on Anniversary of Invasion*, Reuters (Feb. 24, 2023), www.reuters.com/world/europe/eu-war-anniversary-sanctions-against-russia-stalled-diplomats-2023-02-24/.

60 *EU Agrees 10th Package of Sanctions against Russia*, European Commission (Feb. 25, 2023), https://ec.europa.eu/commission/presscorner/detail/en/ip_23_1185.

61 *Can Sanctions Really Stop Putin?*, New York Times (Apr. 22, 2022), www.nytimes.com/2022/04/22/opinion/sanctions-russia-ukraine-war.html.

62 Nicholas Mulder, *Sanctions against Russia Ignore the Economic Challenges Facing Ukraine*, New York Times (Feb. 9, 2023), www.nytimes.com/2023/02/09/opinion/sanctions-russia-ukraine-economy.html.

CONCLUSION

1 *European Parliament Declares Russia to Be a State Sponsor of Terrorism*, European Parliament (Nov. 23, 2022), www.europarl.europa.eu/news/en/press-room/20221118IPR55707/european-par liament-declares-russia-to-be-a-state-sponsor-of-terrorism.

2 *European Parliament Declares Russia a "State Sponsor of Terrorism" as Putin Launches Fresh Attacks on Ukraine*, Politico (Jan. 30, 2023), www.politico.eu/article/eu-declares-russia-a-state-sponsor-of-terrorism/.

3 *State Sponsors of Terrorism*, U.S. Department of State (Sept. 8, 2012), www.state.gov/state-sponsors-of-terrorism.

4 *S.Res.623 – A resolution calling on the Secretary of State to designate the Russian Federation as a state sponsor of terrorism*, 117th Congress (introduced May 9, 2022), www.congress.gov/bill/117th-congress/senate-resolution/623/text; Julia Mueller, *Senators Introduce Bill Designating Russia "State Sponsor of Terrorism*,*"* The Hill (Sept. 14, 2022), https://thehill .com/policy/international/3643593-senators-introduce-bill-designating-russia-state-sponsor-of-terrorism/.

5 *The U.S. Says the Wagner Group Is a Transnational Criminal Organization. Here's Why*, CBC (Jan. 28, 2023), www.cbc.ca/news/politics/wagner-group-russia-ukraine-putin-prigoz hin-1.6729177; *Treasury Sanctions Russian Proxy Wagner Group as Transnational Criminal Organization*, U.S. Department of the Treasury (Jan. 26, 2023), https://home .treasury.gov/news/press-releases/jy1220.

6 *FACT SHEET: On One Year Anniversary of Russia's Invasion of Ukraine, Biden Administration Announces Actions to Support Ukraine and Hold Russia Accountable*, White House (Feb. 24, 2023), www.whitehouse.gov/briefing-room/statements-releases/ 2023/02/24/fact-sheet-on-one-year-anniversary-of-russias-invasion-of-ukraine-biden-adminis tration-announces-actions-to-support-ukraine-and-hold-russia-accountable/.

7 *New Sanctions Ban Every Item Russia Is Using on the Battlefield*, Government of the United Kingdom (Feb. 24, 2023), www.gov.uk/government/news/new-sanctions-ban-every-item-russia-is-using-on-the-battlefield.

8 *Id.*=

9 *EU Agrees 10th Package of Sanctions against Russia*, European Commission (Feb. 25, 2023), https://ec.europa.eu/commission/presscorner/detail/en/ip_23_1185.

10 *EU Welcomes Co-ordinated First Anniversary Push on Russia Sanctions*, European Commission (Mar. 1, 2023), https://policy.trade.ec.europa.eu/news/eu-welcomes-co-ordi nated-first-anniversary-push-russia-sanctions-2023-03-01_en.

11 *G7 Leaders' Statement*, Prime Minister's Office of Japan (Feb. 24, 2023), at 3, https://japan .kantei.go.jp/content/000123437.pdf.

12 Christina L. Arabia et al., *U.S. Security Assistance to Ukraine*, Congressional Research Service (Feb. 27, 2023), https://crsreports.congress.gov/product/pdf/IF/IF12040; Justin Gomez, *Biden's support for Ukraine has been unwavering, but challenges lie ahead*, ABC News (Feb. 24, 2023), https://abcnews.go.com/Politics/bidens-support-ukraine-unwavering-challenges-lie-ahead/story?id=97424029.

13 Claire Mills, *Military Assistance to Ukraine since the Russian Invasion*, House of Commons Library Research Briefing (Mar. 30, 2023), https://researchbriefings.files .parliament.uk/documents/CBP-9477/CBP-9477.pdf.

14 Gareth Evans, *US Joins Germany in Sending Battle Tanks to Ukraine*, BBC (Jan. 25, 2023), www.bbc.com/news/world-us-canada-64404928.

15 Janek Lasocki, *The Cost of War to Ukraine*, RUSI (Feb. 24, 2023), www.rusi.org/explore-our-research/publications/commentary/cost-war-ukraine.

16 *Conflict Observatory, Russia's Systematic Program for the Re-Education and Adoption of Ukraine's Children*, Ukraine Conflict Observatory (Feb. 14, 2023), https://hub.conflictobservatory.org/portal/apps/sites/#/home/pages/children-camps-1.

17 *United Nations Human Rights Office of the High Commissioner, Ukraine: Civilian Casualty*, OHCHR (last updated Feb. 13, 2023), www.ohchr.org/en/news/2023/02/ukraine-civilian-casualty-update-13-february-2023.

18 *Full Transcript of Zelensky's Speech before Congress*, New York Times (Dec. 21, 2022), www.nytimes.com/2022/12/21/us/politics/zelensky-speech-transcript.html.

Index

This index is alphabetized in Word-by-Word order. All references to sanctions are to sanctions *against* Russia unless otherwise stated. "Invasion" refers to the full-scale invasion of Ukraine by Vladimir Putin begun on February 24, 2022.

Printed in the USA
CPSIA information can be obtained
at www.ICGtesting.com
LVHW022008161223
766613LV00005B/364